The Greenwood Encyclopedia of Clothing through World History

The Greenwood Encyclopedia of Clothing through World History

Volume 1
Prehistory to 1500 CE

Edited by Jill Condra

GREENWOOD PRESS
Westport, Connecticut • London

Library of Congress Cataloging-in-Publication Data

The Greenwood encyclopedia of clothing through world history / edited by Jill Condra.
    p. cm.
    Includes bibliographical references and index.
    ISBN 978-0-313-33662-1 ((set) : alk. paper) — ISBN 978-0-313-33663-8
((vol 1) : alk. paper) — ISBN 978-0-313-33664-5 ((vol 2) : alk. paper) — ISBN
978-0-313-33665-2 ((vol 3) : alk. paper)
    1. Clothing and dress—History—Encyclopedias. I. Condra, Jill, 1968-
GT507.G74 2008
391.009—dc22   2007030705

British Library Cataloguing in Publication Data is available.

Library of Congress Catalog Card Number: 2007030705
ISBN: 978-0-313-33662-1 (set)
        978-0-313-33663-8 (vol. 1)
        978-0-313-33664-5 (vol. 2)
        978-0-313-33665-2 (vol. 3)

First published in 2008

Greenwood Press, 88 Post Road West, Westport, CT 06881
An imprint of Greenwood Publishing Group, Inc.
www.greenwood.com

Printed in the United States of America

∞™

The paper used in this book complies with the
Permanent Paper Standard issued by the National
Information Standards Organization (Z39.48–1984).

10 9 8 7 6 5 4 3 2 1

Contents

Preface

The history of clothing and world history go closely in hand, and to trace the evolution of clothing is to trace events that occurred in times and places long ago. Within the context of world events, clothing is a vital piece of material culture that can help to understand what has happened in the past and how it has affected our present. The way in which people dressed throughout time has always indicated, to a great extent, who they are. It also has been an indicator of where they come from, their lot in life, their wealth or poverty, or their occupation. Starting at the cradle of civilization, the following chapters and those in the other volumes trace the evolution of dress from prehistoric times through the classical eras of Rome and Greece to the Middle Ages and onward to the most recent times.

The study of clothing was once solely the provenance of the art historian, interested from the perspective of the paintings and sculptures they studied to understand what the subjects of the art were wearing. This process helped to authenticate and date the art but was not a study unto itself. It wasn't until the last half of the twentieth century that costume/clothing/dress history has become a subject of interest for its own sake. Still closely related to the study of art history, those who study costume have evolved in their own discipline from producing "hemline histories" to developing material culture models, based on anthropology, and other methods to put the clothing they find and study into context.

While a hemline history might look solely at the costumes and their minute details, tracing the evolution of a feature, such as the length of a hemline, to its most recent incarnation, little else about history is included. These original studies of dress were often seen by self-described "serious" historians as elitist and merely the domain of the connoisseurs, implying that, although it may be interesting to look at fashion, it was not exactly important in the face of more rigorous study of military, political, or religious histories, for example. Clothing, and especially fashion, is often seen as frivolous and not the domain of the serious academic, and the original costume historians faced this criticism continually.

In light of this criticism, and as interest in tracing the evolution of clothing became more popular, things began to change. It became obvious that neither costume nor the other aspects of history can be studied in isolation and still provide a full picture and true understanding of history. Tracing the roots of clothing styles by looking at the geography, social setting, political situation, religious affiliation, technological development, pop culture (especially from the 1920s onward), and so forth gives the context from which to look at what people wore and perhaps sheds better light on the reasons they chose to wear the clothes they did. It can also do the reverse and shed light on why certain other social, political, or economic events occurred. Trade, for example, has always been heavily influenced by fashion demands around the world, and many a country has its roots in the trade of textiles used for fashion purposes (e.g., demand in Europe for the fashionable beaver hat allowed for exploration, trade, and development in the newly established colonies of Canada and the establishment of the Hudson Bay Company).

The original clothing histories that concentrated specifically on the clothes themselves remain a gold mine for modern costume and clothing historians and provide a wealth of detailed information about the garments, showing how they were worn and how they were constructed, often showing patterns and details of the textiles that allow students of costume to see every aspect of the garments. Much in the way of general social history can be gleaned from these sources, and taken together with the kind of studies such as the one in this series, a very thorough picture of clothing and world history can be achieved.

PROBLEMS WITH COSTUME EVIDENCE

As many of the authors in these volumes suggest, depending on the era, the sources of evidence to study dress are sometime difficult to interpret and trust as absolute. Unless there is an actual garment, or set of garments, other kinds of evidence must be used to look at the costumes people wore. These sources might include cave drawings, sculptures of the early Greeks and Romans, wall paintings in tombs, hieroglyphics from ancient Egypt, literature, journals, legends, oral histories, paintings of the seventeenth century, or photographs of the twentieth century.

The problem with any of these sources is that the are inherently biased, taken only from the perspective of the painter, photographer, or writer, who is free to embellish or gloss over aspects of the actual situation as he or she feels is fit. Painting a portrait in the eighteenth century, an artist may have been asked to omit a certain less-than-flattering feature of the subject, thus altering the evidence for future study, while presumably pleasing the person who was paying him. It is impossible to know for sure what is true in a depiction of a costume and what is idealized, but nevertheless the evidence is crucial, and the process of gathering as much detail as possible will allow the student of history to piece together a fairly accurate picture of the real thing.

Taking the evidence and backing it up with other sources of historical record only adds to the relative certainty of the claims made about the clothing people wore. Tracing the influences from one set of evidence to the next gives a clearer picture of the whole. The best source of evidence, of course, is the actual garment itself. But, unfortunately, given the organic nature of textiles used until relatively recent times, there are few very early garments surviving intact. As one progresses through time from the early prehistoric period, more and more pieces survive, and these account for the increased amount of information available for the past four centuries or so. Before that, there is little actual material culture left to study. We are fortunate enough to occasionally find the odd textile piece that has been preserved by luck in the dry deserts of Egypt, and there have been the chance discoveries of perfectly preserved "bog people" whose entire person is still intact, clothes and all (even the food they ate just before they died can be determined!). The problem, though, is that as soon as the textiles are exposed to oxygen and humidity, the process of decay begins immediately.

In later time periods, the luscious garments were used and reused, then sold secondhand to poorer people, who wore the garments until they were threadbare and then used them for other purposes. As a result, very few extant pieces survive from before the late sixteenth and seventeenth centuries. For the student of these and later centuries, there are many surviving garments. Yet even these only tell part of the story. This is due to the fact that the extant pieces are usually only the most important garments worn by the wealthiest and most privileged in a society. It is very rare indeed to find a museum well stocked with peasant tunics and aprons. What does survive, and what is so alluring for those of us who adore textiles of any kind, are the beautiful and luxurious gowns, sumptuous skirts, and coats with over-the-top decorations. Often these garments were worn by royalty or courtiers in the great courts of Versailles or Florence in the romantic and exquisite Renaissance. These garments do not, however, represent what everyday people wore in their jobs and occupations. To embark on a study of peasant dress would be a short journey with so little available.

The existing gowns and men's suits, though not showing all facets of society, do represent the most fashionable of the time and are a good representation of the affluence that was shown on the backs of the aristocracy. Their garments were worn as symbols of who they were, where they were stationed in life and society, and to what class of people they belonged. Competition was blatant, and both men and women tried their best, in many eras, to outdo each other in their show of status through their clothing.

It is with all this in mind that costume historians undertake the study of clothing and fashion changes over time. As with any kind of history, the evidence provides only partial information, and so it is even more important to combine all aspects of history, in an interdisciplinary manner, to provide the context for the most accurate picture to be analyzed. Looking at social history alongside the clothing evidence, imperfect as it may seem, gives an excellent taste of the past.

GETTING DRESSED

What people wear on their bodies depends not only on the physical conditions in which they live but also on the availability of resources, the amount of money they have, and their associations within their communities. Clothing is the most personal of effects and can tell more about a person and the life they lead than any other kind of material history. The clothing artifact is precious for historians and anthropologists who study materials of the past. While an ancient piece of pottery or an eighteenth-century chair is valuable to the archaeologist, it indicates only a certain amount about the people who used it. It may inform about the materials available and the technology and design sense of the maker, but not about his size, habits, or personal preferences. On the other hand, clothing can tell a great deal about the individuals who wore the clothes and as such are very valuable to study.

People wear clothes for a number of reasons, including protection from the environment, identification, status, comfort, sexual allurement, beauty, and a myriad of others. It is a recurring theme from chapter to chapter in these volumes that, in all the times and places throughout history, people appear to have dressed for the same reasons as we still do today. How those ideals manifested themselves is what differs from period to period and place to place. For example, what is now considered attractive or a symbol of great status would certainly not have been read the same way in the Renaissance or ancient Egypt—though there are similarities. Precious stones were and remain valuable and show a certain something about the wearer, namely, that they can afford such items. However, the extremely casual nature of clothing in today's society would have been unheard of in times gone by and would have seemed not only unflattering to the human form but also immoral.

Dress has been indelibly linked to manner and morals for centuries, and this is just some of the information clothes can communicate. The functions of dress have varied in detail over the centuries but have remained clear identifiers of the people, place, and time of its wearing.

SCOPE OF THE VOLUMES

There are many terms used in the study of clothing, and they are often used interchangeably to mean what people wore. However, there are some very subtle differences, and it is worth identifying these differences at the outset of this study of clothing in world history. To talk about *clothing* means to talk about the garments people wore, to be sure, but it also encompasses other parts of the decoration and covering of the human form. In this set of volumes, the textiles used for clothing is a great focus, as are the changes seen over time, but there are also frequent glimpses of the other elements that went into personal adornment. Jewelry, headwear, shoes, bags or purses, and other accessories that are held, draped, tied, and attached to the body all affect the clothing of the wearer and the look it achieves. This study undertakes to look at all these things within the parameters of both high fashion, and where possible, peasant clothing.

Dress is a term applied, like *clothing*, more generally to the entire outfit or trend in styles worn by people through the ages. *Costume* implies, increasingly it seems recently, theatrical and special-occasion or fancy dress—things not worn as a norm—but the term is also still used to identify the garments and accessories generally. *Adornment* is another term that identifies objects worn to enhance and dress the body.

These terms are all used as a way of talking about the same or similar things, but depending on the country or culture in question, different terms seem to be more common than others. For example, museums in the United Kingdom tend be called "costume collections," but "dress" is often used in discussion about the garments themselves. For the purposes of this book, all these terms are used purposefully to denote the wearing of garments, both of the wealthy and not-so-wealthy, as well as accessories, cosmetics, hairstyles, and anything to do with how people looked in history.

To make the study as complete and true to the title as possible, historical divisions have been identified into chapters grouped together in the three volumes. All three attempt to cover the important political, social, economic, technological, and cultural history of the times. Introductions to each chapter deal with the major events of the time and place. Each chapter then delves into the clothing people wore and ties the events to the choices people made in their dress.

Early history is covered in volume 1, looking at clothing from prehistoric times to the end of the Middle Ages and Byzantine eras, roughly to 1500. In this volume, discussions focus on several cultures from around the Western world, including Egypt, Greece, Rome, Persia, and the northern portions of continental Europe. Volume 2 follows clothing history from the sixteenth century through the 1800s and looks at clothing in Europe, North America, Latin America, Japan, Korea, India, and China. Volume 3 opens with the postrevolutionary period in Europe at the start of the nineteenth century and covers the history and dress of people throughout the increasingly small world, examining aspects of dress from most regions of the world where there is historical record.

This set of volumes, however, does not claim to cover all of history in all of the world throughout time. This would be an impossible undertaking, so it is with care that the geographical and time divisions have been chosen, as they represent a good sample of the events that were occurring around the world and how these events affected the ways people clothed themselves. Commonalities are evident if close attention is paid to the details within each chapter. For example, rituals surrounding moving from childhood to adulthood are roughly similar in all places and times and usually involve a change in dress style, often accompanied by a ceremony to mark the occasion. Dressing for status and identification is another common theme, as is the idea that children through time and to the present, with few exceptions, have dressed in a strikingly similar manner to their parents after babyhood.

Clothing in every culture and time period is used for ceremonial purposes and carries great meaning and symbolism. Coronation gowns and liturgical attire are painstakingly designed and made, and each element might represent some important idea associated with the monarchy or priesthood. In some eras where religion is of utmost importance to the development of culture, religious garb is studied, but this is not necessarily an important part of clothing in all places or in all time periods and so is not discussed in other chapters at all. It is thus impractical in a work of this huge scope to look at the same aspects of dress throughout. Instead, the time, events, and place dictate the differences in subheadings to most appropriately fit the subject matter. So, during the Byzantine era, religious garb is studied, but once the late twentieth century is covered, religious clothing is no longer emphasized.

Military dress can be a study unto itself, and there are many books and websites devoted to the evolution of armor and military uniforms. In this book, armor is described, for example, in terms of the Renaissance, when it was commonly worn by people; it is also noteworthy as a useful piece of durable material culture, because much has survived where many contemporaneous textile artifacts have long decayed. Military uniforms are revisited in the twentieth century in the context of the two world wars and the effect this look had on regular clothing of nonmilitary men, women, and children.

Looking at different places during the same time period will reveal a certain sameness in the clothing people wore. There was often one prevailing style, with deviations in detail from place to place. When explorers were off discovering new places in the name of their European homelands, they often brought their own distinct styles and textiles, which were traded with the locals, hence creating a merging of styles all over the world. The interchange of goods, especially textile goods, helped to shape the shared fashion choices among many people far away from each other, resulting in features that were often the same or very similar. People in Latin America, for example, in many time periods wore styles very similar to—and with certain aspects exactly the same as—those in France; in the middle of the twentieth century, women in Buenos Aires were seen in the highest of high fashions from the French runways. Cultural highlights might distinguish certain aspects and interpretations of the *haute couture* fashions, but they were also decidedly the same in many respects.

What this book is not is a look at the folk costumes of the countries and times within the scope. While there is the occasional mention of folk dress— the Scottish kilt, for example—there is little discussion of folk attire. That facet of study needs its own series of books with a concrete plan to study all the costumes in cultures, historical and more recent throughout time.

HOW TO USE THIS BOOK

These volumes have been written by some of the best writers in the area of costume studies, who are often specialists in one area or era in clothing history and have spent a good deal of their lives dedicated to the study of clothing history.

In this look at history and clothing, the abbreviations BC (Before Christ) and AD (Anno Domini) have been replaced with the newer parlance of BCE (Before the Common Era) and CE (Common Era).

At the beginning of each chapter, a timeline allows a quick reference to what occurred, both in terms of general history and developments in the areas of clothing and textiles, in the relevant geographical areas. Some of the timelines are more complicated and indicate a greater amount of available information, while others simply outline some of the key world and textile-related events.

Following the timeline are the introductions to the general histories of time and place. These vary according to what happened in the specific period and location and are reflections of economics, political structure and events, monarchies, exploration, technological developments, governments, social pressures and concerns, religion, military history, and international affairs. All of these are meant to provide the reader with the context needed to understand the clothing section that follows.

The portion of each chapter on clothing begins with a general introduction to the themes in dress of the age and place. Then dress is looked at in terms of gender, with men's and women's clothing separately discussed. The important items of clothing are mostly defined within the text, but words that are specific to clothing history and may not be commonly known are also contained in a glossary at the end of each volume. Each chapter is illustrated with images that reflect what is described—paintings, decorations, or photographs of the actual clothing, depending on the time period. While some images are placed within the text, many more are contained in the color inserts in the center of the volume. Children's clothing is covered in a necessarily smaller section at the end of each chapter, owing to the fact that there is often little information pertaining to the children, especially in very early times, and also that children often dressed in the same or similar styles to their parents. Most chapters also contain a number of highlighted boxes with curious or intriguing information about a certain aspect of the history.

At the end of each chapter, there is a list of recommended books for further study, along with a few websites that will help with further research on the topic and time period. These resources are followed by a list of suggestions (by no means exhaustive) of films, documentaries, or television shows that do a good job of depicting the costume history of the time and place in question. There are markedly more such films available for more recent or modern history, of course. The lists vary in terms of the dates they were made and the countries, but all are English-language movies or programs.

TEXTILE TERMS FROM FIBERS TO FABRIC AND CLOTHING

In order to understand some of what is contained in these books it is important to start this process with some of the basic textile and clothing terms needed to read and comprehend the information. Following is a list of the key terms:

Textile: A general term applied to fibers, yarns, and fabrics; anything to do with the production of these things is part of the textile complex.

Fabric: The piece of cloth used to construct garments and other soft goods. It can be a knit, woven, or nonwoven fabric.

Knit fabric: A fabric produced by one continuous yarn interlooping with one or more yarns. It is stretchy and was not commonly used before the seventeenth century.

Woven fabric: A fabric made through the process of weaving on a loom. Looms have been used in different forms since the beginning of time. Weaving is a process whereby a *warp* thread—the lengthwise thread running vertically on the loom—is alternately interwoven with the *weft* threads that run horizontally, creating a pattern. These threads sit at 90° angles to one another and can be made into all kinds of patterns and designs. Woven fabrics were made as early as the discovery of fibers.

Yarns: Threads that are spun (twisted) from loose fibers cultivated in a range of ways. The spun yarn can be further twisted with other yarns to create *plied yarns* of greater bulk and strength. Yarns can be made from natural fiber or manufactured fibers, or a combination of these.

Fibers: The base substance of yarn. These can be *staple length* (shorter) or *filament length* (longer) and are generally twisted to make the yarn used to make fabric. Fibers can be either natural or manufactured.

Natural fibers: Fibers that are either *cellulosic* and come from plants, such as cotton or linen, or *protein*-based and come from animals or insects, such as wool and silk. Except for silk fiber, natural fibers are *staple* (short) length and are twisted into yarns. Silk, a natural filament yarn, is extruded from the silkworm in one continuous strand.

Manufactured fibers: Fibers made from chemicals extruded through a spinerette into long continuous filaments, which can be cut into staple lengths if desired. These include nylon, polyester, and spandex, to name just a few.

Dyes: Textiles are dyed in many different colors and have been for hundreds of years. They can be dyed with natural or synthetic dyes now, but historically dyes were found in nature and applied to natural fibers. Often maintaining color on textiles was a problem, and *mordants* became a necessary part of the dyeing process. Dyes are generally from an organic source, that is, plant or animal matter. Historical sources of natural dyes include berries, insects, flowers, and other naturally occurring substances. Dyes, which are much smaller molecules than pigments, do not adhere to the surface of a fiber or textile material but rather bond with the fiber chemically and color the fibers throughout. Dyes allow fibers, yarns, or whole textiles to be colored at any time during the textile production process. Since their application is so versatile, different effects can be created.

Pigments: When prints were introduced, a different kind of coloring agent than dye was needed. Pastes or pigments are applied to textiles for printing patterns. The color sits on top of the fibers rather than being absorbed into the core of the fiber. Inorganic pigments must be applied, much as paint would be applied, to the textile or fabric as a whole piece, while fibers or yarns are not generally colored with pigments. A modern example of a pigment application would be stamping (direct) or stenciling (indirect), but the principle remains the same.

Prehistoric Clothing

Christel Baldia

TIMELINE

Paleolithic (600,000–8000 BCE)	Hunters wear fur clothing
Mesolithic (8000–3000 BCE)	Hunters and fishers wear clothing made from animals, especially furs and leather
Neolithic (3000–1000 BCE)	People settle into farming and animal husbandry, growing flax and cotton and shearing sheep for fleece that is used for garments, rugs, and blankets made with crude weaving techniques
Bronze Age (2100–1000 BCE)	Sophisticated artisans, farmers, and sailors use wool, linen, and cotton for garments, adding some applied designs for decoration
Iron Age (Hallstatt period 1000–500 BCE; La Tène period 500–50 BCE)	Linen and woolen woven clothing with decorations become common

The development of textile technology did not occur simultaneously in the Old World (Europe and Asia) and New World (the Americas). Rather, each region's technology developed in its own time with the resources that were available, in varied environments ranging from the extreme climates of the Arctic to the tropics and deserts. In this chapter, we discuss prehistoric textiles from all over the world, with a particular focus on examples from North America, which has been given little attention in the past.

PREHISTORY

Much of what we know about the dress of the indigenous peoples of North America is based on the observations of the early

European explorers and travelers who kept diaries and occasionally even drew pictures. However, to extend this study back into the time prior to European contact, material evidence is the only source of information because writing (in the way we know it) did not exist in the Americas, with the exception of the Maya, whose writings recorded only historic events and some political relationships. Most of this material evidence is no longer available for close observation due to degradation over time, and this is particularly true for organic materials such as textiles. Luckily, some fragmentary evidence that can give insights to prehistoric life still remains.

Archaeologists study artifacts of the past, and they specialize in *reading* these prehistoric materials by studying the clues discovered on these artifacts to infer past ways of life and social processes. However, due to the nature of prehistoric dress, specialists from other fields must also be involved in this type of research. These specialists come from the fields of textile science, polymer chemistry, geology, ethnobotany, and various crafts. The craftspeople know or seek to learn about spinning, weaving, or plaiting technology with materials that are often no longer recognized for their economic value. These researchers often replicate materials based on the information from archaeological finds to learn about how they were produced and treated by the original people. Thus dress (pre)history is developed by people with multiple backgrounds studying the same things.

FUNCTIONS OF DRESS AND TEXTILES: THEN AND NOW

Clothes protect against the elements. However, textiles and clothing also have other functions that go beyond just protecting the body. Dress and textiles alike are used as a means of nonverbal communication. Obvious examples would be the use of uniforms to communicate a particular social role and the modern white wedding dress Western cultures use to mark this rite of passage. Both types of clothing communicate important information nonverbally to the onlooker. The female wearing the white dress is about to be married and change her status and role in society. The person in the uniform has some specialized function in society, such as police officer, nurse, or soldier. Therefore, it can be said that clothing visually communicates information about group membership and functions as an identity marker. One can dress down or up to display wealth, education, or social standing, depending on the message the wearer wants onlookers to receive. Early explorers, with this instinct in mind, described the Inca as having used headdresses to indicate group membership.

Headdresses were very important in Native North American cultures. The war bonnet is probably the best known headdress regalia. It was always worn by a warrior or a tribal leader, and the feathers in the bonnet signified one slain enemy for a warrior (or good deeds done for the community, if the bonnet belonged to a nonwarrior tribal leader). In prehistory, war bonnets were only found among the Plains Indians, although during historic times, the symbol was adopted by many different ethnic groups as an identity marker, just as the totem pole, which was originally only used by Pacific Northwest peoples, was adopted widely.

Elaborate turbans and wigs were also worn in prehistoric American cultures. The turbans were not fabric specific but rather constituted a specific way of wearing a fabric. The regional climate, flora, and fauna dictated the kinds of material that would be used to assemble the fabric. Wigs were made of human hair that was interlaced in a specific way.

During the nineteenth century, tribal leaders were observed wearing turbans and wigs among groups such as the Pima in the American Southwest and the Seminole in Florida. Their popularity must be much older, however, because turbans and wigs dating to about 1100 CE have been found in situ, often together, in caves in the arid Southwest and must have been used extensively.

A simpler form of headdress was a headband, often worn over long hair or, in some regions, on a totally bald, plucked head. The headband usually was decorated with different colors or ornamentations. In the Eastern Woodlands, antlers or animal skulls and teeth were sometimes incorporated. Some headdresses were so elaborate that they could be considered masks. These were often worn

Luig Moraque, a Pima man, wearing a traditional turban, c. 1920. Courtesy of the Library of Congress.

only by religious specialists or other significant people within the community, and only for special rituals.

Headdresses could signal the region or town from which they originated. Similarly, the peoples of the Pacific Northwest coast, such as the Kwakiutl, used blankets, clothes, and many other materials to ostentatiously display wealth, and thereby status, during their potlatch festivals.

However, all of these processes are culture bound. What is or is not appropriate can differ from one ethnic group to the other and is not necessarily transferable. For instance, among the Zuni in the American Southwest, the leadership decided to pool money to buy jewelry for a lawyer that the tribe had hired to represent them in court. They felt that he was not dressed appropriately for the occasion, and it was obvious to them that he must not be able to afford elaborate Indian jewelry, hence the gesture of donating a rather valuable necklace. As it turned out, the lawyer was wearing what lawyers wear in mainstream America: a dark suit with a conservative tie. For the Zuni, though, it is the jewelry that counts. The amount of jewelry that one wears reflects the importance of the occasion and the status of the person, even if that person wears work jeans and a plaid shirt. In prehistory, societies had many of the same social mechanisms in place.

Some of the important aspects of cultural mores can be seen in the way particular aspects of dress continue to exist through time. For example, while European cloth and style elements were incorporated into the dress of the Seminole in Florida in the nineteenth century, they continued to wear sashes

Undated photograph of Seminole chief, Tommie Jumper. Courtesy of the Library of Congress.

that were decorated in native patterns with traditional symbols. They also wore pendants that resembled artifacts found in archaeological context dating to the Mississippian culture from almost 800 years earlier. One might argue that the sashes and crescent-shaped pendants were so important that they continued to be used through time, while other elements of dress could be replaced by "foreign" materials without regret or hesitation.

The Mississippian peoples occupied the greater Mississippi River Basin between about 800 and 1350 CE. Sometimes, they are referred to as the Temple Mound Culture because they built big temple mound complexes. Like the Hopewell, they had an extensive trade network. However, unlike the Hopewell, it is thought that they were organized as chiefdoms, possibly theocracies, with distinct status differences between the elites and commoners. There are many commonalities in iconography, burial practices, and artifact assemblages found over a huge area in the American Bottom. Their economy was supported by agriculture, with corn, beans, squash, and other crops planted in the rich river floodplain. Cahokia, modern-day St. Louis, was their biggest city, and it is estimated that it was the home of approximately 30,000 people. Other important ceremonial centers of the Mississippians were Moundville, Alabama; Spiro, Oklahoma; and Etowah, Georgia.

MATERIALS TELL A STORY

To understand prehistoric artifacts, it is essential to determine for what the materials were used. Archaeologists and dress historians generally deal with the remnants of material culture that came from a particular prehistoric context. Anthropologists and archaeologists term this the *remnant system*. To understand the meaning of this term fully, some other terms such as *material culture* must be defined.

A culture is commonly defined as the shared beliefs and values of a people. Their physical objects reflect these shared ideas. Archaeologists find only their material culture leftovers: the bits and pieces that were discarded or forgotten, and then stored or preserved, often by chance, in such a way that they survived through time. These remnants are considered to be a sample of material that once existed. They reflect the technological accomplishments, social processes, and iconography of that time and cultural expression. Often, the depictions of humans in figurines, pipes, or drawings on walls, pottery, and pendants have to be consulted to understand elements of dress, because the actual garments no longer exist. For instance, shells were carved by Hopewell peoples depicting body decorations, tattoos, ear spools, hairdos, and how clothing was worn in general. This can often be correlated to the few artifacts that survived and have been recovered.

Materials Used in Prehistoric Textile Production

It is obvious that nature provided the source of all materials that were used before the invention of man-made fibers. Therefore, all resources that were used in pre-

THE HOPEWELL CULTURE

The Hopewell archaeological culture existed in southern Ohio and parts of Illinois from 100 BCE to about 400 CE. They were characterized by the erection of massive earthworks and burial mounds. The Hopewell had a wide-ranging trade network, through which they acquired many exotic materials, such as shark teeth and shells from the Gulf Coast, obsidian from California, and turquoise from the Southwest. The Hopewell did not practice agriculture as we understand it today, but they did selectively tend a whole range of plants for food and other purposes before corn and beans reached their region. Among the plants they grew were sumpweed (*Iva annua*), goosefoot (*Chenopodium berlandieri*), sunflower (*Helianthus annuus*), little barley (*Hordeum pusillum*), erect knotweek (*Polygonum erectum*), and maygrass (*Phalaris caroliniana*).

historic textile production came from either an animal or a plant source. Animals yielded protein-containing materials, not only skins and leather but also silk and hair fibers from animals such as musk ox, rabbits, and dogs in North America and sheep and goats in the Old World. While hair fibers from wild animals were collected extensively in prehistory, the domestication of sheep, goats, and other animals during the Neolithic period made the access to meat, milk, and fibers easier.

The Neolithic or New Stone Age is associated with the introduction of pottery, the domestication of economically important plants and animals, and the beginning of a sedentary lifestyle and farming. Archaeological evidence shows that this development started independently in several areas of the world at different times. The technology that was adopted varied greatly regionally. The earliest evidence comes from the Old World, beginning in the Fertile Crescent around 9000 BCE and reaching central Europe around 5500 BCE. This time of transition from nomadic hunter-gatherer life to a life of subsistence farming is seen as a major change in society and therefore is sometimes referred to as the Neolithic Revolution. Moving to a sedentary, or at least semisedentary, lifestyle gave rise to new social, cultural, economic, and political institutions. As a result, the utilization of domesticated animals and plants became an important resource for the Old World.

Except for turkeys and dogs, animal husbandry was not carried out in prehistoric North America, but the domestication of economically important plants, such as cotton, did take place. Cotton (genus *Gossypium*) is probably the best-known seed fiber used by humans. It was domesticated independently in the Old and New worlds. Each hemisphere originally had two different wild species.

Archaeological evidence suggests that in the New World, cotton (*G. barbadense*) was already used for garments as early as 2500–1750 BCE in South America. In tropical Mesoamerica, another species, *G. hirsutum*, also referred to as "upland cotton" today, appeared in an archaeological context in the Valley of Mexico by 900 BCE. It then moved north to the American Southwest by 500 CE as the cultivar adapted to shorter growing seasons. While cotton was grown and used in the American Southwest, it never became widely spread beyond this area in North America. After European contact, cotton did not become a major crop until the invention of the cotton gin by Eli Whitney in 1794.

One of the two species of cotton that grew in the Old World, *G. herbaceum*, is native to sub-Saharan Africa and Arabia. It was probably domesticated in Ethiopia or southern Arabia. Its cultivation spread, and we have evidence of cotton being produced in China about 600 CE. The other Old World species, *G. arboreum*, is native to northwest India and Pakistan. It appeared between 3000 and 2000 BCE in the Indus Valley. While cotton is normally thought of as being white, it actually grows in many different shades, including browns, grays, greens, and pinks; white gained preference because it can be easily dyed into any color.

COLORED COTTON HYBRIDS

In the 1980s, Sally Fox once again successfully bred (as had been done in prehistoric times) and marketed varieties of naturally colored cotton she calls FoxFiberR. These hybrids are environmentally sustainable fibers that need no extra processing like dyeing or finishing as most commercial cottons do these days. This is a discovery from prehistoric times that has carried through to modern times.

Besides the seed fiber used in cotton, fibers are also obtained from leafy or stem materials from plants. Good prehistoric examples included the yucca (genus *Yucca*) in the American Southwest or rattlesnake master (*Eryngium yuccifolium*) in the Eastern United States. These materials were often used for the construction of prehistoric sandals, mats, thatch, and baskets where strength and durability were more important than comfort against the skin.

Flax (*Linum usitatissimum*) is a good example of a *bast fiber* that has been widely found in digs around the prehistoric and ancient worlds. Flax was domesticated in the Near East about 8,000 years ago and then slowly moved westward into the Aegean Sea area, India, and Egypt, after which it finally reached central Europe at the beginning of the Neolithic era. Flax seeds have been found from even earlier, but these may not be evidence of their use in textile production because they may have been consumed as food along with wheat. Flax was not available in the New World until its introduction by Europeans in the seventeenth century, when it was grown as a cottage industry. Species belonging to the nettle family (genus *Urtica*) have been used in both New and Old worlds for fiber production, although they are no longer economically important. In Europe, fabrics were constructed from nettle fibers as early as the Neolithic and as late as World War I.

In North America, bast fiber–producing plants such as milkweed (genus *Asclepias*) and Indian hemp (*Apocynum cannabinum*) were also very important in textile production. It is documented in historic records that early travelers and pioneers admired their usefulness and quality. American basswood, or linden (genus *Tilia*), a large tree, also yields fibers from the inner layer of its bark, and these were used extensively. The same genus was used widely in Europe as well; archaeologists have found evidence of its use in the Swiss lake-dwellers' array of material culture.

In some areas of the New World, such as Polynesia, the inner layer of bark from a specific mulberry tree was and still is pounded to make a paper-like material also called tapa cloth, which totally alleviates the fabric construction processes of spinning and then weaving or twining.

Mix and Matching of Materials

The Native American Hopewell culture blended bast fibers with rabbit hair to make use of the warmth and softness of the hair while the bast fibers added strength to the yarns that they spun. In doing so, they exploited the best properties of each material and created a superior and more functional textile.

Other materials were also blended. For example, turkey skins with feathers still attached, were cut into strips and attached to a bast fiber backing to make a warm, soft, and yet stable blanket. Sometimes the feathers were directly attached to a backing. In the arid climate of the American Southwest, several examples of turkey blankets have survived in good condition. These blankets have appeared in different sizes and in burial contexts, close to skeletal remains of adults or children. There are no indications that these blankets would have been used for ceremonial purposes, but this is impossible to fully determine.

DECORATION OF TEXTILES

There are many ways to construct and decorate textiles, ranging from the spinning of the yarn to the actual construction of the fabric by weaving, plaiting, or twining, and, of course, the application of color and other elements such as beads. The decorations range from the functional, such as the attachment of little rattles or noisemakers, to the aesthetically pleasing and perhaps religiously inspired. The latter decorations may have been regulated by the group of religious specialists.

Outside of China, where filament silk was heavily used, only staple fibers (such as linen, wool, or cotton) were available for the creation of yarn. Spinning was done by finger, thigh, and later the use of spindle whorls. Researchers have

ARTIFACTS FROM THE LAKE DWELLERS

From 4000 BCE to 500 BCE, lake dwellers constructed wooden houses on posts at the shores of Switzerland's lakes, the Alpine arc in general, and as far north as Lithuania. Floors and walls were constructed with plaited twigs, and the chinks were filled with clay. Due to the waterlogged environment, these sites have preserved many perishable artifacts such as food items, spinning and weaving implements, and actual textiles—a rarity in prehistoric research. This made it possible to reconstruct Neolithic life ways. Flax fibers have also been found by the Swiss lakes, dating in this area as early as 5000 BCE. Flax seeds were found in earlier levels, but without finding fibers. Therefore this very early find is only indirect evidence of using flax for textiles because flax also could have been grown for the food and oil value of the seeds.

found that the structure of the yarn yields information about what type of spinning was employed when the yarn was constructed. Often the yarns themselves have long been degraded, but the spinning whorls, most often made of clay or stone, have survived through time as a witness of yarn spinning.

The Mississippian culture is a good example for the extensive use of spinning whorls and the elaborate use of many types of decorations in their dress. Different means of constructing the fabric were employed. A heddle loom (as we understand it today) was not introduced to North America until the Spanish explorers arrived, but elaborate and rather complicated twining and plaiting techniques were used to create beautiful structures that may have been made on some type of frame. Some of these textiles are constructed to look like lace, with worked-in, mitered corners as is the case in a textile from Etowah, a Mississippian temple mound site in Georgia. Another technique that was used is demonstrated by the springlike construction of the Tonto shirt that was recovered from the Tonto Ruins in Arizona, dating to about the same time as Etowah. While some types of decoration, such as fringes, were already in use by the Hopewell around 400 CE in the east, the later Mississippian textiles and dress were much more elaborate, suggesting specialized workmanship. Besides using patterning structure as a decorative feature, color was applied by the Hopewell and colorant use became even more elaborate in Mississippian textiles.

TONTO NATIONAL MONUMENT

The Tonto Ruins are well-preserved cliff dwellings in southeastern Arizona. They were occupied between 1150 and 1450 CE. The people farmed in the Salt River Valley and supplemented their diet by hunting and gathering native wildlife and plants. The Salado, the people that lived there, were fine craftsmen, producing some of the most exquisitely constructed polychrome pottery and textiles. The Salado abandoned Tonto around 1450, when the Anasazi also left their dwellings in this region.

Color and Coloration Materials

Color applications in the form of ocher have been noted from as early as the Upper Paleolithic, between 30,000 and 11,000 years ago, in Europe. This mineral-based colorant was also used extensively in North America by Paleo-Indians as early as 13,000 years ago and continued in use until European contact. It is thought that this tradition may have crossed via the land bridge between Asia and North America (Beringia) with the peoples who populated the Americas.

Ocher is used throughout the world in a ritual context, as demonstrated by its occurrence in funerary remains. However, it is not the only colorant that is exploited. The use of coloration and dye developed early in the Old World, as is seen in the Hallstatt materials. The Hallstatt salt mines in Austria have yielded textiles that date to the Iron Age of about 3,000 years ago. The salt from the mines permeated the fibers and helped preserve these textiles, which are mostly made of wool. Due to the rarity of such a discovery, these are highly valued to study textile production from this time period. The natural colors of the sheep's wool were used, but blue, green, and yellow dyes were also incorporated to produce stripes and checkered patterns (similar to Irish and Scottish tartans).

These pieces are considered high quality not only because of the color use but also because of the complex weaving techniques. They provide evidence for fine sewing, cutting, hemming, and decorative stitching, as well as relatively hurried and coarse repair work. It has also been known for a long time that the eastern North American Hopewell decorated their textiles with pigments by painting them. However, based on distinct differences in the physical properties of colorant materials, it is now evident that they dyed fibers as well as yarns.

Pigments and Dyes

Pigments are relatively large molecules that attach to the surface of a fabric. Different binders have been used throughout history, including resin, glue, egg whites, and many other materials, to help facilitate adherence of the pigment to the fabric. Early pigments were generally made from mineral or inorganic sources.

Dyes, on the other hand, are absorbed into the core of the fibers, allowing the fibers, yarns, or fabrics to be colored in richer colors and patterns. One example is to use differently colored yarns to create patterns like a tartan. Some of the Celtic textiles found in the Hallstatt salt mines in Austria show plaid patterns created by using dyed yarn materials. Besides the colorant and structure information acquired from the Hallstatt materials, scientists have found evidence of nits (eggs of lice) attached to the hair fibers used in the fabric construction. Therefore, they concluded that the people had problems with these insects, and the clothes they wore must have been in close proximity to the bodies where the lice fed on the blood of the human host. Other garments were probably "overclothes," worn away from the body.

In North America, coloration became more elaborate in the Mississippian period, as is exemplified in the textiles found at Spiro temple mound complex in Oklahoma. There, drier climates enabled elaborately decorated and colored mantles, sometimes decorated with feathers, to survive. This is also the first time in North America that resist dyed materials were found. The Spiro textiles are housed and studied at the Cooper-Hewitt National Design Museum.

It must be remembered that dyes and pigments are subject to change over time due to exposure to heat and light. Yarns that are now brown may have once been yellow, red, or green at the time of their production and use. Degradation of products frequently alters their appearance. Sometimes all color has turned brown or black, and only complex analysis can provide proof that the textile was ever another color. Museums, therefore, such as the Museum of Natural History in Vienna, have reproductions of some of their ancient textiles on display while the originals are kept in a climate-controlled environment to preserve them for future study.

ENVIRONMENTS CONDUCIVE TO TEXTILE SURVIVAL

It takes a special set of circumstances, and a lot of good luck, for fragile textiles to survive through a long period of time. Prehistoric textiles are all made from organic materials and are therefore very perishable. Therefore, archaeologists often refer to textiles as "perishables," whether they are made from fibrous or skin materials. However, certain materials survive better than others, and often the direct surroundings are responsible for the survival or degradation of the textiles. Circumstances under which textiles are more likely to be preserved are:

- pH compatible with the textile material
- freezing temperatures
- anaerobic or waterlogged conditions
- aridity (low humidity)
- carbonization and mineralization

pH Compatibility

For buried artifacts, the pH of the soil in contact with the materials influences their fate. For instance, hair fibers such as wool will do relatively well in an acidic environment, while cellulose fibers, such as cotton, will completely degrade. However, cellulosics will do well if the surrounding materials have an alkali nature. This situation is generally referred to as "differential survival," and soil composition has a great influence on the preservation outcome.

Freezing

In regions of permafrost such the Arctic and subarctic zones, perishable artifacts have been found to endure through time so we can study them today because the freezing temperatures inhibit the growth of bacteria and fungi that are responsible for much degradation. A well-known example is Ötzi, the "Iceman," who was at least partially covered in ice and snow immediately after he died around 3200 BCE in the high Alps on the border of Austria and Italy.

According to the museum that houses Ötzi, his clothing is composed of a cap, hide coat, grass cloak, leggings, belt, loincloth, and a pair of shoes. Only tanned leather and a grass coat were used. The stitching threads were made mainly of animal sinews and only in part of plants, above all grasses and to a lesser extent bast. The cloak, a twined construction, was worn over a hide coat and determined to a large extent the outward appearance of the man. The cloak was made of long stalks of Alpine grass. Under the grass cloak, the Iceman wore a knee-length upper garment made of goatskin. It consisted of numerous long, rectangular strips of leather that were joined together by regular oversewing on the inside. The arrangement of the leather into vertical strips may have aimed at creating a pattern out of the different colors.

The Iceman's leggings were composed of a number of pieces of leather sewn together lengthwise with animal sinews and tapered near the bottom. They were made of domestic goat hide. The leggings were about $25\frac{1}{2}$ inches (65 cm) long and covered the thighs and lower legs. In this sense, they were not really a pair of trousers but more like two separate sleeves.

Ötzi also wore a belt made of calf leather. A piece of sewn-on leather formed a little pouch that contained five items, including a scraper, a drill, a flint flake, and a bone awl. Among the preserved bits of hide was a $19\frac{1}{2}$-inch-long (50 cm), 13-inch-wide (33 cm) leather fragment. This piece of clothing was made out of long narrow strips of goat hide joined by oversewing with twisted threads made from animal sinews. The originally 40-inch-long (1 m) loincloth was drawn between the legs and fastened at the front and back with the belt.

The shoes originally consisted of an oval leather sole with turned-up edges held in place by a leather thong. A net woven out of grass was attached to this on the inside to hold in place the hay that was stuffed inside as protection against the cold. The shoes were closed with leather uppers attached to the sole by a plain-stitched leather thong. Whereas the sole of the shoe is made of brown bearskin, the uppers are made of deerskin. The uppers were closed using a form of shoelaces. The Iceman's shoes are the oldest ever found.

He also wore a half-spherical bearskin cap consisting of a number of strips of leather. Unlike the other pieces of clothing, even the outer fur has remained intact in this case. Two leather thongs were attached to the lower rim of the cap, to fasten it under the chin.

After Ötzi died, the ice froze and desiccated the body, thereby preserving it until tourists found it in 1991. The Iceman mummy, with his equipment and clothing, gives us unique insight into the everyday life and general appearance of an inhabitant of the Alps during the Late Neolithic (or Copper Age), more than 5,000 years ago. The clothing and equipment that he was using before he met his end is on display in a museum, and researchers have learned invaluable information about Neolithic technology and use of natural resources from this discovery.

Anaerobic Conditions

As in freezing conditions, in waterlogged environments, microorganisms do not have access to the oxygen that they need to thrive. Furthermore, sometimes the organic acids and aldehydes, such as tannins, that are present in this wet environment act to preserve the soft tissues of cadavers and other organic remains, including their clothing and adornments. "Bog mummies" have been instrumental in discovering details about ancient fashions, jewelry, and the food people consumed before they fell or were placed into these bogs. Such evidence gives insights into the social discourse.

The bog bodies have been found all over northern Europe. Best known are the Grauballe Man and Tollund Man from Denmark, who lived during the Celtic Iron Age (c. 400–300 BCE). In Germany, the Windeby Girl is best known. Often the individuals suffered a violent death, which has given rise to some speculations about social norms, justice, and the like. Especially in Europe, some of the clothing and dress from the past has been reconstructed based on what was learned from these remains.

In North America, the Ozette and Windover sites are examples of waterlogged environments that have yielded many perishables. Both are wetland sites dating to the Archaic period and used for an extended time. The Archaic period in North America

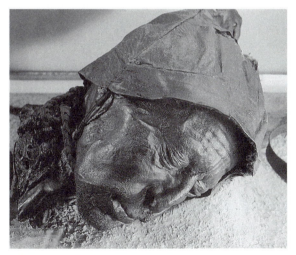

Tollund man. © Werner Forman / Art Resource, NY.

GRAUBALLE MAN

The Grauballe Man is the best-preserved bog body from Iron Age Europe dating to about 290 BCE. He was found during peat-cutting close to the village of Grauballe near Silkeborg in central Jutland in 1952 and is now housed at the Moesgård Museum of Prehistory in nearby Aarhus.

WINDEBY GIRL

An approximately fourteen-year-old girl was found in Windeby, near Schleswig, Germany. The body dates to the first century CE and her death may not have been accidental. Her body was anchored by a large stone and branches from a birch tree, and her eyes had been blindfolded with a strip of cloth woven from brown, yellow, and red threads. It was thought for a long time that she may have been sacrificed, but new research does not support this.

featured a widespread nonagricultural adaptation of hunter-gatherers that moved around seasonally to hunt. Their toolkit included the *atlatl* (spear thrower) and grinding stones. Depending on the region, this period dates from 8000 BCE to 1000 BCE or even as late as the first century CE. Textile remains from this period have been found at the Windover site in Florida, but also in dry rock shelters in the Great Basin.

Ozette, located on the Olympic Peninsula, Washington, was partly covered by a mudslide around 1400–1500 CE. The mud sealed perishable materials from oxygen in an environment that does not usually preserve them. Baskets, mats, tumplines (carrying straps), and many wooden objects have been recovered, amounting to a total of 42,000 artifacts. The modern inhabitants of Ozette assisted the archaeologists and took the artifact recovery as an opportunity to learn more about their ancestors.

Windover, near present-day Titusville, Florida, is a muck pond that was used by early Archaic peoples to dispose of their dead from 6000 to 5000 BCE. More than 160 individuals have been recovered from this mortuary pond. It produced exceptionally well preserved, but fragile, organic materials in addition to the tools and skeletal remains found there. Some of the items were sophisticated basketry, cordage, and wood items previously undocumented for this time in Florida. The textile assemblage exhibit close-simple and close-diagonal twining, both with S-Twist wefts (doubled and tripled), as well as open twining with paired Z-Twist wefts and balanced plain weave. Represented forms include circular or globular bags, hoods, blankets, clothing, and burial shrouds. There was also twisted and braided cordage and composite fiber constructions. This assemblage of materials may indeed constitute the oldest textiles from the American Southeast.

Aridity

A very dry climate also preserves perishable materials. Therefore, in southwestern North America, many cliff dwellings and rock shelters contain ancient perishables. Unfortunately, rodent or other animal activity often damages these items. Furthermore, in many cases, people who used these caves and rock shelters subsequently recycled anything useful that they found nearby.

The Tonto shirt is one of the more spectacular textile finds. Other important discoveries include the oldest twined and coiled baskets found in North America, dating to about 11,000 years ago. Basketry was a very widespread tradition in Native American cultures and was used for various purposes in ancient times. It is often seen as the predecessor that evolved into the production of finer (soft) textiles. Some of the oldest archaeological sites yielding baskets, cordage, and other perishable materials were in caves and rock shelters in the Great Basin region of Nevada, Utah, and parts of Idaho.

Mineralization and Carbonization

Under the right circumstances, the organic portions of fibers or whole textiles can be preserved through mineralization or carbonization. In the first process, the fibers are replaced by minerals from the surrounding areas, such as in soils or metals, to form a cast or mold while still retaining the morphology of the organic structure that they have replaced. This is a form of fossilization, and the resulting structures are called *pseudomorphs*. Pseudomorphs frequently occur when a textile was used to wrap a metal object, especially copper. Over time, copper corrosion products replace the organics in the fibers. Sadly, this material is often merely viewed as corrosion and has traditionally been removed by well-meaning museum workers to make the copper artifact look shiny again. However, pseudomorphs still retain much information, especially about the fabrics that left their impressions. Careful analysis can determine the type of yarn twist and textile structure. It can also be determined whether the replaced materials were protein or cellulose.

A textile becomes carbonized when it has been exposed to a heat source that is hot enough to change its chemical structure, but under circumstances that do not allow total combustion. This carbonization actually stabilizes the materials somewhat. Again, there is much information that can be gained from it. Often these types of remains are found in cremation burial context.

POTTERY IMPRESSIONS

Often, direct evidence of textile production cannot be found because the textiles are completely degraded. However, there are instances of indirect evidence. Textile impressions can be found on pottery, for example, which allow inferences about yarn and fabric construction. Textiles or cords were a popular way of decorating pots all over the world. Paddles wound with cords or covered in fabric were also commonly used to create a tool that made the decoration of the pottery faster and more efficient, while improving the structure of the pot. This method was popular in North America, Europe, Japan, and many other places. Yarn and textile structure can be determined based on the impressions left behind.

Textiles were produced and used extensively in prehistory. Not only were leather and skins used, but an array of fibrous materials from plant or animal sources were employed for the construction of clothing and many utilitarian items such as cords and baskets. Many of the plants, such as milkweed, are no longer identified as economically important, and not too many people today would use bear, buffalo, or dog hair to make their clothes. Nevertheless, in the past, these materials constituted an important resource, and these once-important raw materials may still prove themselves useful at a time when sustainability has become a real concern. Thus the study of ancient textiles may ultimately play a role in the discovery of renewable resources similar to that of ethnobotany in the discovery of new and better medicines. After all, ancient peoples had an intimate knowledge of the landscape and the plants and animals within, something that most people today can no longer claim.

Although we cannot interview the peoples from the past anymore, archaeologists and textile historians can infer that some of archaeological textiles were used in religious or ritual contexts. In other words, they reflect the sociocultural discourse of the past. Studying ancient textiles and learning where these raw materials came from can provide valuable information on the economy of the past, potential trade relationships, and communications that sometimes took place over long distances. It also reflects social processes such as craft specialization. The evolution of craft specialization is the process that freed some individuals to perform highly specialized tasks, while others did the everyday chores, especially food procurement. Textiles touch everybody's lives, in both sacred and mundane ways.

FURTHER READING

Downs, Dorothy. *Art of the Florida Seminole and Miccosukee Indians*. Gainesville: University Press of Florida, 1995.

Drooker, Penelope Ballard, and Laurie D. Webster, eds. *Beyond Cloth and Cordage: Archaeological Textile Research in the Americas*. Salt Lake City: University of Utah Press, 2000.

Menotti, Francesco, ed. *Living on the Lake in Prehistoric Europe: 150 Years of Lake-Dwelling Research*. London: Routledge, 2004.

Spindler, Konrad. *The Man in the Ice: The Discovery of a 5,000-Year-Old Body Reveals the Secrets of the Stone Age*. New York: Harmony Books, 1994.

Teague, Lynn S., and Helga Teiwes. *Textiles in Southwestern Prehistory*. Albuquerque: University of New Mexico Press, 1998.

WEB RESOURCES

"Clothes and Fashion at the Time of the Tollund Man." http://www.tollundman.dk/toej.asp.

Moesgård Museum. "The Grauballe Man." http://moesgaard.hum.au.dk/my.php?sub=80&language=1.

"Sandals of the Anasazi." http://www.centralpt.com/pageview.aspx?id=15887.

South Tyrol Museum of Archaeology. "The Iceman." http://www.archaeologiemuseum.it/f01_ice_uk.html.

"Textiles from Hallstatt." http://members.aon.at/textile-techniken/TKF/textile_e.html.

Egyptian Clothing

Katherine Eaton

TIMELINE

GEOGRAPHY AND ENVIRONMENT

The Egyptian environment was the context in which ancient Egyptian dress and costume was produced and used. Egypt is located in the northeastern corner of Africa. Were it not for the waters of the Nile River, it would be like other North African countries, a tiny strip of semifertile land squeezed between the Sahara Desert and the Mediterranean Sea. Basic knowledge of the annual cycle of this river is essential to understanding many aspects of ancient Egyptian culture, including textile production and seasonally based religious performance.

The Nile begins at Khartoum in modern Sudan, where the White Nile, originating in southern Sudan, and the Blue Nile, originating in the Ethiopian highlands, meet. From there, it runs a twisted course through the Bayuda and Nubian deserts. There are six cataracts along its course, points where rapids make navigation by boat difficult or impossible. In ancient times, the southern border of Egypt was at Aswan, just north of the first (i.e., northernmost) cataract. From there, the Nile continues to cut a narrow path through the desert until it fans out into the delta just north of the most ancient capital city, Memphis, in the vicinity of modern Cairo.

Thus, Egypt had two main agricultural zones, the Nile Valley and the delta. These areas were the focal points of life in ancient Egypt, where crops were grown and most settlements were located. Average annual rainfall is only 4–8 inches (100–200 mm) in the delta, less in southern Egypt. Rain levels in the past may have been somewhat higher than present day, supporting more nomads in the desert areas in the Old Kingdom and perhaps into the Middle Kingdom. However, from its beginning, ancient Egypt was a desert country where agriculture was dependent on irrigation from the Nile River. The annual seasonal cycle of this river was central to life in ancient Egypt.

Moreover, the land of Egypt is the context in which all the evidence about ancient Egypt is preserved. Aspects of the environment have led to accidents of preservation that favor certain categories of evidence—the mortuary memorials of elite individuals, for example—while destroying other categories that were probably more representative of ancient Egyptian culture as a whole, such as the settlements of average people.

Annual Seasonal Cycle

The ancient Egyptian seasons were rooted in the yearly agricultural cycle, which was dependent on the inundation, the annual flooding, of the Nile River. In ancient times, the year was divided into three seasons of four thirty-day months—inundation (*akhet*), growing (*peret*), and harvest (*shemu*). Five days, called *epagominal days*, were added to the end of the year to make a 365-day year. The flax harvest provided the raw material for the linen cloth out of which most ancient Egyptian clothing was made. Linen was ancient Egypt's main cash crop for both domestic production and export, and thus textile production was very important to the ancient Egyptian economy—second only to food production.

Inundation (Akhet)—July through October

Monsoon rains and the melting of snow in the Ethiopian highlands deliver large amounts of water to the Nile from the Blue Nile and Atbara rivers in late spring to early summer. Until dams were built in modern times, the effects were dramatic. Toward the end of the harvest season, in June, the rising river started to fill the hollows and marshes in the southernmost parts of Egypt with water, reaching Memphis about three weeks later. In mid-July, the waters began to rise rapidly. A combination of simple earthen dikes and natural levees guided the water into flood basins. The valley was flooded from mid-August through mid-September, reaching an average depth of five feet (1.5 m). The waters receded gradually, with flood basins being drained in southern Egypt by mid-October, and in northern Egypt, as late as the end of November. In addition to watering the land, the inundation washed harmful salts out of the soil and left deposits of rich silt, which fertilized the fields.

Settlements were built on mounds created by debris accumulated over time. Travel between towns and villages was conducted by boat or along paths atop dikes and levees. The ability to use boats may have facilitated the transport of produce harvested during the previous season. Thus, it is probably not a coincidence that this season was when some of the most important ancient Egyptian festivals, with the largest offerings of grain, bread, and beer, were celebrated, including Osiris's Khoiak Festival and Amun-Re's Opet Festival.

Growing (Peret)—November through February

Once the irrigation basins were fully drained, the fields were plowed. Grain and flax seed were planted. Flax seed was scattered over the damp fields, using "an underarm movement," and then trampled into the ground by animals. According to agricultural scenes preserved in the tombs of elite Egyptians, men seem to have done most of the work involved in planting the crops. However, such scenes presented an idealized view of Egyptian life and may not represent the actual division of labor. Very little is known about any fieldwork that may have been done between sowing and harvest.

Basin irrigation, practiced from the beginning of agriculture in the Nile Valley until the end of the Pharaonic Period, allows only one crop per year. In the Ptolemaic period, new irrigation technology, including the waterwheel (*saqia*) and the Archimedean screw, allowed water to be lifted from canals, permitting multiple cropping.[2]

Harvesting (Shemu)—March through June

The harvest was the most labor-intensive part of the annual agricultural cycle. Flax, which takes only about three months to mature, was the first major crop harvested. Flax grows to about three feet (1 m) in height and has blue flowers. Harvesting flax was particularly demanding, as it was pulled up by the roots so that the fibers would be as long as possible. Women are depicted taking part in the flax harvest alongside men in scenes in elite tombs. In contrast, scenes showing other phases of the agricultural cycle depict very few women working with the men.

Young, green flax is necessary to make the finest linen. However, if harvested too young, the fibers will not be strong enough. Thus, it may be that men and women worked together because as many hands as possible were needed to bring in the flax crop quickly. The longer it is left in the field, the coarser the fibers become. Once it starts to turn yellow, the flax can no longer be used in the production of the finest, most valuable linen. Fully ripened flax could be used only for very coarse cloth and rope. The harvested plants were left to dry and the seeds were collected from more mature plants. Then processing would begin.

The flax harvest did not interfere with the harvesting of the other main crops, emmer and barley, which usually take about six months to ripen. Women are generally not depicted playing a major role in the grain harvest. It might be that women were occupied processing flax, spinning thread, and weaving cloth during this time, although men also participated in processing flax. The harvest season ended with the beginning of the next inundation.

ACCIDENTS OF PRESERVATION AND THEIR CONSEQUENCES

The divide between flood plain and desert in Egypt is striking and abrupt—one can stand with one foot on fertile fields and the other on the seemingly lifeless desert sands. Most daily life activity in Egypt occurs on the Nile flood plain, the area that was covered by water during the inundation prior to the building of dams in modern times. The remains of ancient towns and villages on the flood plain are difficult to excavate for many reasons—people are living on this land now, and excavations would disrupt their lives; remains are located beneath many feet of silt deposited by the Nile and subsequent occupation debris; and the water table is so high that even when extensive excavation is conducted in such areas, delicate materials such as cloth, which deteriorate quickly in damp soil, are rarely preserved. In contrast, the dry, largely unoccupied desert is relatively easy to work in. This is where the elite tombs and royal mortuary complexes were located. Thus, ancient Egyptian archaeology is strongly weighted on the side of what some have called the "archaeology of death."

These environmental pressures, combined with aspects of ancient Egyptian culture and decisions made by earlier generations of Egyptologists, create very significant biases in the record due to "accidents of preservation." The royal family and elite Egyptians invested heavily in their tombs—building them out of stone even as they built their palaces and houses of mud brick. Starting in the New Kingdom, divine temples were also built of stone. Artworks are best preserved in these stone monuments.

Cloth is best preserved in desert sands. Settlement archaeology has dramatically improved over the past few decades, but there is still a great deal of work to be done. Cloth was very valuable, passed on and reused. One letter from a man to his son reads, in part: "And you shall be attentive to take this rag of a kilt and this rag of a loincloth in order to rework the kilt into a red sash and the loincloth into an apron."[3] Thus, although cloth is frequently found at settlement sites, particularly those near the desert edge, it usually consists of discarded scraps and rags.

Most surviving examples of cloth and clothing, in particular the most well preserved examples, come from royal and elite mortuary contexts. Again, this leads to biases. For example, wool does not seem to have been deposited in tombs, perhaps because it was considered ritually unclean. However, remains from workmen's villages on the desert edge associated with royal tombs at Kahun (Middle Kingdom) and Amarna (New Kingdom) reveal that wool was spun and woven at these sites.

The question of bias is even more significant when it comes to depictions of clothing in art. The purpose of scenes in tombs was not to faithfully render an accurate picture of life. These scenes were idealized and functioned on deeper ideological and symbolic levels. There are several trends in representations that disagree with the material remains of cloth and clothing recovered. Some of the most ubiquitous are:

- People were often portrayed wearing archaic costumes, and in some cases there is a considerable lag between when a type of garment appears in the archaeological record and when it appears in the artistic record. Many times, the king and deities were depicted in archaic dress no longer represented on ordinary members of the elite.
- In art in two dimensions, various parts of the human body were rendered from different perspectives—the nose in profile, the eye frontally, shoulders frontally, breast and nipples in profile. Clothing also was illustrated from its most characteristic angle and as a result did not always match up with the body. Interpretation of women's garments is further complicated by the desire to emphasize female sexuality. Sometimes comparison with three-dimensional artworks can help improve understanding, but this is not always the case.
- States of dress or undress in art were emblematic of rank and often do not reflect what people of different orders in society actually wore. Servants and laborers were often depicted nearly naked, even in situations when more clothing would have been essential.

Thus, the records available to reconstruct what the ancient Egyptians wore are heavily biased toward a fantasy version of life constructed by the elites in that society.

Finally, environmental conditions have preserved more sites in the Nile Valley than in the delta, a fact exacerbated by the concentration of population in northern Egypt from antiquity until modern times. Thus, most monuments were reduced to their foundations as they were used like quarries. In contrast, many major temples in southern Egypt, particularly in Luxor (ancient Thebes), are still standing. During periods when ancient Egyptian building activity was concentrated in the north, for example, the Third Intermediate Period, there is much less material to work with than during periods when more investment was made in southern Egypt, as during the New Kingdom.

CHRONOLOGICAL OUTLINE

Over the course of ancient Egyptian history, the environment remained fairly constant. However, the culture was not stagnant. The royal and elite monuments, which provide the bulk of the evidence concerning ancient Egyptian dress and costume, changed considerably over time. Other changes of note are the move to stone for the building of temples, increased contact with foreign peoples, and, of particular interest here, fashions in elite dress and developments in glass production and glazing, which changed jewelry production. Thus, a brief chronological overview is necessary to round out the background knowledge of ancient Egypt.

There are considerable debates regarding many details of ancient Egyptian chronology, particularly prior to the Late Period. This overview is based on the outline provided in Baines and Málek's *Atlas of Ancient Egypt*, which is generally accepted by mainstream Egyptologists.[4] There are three major phases to consider: the Predynastic Period (c. 5000–2950 BCE), the Pharaonic Period (c. 2950–332 BCE), and the Greco-Roman Period (332 BCE–395 CE).

The Predynastic Period: The Beginning of Ancient Egyptian Civilization

Alternating periods of dryness and fertility meant the Sahara drew people in during fruitful times and forced them out in dry times. At the end of the last Ice Age, from about 10,000 to 9500 BCE, the Nile was transformed into what has been called the "wild Nile." Extremely high floods resulted. The Nile cut a single channel, and the flood plain was reduced to approximately its current dimensions. During this time, the material culture of the Nile Valley remained fairly constant and was part of a larger North African complex. About 5000 BCE, a series of Neolithic cultures developed in the Nile Valley, including the Tarifian, Tasian, and Badarian. This is the beginning of the Predynastic Period, the first period that is generally considered in the history of ancient Egypt.

Already in the Predynastic Period, many essential elements of later ancient Egyptian culture were in place. Flax was grown and woven into linen cloth. Burials included provision for the basic necessities of life, indicating a concern about providing for the deceased in the afterlife. These supplies included objects related to personal hygiene and beauty, including combs and cosmetic palettes for the grinding of pigments for eye paint. Although some of these objects were made of valuable materials, such as ivory, social stratification was not strongly marked in the Naqada I period (also called Amratian, c. 4400–3500 BCE). During the Naqada II (also known as Gerzean) and Naqada III (also known as Semainian) periods up to 3000 BCE, this culture spread throughout the Nile Valley and into the delta. Cemeteries show greater social stratification, with a few burials, mostly of males, significantly more richly appointed than those around them.

Most Predynastic representational art is in the form of monochromatic line drawings that do not render the clothing of figures in detail. However, a wall painting dating to the Naqada II period from tomb 100 at Hierakonpolis done in whites, browns, and black, clearly depicts men wearing white kilts or loincloths. One figure wears a white garment with black spots, which, judging a similarly patterned object held by another figure, might be a depiction of the ceremonial leopard skin worn in certain ritual contexts.

At the end of this period, Egypt became politically united. The earliest kings of Egypt, known from their tombs at Abydos, were not included in later king lists. Modern scholars have designated this time period as Dynasty 0 or the Late Predynastic Period (c. 3100–2950 BCE). All of the primary features of the pharaonic style in art appeared at this time, including the use of registers and ground-lines; the depiction of figures of different rank on scales reflecting their status; the representation of objects and people from composites in which their parts are viewed from their most characteristic angles; and elements of royal regalia, including the red and white crowns, *sed*-festival cloak, bull's tail, beard, and mace.

Pharaonic Egypt

From the end of Dynasty 0, ancient Egyptian history is conventionally divided into thirty dynasties, based on a list compiled by Manetho about 300 BCE. Manetho's chronology has been supplemented by earlier lists and archaeological evidence, such as monuments and texts recording the year of the king's reign in which they were built or composed. It is probably not accidental that there were thirty dynasties listed. Thirty was a very significant number to the Egyptians. It was the length of a month in days and a generation in years. Modern scholars divide the Pharaonic Period into eight segments: the Early Dynastic Period, Old Kingdom, First Intermediate Period, Middle Kingdom, Second Intermediate Period, New Kingdom, Third Intermediate Period, and Late Period. The Pharaonic Period essentially ended when Egypt was conquered by the Persians for a second time in 343 BCE, although the Late Period is generally considered to have ended only with the Macedonian invasion in 332 BCE.

The Early Dynastic Period (c. 2929–2575 BCE)

The Early Dynastic Period, also called the Archaic Period, is composed of Dynasties 1–3 (c. 2929–2575 BCE). A major change at the beginning of this period was the building of large brick mastabas by members of the elite. *Mastaba*, which means "bench" in Arabic, designates a type of large rectangular building, constructed over a tomb shaft. Some people include the 3rd dynasty (c. 2649–2575 BCE) in the Old Kingdom. In fact, there was no decisive break between the Early Dynastic Period and the Old Kingdom, which are quite artificial. Egyptian society changed gradually, but significantly over this time period. The theme of provisioning for the afterlife, evident in Predynastic Period graves, continued in elite tombs and was extended. The tomb and other elements of memorial complexes developed features of palaces, indicating that they were to be houses for the dead. The use of stone in mortuary monuments was greatly expanded, particularly in the 3rd dynasty, when King Netjerykhet—better known as Zoser or Djoser—built the first pyramid, by expanding his stone mastaba into a step pyramid surrounded by subsidiary stone buildings.

A commonly illustrated item of dress during this time period was the archaic wraparound. Although it stopped being depicted on regular people in art during the Old Kingdom, it may have gone out of use in daily life before that point. The king and deities continued to be shown wearing variations on these garments even in the Greco-Roman Period. Most other trends in dress established in the Old Kingdom had already begun to develop by the end of the Archaic Period.

The Old Kingdom (c. 2575–2150 BCE)

The Old Kingdom was composed of Dynasties 4–8. The first king of the 4th dynasty, Snefru, developed the true pyramid (as opposed to Zoser's Step Pyramid), which was the primary form used for royal burials until the beginning of the 18th dynasty. The largest and most imposing pyramids are the great pyramids at Giza, which belonged to three 4th-dynasty kings—Khufu, Khephren, and Menkaure. Starting in the 5th dynasty, pyramids were both smaller and more cheaply built—today they look like piles of rubble.

In contrast, elite tombs became more elaborate over the course of the 5th and 6th dynasties. Most elite cemeteries consisted of fields of stone mastabas clustered around the royal burial sites in the area of Egypt's capital, Memphis, near modern Cairo. The earliest were almost solid, with only a small offering chapel and a shaft leading to the burial chamber. Over time, more and more rooms were added. In addition, local elites started building tombs in their provinces. These tended to be cut into the rock cliffs marking the divide between the high and low deserts.

Much of the decorative artwork from royal monuments focused on the relationship between the king and the gods. Beginning at the end of the 5th dynasty, the burial chambers of kings and some queens were inscribed with mortuary texts, called Pyramid Texts. The themes of mortuary decoration in the tombs of both the provincial and central elite indicate that provision for the afterlife was still a primary concern. This included an ever-expanding variety of idealized depictions of agriculture, craftsmen at work, fishing and fowling, banqueting, festivals, and other so-called scenes of daily life. Such scenes were not intended to be faithful renditions of life in ancient Egypt, however, and evidence from them must be used with caution. Their themes are inextricably intertwined with the offering ritual and funerary scenes, with which they have often been contrasted. "Daily life" scenes often show the sources of ritual offerings and burial equipment. Moreover, many contain coded references to rebirth in the afterlife and other aspects of mortuary ritual, although decorum forbade the explicit visual depiction of such subject matter, including any visual representations of deities or the king, in private tomb chapels until the New Kingdom.

During the Old Kingdom, men in the fields were shown wearing primarily cloth loincloths and short wraparound kilts with sashes and straps. Two contrasting depictions of elite men often appear in their tombs—in young adulthood and as mature, older men. The younger figure generally wears a short kilt and has a slender waist and flat or slightly muscular chest. The older official wears a longer kilt and has a bit of a belly and sagging pectoral muscles.

Elite women are always portrayed as young and slender. Although the so-called sheath dress is the most commonly depicted women's garment, it is not clear what it corresponds to archaeologically. In contrast, the most commonly encountered garments among surviving textiles for women—long-sleeved V-neck dresses—never appear in the artistic record. Female laborers were illustrated wearing sleeveless V-neck dresses as well as loincloths and skirts. Cloaks would have been worn by all for warmth but appear to be rather underrepresented in the artistic record.

The Old Kingdom ended in twenty years of kings with ephemeral rules. The breakdown of the Old Kingdom has been attributed to various causes ranging from the political (e.g., weak kingship or administrative problems) to the environmental (e.g., low Nile inundations). Several overlapping trends in mortuary traditions occurred during the Old Kingdom—royal monuments became smaller and more cheaply built, while elite monuments became more complex and more elaborately decorated. Recent studies of poorer cemeteries indicate that a middle class had begun to form in the later part of the Old Kingdom.

The First Intermediate Period (c. 2125–1975 BCE)

Dynasties 9 and 10, based in Heliopolis, competed with Dynasty 11, based in Thebes, during what is known as the First Intermediate Period. Warfare discouraged contact between artists of different regions, and thus provincial artistic styles developed. This time period also seems to have been one of economic contraction. Royal monuments are rare and generally quite modest. Nonetheless, "quite large numbers of modest monuments, made for lower strata of society than hitherto, are preserved."[5] This impression is supported by recent studies in nonelite cemeteries that indicate that the social processes related to the creation of a "middle class" during the later Old Kingdom intensified during this period.

The relaxation of certain points of decorum is perhaps a related phenomenon. For example, throughout most of the Old Kingdom, the king was depicted with his kilt wrapped left over right, while officials wrapped their kilts right over left. Private officials had certainly adopted the royal fold by the early 11th dynasty, and it became more common thereafter. The king rarely is depicted with a private fold.

The Middle Kingdom (c. 1975–1640 BCE)

Egypt was reunited by Nebhetepre Mentuhotep (variously called I or II), a king of the Theban-based 11th dynasty. Dynasties 12–14 formed the remainder of the Middle Kingdom. The kings of Dynasties 13 and 14 generally had very short reigns, indicating significant political instability. Other notable trends are increased engagement in Nubia, the land to the south of Egypt, where a system of forts was established, and increased immigration from western Asia. The contact between Egypt and its neighbors would continue to grow over time.

Throughout the Middle Kingdom, kings continued to build pyramids for themselves, and court officials located their tombs near the monument of the king they served. Provincial officials also built tombs in their hometowns until the process was halted quite abruptly during the reign of Senwosret III. The decorative schemes in elite tombs remained broadly similar to those in Old Kingdom tombs. However, coffins were decorated with mortuary texts (Coffin Texts), similar to those inscribed in royal pyramids from the end of the 5th dynasty. There is considerable debate surrounding the dating of coffins, and this trend may even have begun in the First Intermediate Period.

During the Middle Kingdom, men seem to have continued to wear all the items that they had during the Old Kingdom and also added leather loincloths and longer wraparound kilts (extending from the armpits to mid-calf). Women continued to wear all the items that they wore during the Old Kingdom. Both men and women may have added shawls. The Middle Kingdom is also the period to which the earliest examples of bag-tunics date, although they do not commonly appear in art until the New Kingdom. This time lag between the introduction of a new garment and its depiction in art may have been dictated by decorum.

The Second Intermediate Period (c. 1630–1520 BCE)

The period of transition between the Middle Kingdom and Second Intermediate Period is quite unclear, but it seems that the kings of Dynasty 14, if they existed at all, probably overlapped considerably with those of Dynasties 13 and 15. Dynasties 15 and 16 (which overlapped) were made up of foreign rulers called the Hyksos, who ruled the northern half of Egypt from their capitals of Sahkam and Tel el-Dab'a in the delta. Meanwhile, Dynasty 17, a native Egyptian dynasty based in Thebes, ruled the south. The last kings of the 17th dynasty expelled the Hyksos from northern Egypt, once again reuniting the country. Increased contact with western Asia, which continued in the New Kingdom, seems to have led to great technological change, with advances in metalwork, weaponry, and, of more relevance here, the vertical loom, glass production, and glazing techniques.

The New Kingdom (c. 1539–1075 BCE)

The New Kingdom was a period of increased engagement with the outside world, greatly fueled by imperial expansion. Clothing styles changed dramatically in the New Kingdom, with new forms illustrated and some types of clothing occasionally encountered in Middle Kingdom contexts appearing to have gained dramatically in popularity—namely, the use of complex wraparound dresses for women, leather loincloths for men, and bag-tunics for men and women from all walks of life. Meanwhile, women appear to have stopped wearing V-neck dresses, although they were still depicted in art, particularly on goddesses. The introduction of the vertical loom, which seems to have been operated by men, represents a major change in cloth production and particularly in the gendered nature of the work.

The New Kingdom can be split into three parts: the early 18th dynasty (1539–1353 BCE); the Amarna Period and its reconstruction (c. 1353–1292 BCE); and the Ramesside Period, composed of Dynasties 19 and 20 (c. 1292–1075 BCE).

Early Dynasty 18

Egypt was united by Ahmose. Although he was the son of the last king of the 17th dynasty, Ahmose is traditionally held to be founder of the 18th dynasty. This was a time of expansion, when Egypt became one of the first empires, controlling both lower Nubia and large portions of Syria-Palestine. For the first time, divine temples (as opposed to royal memorial temples) were built entirely of stone, including Luxor Temple, which was begun by Amenhotep (sometimes Amenophis III). These projects often involved thanks to the gods for victory in battle and were in no small part funded by these victories.

Ahmose built the last royal pyramid, at Abydos. Most New Kingdom kings built rock-cut tombs in the Valley of the Kings at Thebes, with memorial temples along the edge of the flood plain on the west bank of the Nile. High officials also built rock-cut tombs at Thebes, although recent work is revealing more and more about New Kingdom mastaba-tombs in the Memphite area as well. Decoration in private tombs focused on the same themes as earlier, but some favored high officials began to include depictions of the king in their tombs, a practice previously forbidden.

The Amarna Period and Its Reconstruction

After the reign of Amenophis III, his son Amenophis IV came to the throne. This king had radical religious ideas. He rejected the traditional gods of Egypt, including the state god Amun, for whom he was named, in favor of the singular sun disk. Called Aten, the sun disk was depicted as a solid circle with rays ending in hands holding *ankh* signs, representing the life-giving powers of the sun. In about his fifth year, Amenophis IV changed his name to Akhenaten, in tribute to his only god, and moved the capital of Egypt to a virgin site, called Akhetaten, "horizon of the Aten." Here, tombs were built for the royal family and high officials. This city is better preserved than any other ancient Egyptian city. Of particular importance here are textile remains from the worker's village at Amarna. In about his ninth year, Akhenaten closed the temples of the other gods of Egypt and sent out teams to erase the name of Amun from existing monuments.

Art during this period is very different from earlier and later work in both content and style. The only deity depicted was the Aten, a sun disk placed at the top of the scene, with rays extending down and ending in hands. Previously and subsequently anthropomorphized versions of deities generally met the king face-to-face in artwork. Thus, this change had a profound impact on the composition of scenes. Only the king and the queen could commune directly with the sun god; private devotion focused on the royal family. One of the most striking aspects of Amarna Period art is the way in which human figures are rendered. To put it most succinctly, the figures are pear shaped, with thick thighs, a large posterior, and drooping belly. This effect is enhanced by the contrast with narrow shoulders and chest and spindly arms and lower legs.

Akhenaten's religion did not long outlive him. The end of Akhenaten's life is shadowy and the identity of his immediate successor is debated. It is clear that the first steps to reinstate the traditional religion were taken by Akhenaten's son, Tutankhamun (born Tutankhaten). A very important find from this time period was the largely intact (having been robbed in antiquity) tomb of the boy-king Tutankhamun, which included many examples of textiles and jewelry. Nonetheless, the ruling family was clearly in decline. After the brief rule of King Ay, Horemheb, a military ruler of nonroyal birth took the throne. However, as he had no sons, it was left to his successor, Ramesses I, to start a new dynasty.

The Ramesside Period

Ramesses I had male heirs to inherit the throne—his son Seti I and grandson, Ramesses II. Finally, after three decades of disruption, a new royal family, the 19th dynasty, could establish itself and complete the restoration of the old religion. The building program of Seti I, which was completed and expanded by his long-lived son Ramesses II, is unparalleled in the number and degree of preservation of buildings that are still standing today. While the survival of this material is doubtless due in part to accidents of preservation, it is clear that the general trend in building during this time was one of enlargement and expansion, perhaps fueled in part by the new ruling family's need to demonstrate its legitimacy. Ramesses II, commonly called Ramesses the Great, ruled for a remarkable sixty-six years, during which time his empire was strong and stable and his building projects enormous. Given his achievements, it is not surprising that the kings of Dynasty 20 decided to name themselves after him, although none lived up to his namesake.

A very important source for this time period is the workmen's village at Deir el-Medina. This village was established to house the workers and craftsmen who built the royal tombs in the Valley of the Kings. Established early in the 18th dynasty, most of the material recovered from the site dates to the Ramesside Period. Throughout the period, elite tomb decoration tended to focus on themes previously forbidden by decorum, including vignettes from the *Book of the Dead* and many depictions of the deceased in the presence of deities.

The Third Intermediate Period (1075–715 BCE)

During the Third Intermediate Period, the native Egyptian kings of Dynasties 21 and 24 competed with the Libyan kings of Dynasties 22 and 23. The kings of the 21st and 22nd dynasties were buried within the Amun Temple enclosure at Tanis, where they could be better guarded than the New Kingdom tombs in the Valley of the Kings were. This precaution was not in vain because the burials survived essentially intact, with splendors rivaled only by the Tomb of Tutankhamun, including golden jewelry inlaid with precious stones. During this time, the high priests of Amun at Thebes controlled southern Egypt.

The Late Period (715–332 BCE)

Egypt became reunited by a force from without, the Nubian 25th dynasty, which was interrupted by Assyrian invasions. Egyptians regained control in Dynasty 26, called the Saite Period. During this time period, there was a great deal of copying of older styles in art, including depictions of dress. The Persian invasion, resulting in another foreign dynasty, Dynasty 27, ended this period. Native Egyptians again gained control, forming Dynasties 28–30. The rule of the last king of the 30th dynasty, Nectanebo II, came to an end when the Persians invaded again in 343 BCE. Egypt would not be ruled by a native Egyptian again until 1952 CE.

The Greco-Roman Period (332 BCE–395 CE)

In 332 BCE, Egypt became part of Alexander the Great's Macedonian Empire, along with the rest of the Persian Empire. Upon Alexander's death, Egypt was handed over to one of his generals, Ptolemy. He and his successors ruled Egypt as pharaohs until 30 BCE, when the Romans took over. Throughout this time period, called the Ptolemaic Period after the name of the royal family, Greeks immigrated to Egypt, settling primarily in Alexandria and the Fayum region. Great changes occurred, as new forms of irrigation allowed a second crop to be produced each year and coinage was introduced. However, traditional Egyptian religion was maintained, with the Ptolemaic kings and Roman emperors styling themselves as pharaohs on temples newly built in the traditional Egyptian style. The degree of interaction and influence between the Greek and Egyptian populations is a matter of considerable debate. For the dress of the Greek and Roman populations in Egypt, refer to chapter 4.

MATERIALS AND MODES OF PRODUCTION

Most clothing in ancient Egypt was made of linen, although there is evidence for the limited use of other fibers, especially wool. Sandals and, during some time periods, loincloths were made out of leather. Beads made of gemstones and glazed composite were used in jewelry production, to adorn items of clothing, and strung together to make items of clothing. Finally, sometimes clothing and adornments were made of highly perishable materials, including flowers and perhaps feathers.

Linen

Linen is made from the fibers of the flax plant. Once the flax is harvested and dried, it is processed to produce linen thread and woven into cloth. Sometimes either the thread or the cloth was dyed, although other decorative elements appear to have been more common, particularly prior to the New Kingdom.

Processing Flax to Make Linen Thread

There are three main steps involved in making raw flax into linen thread: separating the bast fibers, used to make the thread, from the useless parts of the stem; roving; and spinning the cleaned fibers into thread. The flax was first *retted*, soaked for 10–14 days in order to break down the hard, outer parts of the stem. After drying the flax, most of the remaining woody parts of the plant were separated by beating, or *bruising*, the stems. The last remaining bits of debris were then *scutched* or combed out, using a pair of sticks. Next, the cleaned bast fibers were *roved*, a process in which fibers were drawn out, spliced together with a twist, and perhaps secured using saliva. The resulting lengths of fiber, or roves, were wound into balls or coils, which were placed into bowls or baskets. The rough threads passed through loops, rings, or lids with holes so that the fibers would not become tangled as they were spun into finished thread, either by hand or with the use of a spindle.

Three methods of spindle spinning were illustrated in ancient Egyptian tomb paintings. In all methods, fibers are drawn out of the rove, twisted by the motion of the spindle, and then wound on the shaft of the spindle. The main difference is the way in which the spindle is spun. In the grasped-spindle method, the thread passes through rings or a forked stick and the spinner uses both hands to turn the spindle. In the support-spindle method, one hand is used to hold up the fibers while the other hand spins the spindle. The most frequently depicted procedure, which also produced the finest threads, was the suspended- or drop-spindle method, in which the spindle was first rolled on the thigh and then dropped, with the weight of the spindle, called the whorl, maintaining the spin. Spindles are quite common in the archaeological record and support the view that illustrations of spinning in tomb paintings and models are generally accurate.

Weaving Technology

Weaving began with the measuring of the warp threads on a warping board, which might be a frame or simply pegs in the wall, as found in the workmen's village at Amarna. The warp was then transferred to the loom, where it formed the foundation of the cloth. From the Predynastic period until the start of the New Kingdom (c. 1500 BCE), weaving was done using horizontal looms, often simply composed of a pair of crossbars pegged to the floor. Although no looms survive, there are numerous depictions of them in art. The earliest view of a horizontal loom, dating to the Predynastic Period, was drawn on a bowl deposited in the tomb of a woman at Badari. Middle Kingdom representations of looms survive in both three and two dimensions. In two-dimensional art, horizontal looms are shown as if the viewer were looking down at them, with the women weavers sitting to the sides because that is the angle from which the details of the things and people rendered are most visible. Titles appended to names (such as "weaver") and economic documents indicate that weaving was done almost exclusively by women during the Old and Middle kingdoms.

Around the beginning of the New Kingdom, the vertical loom was introduced, along with other technology, probably from western Asia. One of the earliest pieces of evidence for the use of the vertical loom in Egypt appears in a scene depicting its use in the tomb of Thutnofer, who served under Thutmose III (*R.* 1479–1425 BCE). With the introduction of the vertical loom, men began weaving and horizontal looms ceased to be shown in art. Nonetheless, vertical looms were made with large wooden beams, which were very costly imported goods in ancient Egypt. Thus, it seems probable that weaving in homes continued to be done on the traditional ground loom and was still primarily women's work. Although no looms survive, this supposition is supported by the textiles themselves, which often have a weft fringe, a feature associated with depictions of horizontal, but not vertical, looms.

Once the loom was prepared, the actual weaving could begin. Quite simply, weft threads were passed between the warp threads. The most basic form is the *tabby weave* or *plain weave*, in which the weft thread passes over one warp thread and under the next. At the end of the line, the thread returns in the opposite direction, with the weft thread going under threads it had gone over in the previous line, and vice versa, forming an interlocking structure. There were countless variations on this basic pattern. One of the more common patterns is the *basket weave*, in which a group of weft passes follow the same pattern and then alternate in groups. Some 11th dynasty textiles have loops, rather like terry cloth; one in particular displays a pattern of stripes and zigzags made by leaving loops of thread as it was woven. It is common for depictions of garments to display stripes and other simple geometric designs from the Archaic Period onward, although it is generally not clear if these were part of the weave, pleats, or representations of clothing made from matting.

The most intricate patterns were *tapestry weaves*, in which different colored threads were interwoven only in the areas where they were required to form a pattern. This is a very labor-intensive process, which appears to have been introduced to Egypt at roughly the same time as the vertical loom. The earliest examples of tapestry-woven fabrics come from the tomb of Thutmose IV (*R.* c. 1400–1390 BCE) and appear to be heirlooms passed down from his father, Amenophis II (*R.* c. 1426–1400 BCE), and grandfather, Thutmose III (*R.* c. 1479–1425 BCE). Tapestry-woven fabrics quickly became a marker of status among the elite, with those who could not afford the most costly fabrics opting for simpler patterns and sometimes supplementing very simple designs with painted decoration.

Dyes and Other Decorative Elements

Most linen is naturally beige, ranging from shades of white to golden brown. Garments depicted in artwork are usually bleached white. White linen was required for ritual purity and may have been shown on people in artworks from tomb contexts for that reason. However, bleaching garments might not have been as widespread among workmen as the idealized tomb paintings seem to indicate. Large amounts of beige and brown linen excavated at the workmen's village at Amarna might indicate that common people often left their linen clothing its natural shades of beige and light brown.

The earliest dyes used in Egypt were ochers, which may have been employed as early as the Predynastic Period, although some do not consider these to be true dyes, as the cloth was colored by painting pigments onto the cloth, merely coating the fibers. However, dyes were used on leather and matting in this early period. True dyes for linen may have been developed as early as the Middle Kingdom. Mordants were required in order to fix the dye in the fabric. Alum was the most likely mordant to have been used in ancient Egypt, based largely on what is known of the available resources.

The earliest evidence for linen cloth woven from colored threads comes in the form of tapestry-woven cloth from early 18th-dynasty royal tombs. The three main colors obtained were blue, probably from woad (early reports of the use of indigo for blue have not been substantiated); shades of red and pink, from madder; and yellow, perhaps obtained from safflower, pomegranate, or iron buff. Purple tones and dark browns were made by mixing red and blue. Green cloth, produced using a mix of blue and yellow, is rare in the archaeological record. However, in the daily temple ritual, a trio of cloths—white, green, and red—was offered to each deity, so the impression that green cloth was less common might be due to accidents of preservation.

Linen clothing was also embellished in other ways. Some decorative elements, including fringes, looped patterns, and complex tapestry patterns, were incorporated during weaving. There is also limited evidence for the use of embroidery and appliqué, primarily from royal contexts. Other embellishments were sewn on—beads, rosettes, bits of gold; it is often difficult to determine whether depictions of such elements represent part of the clothing or elaborate pieces of jewelry. Finally, many garments were shown formed into complex shapes. Because of the natural pectin in the flax fibers, new garments could take on quite stiff shapes, as in the triangular-fronted kilts favored by elite men. They could also hold elaborate pleats.

Other Fibers

Textiles made of sheep's wool have been found in ancient Egyptian contexts from as early as the Predynastic Period, but they are generally not from tombs. The worker's villages at Kahun and Amarna provide evidence that wool was spun, woven, and dyed in Egypt. Goat hair was similarly used. Wool and goat hair would certainly have made warmer cloaks than linen. Human hair was used to make wigs. Examples of textiles made of palm fiber, grass and reeds, and hemp and ramie have all been reported from Pharaonic Period sites, but doubts remain concerning these identifications. Cotton imported from India and silk imported from China were both introduced to Egypt in the Greco-Roman Period.

Leather

Sandals were often made of leather. Otherwise, the use of leather in clothing appears to have been quite limited. A garment that looks similar in form to the archaic wraparound was made out of leopard skin and secured over the shoulder with ties. This garment went out of fashion in the 4th dynasty, somewhat earlier than the archaic wraparound. A full leopard hide, complete with legs and head, was worn by the deceased's eldest son and by priests during the performance of certain rituals throughout ancient Egyptian history. Beginning in the Middle Kingdom, men and boys wore leather loincloths, a fashion that may have been imported from Nubia.

Precious Stones

Elite women and goddesses are often depicted wearing beaded net-dresses over their white linen garments. Even some servant statues appear to show women with beaded overskirts. Some aprons and kilts were beaded, or were worn with beaded nets over them, as well. Elite Egyptians, royalty, and deities are rarely portrayed without considerable amounts of jewelry.

The desert areas around the Nile—the Eastern Desert, Western Desert, and Sinai Peninsula—were rich in raw materials from which jewelry could be made, including copper, gold, and gemstones. In addition, imports of lapis lazuli and silver were highly valued, often even more than gold. The widest variety of local stones were used to make beads, pendants, and amulets during the Predynastic Period—agate, chrysoprase, cornelian (or carnelian), onyx, red and green jasper, fluorspar, garnet, malachite, microline, olivine, amethyst, milky quartz, serpentine, steatite, and turquoise. Although almost all of these continued to be used in jewelry to some degree, cornelian, red jasper, amazonite, and turquoise were among the most widely valued gemstones throughout the Pharaonic Period. Lapis lazuli was one of the most highly prized stones until at least the Third Intermediate Period. Most ancient Egyptian jewelry—even simple beads—were believed to protect their wearers in a variety of ways; that is, they had amuletic value. However, these popular stones appear to have been considered particularly important in this respect. Other stones came to be associated with specific amulets, for example hematite was associated particularly with the plummet, carpenter's square, and headrest amulets.[6]

There were also changes over the course of the Pharaonic Period. For example, amethyst became particularly popular in the Middle Kingdom, then fell out of use in the New Kingdom only to be revived in the Roman Period. It is unclear whether such changes were the result of fashion or supply. In the case of onyx, which was always used in a small way but became very popular in the Third Intermediate Period, supply might have been an issue; the Ptolemies and Romans imported the stone from India.[7]

During the Ptolemaic and Roman periods, several stones started to be used for jewelry for the first time. In some cases, as with beryl (emerald) in the Ptolemaic Period, the introduction appears to correspond with the discovery of a source in the Eastern Desert. This might also have been true for peridot, first found in the Ptolemaic Period in Egypt.[8] Others stones had long been known, but perhaps it took a foreign eye to appreciate their potential as gemstones. For example, the Romans appear to have been the first to use yellow jasper in jewelry, even though it had been used in the making of sculptures since the 18th dynasty.[9]

Glass and Glazed Ward

Egyptian *faience*, a nonclay ceramic usually composed of glazed powdered quartz (quartz frit), was a common material for inexpensive jewelry from the Predynastic Period, when it was first developed, throughout ancient Egyptian history. Jewelry-making again changed radically at the beginning of New Kingdom as the result of technological advances in glass production. Objects made of glass predating the 18th dynasty are extremely rare, often of questionable date or possibly the result of accidents. In ancient Egypt, glass "gemstones" were not considered to be cheap imitations but were valued in their own right. In fact, glass was so highly valued that milky quartz and rock crystal, both very commonly found in the deserts, would be laid over red cement "probably in imitation of cornelian or red glass."[10] Advances in glassmaking led to the development of a wider array of faience colors, as well. These changes were complemented by the development of the open-face mold, which allowed great increases in productivity.

Flowers and Feathers

Some garments are depicted with a scale-like patterning that are sometimes called *feathered dressed*. These were worn predominantly by women, but there are also depictions of gods wearing short archaic wraparound garments with this sort of patterning.[11] Examples of this pattern have been found in tapestry-woven garments, including on a glove from the tomb of Tutankhamun, and made of metal and jewels, as in a jeweled corselet also from Tutankhamun's tomb. Although no examples actually made of feathers have been recovered archaeologically, examples of broad collars made with perishable flowers have survived and were probably used on ceremonial occasions. Feathers, particularly ostrich feathers, were also used in headdresses.

TYPES OF CLOTHING

Egyptian clothing was quite simple in construction and was in two basic forms: cut-to-shape and wraparound. Because wraparound garments were simple lengths of cloth, determining the identity of surviving examples is complicated. Since some types of garments, most notably dresses, could be made by both methods, the two styles and their various methods of manufacture will be discussed separately.

In the following discussion, two items of clothing that became outmoded very early in Egyptian history, although they continued to appear in illustrations of deities—the archaic wraparound and penis sheath—are examined first. After that, the most commonly depicted items of dress prior to the New Kingdom—loincloths, kilts for men, and dresses and skirts for women—are addressed. Starting in the New Kingdom, the bag-tunic became one of the most widely depicted garments on both men and women, although these garments had probably already been around for a while. This section closes with the sashes, aprons, and straps that held these outfits together; the cloaks, blankets, and shawls worn over them for warmth; and headgear and sandals, which completed the look.

Archaic Wraparound

The archaic wraparound was formed from a simple, rectangular piece of cloth. It is depicted as extending anywhere from midthigh to midcalf in length. One corner was draped over the left shoulder, and the cloth was then wrapped around the body and tied at the left shoulder. In some cases, a shoulder strap was formed; in others, the cloth covered the left arm. A garment that looks quite similar in the artistic record was made out of leopard skin and secured over the shoulder with ties.

Worn by both men and women, the archaic wraparound gets its name because it is most commonly seen during the Early Dynastic, or Archaic, Period. Nonetheless, men from all ranks of society were depicted wearing it until at least the 5th dynasty. Male laborers were typically represented in short versions, tied with a sash. The king and gods also often wore short examples, theirs secured with elaborate sashes and aprons. Women's archaic wraparounds, worn mostly by servants, were generally about midcalf length. Some servant statues had patterns or beaded overskirts, but there do not appear to be any depictions in which women tied their archaic wraparound with a sash.

No examples of this garment have been recovered archaeologically. However, examples could be indistinguishable from many later garments because in construction it was simply a large, rectangular piece of cloth. Thus, unless marks of use, indicating how it was tied, were present, there would be no way to distinguish it from other wraparound garments of similar size, such as dresses and cloaks. Moreover, there is no reason to suppose that a single wraparound garment might not be wrapped in different ways for different purposes. For example, the same length of cloth could theoretically have been used as both a short archaic wraparound and a long kilt. Although there are no examples with patterns of wear consistent with multiple uses, garments with patterns of wear that have been analyzed are very, very rare.

By the New Kingdom, the archaic wraparound was depicted being worn only by the king and deities. It is not clear whether these garments were used ceremonially or shown only in art. In Ptolemaic temple scenes, any type of short kilt could be combined with a "corset," which sometimes featured one or two shoulder straps. These outfits may have evolved from the archaic wraparound and may never have been worn in real life.

Penis Sheath

The penis sheath is a rarely depicted item of clothing. Even in the earliest illustration, on the Narmer Palette (Dynasty 0), it appears to be nonfunctional and may already have been outdated. It is most frequently represented being worn by fecundity figures, minor deities associated with fertility, the most famous of whom is Hapy, personification of the Nile River. Penis sheaths do not appear to have been worn by ancient Egyptian men, although some foreign people were depicted wearing them.

Loincloths

There were two types of loincloths routinely worn in ancient Egypt: linen and leather. Linen loincloths were by far the more common, being worn by both men and women, although men are more often wearing them. Although women may have used them primarily as underwear and they have been found in women's tombs, loincloths are generally not depicted in art, which favors tight-fitting or diaphanous garments on female figures. Workers and female performers—particularly dancers and acrobats—are frequently portrayed wearing only loincloths.

Linen loincloths were cut-to-shape garments, composed of two triangles sewn together down the middle. The top was hemmed and the other edges rolled and whip-stitched. Cords were often attached to the top two corners, to be fastened around the waist. The third corner would be pulled between the legs and tucked in. Artistic depictions indicate that loincloths were generally tucked in so that the excess fabric did not hang loose.

Some kilts show a small triangle of cloth peeking out at the front. Although these have been identified as pointed aprons worn under kilts,[12] they could also represent the front tip of a loincloth that was not tucked in but rather drawn through the waistband, with the extra fabric hanging on the outside (in the manner of cloth loincloths worn beneath leather loincloths). This would allow elite men to show off the high-quality linen used to make their loincloths, subtly displaying their wealth at court.

Leather loincloths were only worn by men, and possibly boys, primarily during the New Kingdom, although they were introduced during the Middle Kingdom. Unlike cloth loincloths, leather loincloths were roughly rectangular. The body was formed from a single piece of leather, usually displaying highly decorative cutwork patterns consisting of patterns of holes, staggered rows of slits, or diamond-shaped cutouts. These features would also have allowed air to circulate, making the garments much more comfortable. A band was attached around the edges, extending to form straps extending at each corner. Leather loincloths were generally worn over cloth loincloths, with the excess fabric from the cloth loincloth hanging in front, rather than being tucked in.

Leather loincloths were commonly worn by two groups of men. The ones cut into delicate nets, which could not withstand wear and tear, may have been ethnic identifiers being worn by Nubians and by Egyptian officials connected with Nubia, including the king. More sturdy examples would have been worn by workers, such as craftsmen, sailors, and members of the military to protect undergarments from hard wear.

Kilts

Kilts and skirts were wraparound garments worn by men and women, respectively. They could be secured anywhere between the armpits and the waist at the top, and hang down anywhere from the midthigh to the ankle at the bottom. The simplest type, commonly depicted from the 1st dynasty onward, is the "classical-wrap around kilt."[13] This was quite simply a length of cloth, wrapped around the body, tucked in at the front, and usually secured with a sash. Throughout most of the Old Kingdom, the king was shown with his kilt wrapped left over right, while officials wrapped their kilts right over left. Elites had usurped the royal fold by the start of the Middle Kingdom.[14]

Short kilts generally have a rounded edge hanging down from the waist. This does not appear to have been specially made but was simply an artifact of wrapping, "as less cloth is used around the waist than around the hips, the kilt is naturally pulled to one side."[15] Longer kilts and skirts generally have a straight edge. Kilts might be decorated with fringe, tassels, or pleating. Some kilts are seen to have a stiff, triangular piece in front. Although some have interpreted these as separate aprons, the weight of scholarly opinion favors the view that the triangular front was formed by folding the excess fabric into the kilt and tucking it into the belt.

These large wood and bronze statues of Tutankhamun as royal Ka show a kilt style. © François Guenet / Art Resource, NY.

During the Old Kingdom, men often contrasted depictions of themselves wearing two different styles of kilt secured around the waist—a short one representing vigorous, youthful adulthood, and a longer one, representing the mature official. During the Middle Kingdom, an even longer kilt that tied much higher than Old Kingdom examples—sometimes even just under the arms—was frequently illustrated. Some two-dimensional depictions are transparent, revealing a short kilt beneath. In sculpture, they are always opaque—however, it is not possible to render cloth that does not cling to the body as transparent in three-dimensional stone or wood sculptures, and thus it is not known whether these garments were sometimes diaphanous or were simply rendered as such to demonstrate layering, or if the older-style kilt beneath the new was meant to display an attachment to tradition, even if it would not actually have been worn.

In the 18th dynasty, much more elaborately draped kilts came into fashion. The most common was the *sash kilt*. It could be draped in various ways, but the most usual was for the cloth to be wrapped around the hips once and then knotted at the front, with the ends hanging down. There was also a *scalloped-edge kilt*, which may have been a variation of the sash kilt. These new kilts were often layered over bag-tunics and earlier styles of kilt. In these cases, the sash kilts were generally opaque and the other forms peek out from beneath. As with the Middle Kingdom layering, it is not always clear which combinations would have been worn and which may have been rendered for other reasons.

One word for kilt in ancient Egyptian is *shendyt*, which can be written with an ideogram (𓄼). This type of kilt, so routinely depicted in art, has yet to be identified archaeologically. It tends to be worn in scenes of vigorous activity, such as running, hunting, and combat. Vogelsang-Eastwood described a similar garment as a kilt with an apron beneath.[16] Whatever the form of its construction, the Egyptians certainly seem to have considered this to be a single garment.

Dresses and Skirts

Two main types of dresses have been recovered from archaeological contexts: wraparound dresses, which are discussed along with skirts, and V-neck dresses. The most frequently seen dress in art is the so-called *sheath dress*, which does not clearly correspond to either type of dress surviving from the archaeological record. Any type of dress could be adorned by wearing beaded overdresses, which were also worn on their own for erotic effect.

Skirts and Wraparound Dresses

Skirts and simple wraparound dresses were formed by wrapping a rectangular piece of cloth around the body. There were two garments which strongly indicate that wraparound dresses were worn. Two rectangular pieces of cloth show stress marks and creases consistent with the wear patterns one would expect from a wraparound dress.[17] There were very few clear depictions of these garments in the artistic record prior to the New Kingdom, but the sheath dress might have been an artistic rendition, shown as much more form fitting than an actual garment could be in order to emphasize female sexuality and the more sedentary life of elite women.

During the New Kingdom, more complicated wraparound dresses with elaborate pleating began to be depicted. In one configuration, reconstructed by Bonnet, one top corner of the fabric was held at the left side of the waist. The material was then brought behind the body and the other top corner was brought over the left shoulder and under the left arm. The two corners were then knotted in front of the body. The right breast was left exposed. The left breast and upper left arm were covered.

Vogelsang-Eastwood reconstructed another wrap as follows: if the cloth were laid out, the upper right corner would be drawn over the person's shoulder. The left edge of the fabric would be pulled over the other shoulder and brought in front of the body, so that the bottom edge of the material would come across the arm near the elbow. The top left corner would then be wrapped around the body again and then knotted with the top right corner at the heart. Finally, there was a style in which the top corners were brought over the shoulders and knotted, and the front was left open or held closed with a sash.[18]

Cut-to-Shape or V-Neck Dresses

A significant number of cut-to-shape dresses with V-shaped necklines dating to the Old and Middle kingdoms have been found. These come in two forms with significant differences. The sleeveless V-neck dress was a cut-to-shape garment made from a single piece of cloth. It can be distinguished from the sheath dress, both in art and in preserved examples, because it has no seam below the bust. V-neck dresses with sleeves were constructed quite differently. The body was a simple tube. Two additional pieces of cloth extended from the neck to the wrist on each side of the body. The arm portion was a simple tube, with the shoulder portion attached to the body of the dress, forming a seam across the bodice.

Long-sleeved examples outnumber sleeveless examples in the archaeological record. The opposite state of affairs exists in artistic representations of attire, with sleeveless V-neck dresses commonly depicted, but no clear examples of V-neck dresses with sleeves. Some V-neck dresses, both with and without sleeves, were pleated horizontally.

Although women continued to be shown wearing sleeveless V-neck dresses until at least the Third Intermediate Period, it is not clear whether such dresses were actually still worn. No examples of V-neck dresses dating after the Middle Kingdom have been found, and it was not unusual for the Egyptians to portray people, and especially deities, in archaic dress.

The Sheath Dress

The most frequent type of dress in Egyptian art, particularly prior to the New Kingdom, is often called the sheath dress. For a long time, this dress was believed to have been made of a tube of cloth with straps attached. However, it was often noted that such a garment would be very difficult to wear. Furthermore, when women are depicted walking or kneeling with one knee raised, "the dress mysteriously stretches by just the right amount."[19] For possible symbolic and social reasons, women were usually portrayed in tight, restrictive clothing.

Of the nearly twenty dresses found to date, none are in this form. Although arguments from absence must be considered to be shaky ground, it is notable that the types of dresses most commonly found prior to the New Kingdom do not appear to have been depicted in art—in particular, the long-sleeved V-neck dress. Vogelsang-Eastwood has suggested that the sheath dresses were in fact skirts or wrap-dresses worn with straps arranged in various configurations over the shoulders and breasts. Others have suggested that sheath dresses were sleeveless V-neck dresses. However, sleeveless V-neck dresses do not feature a seam beneath the breasts, a characteristic feature of depictions of the sheath dress. The lines of surviving bead-net dresses are actually closest in form to the sheath dress.

Bead-Net Dresses

In the ancient Egyptian story collection *Three Tales of Wonder*, King Khufu was looking for entertainment. It was suggested that he have the beautiful girls of the palace row around his lake. His instructions regarding the women were:

> Let there be brought to me twenty women with the shapeliest bodies, breasts, and braids, who have not yet given birth. Also let there be brought to me twenty nets and give these nets to these women in place of their clothes![20]

Somewhere between clothing and jewelry, lies the bead-net dress. Like much jewelry, bead-net dresses were made of beads strung together. Two examples have been found. One, from an undisturbed burial, included enough of the original threading that archaeologists were able to reconstruct it. Depictions in art indicate that bead-net dresses were generally worn over either sleeveless V-neck or sheath dresses, the two forms of cloth dress most commonly represented. Patterned garments from ancient Egypt were rare, particularly prior to the New Kingdom. However, most representations of patterned clothing are consistent with the employment of beading, whether they were woven into the fabric, sewn on, or worn over in the form of a bead-net dress. It is likely that different methods could be used to achieve the same effect, as with the feathered patterns made in both tapestry and metal or the broad collars variously made out of beads, tapestry, painted decoration, and flowers.

Bag-Tunics

Bag-tunics (*meses*) were constructed by folding a rectangular piece of cloth in half and sewing up the sides, which usually were selvages. Holes were left for the arms near the fold at the top, and sleeves were sometimes attached. A hole and slit was usually cut for the head, the edges rolled and whip-stitched. Ties were often added so the slit could be closed. Bag-tunics came in two sizes: long (full-length), which fell to calf or ankle length, and short (half-length), which fell to between the hip and the knee. In both cases, the bottom was generally either hemmed or fringed. Nonetheless, there are examples with idiosyncratic features, such as in the construction of the neck hole or having hems around the arms in cases where selvages were not at the sides. Short bag-tunics were worn only by males.

The earliest bag-tunic found to date is a short one from an 11th-dynasty tomb at Thebes.[21] Bag-tunics of both lengths begin appearing in tomb art in the Middle Kingdom. By the New Kingdom, bag-tunics were clearly the most commonly worn garments, based on recovered garments, textual sources, and art historical material.

The only colored bag-tunic found to date was a very elaborately decorated example from the tomb of Tutankhamun. It was a

> yellow tapestry woven tunic, striped green and brown, with bands of flying ducks in green and another ornamented in rows of rosettes, with a band of inscription down the front and a tapestry-woven collar . . . which seems to be a woven version of the usual floral broad collar.[22]

Simpler striped tunics were also found in Tutankhamun's tomb, made by incorporating colored threads into the warp. Fragments of cloth from the workmen's village at Amarna also have colored stripes, indicating that this was probably standard practice in the 18th dynasty.

An alternative to incorporating decorative elements into the fabric was attaching beads, sequins, or woven bands. Embroidery was rare, but there are examples of it from the tomb of Tutankhamun. In artistic depictions, bag-tunics are often described as "pleated"; however, it is not clear whether the depictions in question represent pleats or simply folds in the cloth.

Actual surviving examples leave little doubt about the inaccuracies of these representations. Bag-tunics would have been very bulky and loose fitting. They are often shown with no more than a small, round neck opening—far too small to get one's head through. The fabric is often shown as being diaphanous, even though, with the exceptions of a few examples recovered from royal tombs, bag-tunics were made from fabrics that were "heavily close-woven and consequently bulky weaves."[23] Garments in the artistic records generally tend to be depicted as more close fitting than they would have been in reality.

Nonetheless, it is only from the artistic record that it is possible to see the approximate way in which these garments were worn. Depictions in art indicate that full-length bag-tunics were worn by men, women, and children of all classes, from laborers to royalty. However, whereas men are frequently portrayed wearing short kilts over their long bag-tunics, or tying them with broad sashes, women are generally wearing them alone. Short bag-tunics were invariably worn by men. Some excavation reports call short bag-tunics "shirts," and they were generally worn with a kilt and sash or apron, in the manner of a shirt. Some tiny bag-tunics were left as votive offerings at a shrine dedicated to the goddess Hathor.

Sashes, Aprons, and Straps

Sashes, aprons, and straps could be worn by themselves or be used to hold together the baggy tunics and wraparound garments usually worn by the ancient

Egyptians. A sash is essentially a belt made of cloth, rather than leather. In art, there are some views of men wearing only a sash, with the ends covering the genitals in the manner of an apron. In other cases, more pieces of cloth were added, making a true apron. There are also many depictions of kilts that may actually be kilt/apron combinations, but the visual record is not clear and no examples of aprons from the Pharaonic Period have survived. In some cases, items peeking out from kilts that have been identified as aprons might have been loincloths. Nonetheless, there are many illustrations of the king and deities with highly decorative panels hanging in front of their kilts, which almost certainly represent elaborate, jewel-encrusted aprons.[24]

Three types of sash are preserved. The simplest, a rope knotted at each end, was found with a loincloth. The type most commonly depicted in artwork and most frequently found archaeologically was a simple strip of cloth, hemmed along its length. The ends were usually plaited but in some cases hemmed as well. Finally, some sashes that were woven with decorative patterns have been found. So far, this type of sash has only been found in royal contexts, and depictions of it in art are almost exclusively found on "objects relating to deities or the court."[25]

Like sashes, straps were narrow lengths of cloth. However, straps were tied around the body in one of several configurations. They could be worn alone, usually by men or performers of either gender, or over other clothing. The simplest configuration was a single strip placed over one shoulder, arranged diagonally across the body, and either tucked into a sash or wrapped around in the manner of a sash. However, there are some depictions of quite elaborate arrangements wrapped around the body in a series of X-shaped configurations, particularly in the portrayal of dancers and acrobats. In other cases, straps went over one shoulder and under the other arm, or were simply "worn over both shoulders with the ends hanging down over the chest."[26] Some appear to have been either striped or pleated.

Cloaks, Blankets, and Shawls

Cloaks, blankets, and shawls were all generally quite simple garments, often just a piece of particularly thick rectangular cloth, worn over other clothing for warmth. The use of cloaks and blankets had considerable overlap. The possible remains of a woolen blanket have been found at the workmen's village at Amarna. Blankets could be made out of linen, sometimes incorporating loops of weft thread on one side that would trap air, providing insulation. There was also a ceremonial cloak, called the *sed*-festival cloak, worn from the Early Dynastic Period onward in the celebration of this ritual of royal renewal.

Objects identified as knotted cloaks were depicted in one Old Kingdom tomb being held out, open. They were made from a large rectangle of linen, leopard skin, or, since they are sometimes shown as brightly colored, wool. At the top, a narrow piece of cloth was attached, its ends forming ties at each of the two top corners. In the Middle Kingdom, it became more popular for the elite to commission statues in which they were represented wearing cloaks, although there is no reason to suppose that the weather was colder during that time period, as some have suggested.

Cloaks could be arranged in many different configurations. These generally fall into two categories: knotted and wrapped. The latter form is much more widely seen in art. Figures wearing cloaks wrapped around both shoulders appear in statuary from the Predynastic Period onward. In the Middle and New kingdoms, depictions of cloaks worn over one shoulder become more common. There are also more complex configurations in which the cloak is wrapped around the body several times, with the end draped over the shoulder and/or tucked in.

Although several "shawls" have been listed in excavation reports, including from the tomb of Tutankhamun, no clear examples have been analyzed in detail. Shawls are unusual in the artistic record as well, and it may be that it "was not a typical, everyday Egyptian garment."[27] Cloaks, however, appear to have been far more numerous.

Headgear

Status was often expressed in headgear such as caps, kerchiefs, and headbands. It is not clear whether caps were regularly worn in ancient Egypt. (Crowns and other items of royal and divine regalia will be discussed later.) According to Howard Carter, Tutankhamun's mummy wore an elaborately decorated skull-cap beneath the royal headdress. It would not be surprising if elite people often wore such caps between their wigs and their shaven heads, although there does not appear to be further evidence for this practice. Caps do appear to be commonly illustrated in tomb paintings, where they were worn by people working in the fields and at other dirty work. Nonetheless, examples of these sorts of caps have not survived and may actually be depictions of kerchiefs.

The construction of kerchiefs consisted of a square or rectangular piece of cloth with a strip of cloth sewn along its top edge, with its ends forming ties at either corner. The lower edge was often curved, and all edges were generally hemmed or rolled and whip-stitched. The top end, with the ties, was laid across the brow, with the cloth covering the top of the head. The ties were then drawn over the ears and tied behind the head, sometimes underneath the kerchief and sometimes on top of it. Kerchiefs came in different sizes—the smallest just covering the top of the head and the largest covering the back of the head and neck and falling below the shoulders. Longer kerchiefs were sometimes bound at the nape of the neck like a ponytail. Both the royal *khat*-headdress and *nemes*-headdress were essentially types of kerchief. Finally, laborers are often depicted with a simple length of cloth tied around their brows, no doubt to keep the sweat out of their eyes.

Sandals

Most ancient Egyptian sandals (*twt*) were probably made of reeds, although leather was also popular for those who could afford it. Examples have also been found of gold and wood (in the tomb of Tutankhamun); it is not clear whether these would have been worn or were just burial goods. Even the king is often depicted barefoot. He had a sandal-bearer, who followed him and held his sandals when he was not wearing them.

Jewelry

When one thinks of ancient Egyptian jewelry, one's mind is immediately drawn to the gold of the royal tombs of Tutankhamun (Dynasty 18), the Third

Intermediate Period kings within the Amun Temple enclosure at Tanis, and other spectacular finds. However, much ancient Egyptian jewelry has been recovered from surface graves belonging to people who could not even afford to build tombs. These were made from metals and semiprecious substances, as well as cheaper materials. In particular, pieces of glazed composition, "although fragile, were cheap to produce and easy to replace.... The glazed composition components were turned out in their thousands from open-backed moulds."[28]

In the Ramesside Period, documents record necklaces valued at between 5 and 13 *deben*, rings between half a deben and 5 deben, and some amulets for between 1 and 3 deben.[29] Thus, jewelry was as affordable as the most basic items of clothing at that time—bag-tunics, averaging about 5 deben—and considerably more affordable than finely woven clothing.

Throughout Egyptian history, both men and women adorned their plain, white linen clothing with jewelry. Some forms of beaded clothing were essentially very large pieces of jewelry, and it is difficult to draw the line between clothing and jewelry in some cases. For example, female entertainers and serving girls were sometimes depicted wearing nothing but jewelry or bead-net dresses. In these cases, the jewelry served to emphasize the woman's sexuality. Another such case is the royal apron, a garment elaborately decorated with the royal name, *uraei*—coloras that the king and some deities wore on their brows and which often adorn the King's apron, and other motifs that were royal prerogatives.

Many of the forms used had amuletic value and were believed to protect the wearer in some capacity. Beads of different shapes, colors, and substances could be strung together into bracelets, necklaces, broad collars, and other forms to provide personalized protection for the wearer. Other types of jewelry were signs of rank, most notably the *shebyu*-collar, a necklace made of disks of gold and awarded to high officials by the king himself beginning in the New Kingdom. It is worth emphasizing again that men wore elaborate jewelry as much as women did.

The most commonly encountered types of jewelry were, moving from the top of the body downward:

- Headbands, diadems, and circlets first appeared in the Predynastic Period and were worn by both men and women.[30] Additional hair adornments hanging down from these bands or attached directly to braids or ringlets seem to have been worn primarily by women. (See also the sections on headgear, hair and wigs, and royal and divine regalia.)
- Earrings of various forms were introduced during the Second Intermediate Period. Initially worn only by women, men began wearing earrings as well by the end of the early 18th dynasty. It has been suggested that they were introduced from abroad—either from Nubia by the Pan-grave people who served as mercenaries in Egypt or (somewhat less likely) from western Asia by the Hyksos.[31]
- Necklaces made of strings of beads are among the most commonly encountered pieces of jewelry from ancient Egypt. They could also incorporate amulets, pendants, or pectorals. Multiple strings were often worn, sometimes with broad collars as well. Chokers are often depicted in art, however no clear examples have survived.[32]
- Broad collars are "perhaps the most characteristic form of Egyptian jewelry."[33] They extended in a circle, radiating from the neck to the outer shoulders. Broad collars could be either pieces of jewelry or decorations incorporated into the clothing. Independent broad collars made of beads, as well as combinations of beads

and flowers, survived. However, decoration mimicking that of such jewelry was also painted or added in tapestry around the neckline of bag-tunics.

- Armlets, bracelets and anklets often came in matched sets and can be difficult to distinguish from one another in the archaeological record if they are not found in situ on a body. Bracelets, however, tend to show the most variety, ranging from delicate strings of beads to thick golden bangles inlaid with stones.
- Rings worn on the fingers took many forms, but perhaps the most popular were the scarab rings, representing the *kheper*-beetle (𓆣). The underside of the beetle was often inscribed with the owner's name. Plain signet rings were also popular and had a practical function as well—pressed into clay or wax, they were used to seal storerooms, shrines, letters, and the like.
- Girdles and belts were associated with male burials in the Predynastic Period. By the 12th dynasty, though, girdles had become "the prerogative of women."[34]

Thus, although there was some change over time, most forms of jewelry appeared throughout ancient Egyptian history and were worn by both men and women.

HAIR AND WIGS

Although hair fashions changed over time, a few general trends held. At any given time, there was a limited range of acceptable hairstyles for the elite and their household servants. Both elite women and men are often depicted with curled or braided hair. Robins observed that "wigs would have had the same social significance for women as for men: to hide thinning and graying hair, and to demonstrate the ability to appropriate the hair of others for one's own use."[35]

Shaven heads were required for priestly service, and most elite men, male entertainers, and male household servants had shaved heads. The elite men would wear wigs. Although women also wore wigs, they were much less likely to shave their heads. Female entertainers and household servants often wore hairstyles like those of elite women. Women may have tended to keep their own hair, because a women's hair was considered sexually appealing. The image of a woman braiding her hair was a common erotic motif in love poetry and literary tales, as in this New Kingdom love song:

> My heart thought of my love of you,
> When half of my hair was braided;
> I came at a run to find you,
> And neglected my hairdo.
> Now if you let me braid my hair,
> I shall be ready in a moment.[36]

Although long and short wigs were worn in most periods, there were subtle variations over time. For example, short wigs were worn by men from the Old Kingdom through the early 18th dynasty. Women generally favored longer wigs but did wear short wigs during the Middle Kingdom. For men of the early 18th dynasty, long wigs were markers of status and were not depicted being worn in the presence of a man's superiors (e.g., parents, the king). The *Nubian wig*, a multilayered, shoulder-length wig, became the most popular hairstyle for both elite men and women during the later 18th dynasty and again during the 25th

(Nubian) dynasty. From that point on, archaism in art was ubiquitous, with styles from all different periods being placed side by side, so it is not possible to assess changes in hairstyle based on artistic representations from that point forward.

Ancient Egyptian wigs are the oldest surviving wigs. They were made of human hair impregnated with a mixture of beeswax and resin. One example was composed of a combination of curls and plaits. The strands were attached to a mesh foundation, one end being looped over by about a quarter-inch (6 mm) and secured with a mixture of two-thirds beeswax and one-third resin. This mixture has a melting temperature of 140°F (60°C) and thus should have held firm even on the hottest Egyptian days.[37]

Aside from some entertainers and household servants (mostly female), most nonelites probably did not wear wigs. However, if their depictions of themselves in their tombs near the village of Deir el-Medina are to be trusted, the highest-status craftsmen—the men who worked on the royal tombs in the Valley of the Kings—and their wives did wear wigs. Nonetheless, most nonelites, including laborers and most craftsmen, were shown in a much wider range of hairstyles than the elites were. Their hair could be grey or reddish brown, in addition to the standard black. The women usually had long hair, but quite simple in style, and sometimes even tied back rather carelessly. Like elite men, nonelite men are commonly depicted with short curled hair, in the general shape of a modern "bowl cut." On elite men, these were probably wigs, but on nonelites it was more likely a rendition of their natural hair. Men might also be portrayed with disheveled hair, balding on the top, and even with stubble on their faces.

Throughout most of ancient Egyptian history, most elite men were shown as clean-shaven or with a small, square, or rectangular goatee, although there is some variation over time. For example, there are numerous depictions of men with moustaches from monuments of the 3rd and 4th dynasties. The king and deities often wore a long ceremonial beard, held on with straps, which curled at the bottom. Large, bushy beards and small, pointed beards were worn only by foreigners.

PERFUMES AND COSMETICS

Perfumes and cosmetics were worn by both men and women in ancient Egypt. In the Predynastic Period, both men and women were buried with cosmetic palettes for grinding pigment for eye paint, kohl containers, and other objects associated with personal adornment. In the Pharaonic Period, precious substances such as perfumes and eye paint were standard mortuary offerings presented to all the deities, male and female, in the course of daily ritual services. Ointments would protect the skin from the dry, desert air. In banqueting scenes, men and women alike wore on their heads cones of perfumed fat, which would melt over the course of the evening, perfuming their wigs.

Eye paint was also used by both men and women among the elite. Clearly, this type of adornment had aesthetic value:

> My longing for you is my eye-paint,
> When I see you my eyes shine.[38]

However, eye paint may have served a practical purpose. Sandstorms and smoky rooms caused many health problems, including chest infections and eye problems. Eye makeup may have prevented some eye problems. It was even used on wounds; experiments have confirmed that the copper compounds out of which green eye paint was made in the Old Kingdom would have served as an effective antibacterial agent (as called for in the Edwin Smith Surgical Papyrus), without serious risk of copper poisoning.[39] By the Middle Kingdom, the green eye paint had been replaced by galena (a dark gray ore of lead).

DRESS AND SOCIAL RANK

From something as simple as the wearing of clean, white garments to complex adornment with expensive jewelry, social rank was expressed through dress in ancient Egypt. Nonetheless, many considered it improper to judge a person based on appearances, as indicated in this passage from the New Kingdom "Instruction of Any":

> Do not confound a man in the law court,
> In order to brush aside one who is right.
> Do not incline to the well-dressed man,
> And rebuff the one in rags.
> Don't accept the gift of a powerful man,
> And deprive the weak for his sake.[40]

In ancient Egyptian literature, fine clothing is often described as one of the great pleasures of life. For example, a song celebrating the pleasures of life, reportedly copied from the tomb of a King Intef (either Dynasty 11 or 17; the surviving copies date to the New Kingdom), the singer exclaims:

> Follow your heart as long as you live!
> Put myrrh on your head,
> Dress in fine linen,
> Anoint yourself with oils fit for a god.
> Heap up your joys,
> Let your heat not sink![41]

The remainder of this section below begins with descriptions of the conventions of Egyptian art in depictions of elites and elite dress, including issues surrounding age and gender. In comparison, deities distinguished by their regalia, and in some cases animal heads, were often shown dressed in archaic fashions and generally did not display even those few signs of old age that were permitted among the elites. The garments worn by royalty were essentially the same as those worn by the elites and deities during any given period. Many of the artistic conventions applied to members of the elite were relaxed in depictions of nonelites and foreigners.

The Elite

Elite families were portrayed as forever prosperous and healthy. Elite men were shown striding in two major modes, as vigorous youths with strong, slender figures, and in a state of prosperous maturity, with a good deal of fat on the belly and chest, but still in good health and with all their hair. Elite women did not generally stride and were depicted only as young and slender, usually with their feet together. In general, signs of age among members of the elite are rare in visual art, although during some periods a "careworn" expression gained popularity (e.g., Sesostris III of Dynasty 12). A similar willingness to portray a few facial lines, but still befitting the dignity of an elite individual, is found in representations of Queen Tiye of the 18th dynasty. Such fashions in the rendering of royal faces were often copied by members of the elite, who were not seeking faithful portraits of themselves but rather idealized renditions—and who could be more ideal than the king? In other cases, people of the older generation were depicted in slightly archaic hairstyles, but not as elderly.[42]

Decorum demanded that members of the elite be represented according to certain conventions, with each part of the body shown from its most characteristic angle—the eye, waist, and shoulders depicted frontally; the nose, breast, buttocks, legs, and feet in profile. In two-dimensional art men are generally painted a reddish-brown color, whereas women are painted yellow. These colors are emblematic of the separate spheres of men and women—men outside the home and therefore exposed to the sun, and women inside, in the shade and therefore paler.

Gender division was also reflected in clothing. During the Old and Middle kingdoms, women generally are illustrated wearing a sheath dress, generally depicted as so close-fitting—almost like a second skin—that they would have been impossible to move in. This emphasized the woman's fertility—the pubic triangle was a particular focus. Remains of actual clothing recovered archaeologically reveal the inaccuracy of the representations—they do not even appear to have been tailored to fit individual figures.

Surviving examples of clothing indicate that women's dresses were never as tight as their representations in art would suggest. Nonetheless, when the sheath dress gave way to the bag-tunic as the primary mode of dress, women's clothing clearly appears to be less restrictive. One wonders whether this change in artistic conventions has broader implications on the position of women in society.[43] In any case, female sexuality continued to be emphasized by rendering the garments transparent. In contrast, the genitals of elite men are almost always completely concealed.

Thus, one of the most striking differences between portrayals of men and women in ancient Egyptian art is the degree to which female sexuality is stressed. The ideal of feminine beauty is praised in a New Kingdom love poem:

> The *One*, the sister without peer,
> The handsomest of all!
> She looks like the rising morning star
> At the start of a happy year.
> Shining bright, fair of skin,
> Lovely the look of her eyes,
> Sweet the speech of her lips,
> She has not a word too much.
> Upright neck, shining breast,
> Hair true lapis lazuli,
> Arms surpassing gold,

Fingers like lotus buds.
Heavy thighs, narrow waist,
Her legs parade her beauty;
With graceful step she treads the ground,
Captures my heart by her movements.[44]

Prepubescent children of all ranks, from laborer to god, male and female, share a common iconography from at least the Old Kingdom on. They are generally depicted naked, often holding a finger to the mouth, as in the hieroglyph for child, (🖼). Of course, the same climatic considerations that make it probable laborers wore more than they are generally depicted as wearing hold for children as well. Reference is made to the clothing of infants and young children in several texts. Subtle distinctions were used to mark gender and rank in some cases. Male and female children sometimes were distinguished by their skin color, with girls being colored yellow and boys a reddish-brown.

Children were also shown with their heads shaven. In some cases, a long piece was left on the right side of the head, called the "side-lock of youth." This side-lock could be braided or curled in several styles. During some periods, it was worn primarily by elite children. Elite children were also more frequently depicted wearing jewelry. Nonetheless, the main marker of a child's status in art was the adults with whom he or she was associated. Although the king is often illustrated as a miniature of himself suckling or sitting on the lap of a goddess or his mother, he can be portrayed as a typical child as well, as can deities like "Horus the Child" and the moon god Khonsu.

Deities

Deities tend to be depicted in more archaic dress than people, for example, in garments such as the archaic wraparound and sheath dress long after they had gone out of fashion among the elite. Certain deities were associated with different animals and were represented with the heads of that animal. For example, Re, Horus, and others were associated with falcons and rendered with a falcon head; likewise, Thoth had an ibis head and Sakhemet the head of a lioness. Many deities, both human- and animal-headed, are shown wearing royal crowns; however, subtle yet significant differences often distinguish royal crowns from divine crowns, such as the form of horns or streamers. A common headdress among goddesses, including Isis and Hathor (who was sometimes depicted in the form of a cow), is the cow horns with sun disk (🖼). Some deities can be identified based solely upon their headdress or a unique combination of headdresses worn by no one else. For example, the goddess Mut wears a vulture headdress surmounted by the double crown (🖼). Other deities, such as the god Shu (🖼) and the goddess Nephthys (🖼), wore hieroglyphs of their names upon their heads.

Royalty

The king and queen were represented in essentially the same garments as those worn by the elites and deities during any given period, as befitting the position of the royal couple as vessels through whom divine rule could be manifest on earth. This included such prosaic items of clothing as the short kilt, which was worn not only by the regular elite but even by craftsmen and some laborers. However, royal garments were made of the finest material—the finest grade of linen was called *royal linen*. Of course, the primary way in which the king and queen were distinguished from ordinary members of the elite and deities was through their regalia.

The King

Depictions of the king were clearly distinguished by several features reserved for him—a narrow apron decorated with the royal name in cartouches and uraei; a bull's tail, secured around the waist; and a long artificial beard, which appears to have been strapped on. More than anything else, the king was distinguished by his headdresses, which during most periods displayed a uraeus at the brow, indicating the king's divinity.

The only crowns that have survived from ancient Egypt are diadems with uraei, all made of metal. Thus, the true crowns can be described only from their depictions in artwork. The three most ancient and commonly encountered royal headdresses are the red crown (*deshret*), emblematic of Lower Egypt and probably made of metal; the white crown (known by many names, including

A carving of Pharaoh, with the crowns of Upper and Lower Egypt, makes offerings to the crocodile god Sobek, in the Temple of Sobek and Horus. This was one of the healing temples to which pilgrims came to regain their health. © Erich Lessing / Art Resource, NY.

hedjet), emblematic of Upper Egypt and perhaps made of leather; and the double crown (*pschent*), composed of the white crown set within the red crown.

The king also wore head-cloths arranged in two different ways—called the *nemes*-headdress and the *khat*-headdress or *bag wig*. Both were made by securing a rectangular piece of cloth with a band stretching over the brow and above the ears in the manner of a kerchief. The *nemes*-headdress was generally made with striped fabric, and the excess fabric was "tied into a kind of tail at the back while at each side of the face two strands or lappets hung down."[45] In contrast, the *khat*-headdress was generally plain, with the pieces of cloth arranged as lappets on the *nemes*-headdress tucked up under the band instead.[46]

Another frequently seen royal crown is the blue crown (*khepresh*), along with its relative, the cap crown. These may originally have been made of leather or cloth, strengthened with metal rivets, based on its circular patterning. Later depictions often lack this patterning and may have been made of metal. The blue crown was clearly associated with battle. It first appeared in the 18th dynasty, perhaps a variation on the cap crown, which had been called *khepresh* earlier. The blue crown was a great favorite among the kings of the Saite Period, who used it to distinguish themselves from the Nubian kings who ruled before them and generally wore the similarly patterned cap crown. These may, in fact, be two variations of the same crown.

A final ceremonial crown, starting in the 18th dynasty, was the *aetef*-crown 𓋚, also known as the "rush crown." Its body is essentially the same shape as the white crown, adorned with a pair of ostrich feathers on the sides. The top often has a tuft, indicating that it may have been made of reeds (hence its alternative name). Sometimes this feature is replaced by a small sun disk. The rush crown was also tripled to form the *hmhm*-crown.

As time went on, more and more variations on these basic royal headdresses were developed. Some of these involved adding elements such as streamers, sidelocks, horns, feathers, and sun disks. The details were often very significant; for example, during certain periods, the presence or absence of different types of streamers could "distinguish a divine crown from a royal one."[47] Other crowns were composed by compounding different crowns and headdresses. For example, various crowns were depicted upon the *nemes*-headdress or within the red crown. The most variety appears on the walls of temples of the Ptolemaic Period.

The Queen and Other Royal Women

The words for vulture (*mut*) and mother (*mut*) were homophones in ancient Egyptian, and the ancient Egyptians believed that words that sounded similar were not merely random occurrences. Rather, the use of similar sounds to designate two different things was believed to indicate that there was an underlying connection between them, even if it might not be immediately apparent. Thus, the queen's most distinctive piece of regalia was the vulture headdress:

> The cap is formed by the bird's body, and the wings extend down the side of her wig. The tail and legs of the bird were carved on the back of the wig....The vulture headdress was originally the attribute of the vulture goddess, Nekhbet.... The headdress is first firmly attested for queens in the Fifth Dynasty.[48]

The use of this headdress underscores that the queen, as a woman, was considered first and foremost to be a mother. Her main duty was to provide a royal heir.

A few women in ancient Egypt, the most famous of whom was Hatshepsut, did rule as kings. In these cases, they were depicted as kings, and sometimes even as men rather than women. In addition, during the Third Intermediate Period, when southern Egypt was ruled by the high priests of Amun, women who occupied the office of God's Wife of Amun took on some features of kingly iconography. Like the king, they could perform rituals directly before deities and had their names written in cartouches. Like 18th-dynasty queens, they wear "the sheath dress, tripartite wig, vulture headdress and double feathers."[49]

Nonelites

The vast majority of ancient Egyptians were laborers who lived in simple mud brick structures and were buried in shallow graves, of which there are few remains. Although archaeology provides bits of cloth and pieces of tools and equipment, how to fit these remains together to gain some understanding of the work and dress of laborers comes overwhelmingly from scenes of daily life in elite tombs. The biases inherent in this situation are significant. As Robins observed: "They are only present in so far as they are being productive on the tomb owner's behalf; their own life is totally without interest."[50]

Many of the conventions followed in the rendering of elite figures are general conventions of Egyptian art and were employed in many depictions of nonelites as well. However, conventions were much more likely to be relaxed in the representation of nonelites. Thus, these men and women could be depicted twisted in all directions, from behind, with balding heads and stubble on their faces. In short, they could be portrayed in ways that elite Egyptians would have considered to be beneath their dignity.

Male laborers are often shown wearing no more than a short kilt, loincloth, or apron throughout ancient Egyptian history. Although women may wear just a loincloth or skirt, they are also frequently depicted wearing dresses. Laborers are rarely seen wearing warm clothing. However, this may not reflect the actual situation. With average daily lows of around 47°F (8°C) in January (and highs of only about 65°F/18°C) in Cairo, such clothing would not have been adequate year-round. Average daily lows in Cairo are 18–26°F (10–15°C) below the average daily highs. Such significant daily temperature fluctuations are generally associated with desert environments—in more humid environments, water vapor traps heat in the air, leading to less fluctuation in daily temperatures. Thus, although a 70°F (21°C) average nighttime temperature (summer in Cairo) might sound warm, it feels cold after an average daily high of 96°F (36°C).

Craftsmen, having skills that were in limited supply, were of higher status than laborers. However, at their lowest levels, they were certainly not members of the elite. From the Middle Kingdom "Satire of the Trades," there is this description of the mason's cloths:

> Though he is out in the wind,
> He works without a cloak;
> His loincloth is a twisted rope
> And a string in the rear.[51]

However, in tomb scenes, craftsmen are usually portrayed wearing short kilts, not unlike those worn by members of the elite. Of course, in most cases, they were being depicted in tombs only to display how they were of use to the tomb owner.

A great deal is known about the lives of the most skilled ancient Egyptian craftsmen, who were employed in building and decorating the royal tombs and grouped in villages like those at Amarna and Deir el-Medina. At these levels, craftsmen could attain elite status. The workmen at Deir el-Medina built their own elaborately decorated tombs and had themselves shown in the same fashions as members of the elite at this time.

Entertainers could encompass many levels of society in ancient Egypt as well. Dancers and acrobats are often depicted nude, wearing only a belt and jewelry or in just a loincloth. This places them on par with servant girls. The nonelite nature of their clothing often is combined with their elite-style wigs. Musicians are often represented in elaborate dress like members of the elite. Nonetheless, their lower status in relation to the tomb owner is represented by the twisted positions they are often depicted in, with unusual hairstyles often worn by the women and the occasional baldness of the men, all of which were indicative of lower status. Finally, elite women often served as chantresses in their local temples, and priests would conduct elaborate processions in which divine statues were carried out on procession. These performances were clearly religious in nature, but nonetheless highly entertaining.

Depictions of Foreigners

Although the Egyptians referred to their enemies as the "nine bows," there were really three main groups—the Nubians to the south, the Asiatics to the northeast, and the Libyans and oasis dwellers to the west. In the New Kingdom, the Aegean Islanders and the people of Punt, reached via the Red Sea, also became groups of focus.

Style of dress and manner of hygiene were part of what defined a person as an Egyptian. In the *Tale of Sinuhe*, Sinuhe flees Egypt in fear of his life and lives among the Asiatics. Upon his return, he is cleaned and dressed in proper fashion:

> I was shaved; my hair was combed. Thus was my squalor returned to the foreign land, my dress to the Sand-farers. I was clothed in fine linen; I was anointed with fine oil. I slept on a bed. I had returned the sand to those who dwell in it, the tree-oil to those who grease themselves with it.[52]

Foreigners were portrayed in accordance with fairly standard stereotypes in ancient Egyptian art. Depictions of foreign dress stand out in ancient Egyptian art for the lack of white linen, the unusually patterned garments, headdresses, and hairstyles.

The ancient Egyptians viewed foreigners as forces of chaos. From the earliest times, the ancient Egyptians portrayed foreigners predominantly in submission. In the Early Dynastic Period, enemies were frequently shown nude, in twisted positions beneath the feet of the king. In later times, enemies were depicted in their stereotypical ethnic costume. These illustrations are largely from elite tombs and temple contexts, including scenes of battle, trade missions, tribute, and foreign laborers working in Egypt.

In the New Kingdom, several aspects of Egyptian fashion seem to have been influenced by Nubian fashion, probably introduced by mercenaries. Patterned leather loincloths for men, first encountered in the Middle Kingdom, gained in popularity. The introduction of earrings may also have been due to Nubian influence, although these were also worn by Asiatics, including the Hyksos, who ruled northern Egypt during the Second Intermediate Period. The Nubian wig also became fashionable somewhat later in the New Kingdom. Elite Nubians who worked for the Egyptian government that was occupying their country built Egyptian-style tombs and often portrayed themselves in Egyptian dress.

In the Late Period, Egypt was ruled by several groups of foreigners—Nubians, Libyans, Assyrians, and Persians. Although there was a strong focus on archaism in art during this period, elements of foreign influence in dress sometimes appear. It has often been asserted that Egyptian and Greco-Roman culture in Egypt were kept quite separate. Certainly, there appears to be little direct influence from Greco-Roman dress in the art from the latest ancient Egyptian temples. Tombs were another matter, however. These frequently do display fusions, such as the Egyptian god Anubis depicted in Greco-Roman dress.

SOCIOECONOMIC ASPECTS OF DRESS IN EGYPT

Cloth and clothing was much more valuable in the ancient world than they are today. They were a form of wealth, valuable enough to leave as an inheritance. They could be used as currency or to secure a loan in the barter-based economy of ancient Egypt. References to simple transactions are quite common in ancient Egyptian letters. Unfortunately, these documents themselves are so rare as to be essentially anecdotal evidence for most places and time periods.

Most of the information about the cost of clothing comes from village of Deir el-Medina, on the west bank of the Nile in Luxor, where the workmen who built the royal tombs in the Valley of the Kings lived. This material dates to the Ramesside Period of the New Kingdom. Cloth was identified as one of four grades, starting with the finest—royal linen, then fine thin cloth, thin cloth, and smooth cloth.

A systematic study of ancient Egyptian clothing terminology for all periods of Egyptian history has yet to be undertaken. This makes the interpretation of textual evidence particularly difficult. Nowhere are the consequences of this lack greater than in reading the economic documents, which provide little in the way of context to guide us. Janssen discussed sixteen different names for items of dress involved in economic transactions in the Ramesside Period, only seven of which appear often enough in association with prices to draw any firm conclusions. Only two of these can be confidently identified with specific types of clothing—*meses* with the bag-tunic and *twt* with sandals.[53] The bag-tunic was the most commonly encountered, occurring in forty-five documents, in which they were usually priced at 5 deben.[54] The economic documents also confirm what recovered examples of bag-tunics had already suggested—that they were made of much rougher material than tomb paintings would suggest and were worn by a very broad segment of society.

Two types of garment, the *daiw* and the *sedjw*, are often listed together as a set. Janssen suggested that the *daiw* was a kilt and the slightly cheaper *sedjw*, a loincloth. Nonetheless, the *daiw* has been variously identified as a loincloth, shawl, skirt or kilt, and *ghalabiyah* (a long robe-like garment, the traditional clothing of modern Egyptian workers). Whatever they were, *daiw* were considerably more expensive than bag-tunics, ranging from 11 to 20 deben if made of smooth cloth and from 20 to 30 deben if made of thin cloth. Clearly, the quality of cloth made a substantial difference in the price of the garment.

The identity of the *djayt* is also uncertain, but at least one measured 50 feet (15 m) by 6½ feet (2 m), suggesting that it was a cloak or other large, wraparound garment.[55] At 20–25 deben, a *djayt* cost about the same as a high-end *daiw* but was generally made of cheaper cloth.[56] The *rewdjw* was probably a smaller a wraparound garment. One example, cited in a tomb robbery papyrus, was said to measure 13 feet (4 m) by 6½ feet (2 m).[57] Along with the bag-tunic (*meses*), the *rewdjw* was one of the basic garments given to female slaves. Prices vary from 5 to 15 deben, with one example made of fine thin cloth priced at 20 deben.[58]

It is interesting that some quite small garments tended to demand consider-able prices. For example, the *ideg*, which Janssen tentatively identified as a ker-chief, ranged in price from 8 to 25 deben.[59] Even considering that these were usually made of thin cloth, one would expect that a kerchief requires consider-ably less cloth than a kilt (*daiw*). Similarly, *merew*, which seem to have been cloth strips, possibly used as sashes or straps, cost about 5 deben, the same price as a bag-tunic.[60] In contrast, sandals (*twt*) were generally valued at only 1–3 deben, even when made of leather.

RITUAL, SYMBOLISM, AND DRESS

The ritual use of clothing, of which there is the most evidence, is its presence among burial goods. Since this is how most of the surviving examples of Egyp-tian clothing have survived, it is difficult to separate the above descriptions from the symbolic or ritualistic dress. Most performances (with historical records) from ancient Egypt were religious rituals. Temple priests were members of the elite and dressed as such. However, for their jobs, they had additional require-ments. They had to dress in pure white linen and have a shaved head. In the *Instruction of Merikare*, the king instructs his successor:

> In the monthly service, wear the white sandals,
> Visit the temple, [observe] the mysteries
> Enter the shrine, eat bread in the god's house;
> Proffer libations, multiply the loaves,
> Make ample the daily offerings,
> It profits him who does it.[61]

It is often unclear from the art and texts preserved whether there were any fur-ther costume requirements for priests. Other ritual aspects of dress are the sym-bolic value of color, the amuletic value of much jewelry, and the use of items of clothing as offerings.

Ritual Costume

There are very few elements of ritual costume that are generally agreed to reflect actual cult practice rather than artistic convention. Two are the wearing of the panther or leopard skin and the *sed*-festival cloak. However, most cases in which ritual costumes may have been depicted are much more controversial. Speeches in which ritualists claim to be divine beings are common in ancient Egyptian temple mortuary and, so-called, magical rituals. It is not clear whether the ritual impersonation of deities extended to ritual costumes.

Panther or Leopard Skin

A man's eldest son would serve as his by *ka*-priest. In elite tombs, they are depicted wearing a panther skin slung over their ordinary clothes and present-ing mortuary cult offerings. Often translated as "double," the *ka*-spirit is vari-ously understood as a person's image, life-force, power, or reputation. Perhaps because it and the ancient Egyptian word for food (*ka*) are homophones, the *ka*-spirit was the aspect of the soul to whom the cult offering was directed. These garments were also worn by *sem*-priests, as they carried out various duties, including walking beside divine processional barques, as shown in New Kingdom processional scenes. Imported from farther south in Africa, these skins were undoubtedly luxury goods.

The Sed-Festival Cloak

The *sed*-festival, also called the "jubilee festival," was a rite of royal renewal. The earliest depictions date to the Early Dynastic Period, and it continued to be illustrated in temples through the end of the Pharaonic Period with the same group of motifs. One of the high points of the festival was when the king displayed his continued vitality by running a circuit in an open court. During his run, the king is represented simply wearing his usual attire. The king then sat in a kiosk approached by a small set of stairs (𓊃), wrapped in the *sed*-festival cloak and watching performances.

A similar cloak appears to have been worn in the Opening of the Mouth ceremony, when the *sem*-priest spends the night sleeping in front of a statue that is being ritually activated.[62] It is notable that in both these cases, the need for warmth—sitting still after a vigorous run and sleeping at night—would have dictated the use of a warmer garment.

Ritual Impersonation of Deities

Whether or not masks were used in ancient Egypt is the topic of significant debate. Many ritual texts have utterances in which speeches are attributed to deities, some of whom are generally depicted with animal heads. In many mortuary scenes, for example, the jackal-headed god Anubis is shown attending to the corpse. Did priests and embalmers actually wear Anubis masks, or do these scenes reflect a rendition of a spiritual reality (the inhabiting of the officiant by the deity) that was not actually reflected in costume? The answer to this question might be different for different periods. There seems to be little reason to doubt that masks were used during the Late Period, at least in limited contexts. Terra-cotta jackal masks dating from the Late Period, although they would have been awkward to wear, were nonetheless unlikely to have been used for any other purpose. A clear depiction of a priest wearing a jackal mask (the mask is rendered as transparent so one can see the wearer beneath) from the Ptolemaic temple of Hathor at Dendera, shows that the wearer did need to be guided.[63]

The use of such masks during earlier periods might be suggested based on depictions of processional scenes in which the jackal-headed Souls of Nekhen carry palanquins (for example in the Great Hypostyle Hall at Karnak, and in some *sed*-festival scenes) along with the falcon-headed Souls of Pe. The two earliest objects identified as masks to be used in performances, from the Middle Kingdom town of Kahun, are severely damaged and highly disputed. There are also numerous demon statues that are clearly portrayed as wearing masks.

There are other possible elements of costume to consider. In art, deities were distinguished by their archaic dress and hairstyles and their distinctive regalia. When people were speaking in the names of deities during rituals, did they wear costumes? Examples of "archaic" styles of dress have not been recovered archaeologically. The lack of surviving examples of archaic garments from tomb contexts, particularly royal tombs like that of Tutankhamun, might suggest that such garments were not worn ritually. Yet, in an area such as ancient Egyptian textiles, in which evidence is so limited, arguments from absence are very weak. Moreover, these garments would have been used primarily in temple contexts. Finally, in many cases whether a garment was the current fashion or archaic may have been simply a function of how a plain rectangular piece of material was wrapped around the body.

Artificial versions of the side-lock of youth may have been worn by certain priests when they were serving in the capacity of Horus, son of Osiris, in the course of temple ritual, or together with a round wig when serving as the Iunmutef priest or high priest of Ptah at Memphis.[64] By the Ptolemaic period, the side-lock was a common attachment to crowns depicted in temple contexts. The side-lock identified the ritualist as the son of the recipient of the ritual. In cases when the round wig was worn as well, that would underscore "the wearer's actual adult status."[65]

In contrast to masking, there seems to be little debate about whether these hairstyles were actually worn by priests, even though there seems no reason to be more certain of their use in ritual than of the use of masks.

Color

Color had great symbolic significance for the ancient Egyptians. It was so important that items of clothing were often named after their color. A brief note on the ancient Egyptian writing system is necessary to explain this. The hieroglyphic writing system works on the rebus principle, with pictures of everyday things being used to represent their sounds. For example, using the rebus principle, it is possible to write the word *belief* with pictures of a bee and a leaf. In addition to these signs which represent sounds (phonetic signs), there were signs which indicated broadly what the word referred to (determinatives or class indicators). For example, a boat symbol ends various words for different types of boat, and a book roll symbol often ends words for abstract ideas.

Names of items of clothing sometimes feature a color name written phonetically followed by a determinative indicating what item it was. For example, the word *white*, written with a mace (), can be used to designate: white clothes (*hedj*), white linen (*hedjet*), white crown (*hedjet*), or white sandals (*hedjty*).[66]

The Egyptians recognized four major color groups—red, yellow/white, green/blue, and black—although more subtle distinctions were often made. Some symbolic associations extended between categories, for example, although yellow and gold were most strongly associated with the sun, red, white, and blue (particularly blue faience) all had solar associations in some contexts.

Red was associated with a constellation of extremely powerful and potentially destructive forces—the sun, fire, blood, and the desert—the red land so often contrasted with the fertile black land of the Nile flood plain. The red desert was the land of Seth, murderer of Osiris, and was thus associated with anger and chaos. The word for red, *desher*, is from the same root as the word for "wrath" (*desheru*), and a person who was furious was said to be "red of heart."[67] Since those forces which can give life can also take it away, red was considered to be a dangerous color. However, different red stones were associated with different qualities. For example, red jasper seems to be linked with only the positive aspects of red, perhaps because the ancient Egyptian word for red jasper (*khenmet*) forms a pun with the verb "to delight" (*khenem*).[68]

As a solar color, red was sometimes interchangeable with white and yellow. Yellow, and its metallic variation gold, were primarily associated with the sun, "eternal and imperishable."[69] White was also a solar color and could serve for yellow in some contexts. However, it was also associated with silver and, therefore, the moon. White was most strongly associated with cleanliness and ritual purity.

"Green" could refer to a broad complex of greens and blues. The use of separate words for blues did not become common until the New Kingdom. Although the symbolic significance of green and blue had significant overlap, there were some distinctions. Green was associated with freshness and growth, particularly plant growth. By extension, it was associated with fertility and rebirth. Although the Egyptians often included blue in the same category as green, blue stones sometimes had their own particular symbolic associations. Blue was strongly associated with water, particularly the celestial waters of the sky, upon which the sun barque sailed, and the primordial waters from the inundation sprang. These waters rejuvenated the sun nightly, and the earth annually. Thus, blue was associated with rebirth and, by extension, recovery from illness. Blue faience also was associated with the sun, and thus carried many of the same symbolic associations.

Finally, black embodies a paradox. It represents death, the underworld, and funerary deities such as Osiris and Anubis. However, death was seen as necessary for new life. The land of Egypt was flooded each year by the inundation, which left behind a thick layer of black silt. It was out of this black silt that the life of the land was renewed each year. Thus, black and green could sometimes substitute for each other.

Amulets

Amulets were essentially good-luck charms. They came in all different sizes and materials. Much jewelry was composed of beads and pendants with amuletic value based on color, shape, or material. Some of the most commonly encountered amulet shapes and their associations are:

- ☥ The *ankh*-sign was emblematic of life.
- ☩ The *djed*-pillar, or column, was emblematic of stability.
- 𓂀 The *wadjet*-eye was the eye of the god Horus, the eye that Seth, murderer of Horus's divine father Osiris, king of the gods, wounded in their contest for the kingship. It was associated with the moon, which was wounded and healed each month. This symbol was believed to provide general protection to its wearer.
- 𓆣 The *kheper*-beetle, or scarab, is a type of beetle that is also called a "dung beetle" because they roll balls of dung around. The ancient Egyptians connected this practice to rolling the sun across the sky. The ancient Egyptian name for this insect forms a pun with the verb "to come into being."
- 𓊃 The *sa*-sign (its phonetic value) was associated with protection (also pronounced *sa*). The sign may represent some sort of papyrus shelter.
- 𓎬 The Isis-knot was a symbol of protection, particularly for pregnant women. Tying knots, often in strips of linen that would subsequently be worn around the neck, was a common ritual act used to prevent and heal illness.

- ◯ The *shen*-ring, a circle without beginning or end, was emblematic of eternity and protection. Encircling was considered to be a powerful magico-religious act. This sign also had strong solar associations.
- The fish was worn to protect against drowning, usually by children or young women, and often in the hair.[70]
- Cowrie shells were associated with fertility, because of their vulva-like shape. They were often worn in girdles by young women, particularly servants and entertainers.[71]
- Amulets of many different deities were commonly worn and placed on corpses. Perhaps those most widely worn during life were those, such as Taweret and Bes, that protected pregnant women.

Votive Shirts

If the offering of votive cloths and shirts was a common practice in Egypt, the evidence has rarely survived. Three votive textiles survive from Deir el-Medina, all devoted to goddesses—two to Taweret and one to Hathor and the deified king Amenophis I. Thirty-five textiles decorated with painted scenes of Hathor, usually set within a painted border, were found in that goddess's temple at Deir el-Bahri, on the west bank across from Luxor. They date from the mid-18th to mid-19th dynasties of the New Kingdom. They are inscribed with the names of their donors, most of whom were women; all of the male donors were priests of Hathor. Most of the textiles were simple, rectangular cloths, but five were described as "shirts." The "shirts" were all constructed out of relatively coarse linen in the manner of tiny bag-tunics, three with arms and two sleeveless. At least one garment was not even large enough for a baby. Three of these shirts have broad collars painted around the neck opening.

The inscriptions on the shirts indicate that they were all donated by women but say nothing about their intended purpose. Pinch explored three explanations for the use of these garments, each of which has a particularly evocative piece of evidence supporting it, accompanied by significant reasons for doubt.[72] In fact, none of these purposes appears to be contradictory, and it is possible that the shirts functioned on multiple symbolic levels.

The first suggestion is that these small garments were baby cloths, offered in hopes of receiving help in conception or childbirth—or in giving thanks for success. Prayers to Hathor for these purposes are commonplace. Nonetheless, it is curious that none of the shirts or textiles put this request into writing. Second, it may have been that the garments "in some way represented the body of the donor, and that by offering a shirt, the donor was placing her body under the protection of Hathor."[73] This proposed use would not contradict the proposal that they were offered for reproductive assistance, as protecting the woman's body in childbirth might have been the concern. Finally, these shirts may have been offered as clothing for Hathor to wear—and may even have been worn by the divine statue of the goddess. In support of this interpretation, it is particularly notable that "the way in which a Hathor mask is painted inside the neck-opening of one of the shirts suggests that the goddess was thought of as wearing this garment."[74] This use might be understood as complementary to both the protection of the donor and the request for reproductive success. Utterances to be recited during childbirth often associate the women with a goddess.

NOTES

1. The dates in the timeline are calculated from ancient lists, especially the Turin royal papyrus, and from various other sources. The margin of error rises from a decade or so in the Third Intermediate Period and New Kingdom to perhaps 150 years for the 1st dynasty; dates for the third millennium are given for whole dynasties and are rounded, as are numerous later dates. From the 12th dynasty on, possible sequences of dates can be calculated from astronomical evidence; currently accepted sequences are used here. Dates from 664 BCE on are precise to within a year.

The timeline was compiled by John Baines, professor of Egyptology, University of Oxford. He is coauthor with Jaromir Malek of *Cultural Atlas of Ancient Egypt* (2nd ed., 2000) and author *of Fecundity Figures: Egyptian Personification and the Iconology of a Genre* (reprinted 2001).

2. Alan K. Bowman and Eugene Rogan, "Agriculture in Egypt from Pharaonic to Modern Times," in *Agriculture in Egypt from Pharaonic to Modern Times*, ed. Alan K. Bowman and Eugene Rogan (Oxford: Oxford University Press for the British Academy, 1999), 2.

3. Wente, Edward F., trans., *Letters from Ancient Egypt* (Atlanta: Scholars Press, 1990), 153.

4. John Baines and Jaromír Málek, *Atlas of Ancient Egypt*, rev. ed. (New York: Facts on File, 2000), 30–55.

5. Baines and Málek, *Atlas of Ancient Egypt*, 35.

6. B. Aston, J. Harrell, and I. Shaw, "Stone," in *Ancient Egyptian Materials and Technology*, ed. Paul T. Nicholson and Ian Shaw (Cambridge: Cambridge University Press, 2000), 38.

7. Aston, Harrell, and Shaw, "Stone," 27.

8. Aston, Harrell, and Shaw, "Stone," 46.

9. Aston, Harrell, and Shaw, "Stone," 30.

10. Aston, Harrell, and Shaw, "Stone," 52.

11. Gay Robins, *The Art of Ancient Egypt* (Cambridge, MA: Harvard University Press, 1997), fig. 134.

12. Gillian Vogelsang-Eastwood, *Pharaonic Egyptian Clothing* (Leiden: E. J. Brill, 1993), 39–41.

13. Vogelsang-Eastwood, *Pharaonic Egyptian Clothing*, 53.

14. W. Simpson, "A Protocol of Dress: The Royal and Private Fold of the Kilt," *Journal of Egyptian Archaeology* 74 (1988): 203–4.

15. Vogelsang-Eastwood, *Pharaonic Egyptian Clothing*, 55.

16. Vogelsang-Eastwood, *Pharaonic Egyptian Clothing*, 32–33.

17. Vogelsang-Eastwood, *Pharaonic Egyptian Clothing*, 99–101.

18. Vogelsang-Eastwood, *Pharaonic Egyptian Clothing*, figs. 7:13–7.15; Bernard Bruyère, *Rapport sur les fouilles de Deir el Medineh, 1934–1935*, part 2 (Cairo: Institut Français d'Archéologie Orientale, 1937), fig. 30.

19. Gay Robins, "Problems in Interpreting Egyptian Art," *Discussions in Egyptology* 17 (1990): 46.

20. Miriam Lichtheim, *Ancient Egyptian Literature* (Berkeley: University of California Press, 1973), 1:216.

21. Vogelsang-Eastwood, *Pharaonic Egyptian Clothing*, 150.

22. Elizabeth Riefstahl, *Patterned Textiles in Pharaonic Egypt* (Brooklyn, NY: Brooklyn Museum, 1944), 25.

23. Rosalind Hall, "The Pharaonic *mss* Tunic as a Smock?" *Göttinger Miszellen* 43 (1981): 31.

24. Riefstahl, *Patterned Textiles*, 39.

25. Vogelsang-Eastwood, *Pharaonic Egyptian Clothing*, 80.

26. Vogelsang-Eastwood, *Pharaonic Egyptian Clothing*, 85.

27. Vogelsang-Eastwood, *Pharaonic Egyptian Clothing*, 158.

28. Carol Andrews, *Ancient Egyptian Jewelry* (New York: Harry N. Abrams, 1991), 122–23.

29. Jac. J. Janssen, *Commodity Prices from the Ramessid Period* (Leiden: E. J. Brill, 1975), 306–11. Although the ancient Egyptians had no currency, they had standard measures. Thus, prices discussed herein are discussed in *deben*, a standardized measure of copper or bronze, weighing about 3.2 ounces (91 g) (ibid., 101).

30. Andrews, *Ancient Egyptian Jewelry*, 102.

31. Andrews, *Ancient Egyptian Jewelry*, 109–11.

32. Andrews, *Ancient Egyptian Jewelry*, 117.

33. Andrews, *Ancient Egyptian Jewelry*, 119.

34. Andrews, *Ancient Egyptian Jewelry*, 140.

35. Gay Robins, "Hair and the Construction of Identity in Ancient Egypt, c. 1480–1350 B.C.," *Journal of the American Research Center in Egypt* 36 (1999): 66.

36. Lichtheim, *Ancient Egyptian Literature*, 2:191.

37. J. Cox, "The Construction of an Ancient Egyptian Wig (c. 1400 B.C.) in the British Museum," *Journal of Egyptian Archaeology* 63 (1977): 67–68.

38. Lichtheim, *Ancient Egyptian Literature*, 2:192.

39. Guido Majno, *The Healing Hand: Man and Wound in the Ancient World* (Cambridge, MA: Harvard University Press, 1975), 111–15.

40. Lichtheim, *Ancient Egyptian Literature*, 2:158.

41. Lichtheim, *Ancient Egyptian Literature*, 1:196–97.

42. Robins, "Hair and the Construction of Identity," 65.

43. Robins, "Problems in Interpreting Egyptian Art," 47.

44. Lichtheim, *Ancient Egyptian Literature*, 2:182. The ancient Egyptian terms *senet* ("sister"), as in the first line, and *sen* ("brother") referred to female and male members of the same generation, even when they were not literally siblings.

45. Ian Shaw and Paul T. Nicholson, *The Dictionary of Ancient Egypt* (London: Henry N. Abrams, 1995), 74.

46. M. Eaton-Krauss, "The *Khat* Headdress to the End of the Amarna Period," *Studien zur Altägyptischen Kultur* 5 (1977): 22.

47. Eleni Vassilika, *Ptolemaic Philae* (Leuven: Uitgeverij Peeters, 1989), 83–84.

48. Robins, *Art of Ancient Egypt*, 67.

49. Robins, *Art of Ancient Egypt*, 214.

50. Robins, "Problems in Interpreting Egyptian Art," 48.

51. Lichtheim, *Ancient Egyptian Literature*, 1:187.

52. Lichtheim, *Ancient Egyptian Literature*, 1:233.

53. Janssen, *Commodity Prices*, ix and 249–98.

54. Janssen, *Commodity Prices*, 262–63.

55. Janssen, *Commodity Prices*, 280.

56. Janssen, *Commodity Prices*, 282, 526.

57. Janssen, *Commodity Prices*, 284.

58. Janssen, *Commodity Prices*, 285–86.

59. Janssen, *Commodity Prices*, 282, 526.

60. Janssen, *Commodity Prices*, 286–87.

61. Lichtheim, *Ancient Egyptian Literature*, 1:102.

62. R. Gillam, *Performance and Drama in Ancient Egypt* (London: Duckworth, 2005), 71.

63. Heinrich Schäfer, *Principles of Egyptian Art*, rev. ed. (Oxford, England: Griffith Institute, 1986), 122, fig. 87.

64. Robins, "Hair and the Construction of Identity," 62.

65. Robins, "Hair and the Construction of Identity," 62.

66. Raymond O. Faulkner, *A Concise Dictionary of Middle Egyptian* (Oxford, England: Griffith Institute, 1986), 181.

67. Wilkinson, 1994, 106.

68. Andrews, *Ancient Egyptian Jewelry*, 103.

69. Wilkinson, 1994, 108.

70. Andrews, *Ancient Egyptian Jewelry*, 171.

71. Andrews, *Ancient Egyptian Jewelry*, 130.

72. G. Pinch, *Votive Offerings to Hathor* (Oxford, England: Griffith Institute, 1993), 131–32.

73. Pinch, *Votive Offerings to Hathor*, 131.

74. Pinch, *Votive Offerings to Hathor*, 131–32.

FURTHER READING

Ancient Egypt—General

Aldred, Cyril. *Jewels of the Pharaohs: Egyptian Jewelry of the Dynastic Period*. New York: Praeger, 1971.

Andrews, Carol. *Ancient Egyptian Jewelry*. New York: Harry N. Abrams, 1991.

Aston, B., J. Harrell, and I. Shaw. "Stone." In *Ancient Egyptian Materials and Technology*, ed. Paul T. Nicholson and Ian Shaw, pp. 5–77. Cambridge: Cambridge University Press, 2000.

Baines, John. "Ankh-Sign, Belt and Penis Sheath." *Studien zur Altägyptischen Kultur* 3 (1975): 1–24.

Baines, John, and Jaromír Málek. *Atlas of Ancient Egypt*. Rev. ed. New York: Facts on File, 2000.

Barber, Elizabeth Wayland. *Women's Work, the First 20,000 Years: Women, Cloth, and Society in Early Times*. New York: Norton, 1994.

Bonnet, Hans. *Die ägyptische Tracht bis zum Ende des neuen Reiches*. Reprint 1964, Hildesheim: Untersuchungen zur Geschichte und Altertumskunde Aegyptens 7, 1917.

Bowman, Alan K., and Eugene Rogan. "Agriculture in Egypt from Pharaonic to Modern Times." In *Agriculture in Egypt from Pharaonic to Modern Times*, ed. Alan K. Bowman and Eugene Rogan, pp. 1–32. Proceedings of the British Academy, No. 96. Oxford: Oxford University Press for the British Academy, 1999.

Bruyère, Bernard. *Rapport sur les fouilles de Deir el Medineh, 1934–1935*. Part 2. Cairo: Institut Français d'Archèeologie Orientale, 1937.

Capel, Anne, and Glenn Markoe, eds. *Mistress of the House, Mistress of Heaven: Women in Ancient Egypt*. New York: Hudson Hills Press, 1996.

Carnarvon, George, and Howard Carter. *Five Years' Explorations at Thebes*. London: H. Frowde, 1912.

Cox, J. "The Construction of an Ancient Egyptian Wig (c. 1400 B.C.) in the British Museum." *Journal of Egyptian Archaeology* 63 (1977): 67–70.

Driel-Murray, Carol. "Leatherwork and Skin Products." In *Ancient Egyptian Materials and Technology*, ed. Paul T. Nicholson and Ian Shaw, pp. 299–319. Cambridge: Cambridge University Press, 2000.

Eastwood, Gillian. "Preliminary Report on the Textiles." In *Amarna Reports*, comp. Barry J. Kemp, 2:191–204. London: Egypt Exploration Society, 1985.

Eaton-Krauss, Mary Anne. "The *Khat* Headdress to the End of the Amarna Period." *Studien zur Altägyptischen Kultur* 5 (1977): 21–39.

Faulkner, Raymond O. *A Concise Dictionary of Middle Egyptian*. Oxford: Griffith Institute, 1986.

Gillam, Robyn. *Performance and Drama in Ancient Egypt*. London: Duckworth, 2005.

Green, L. "Hairstyles." In *Oxford Encyclopedia of Ancient Egypt*, ed. Donald B. Redford, 2:73–76. Oxford: Oxford University Press, 2001.

Hall, Rosalind. *Egyptian Textiles*. Aylesbury, England: Shire Egyptology, 1986.

———. "A Pair of Linen Sleeves from Gurob." *Göttinger Miszellen* 40 (1980): 29–39.

———. "The Pharaonic *mss* Tunic as a Smock?" *Göttinger Miszellen* 43 (1981): 29–38.

Hayes, William. *Scepter of Egypt*. 2 vols. New York: Metropolitan Museum of Art, 1990.

Janssen, Jac. *Commodity Prices from the Ramessid Period*. Leiden: E. J. Brill, 1975.

Jick, Millicent. "Bead-Net Dress." In *Mummies and Magic*, pp. 78–79. Boston: Museum of Fine Arts, 1988.

Kemp, Barry. *Anatomy of a Civilization*. 2nd ed. London: Routledge, 2005.

Leahy, Anthony. "Royal Iconography and Dynastic Change, 750–525 BC: The Blue and Cap Crowns." *Journal of Egyptian Archaeology* 78 (1992): 223–40.

Lichtheim, Miriam. *Ancient Egyptian Literature*. 3 vols. Berkeley: University of California Press, 1973–1980.

Lucas, Alfred. *Ancient Egyptian Materials and Industries*. London: Edward Arnold, 1962.

Majno, Guido. *The Healing Hand: Man and Wound in the Ancient World*. Cambridge, MA: Harvard University Press, 1975.

Manniche, Lise. *Sacred Luxuries: Fragrance, Aromatherapy, and Cosmetics in Ancient Egypt*. Ithaca, NY: Cornell University Press, 1999.

Murray, Mary Anne. "Cereal Production and Processing." In *Ancient Egyptian Material and Technology*, ed. Paul T. Nicholson and Ian Shaw, pp. 505–36. Cambridge: Cambridge University Press, 2000.

———. "Glass." *Ancient Egyptian Materials and Technology*, ed. Paul T. Nicholson and Ian Shaw, pp. 195–224. Cambridge: Cambridge University Press, 2000.

Nicholson, Paul T., and Edgar Peltenburg. "Egyptian Faience." In *Ancient Egyptian Materials and Technology*, ed. Paul T. Nicholson and Ian Shaw, pp. 177–94. Cambridge: Cambridge University Press, 2000.

Nicholson, Paul T., and Ian Shaw, eds. *Ancient Egyptian Materials and Technology*. Cambridge: Cambridge University Press, 2000.

Pinch, Geraldine. *Votive Offerings to Hathor*. Oxford, England: Griffith Institute, 1993.

Redford, Donald B., ed. *The Oxford Encyclopedia of Ancient Egypt*. Oxford: Oxford University Press, 2001.

Richards, Janet. *Society and Death in Ancient Egypt: Mortuary Landscapes of the Middle Kingdom*. Cambridge: Cambridge University Press, 2005.

Riefstahl, Elizabeth. *Patterned Textiles in Pharaonic Egypt*. Brooklyn, NY: Brooklyn Museum, 1944.

Robins, Gay. *The Art of Ancient Egypt*. Cambridge, MA: Harvard University Press, 1997.

———. "Hair and the Construction of Identity in Ancient Egypt, c. 1480–1350 B.C." *Journal of the American Research Center in Egypt* 36 (1999): 55–69.

———. "Problems in Interpreting Egyptian Art." *Discussions in Egyptology* 17 (1990): 45–58.

———. *Women in Ancient Egypt*. Cambridge, MA: Harvard University Press, 1993.

Roehrig, Catherine. "Women's Work: Some Occupations of Non Royal Women as Depicted in Ancient Egyptian Art." In *Mistress of the House, Mistress of Heaven: Women in Ancient Egypt*, pp. 13–24. New York: Hudson Hills Press, 1997.

Schäfer, Heinrich. *The Dictionary of Ancient Egypt*. London: Henry N. Abrams, 1995.

———. *Principles of Egyptian Art*. Rev. ed. Oxford, England: Griffith Institute, 1986.

Shaw, Ian, and Paul T. Nicholson. *The Dictionary of Ancient Egypt*. London: Henry N. Abrams, 1995.

Simpson, William. "A Protocol of Dress: The Royal and Private Fold of the Kilt." *Journal of Egyptian Archaeology* 74 (1988): 203–4.

Troy, Lana. *Patterns of Queenship in Ancient Egyptian Myth and History*. Uppsala Studies in Ancient Mediterranean and Near Eastern Civilizations, No. 14. Uppsala: University of Uppsala, 1986.

Wilkinson, Richard H. Symbols and Magic in Egyptian Art. London: Thames & Hudson, 1994.

Ancient Egypt—Clothing, Textiles and Bodily Adornment

Andrews, Carol. *Ancient Egyptian Jewelry*. New York: Harry N. Abrams, 1991.
Hall, Rosalind. *Egyptian Textiles*. Aylesbury, England: Shire Egyptology, 1986.
Riefstahl, Elizabeth. *Patterned Textiles in Pharaonic Egypt*. Brooklyn, NY: Brooklyn Museum, 1944.
Vassilika, Eleni. *Ptolemaic Philae*. Leuven: Uitgeverij Peeters, 1989.
Vogelsang-Eastwood, Gillian. *Pharaonic Egyptian Clothing*. Studies in Textile and Costume History, No. 2. Leiden: E. J. Brill, 1993.
———. "Textiles." In *Ancient Egyptian Materials and Technology*, ed. Paul T. Nicholson and Ian Shaw, pp. 268–98. Cambridge: Cambridge University Press, 2000.
Wente, Edward F., trans. *Letters from Ancient Egypt*. Atlanta: Scholars Press, 1990.

WEB RESOURCES

Egyptology Resources. http://www.newton.cam.ac.uk/egypt.
Grajetzki, W., S. Quirke, and N. Shiode. *Digital Egypt for Universities*. Petrie Museum of Egyptian Archaeology. http://www.digitalegypt.ucl.ac.uk. *See especially* "Textile Production and Clothing," by H. Granger-Taylor and S. Quirke, http://www.digitalegypt.ucl.ac.uk/textil/index2.html.
Johnstone, J., et al. *Textiles in the Petrie Schools' Pack*. Petrie Museum of Egyptian Archaeology. http://www.petrie.ucl.ac.uk/Textiles%20in%20the%20Petrie%20Museum.doc.

MOVIES

Egypt's Golden Empire (PBS, 2002)
Cleopatra (1999)

Persian Clothing

Sara M. Harvey

The Middle East was the cradle of civilization, founded between the Tigris and Euphrates rivers as Mesopotamia, "the Land between the Rivers," in 3500 BCE. Ancient Mesopotamia extended across the present-day countries of Iran and Iraq. From this great land came the first forms of writing, sustainable agriculture, innovations in metalworking for technology and weapons, and accurate astronomical observations that were the basis of centuries of study.

This fertile and culturally rich region was also the target for invaders. Mesopotamia was ruled and overthrown by many civilizations. The Sumerians were conquered by the Babylonians. The Babylonians were supplanted by the Assyrians. The Chaldeans overthrew the Assyrian Empire and ruled for more than a hundred years until they were destroyed by the Persians in 539 BCE. The wealth, trade routes, and cultural singularities in this area, including the Hanging Gardens of Babylon, were assimilated by the succeeding cultures and created a lineage of greatness nearly unmatched in the history of the world.

HISTORY

Mesopotamia was a fertile area where crops and herds flourished. Homes were decorated with hanging drapes of wool, either plain woven or figured with complex images. Some linen has also been found in excavations, and flax is mentioned in ancient records, but wool was the textile of choice and was exported at great profit for the region. Rudimentary silk production was also developed in this area and added to the wealth of the Persians.

Originally a band of Indo-European nomadic tribes, the Persians were quick to rise up and take control over the Middle East. The Persian Empire was the last of the string of powerful invasions into the region and the last of the great Middle Eastern kingdoms, ruling from 539 to 330 BCE. By 486 BCE, the Persian Empire controlled the entirety of Mesopotamia and the Arabian Peninsula, reaching nearly to Egypt, India, and Greece. The Persian ruler Cyrus the Great had his sights set on ruling the world and forming an empire over which he held absolute control. The Zoroastrian religion of the Persians, focused on a battle between Ahura-Mazda's forces of good and light and Ahriman's forces of evil and darkness, fed into Cyrus's megalomaniacal ambitions as he established himself as a champion of Ahura-Mazda to bring about the rule of light over a dark world. When Cyrus captured Babylon, he freed the Hebrews that had been exiled there, claiming that the Hebrew god Yahweh had come to him in a dream and allied himself with Ahura-Mazda. Upon his death in 529 BCE, Cyrus had conquered and ruled a massive territory.

Cyrus's son Cambyses spread the Persian influence into Egypt, but his power was spread too thin and the Chaldeans in Mesopotamia proper, as well as the Medes east of the Tigris River in Persia's original lands, staged revolts that were not quelled until after Cambyses' death. When Cambyses' son, Darius I, assumed power, he cleverly divided the empire into autonomous provinces called *satrapies* that were united under an oath of fealty and strictly tithed. This gave the unruly provinces the sense of independence they desired while still keeping them under a tight reign.

Darius expanded the borders of the Persian Empire to their widest limits, reaching Macedonia, just outside of Greece. However, the Greek cities of Asia Minor then revolted against the Persians, not so much because of their rule as the costly tribute the Persians demanded. The Athenians were essential to the Persian defeat of Sardis, the capital of Lydia, in 498 BCE, but their offensive did not last, and it did not take long for the Persians to retake almost all of Asia Minor. Incensed at the Greek audacity, Darius planned to conquer the whole of the Greek peninsula and bring it under Persian rule. Accordingly, in 490 BCE, he led the Persian army into Greece and engaged the Athenians at the battle of Marathon. The Greek army was led by a Persian deserter, Miltiades. This proved to be a decisive victory for the Greeks, possibly one of the most important battles in Greek history. If the Persians had prevailed, the subsequent culture of Greece would have been heavily influenced by Persian character.

But the Persians were not dissuaded in their desire to control the Greek peninsula. Only a decade later, the new Persian ruler, Xerxes I, pressed into Greece again. His forces were met and turned back by the Athenians with the help of the Spartans, who had held back the initial Persian incursion with a very small but highly skilled fighting force. After this victory, the Greek city-states came together into a confederation led by the politically astute Athenians, and their newfound strength would deter any future invasions from Persia, or any other hostile forces. The Persians retreated back to Mesopotamia, but retained control over most of their original territory in the Arabian Peninsula. Although

An undated hand-colored print of Babylonian leader and Persians wearing different types of dress and accessories. © North Wind / North Wind Picture Archives.

issues with succession and population revolts plagued the empire, Persia would remain a powerful force in the ancient world for over a century.

The end of the Persian Empire came at the hands of Alexander the Great, who invaded Persia in an act of retribution for the Persian aggression toward Greece. Although Darius II commanded a superior force, Alexander's brilliance in tactics brought him victory after victory, pushing the Persians back across the Euphrates River into Mesopotamia. In 331 BCE, Alexander crossed the Euphrates and marched into Babylon as Darius II fled into exile, where he was eventually assassinated. The Persian Empire was subsumed by the Greek Empire as Alexander pushed his influence across the Middle East and into Egypt. Hellenistic culture became intertwined with Persian culture as colonization by the Greeks continued through 250 BCE. Trade with China and India thrived in this era, blending not only cultures but also religion. From remaining statuary and artwork, scholars have determined that a mix of Zoroastrianism and Buddhism was practiced across Persia during this time period.

After the death of Alexander the Great's successor, Seleucus I Nicator, in 281 BCE, there was a resurgence in Persian culture. Seleucus and his descendants helped to forge a powerful state that enjoyed strong trade relations with its neighbors, but the Persians eventually freed themselves from the Seleucid rulers in 238 BCE. This was the beginning of the Parthian Empire, although it would not become a unified country until around 170 BCE when Mithridates I took the throne. Under his rule, the Parthian Empire grew to a major force in the ancient world and held power until 288 CE. It controlled areas of modern-day Iran, Iraq, Turkey, Armenia, Georgia, Azerbaijan, Turkmenistan, Afghanistan, Tajikistan, Pakistan, Syria, Lebanon, Jordan, Palestine, and Israel.

Persia knew a period of peace and prosperity during the time of the Parthian Empire, although in 56 BCE the Roman leader Crassus brought 40,000 troops to the western border of Persia. The Persians under the rule of Orodes II, the great-grandson of Mithridates I, soundly defeated the Romans. This did not stop the Roman forces from continuing to skirmish with the Persians at their shared border, and the Romans launched several major campaigns on Persia between 116 and 232 CE, but none of these were successful. Eventually, as wealth and power percolated down to the lesser nobles, they began to vie for power and defy the king. The structure of the government weakened, allowing for successful Roman incursions into Persia. As rulers came and went, respect for the monarchy all but vanished and Persia was plundered by Rome.

In 224, a Parthian governor overthrew the king and established the Sassanian Empire, which would rule the region until the Islamic conquest in 641. Although the Sassanian period was one of great wealth and power, it struggled with internal issues of religion. The Sassanian rulers sought to reinstate Zoroastrianism, but the Persian people had adopted other faiths such as Christianity and Buddhism. Despite the religious factions at odds with one another, the Sassanian Empire was very centralized and held a firm grip on power. Eventually Zoroastrianism was instituted as the official state religion and all other faiths were persecuted, especially the Eastern Orthodox Church because of its ties to Byzantium and Rome. Over time, the Romans were able to wear down the Persians and take control of the outlying areas. By 650, the Romans had destroyed the Sassanian Empire and cleared the way for the Islamic conquest of the entire region. Zoroastrianism was replaced by Islam, and the last Sassanian king, Khosrow II, was murdered by his son, Kavadh II Shiruya, who succeeded him and embraced the Arab caliphate.

The Samanid Empire rose from the Transoxanian region and was the first native Persian dynasty to rule since the Arab conquest. Although they were Islamic, they allowed Zoroastrianism to be practiced in some of the western regions of Persia. The Samanids ruled from 875 to 999, and their dynasty was known as a time of great artistic achievement. Art, literature, architecture, textiles, and literature flourished under the Samanids.

In the eleventh century, Turks began to immigrate into Persia. They established themselves in the northwest of the area, defeated local rulers, and settled themselves into small dynasties. This incursion was countered by the Mongols in the thirteenth century. The Mongols were harsh rulers, often destroying crops and farmland to frighten the residents into submission. The Mongol conquest lasted well into the fifteenth century and caused a great deal of economic decline. Success went back and forth between the shamanistic Mongols and the Islamic Persians, and eventually the cruel Mongols were driven back after their leader Gharzan Khan converted to Islam. Persia began the process of rebuilding its cultural centers, only to have them destroyed once more by the return of the Turks in the fifteenth century.

The last major empire to rule Persia was the Safavid Empire, which ruled between 1502 and 1736. Although they were able to consolidate power, the rich resources of Persia's past were lost. The Silk Road was no longer a major trade route; sea routes were favored by most countries. The Safavids returned to their roots and began to rebuild their economy with the carpet trade using native wool. They were able to amass a great deal of wealth and created numerous palaces and city centers. But by 1723, the power structure began to disintegrate and the Ottoman Turks were able to take control. Russia also stepped in to take over parts of the country at this time, as did the Afghans. The Safavid general Nader Khan was able to reclaim most of Persia's lands back from the invaders by 1735.

THE SILK ROAD

The Silk Route, or Silk Road, developed around 126 BCE. It was actually a series of trade routes about 6,000 miles (7,600 km) long that connected Asia to Italy. The routes were varied in the path they took over both land and sea. Though the name would suggest that only silk was traded this way, in fact many goods were transferred back and forth between the regions along the treacherous and sometimes dangerous road. Silk and textiles were important commodities in demand in Persia and later in Rome, and trade on the Silk Route was a significant factor in the development of the great civilizations of China, Egypt, Mesopotamia, Persia, India, and Rome.

TEXTILES

The Persian textile trade was a mainstay of the region's economy. From the early days of Babylonian rule, wool from Mesopotamia and the Arabian Peninsula was highly prized. But the placement of the Persian Empire on the famed Silk Road gave it an edge in the silk trade. For centuries, Persia wove with Chinese silk, but beginning in the third century CE, scholars suspect that Persia established its own sericulture. The elaborate Persian drawloom weaving was thought to come through the knowledge of Syrians captured as prisoners of war during the battle of Antioch during the mid-third century. Once the silk industry was well established, the Parthian Persians began to export both silk yarn and woven silks to Byzantium and Central Asia. In the succeeding Sassanian Empire, Persian sericulture achieved great renown, and the intricate woven silks that were produced were some of the most coveted textiles in the world.

The Persian style often depicted mystical beasts enclosed in a circle bordered with large dots known as *pearl roundels*. These pearl roundels were the defining motif of Sassanian Persian weaving. Many theories have surfaced regarding their origin. Some claim that the motif was derived from China, a country that employs pearls in much of its weaving and embroidery designs. But the Assyrian kings, too, had always worn pearls as symbols of their rank, and that practice was passed down through dynasties of Persian rulers throughout the centuries. Scholars also believe that the inclusion of the beasts within a circle may have come from Greek coins that featured the heads of rulers encased in a circle that formed the border of the coin. The combination of this round enclosure with pearls and the sacred beast within created a striking visual impact of royal iconography.

The most common type of creature featured inside these pearl roundels was the *senmuru*. The senmuru was a benevolent half-bird and half-dog creature that perched on the tree that grows between heaven and earth. The senmuru is

Persian dignitary dressed in Persian trousers and Kyrbasia cap (dress of a traveller). Silver statuette from the court of Artaxerxes I (464–424 BCE). © Erich Lessing / Art Resource, NY.

associated with the growing season, rain, the fertility of the soil, and the king, who was seen as a divine ruler in the Zoroastrian faith. The crescent moon was often depicted with the senmuru and usually placed on the edges of the pearl roundels. Only the king could wear garments woven with the senmuru motif, and the crescent moon was reserved for the king and other members of the royal family.

For the wealthy of Persia, other designs were devised. The most popular of these were the ram and the boar. These animals were representative of the Zoroastrian god Verethranga and were sometimes shown wearing necklaces or collars indicative of Persian royalty. Scenes from Zoroastrian texts and epic poetry of the time were also often depicted in silk, as well as interpretations of royal hunts. Servants of these rich Persians were also dressed in woven silk, with designs of domestic birds: roosters, hens, ducks, and other waterfowl.

These textiles were a uniform width, suggesting a loom width of approximately $31\frac{1}{2}$ inches (80 cm). The silk was primarily constructed as a compound weft-faced twill. The repeats are usually rather large, several inches across and feature the figures either *confronting* (facing) or *adorsing* (back to back) one another. These figures also confront or adorse one another on a central axis, a specific characteristic of Persian weaving. Many of the designs were similar to carvings and frescoes found throughout Persia and the Middle East. It is unknown which art form inspired the other, but there is no doubting the similarities.

After the Islamic conquest of Persia, sericulture and the silk trade helped Persia hold onto its national identity in the face of the incursions, but the rules for decorative woven motifs changed. The caliphate Sunni Muslims banned depictions of humans and animals in their artwork and tolerated only abstract or geometric motifs. This was true not only in textiles but also in ceramic tiles and paintings. On the other hand, the Shi'a Muslims, who followed Muhammad's son-in-law Ali, were very fond of rendering the human form. Surface decoration was a very important means of expression, and textiles were held in very high regard. Although the Shi'ites did not abandon their human and animal figures, they incorporated the geometric motifs of the Sunnis into their own designs. These unique designs were in high demand across the world, from China to Europe. Prior to the fourteenth century, when Italy developed its own sericulture and silk trade, the majority of silks in Europe came from Byzantium and Persia. Talented Persian silk weavers and embroiderers were brought to Sicily, Italy, and Byzantium to create textile treasure for export to Europe.

After the Mongol invasion, the Persian silk industry was all but destroyed. Later, when the Safavid dynasty came to power and instituted Shi'a as the state religion, silk weaving became a priority once more. The Safavids also focused attention on carpet weaving to keep the fledgling economy afloat. With the Shi'ites in power, there were no prohibitions on depicting human or animal figures. By the fourteenth century, silk weaving had become Persia's preeminent industry once more. In addition to the highly detailed weft-faced twills, the Persians became masters of weaving velvet. At first, they embellished the velvet pile with simple textural variations of cut loops, uncut loops, and long and short pile. But soon the textile masters developed methods of creating voids in the pile that could be filled with intricate weaving or embroidery in a variety of colors. Persians also mastered intricate brocade techniques that were in high demand around the world. As the Safavid Empire declined, however, so did the quality of the silks produced. By the eighteenth century, Persian textiles had become indistinguishable from any other silks being produced.

MEN'S COSTUME

Costume for men in the ancient world consisted mainly of robes and long tunics, made primarily of wool and linen. In Persia, wool was the fiber of choice for the purposes of dress. With the lucrative trade through Persia and Persian territories, dress in the region was rich and elaborate. Dress of the royalty, as shown in existing illustrations, was covered in surface design, either woven or embroidered, but this was not indicative of the dress of the people, even though it was more often depicted than the clothes of the common people. The later dynasties provide much more information about the types of textiles worn by the Persian people, and there is relatively little knowledge about earlier styles of dress.

Persia was well situated on the Silk Road and had the wealth and influence to engage in fashion. While the basic elements of Middle Eastern dress were passed down from the Babylonians and Assyrians, the Persians were also influenced by textiles and garments from India, China, and Greece. Tunics were constructed with wide, draping sleeves, sometimes worn open. This *candys*, a long undertunic that was the precursor to the caftan, developed from the ubiquitous Sumerian shawl and spread

A clay plaque shows a man wearing the typical Parthian dress of a belted tunic worn over loose baggy trousers, possibly from Uruk, southern Iraq, first-second century. © HIP / Art Resource, NY.

An undated hand-colored print of upper-class citizens of ancient Media, part of the Assyrian and Persian empires. © North Wind / North Wind Picture Archives.

across the ancient Middle East. Persians also wore the full-length, wide trousers common to the region. Simple people, farmers and laborers, wore a loincloth indicative of Indian styles, often coupled with a head wrap and nothing more. A square piece of fabric wrapped around the hips like a sarong was also worn by men of all classes; the richness of this fabric would show class divisions.

The multitude of conquests and invasions brought additions to the Persian wardrobe, even after the trade on the Silk Road dwindled and finally vanished altogether. Tailored jackets came in from the Mongols, and metal belts were inspired by Indian examples. Fitted trousers came into the Persian costume with the invasion of peoples from the Steppes.

Persian costume, like that of all Middle Eastern cultures, progressed from a draped type of garment, consisting of a loincloth and some sort of cloak or wrap, toward a more fitted but still minimally structured type of apparel such as a robe or gown worn by itself or over loose-fitting trousers. As fashion evolved, the newer styles were adopted by the upper classes, while the lower classes had to make do with simpler attire. All over the Middle East, these garments were common, and what set Persia apart was not the construction of the garments but the sumptuous textiles from which they were made.

FOOTWEAR AND HEADWEAR

Footwear consisted primarily of sandals and soft leather shoes, either slippers or taller boots (see color insert). Head and hair dressing in Persia was also fairly similar to what was common in the larger region of the Middle East. Men wore beards, often oiled and curled. Hats were either wrapped lengths of fabric or plain wool felt caps. A tall, straight-sided hat similar to the fez was popular with the ruling classes and clerics. Men of wealth and station also wore a metal circlet, often encrusted with jewels, over their curled or braided hair. Persians had a taste for large jewels and set these stones into not only their headbands but also chest plates, flat collar-like neck pieces, and belts. In addition, the Persians were fond of weaving or embroidering gold and other metallic threads into their textiles, and they devised clever ways to attach small metal plates and discs, as well as cabochons of ruby, garnet, lapis, and coral, to their garments.

WOMEN'S CLOTHING

Very little is known about the dress of Persian women. It was considered highly improper to depict women in art, and the only images that have ever been found were stylized goddesses.

For the most part, Middle Eastern garb was fairly unisex. Both men and women wore flowing tunics or robes over full trousers. Women often wore their tunics looser, longer, and with longer, fuller sleeves. The fabrics were sumptuous and colorful and figured with the latest fashions in weaving and embroidery.

Women also wrapped themselves in shawls and veils, often covering the head and hair. The necessity of veils and other head coverings would vary by empire and dynasty. Generally, a veil signified a married woman of station. Some veils covered the head lightly but were not designed to completely cover the hair or face. Others were made specifically to hide the hair, and some hid both the hair and the face. Most women veiled their faces only in public. Slaves, prostitutes, and concubines were prohibited from wearing veils. Veiling customs have remained very strong in the Islamic Middle East through the current time.

Women's hair was worn in a variety of styles, depending on the dominant influence. Styles could be elaborate, arranged with curls and crimps and braids, worn long and curled to the shoulder, or more simply bundled up into a bun, twist, or chignon. Hair styles were modestly decorated with pins and cabochons. Women also wore jeweled collars, bracelets, belts, and armbands that accentuated their dramatic textiles.

CHILDREN'S CLOTHING

There is extremely little evidence for the dress of children in Persia. Children were considered valuable possessions, and older Babylonian texts state that children could be sold or given into slavery to settle a debt or used as collateral.

Children wore simple garments of linen and wool, such as a loincloth-and-tunic combination. Costly textiles would not likely be used for children's clothing, nor is there any reference of children being dressed in jewelry—not even the children of the royal family. Children who were not sold or indentured were often apprenticed to a trade at a young age and dressed in the manner befitting their station as a miniature adult from that point forward.

FURTHER READING

Boucher, François. *20,000 Years of Fashion: The History of Costume and Personal Adornment.* Expanded ed. New York: H. N. Abrams, 1987.
Harris, Jennifer, ed. *Textiles: 5,000 Years.* New York: H. N. Abrams, 1993.
Tortora, Phyllis, and Keith Eubank. *Survey of Historic Costume.* 4th ed. New York: Fairchild, 2005.
Whitfield, Susan. *Life along the Silk Road.* London: John Murray, 2002.

WEB RESOURCES

Hooker, Richard. "Mesopotamia: The Persians." *World Civilizations.* http://www.wsu.edu/~dee/MESO/PERSIANS.HTM
Iran Chamber Society. http://www.iranchamber.com.
"The Parthian Empire." http://www.parthia.com.
"Persia." *The Columbia Encyclopedia,* 6th ed. (2001–2005). http://www.bartleby.com/65/pe/Persia.html.

Greek Clothing

Jennifer Chi and
Larissa Bonfante

TIMELINE

3000–1500 BCE	Minoan civilization on Crete; Aegean bronze age
2000–1000 BCE	Greek-speaking Mycenaeans arrive from the north
1500 BCE	Apogee of Minoan-Mycenaean civilization; Agia Triada Sarcophagus
1200 BCE	Collapse of Mycenaean society; Trojan War
1000–750 BCE	Iron Age; Geometric period; Greeks in Ionia and southern Italy
750–600 BCE	Orientalizing period; first Olympic Games held in Olympia (776 BCE); development of the alphabet, Greek myth; sculpting of nude kouroi and Daedalic korai (Auxerre Kore)
600–480 BCE	Archaic period; Peisistratid tyrants (to 510 BCE); Ionian korai, long chiton, diagonally draped mantle; draped himation for men; nude athletes
490–480 BCE	Persian wars
480–400 BCE	Classical period; democracy in Athens
460–430 BCE	Age of Pericles; Parthenon
431–404 BCE	Peloponnesian War
350 BCE	Praxiteles' nude Aphrodite of Cnidus
350–330 BCE	Alexander the Great conquers Persia, Egypt, and the East
300–31 BCE	Hellenistic period; beardless, young, heroically nude ruler portraits modeled on Alexander; women adopt belted, empire-style chitons, draped mantles (Baker Dancer, Tanagra figurines), Melon coiffure

THE ANCIENT GREEKS

The ancient Greeks are often considered to be the "founders" of Western civilization. Influences however, also came from the Middle East, and the Greeks drew freely from contact (through trading and invasion) with the Persians and Egyptians over their long history.

The *Minoan* was a distinct civilization on the island of Crete between 3000 and 2000 BCE. The ruins of this society at Knossos, discovered in 1900, provide evidence of sumptuous palaces with plumbing and baths and show how these people lived a comfortable if not lavish lifestyle well before modern times. The Minoans worshipped numerous gods and goddesses and were generally accustomed to peaceful and pleasant lives. By 1600 BCE, civilized life was known to exist all along the Aegean Sea coasts and islands.

The *Mycenaean*, unlike the Minoans, were traders and warriors, who struggled with the Cretans to control commerce and land in the eastern Mediterranean Sea. The destruction of this civilization occurred around 1400 BCE, after which the Greeks began to thrive and set themselves apart as great thinkers and developers of city-states, government, law, architecture, and sophisticated economies.

The so-called dark ages of Greek history occurred from about 1150 to 800 BCE, when the Dorian conquerors came down from the north with their barbaric tribal society based on clan and family, with a simple economy and no law or governmental organization. The mingling of the barbarians with the people they had conquered, along with the elements from the Middle East, led to the development of the essential characteristics of classical Greek antiquity, or the *Homeric Greeks*. This name comes from the poet Homer, believed to have lived in the eighth century BCE. Homer was an example of the sophisticated thinking and literature produced by the ancient Greeks. He wrote the *Iliad* and the *Odyssey*, epic poems that give great clues about the customs and life of the society in which he lived.

The first city-states started to emerge following the first Olympic celebration in 776 BCE. The city-state (*polis*) was a government and place to live and trade. Each one covered only a couple of square miles, typically built around a hill to protect it. Normally there was a fortress (*acropolis*) crowning the hill, such as the one in Athens. Each city-state had its own distinct personality and was fiercely independent. The city was serviced for food by the rich ocean and agricultural land that surrounded it, and the population was only a few thousand on average. Each city-state, as their descendants do today, considered itself a separate and sovereign government, run by *citizens*, the most privileged and well-respected men of the state. The affairs of the city belonged to all citizens, who also saw the city-state as their church (believing in the same pantheon or group of gods), school, recreation club, gymnasium, marketplace, and home. Citizens were expected to be active participants in the affairs of the city, and people spent hours discussing their views of the cherished city-state and its affairs, including art, architecture, politics, philosophy, and trade.

Eventually, one city-state would overtake another, and political fragmentation became a persistent problem. The tiny states ended up enmeshed with each other in rivalries, and as each city-state had its own army, they ultimately destroyed each other in war. The biggest and most important city-state was Athens, a center for creativity that is arguably unparalleled in Western history. Other significant city-states included Miletus, Ephesus, Thebes, Argos, Corinth, and Sparta.

The Spartans, the antithesis of the Athenians, were descendants of the warring Dorians and were a proud, aloof people. The Spartiates, or actual citizens, were only a small number, especially compared to the large number of serfs they ruled, a fact that forced them to become a militaristic state in order to maintain control. Both men and women were known to be in top physical shape. There was little in terms of personal choice for the individual, and even the members of the assembly were not allowed to debate proposals brought forward by the council of elders, only to vote in favor or not by shouting their support. Spartans were not open to outsiders or change, and they developed an army that was the most well respected and feared in all of Greece. Spartan foot soldiers were called *hoplites* and fought with spears or short iron swords, protecting themselves with round bronze shields and protective armor.

There was a distinct lack of family life in Sparta. The men were expected to live and dine predominantly with their regiments, while the wives and children often lived elsewhere. Infants were taken to the sea's edge and examined, and if there were any signs of weakness, the child would be abandoned or tossed over the cliff. Boys were taken from their mothers by the state after the age of seven to launch their lifelong regimen of fitness and military instruction. Girls were also expected to maintain physical fitness and underwent drills to ensure their fitness to bear children. Unlike in later societies, celibacy was punished, and mating was encouraged in order to maintain the supremacy of the fighting Spartans. The Spartans maintained their supremacy despite struggles with Athens in the Peloponnesian War of c. 431–404 BCE, which they won (but were significantly weakened in the process).

In Athens, the lifestyle was just the opposite. Athenians sought to create a life full of a balance, where physical fitness was enhanced by thought and words. As a result, literature flourished. Because of the abundant written material, the history of Greece is well known to modern historians. Athens welcomed foreign influence and ideas, unlike Sparta.

Two turning points in the history of Athens were in the form of war: the Persian War, in which the Greeks were victorious, and the Peloponnesian War, in which the Athenians were defeated by the Spartans. In between these two wars, though, was a time when the Greeks flourished in creativity. This was the Age of Pericles (460–430 BCE), named after the leader of Athens during this golden age. Public works projects abounded. Debate was encouraged in the assembly, and skilled orators were encouraged to speak and convince others of their views. Democracy was a valued concept, and by 500 BCE, the ultimate power lay in the hands of an assembly of citizens, all men.

Athens was populated with thousands of public officials to enforce the laws, from building inspectors to tax collectors, who were chosen by lot annually so no one man could be influenced by holding office for too long. Of the approximately 200,000–250,000 inhabitants of Athens at the height of its power, 40,000–60,000 were male citizens and the same number of women citizens. Beneath these men in status were the resident aliens (50,000), who were mainly traders and craftsmen, and at the very bottom of the social ladder were the slaves, who numbered around 50,000. The slaves were mostly not Greek and were part of every city-state. As the philosopher Aristotle said, they were useful for relieving male citizens of heavy manual labor, freeing them to devote time to greater leisure and cultural activities.

Most citizens were men of modest means and were merchants, farmers, or artisans who produced wine, olive oil, metal weapons, textiles, grain, ships, and other varied products needed for life in the city-state or for warfare. Civic celebrations were a big part of life in Athens and were free for men to attend and enjoy the drama, dance, and athletic events. There was separation of public and private, and though they had their own festivals and priestesses, and were important to the life of the city, respectable women were not seen outside the home except for marriages, funerals, and religious festivals. They could not own property and were essentially uninvolved in public activities, especially politics and divorce or marriage procedings, which were handled by men only. Men had wives but also were free to be with prostitutes or slaves. If they could afford to, they took up with *heterae*—noncitizen female high-class prostitutes, or courtesans—who were intelligent and charming. Unlike in Sparta, children were doted on, with boys being educated by private tutors and girls receiving little formal education. At age eighteen, boys took up their military duty for two years.

The Greeks believed in many gods and had hundreds of anthropomorphic gods such as Zeus, Poseidon, and Pluto with whom they tried to gain favor. Many myths surrounded the gods, to whom they prayed and worshipped, and the underworld was a terrifying place to be avoided.

The Greeks had a high level of cultural awareness, excelling in all areas important to human history. Not only were art, architecture, and craft significant in their contribution to human history, but in the areas of language and philosophy, the Greek thinkers are said to have laid the foundation for all modern scientific thought. Information about the ancient Greeks can be gleaned from a number of written sources. As the Greeks were well populated with bards, philosophers, and poets, there is much written material that gives rich information about the time.

Socrates, commonly considered the greatest teacher of the fifth century BCE, was convinced of higher truth and spent his life seeking to find the truth by posing questions. He believed that "the unexamined life is not worth living." The "Socratic method" is a philosophical process by which questioning and examining definitions—of *right, justice, beauty*, and similar concepts—people would consistently move forward in their development and enlightenment.

Socrates' most brilliant student was Plato, who was responsible for writing much of what is known about Socrates. Plato continued where Socrates left off, after the elder philosopher was condemned to death by an Athenian jury of peers for corrupting the youth of Athens and doubting the gods. Plato's dialogues often had Socrates as the main orator and continued the ideas of Socrates after his death. In 385 BCE, he founded the Academy in Athens, which became the most influential center for learning in Antiquity, surviving for nine hundred years. The "Doctrine of Ideas" set out to explain the universe in philosophical terms and later was adaptable to the teachings of Christianity.

Aristotle, Plato's pupil at the Academy, was more interested in the evidence of the senses (ranging from the intellectual ideas in political thought and poetry to the purely scientific) and collected and classified more items than anyone else in Antiquity. He believed that men could gain understanding of life and purpose through the things and interrelations that give guidance to their lives to achieve pure spirit, which would bring them close to God, who was the source of Forms and pure in spirit. Aristotle also studied government and political organization in his work *Politics* and identified three basic types of government: rule by one, rule by a few, and rule by many. The "golden mean" devised by Aristotle is the principle that in most affairs humans should find the desired mean, or midpoint, between extremes; it calls for the best performance of mind and body in harmony.

The Greeks invented many varieties of poetry, including the *epic* poem and the *lyric* poem. Homer is the father of the epic poem, which is the story (at great length) of heroes and great deeds, usually recited to the music of a stringed instrument. Homer wrote in the emerging Greek language with an alphabet based on the Phoenician alphabetic system. Though well established as the author of the two poems the *Iliad* and the *Odyssey*, no one knows exactly who Homer was or where and when he lived. His poems are set in general terms during the Trojan Wars.

Drama, both tragedy and comedy, was considered by Aristotle to be a higher form of art. Greek drama was theatrical and involved dance and song. It was more of a spectacle that was tighter in structure and gave a greater chance for people to look at their lives and reflect on their situations through the trials and settings of others who may reflect their own ordeals. Comedy was initially slapstick performances to honor the god Dionysus (who personified fertility, joy, and mirth), but gradually it became more sophisticated and satirical. Aristophanes, whose works are the only surviving record of comedy of this time, ridiculed politicians, poets, and philosophers with whom he did not agree. His most famous satires are *The Cloud* and *Lysistrata* from the late 400s BCE. Drama was performed in theaters built on hillsides with seating angling down to a central circle where the performers would act out the tragedies or comedies, in full costume and with sets.

Greek architecture and sculpture present another insight into the ancient Greeks. While words allow for a certain level of understanding, it is the visual record that can be examined to further complete that understanding. Architecture from ancient Greece is a glorious representation of the achievements of the society. The Greeks used the post-and-lintel method developed by the Egyptians, where columns placed at intervals supported the stone roof. Examples of this include the Temple of Hera at Paestum, Italy, and, of course, the Parthenon in Athens. The columns were distinctive, and their designs were in the Doric, Ionic, and Corinthian orders, the differences being in the design of the bases and capitals of the columns. The Parthenon, designed in 450 BCE, still stands today and embodies the ideal of the Greek ideal of the golden mean. It has subtle curves rather than straight, stiff lines and was originally painted with soft pastel colors and scriptures, which have faded. The visual image presented by this piece of architecture was paramount, and the painstaking attention to detail is referred to constantly as an architectural ideal.

Images of men and the gods were translated into sculpture by Greek artists, whose passion for beauty is evident in the statues they produced. Only very few original Greek sculptures remain, and the main source of information on sculpture comes from Roman reproductions from later times. Again, the attention to detail and the well-defined ideal of beauty are evident in the bodies that were depicted by Greek artists. The most famous include the Discus Thrower, which, though nude, shows the characteristic interest in the human form; "Hermes with the Infant Dionysus"; and the Venus de Milo. The latter two are excellent sources of information for the costume historian and show incredible attention to draping of textiles over the three-dimensional body form. The statues are carved from cold marble, yet they show a flow and movement of cloth that seems quite real. Other artistic forms that allow for greater understanding of what the Ancient Greeks wore are the fragments of vases, which were clearly decorated with scenes of people in a myriad of activities and scenes. These will be discussed in greater detail below.

While Ancient Greek history is long and complex, there are several manners in which to embark on a study of the culture and dress. Dividing the great amount of time into periods and addressing each with respect to the dress is the most straightforward. This look at costume will start with the Aegean Bronze Age, including a look at the Minoan and Mycenaean dress, followed by the Geometric period, Orientalizing period, and Archaic period, and finishing with the Classical and Hellenistic periods.

Clothing of the Ancient World

Ancient Greek, Etruscan, and Roman dress has been a subject that has both interested and perplexed scholars for more than a century. Many of the early discussions focused on the actual reconstruction of a garment type—how were garments made, and how did they compare to the way they were rendered in artistic representations? Some scholars have focused on a particular garment type, attempting an interpretation of its meanings, or on a particular figure—mortal or divine—analyzing the choice of dress.

To present the attire of mortals and of gods from the cultures of the classical world would require a long handbook. In order to give a basis here for the study of ancient dress, the following survey deals with real costume, that is, representations of actual ancient dress. It does not include images of the gods and goddesses of classical antiquity, nor mythological creatures and their attributes and dress. This decision allows for a more focused presentation of ancient dress from the Aegean Bronze Age to, in the next chapter, the Late Antique period in Rome. For gods and goddesses and mythological figures, information on their dress can often be found in the *Lexicon Iconographicum Mythologiae Classicae* (LIMC). In this discussion of Ancient dress, the overall goals are to provide vivid descriptions of garment types, to include the most recent discussions and bibliography of ancient dress, and to present controversial questions surrounding this fascinating area of study in the classical world.

Fabric Production

Fabric production is often seen in Greek literature as the work of goddesses or female mythological characters or heroines and is ever present in Greek mythology. Athena, the patroness of Athens and of artisans, for example, was said to be the first to work with wool fibers and fabrics. Wool came from the sheep that were raised and kept in the hills above Athens. The sheep were shorn and the fibers spun and woven by artisans and female heads of households in the city-state for use in everyday and special clothing. Rituals, as with most other things in Greek life, surrounded the production and use of special fabrics, which often played a role in ceremonies, ranging from the rite marking the transition from childhood to adulthood, to the offering of wool garments and beautiful fabrics in funeral ceremonies. Wool was most often used for outer garments, and linen was used for garments that were worn closer to the skin. Linen, a fiber that comes from the flax plant, was imported from Egypt, Asia Minor, and the Middle East. Later, silk fabric was also used in Greece, likely originally from Asia. Silk was a precious fiber, used by the wealthy for ceremonial reasons, and was uncommon in everyday garments and household products.

Linen and wool are often depicted as being left undyed in their natural colors. The wool was the color of the sheep from which it came, ranging from creamy white to much darker browns. Linen, in its raw form, is a beige or buff color but is very easy to dye and accepts color very well. Fabrics are thought to have been dyed in many various colors, but it is difficult to see this based on many of the vases and pictorial representations from which scholars have studied costume. If they did dye the fabrics, they used naturally occurring pigments from plants and animals or insects. To add to the decorative effect of the plain woven linen or wool fabrics, Greek women perfected the art of pleating, which allowed for texture to be created in permanent pleats, or they wove the fabrics to add visual interest and beauty. As the garments were rarely tailored or even sewn by the women in the household who were responsible for clothing and household textile production, the weavers had the arduous task of weaving the fabric for the individual's size so as to minimize waste of fabric and avoid the need to cut or sew the garments.

AEGEAN BRONZE AGE

When the future Mycenaeans came from the north about 2000 BCE and settled in mainland Greece, they encountered a more developed culture, one that had its own written language (Linear A), specialized craft production, centralized government, and strong artistic self-identity. Called the Minoan civilization by modern scholars after the mythical King Minos, this culture was located on the island of Crete, where great palaces formed the economic, social, artistic, and religious centers. Crete is a large island located south of the Aegean Sea, and the sea's natural defenses allowed the Minoans to develop a sophisticated and peaceful culture. At the same time, they became great seamen; trade with foreign cultures such as Egypt and the Near East stimulated an unprecedented economic boom and created a distinct sense of self-identity that expressed itself in their language, religion, and dress.

Around 1500 BCE, the northern tribes that had settled on the mainland adopted and adapted such elements of the Minoan civilization as the practice of writing (though they never gave up their own pre-Greek language) and certain artistic motifs and techniques. They are called the Mycenaeans after the great city in ancient Greece where their civilization was first recognized. Their art and much of their culture were so close to that of the Minoans that much of the dress from this period is referred to as the Minoan/Mycenaean.

Evidence of Minoan dress comes from several different sources. The first and most obvious is their own artistic representations. Wall paintings, in particular, provide us with an idea of certain garment types, both male and female, as well as indicating the rich color schemes used in garment decoration. There are also several preserved examples of foreign representations of Minoan dress, most notably Egyptian wall paintings depicting what appear to be Minoan emissaries visiting Egyptian royalty. It seems that the artists were familiar with the costumes they were depicting. Texts give information about the process of weaving and the sophisticated workshops that developed around the manufacture of textiles, as well as raw material employed by weavers. Most garments appear to have been made of linen, a lightweight fabric suitable for Crete's hot and arid climate. Wool is also mentioned as another material favored by the Minoans.

Recent scholarship surrounding Minoan/Mycenaean dress has focused on attempts to reconstruct the actual garments worn by Minoans, in particular those worn by women. While this process provides useful discussions of the actual form of the clothing depicted, it also brings out a number of fundamental problems involved in the study of ancient dress and textiles. How, for example, were costumes made? How much tailoring was used in garment manufacture? Who wore these costumes—the aristocracy, religious figures, or everyday people? And were the costumes represented actually worn or did artists create garment types more as symbolic expressions of particular concepts and ideas?

One costume combination frequently discussed by scholars is worn by the Snake Goddess, a female figure, shown brandishing snakes in both hands and commonly identified as a religious figure, either priestess or goddess. What is most striking about her costume is the form-fitting, open bodice she wears that fully exposes her breasts. This provocative bodice is worn in combination with a flounced skirt, over which is placed an apron-like garment with a rounded edge. In other depictions, brightly colored linen is shown on wall paintings, with the most common colors being yellow, red, and blue. The garments frequently have solid borders as well as interesting and varied patterns.

While earlier scholarship identified this costume as that worn by women in daily life, the combination seems to have been special ritualistic or ceremonial dress. The depiction of nudity in art—either partial or complete—had a special purpose. In the case of the Snake Goddess, the open bodice clearly emphasized her full breasts. Her nudity was perhaps meant to represent divine epiphany, as well as her special function as a fertility goddess. The women depicted in the wall paintings most likely wear the same garments in fulfillment of a religious ritual. Finally, the same combination can sometimes be found in Mycenaean art, where it is worn by both goddesses and women involved in ritualistic activities. The scenes suggest that, for Aegean women, there were varying types of garments, some that were prescribed for specific activities and others worn in daily life.

Another monument that records ritual dress is the Agia Triada Sarcophagus, a limestone coffin covered in plaster and painted with religious scenes. On one side, both men and women participate in the act of libation. One female on the left wears a short-sleeved robe with banded borders and a stripe running down its center front. The other wears two garments—a short-sleeved shirt also decorated with solid borders and a shorter belted skirt with rounded bottom hem. The shaggy hair represented on the surface and the rounded borders indicate that the skirt was made of animal skin. Garments were made of skin in prehistoric times, with their use continuing in many cultures for religious purposes and activities.

Of the five male figures represented on the Agia Triada Sarcophagus, a lyre player behind the women wears a long-sleeved red robe, again delineated by solid borders. This may be the beginning of the Greek tradition of wearing a long dress for musical performances, suggesting that there was continuity in ritual dress for certain ceremonies. The men approaching the deceased and bearing gifts, two animals and a boat, all wear belted animal-skin skirts, which are slightly shorter than those of the females. They also seem to have bare torsos. In Aegean art, males and females are differentiated by the color of their skin. The dark skin of the men means that they were involved in outdoor activities, while women traditionally carried on their work indoors, hence their light skin. The image of the dead man here is slightly smaller than those of the live figures and is covered in a shroud-like garment that is draped around his arms. The pattern on the shroud is similar to that of the animal-skin skirts and may imply that this is made of the same material.

A garment that suggests activity, since it covers the sexual organs while avoiding complete nudity, is depicted in a number of monuments of this period. On the famous fresco at Knossos showing three figures involved in bull-jumping, the male figure in the act of jumping over the bull wears these shorts, called *perizoma* in Greek. Here and elsewhere in Minoan/Mycenaean art, it consists of a type of loincloth placed over the genitals and held in place by a thick belt cinched tightly around the waist. Young men wear this kind of garment in a variety of contexts, the most common of which are athletic or hunt scenes. In these cases, the perizoma allowed for greater freedom of movement. Many statuettes and paintings, however, depict young men worshipping who are also wearing this same garment. In this case, the garment was simply meant to suggest their youthful status, because it was young men who took part in strenuous activities.

In the bull-jumping scene, two women are also shown wearing this athletic garment, clearly because, like the men, they are involved in this sport. Women are, however, never depicted in hunt or ritual scenes wearing the perizoma. Instead, they are usually dressed in long robes, as on the Agia Triada Sarcophagus. However, women, as we have seen, could be shown with their breasts exposed in ritual situations. The perizoma, which never stopped being used in order to avoid complete nudity, could be made of cloth or leather.

GEOMETRIC PERIOD

Unfortunately, the Geometric period boasts little in terms of material evidence in comparison to later periods. The primary source of information comes from figural depictions on vases and small-scale decorative objects. Figures are normally depicted in outline, which makes it difficult to discuss details of the form and construction of the garments that men and women wear. Women are, however, normally dressed in what seem to be straight tunics, which from their form appear to be woolen and are sometimes decorated with geometric and linear patterns. Men are most frequently depicted as soldiers, wearing body armor and helmets, suggesting that warfare formed a significant aspect of Geometric life. Being a warrior indicated a man's high status in society.

When complete nudity is represented in Geometric art, it is not realistic and is meant to distinguish between the sexes. In some senses, this can be compared to the artistic motif of dark skin/light skin used in Minoan and Mycenaean art, as well as in later periods.

ORIENTALIZING PERIOD

The seventh century BCE was a period of great interaction between Greece and the East, or Orient—so much so that it is frequently called the Orientalizing period. There is a larger amount of material evidence from this than from previous periods, as well as a certain amount of literary evidence—mostly derived from Homeric epic—therefore allowing a more specific discussion of garment types and form.

There is much more information about female costumes than male from this period. For women, the most distinctive combination of garments was a tube-like dress worn with a short capelet. This can be seen on the smaller than life-size Auxerre *Kore* (girl), who is shown barefoot and wears a wig-like hairstyle typical of the so-called Daedalic sculptural style of seventh century BCE. The tightness of the dress should be seen more as an artistic convention than a realistic representation of the garment. The straight shape and the lack of folds suggests that the garment was most likely made of wool. The dress is pulled tightly at the waist, with a wide belt that is buckled in front, suggesting that it was made either of leather or metal. The tube-like skirt is elaborately decorated with squares that were originally brightly painted to reflect the sophisticated weaving of such luxurious garments from this period. Such elaborate garments are mentioned by Homer as part of the treasures of princesses and as gifts given by royalty to each other. The *Iliad* and the *Odyssey* record these and other costumes from the earliest periods of Greek culture. The Auxerre Kore's shoulders and upper arms are covered by a capelet, also apparently of heavy wool. Some scholars have argued that this capelet was in reality always formed by pulling up fabric from the back and pinning it at either side of the neckline. But the continuation of the border of the capelet on the back of some examples indicates that this was an actual garment worn in real life. Perhaps both garment options were available for women of this period.

A statuette of the Lady of Auxerre in Daedalic style (Cretan-style dress, Egyptian-style wig), 640–630 BC. The Art Archive / Musée du Louvre Paris / Gianni Dagli Orti.

In Near Eastern art, which was so influential in Greece during this period, the image of the nude goddess was one of the most characteristic and traditional aspects of the visual vocabulary. This motif appeared in Greece in the seventh century BCE, clearly reflecting Near Eastern influence. On a relief from the temple of Gortyn, on Crete, Apollo is depicted with two standing nude female figures. The women flank a striding image of Apollo, unfortunately only partly preserved. These three figures have been interpreted as representing Apollo, flanked by his mother Leto and his sister Artemis. Since the majority of Apollo is missing, it is unknown whether he was depicted nude or wore a perizoma. Later evidence from the Archaic period suggests that men were still wearing the perizoma. The nudity of the female figures was reserved for female divinities during this period and supports their identification as goddesses. The tall headdresses, the *polos* hat worn over their wiglike hairstyle, was also used to signify divinity in this period. Typical of the female nudity from this early period is its sexually explicit character in which the reproductive organ is clearly demarcated, as in the Gortyn relief. Nudity as a signifier of female divinity, however, does not survive into the later Archaic period, perhaps reflecting the diminishing importance of Near Eastern culture.

ARCHAIC PERIOD

The Archaic period (600–480 BCE) saw the beginning of what is considered the Greek identity, which revolved around the polis or city-state system. Though these self-governing cities were highly individualistic and competitive, they shared a common language and a polytheistic religious system (with many gods) with a male god as its chief divinity. Central to their culture were several pan-Hellenic sanctuaries, among which Olympia, on the west coast of the Peloponnesus, was the most important. Here, the Greek city-states met to worship and to compete in athletic Games every four years in honor of Zeus, the chief Olympic deity. A direct and extremely important outcome of these meetings was the beginning of written records in the form of lists recording victorious competitors.

On mainland Greece, among the most prominent city-states were Athens, Sparta, and Corinth. On the other side of the Aegean were the coastal cities of Ionia, whose sophisticated cultures depended in part on their close geographical relationship with the cultures of the East—Samos, Ephesus, and Halicarnassus were among the most prominent.

The course of the Archaic period saw the development of Sparta as a militaristic entity and Athens as a cultural center. By the end of this highly competitive period, and partially through its relationship with Ionian cities, Athens would dominate. The city's victory over the Persians established its political supremacy by the Classical period.

Extremely important to the artistic development of Greek art was the introduction of life-size and larger-than-life-size sculpture in the early Archaic period. The introduction of statues on this scale is frequently attributed to the Greeks' contact with Egypt, who for millennia had been creating monumental statuary. Others have argued that life-size statues found on Crete from the Orientalizing period could have influenced the output of Greek sculptors. Either way, this technological innovation would dramatically change the development and overall character of Greek art from the Archaic period forward.

Women's Clothing

Great diversity is evident in Archaic female costume, with regional differences apparent in style, drapery patterns, and textiles. In mainland Greece, as evidenced by the Athenian Acropolis, statues of *korai* (unmarried young maidens) express a love of elaborate combinations of colors, forms, and textures, all of which emphasize the quality of luxury and youthful beauty. The basic shape of their garments was most often square or rectangular, but they could be draped in what appears to be an endless variety of manners. Among of the Acropolis korai, for example, the combination of a multiplicity of drapery patterns and garments makes their dress often difficult to "read" or understand. It is interesting to note that, unlike some other contemporary cultures, tailoring was not used. The process of weaving was a time-consuming one and cutting fabrics meant waste, so they maximized the use of their favorite fabrics by not tailoring the garments to fit the body's natural shape.

One aspect that adds difficulty to the study Archaic costume is terminology. While some ancient names can be connected with actual garments, there are many names mentioned in literary sources that have not been identified in the visual record. There are also representations of costumes for which we do not know the ancient names. Within the following discussion, standard terminology for unidentified garments will be employed unless the ancient name is known.

A good example of the classic Athenian costume combination is represented by Kore 680. She wears a luxurious thin linen *chiton* (a tunic-like undergarment), which she would have pulled up with her left hand in a graceful gesture. The word *chiton*, which appears frequently in literature, was imported along with the garment from the Near East, embodying the lavish nature of Ionian culture. The garment consisted of a rectangular piece of finely woven linen that was sewn or buttoned at the shoulders to create openings for the neck and arms. The fineness of the material allowed the chiton to cling to the kore's form. Frequently defined by tight pleats, they could either be crinkly or straight, normally reaching to the kore's ankles. This sometimes caused her to grasp the folds at her side allowing for easier movement. Some scholars have also suggested that this was a gesture symbolic of dance; lyric poets from the eighth to the sixth century BCE frequently describe dances for maidens in honor of various, often female, gods.

Kore 680, from the Acropolis, wears a very common Archaic female garment, a "diagonal mantle," the Greek name of which we do not know. Although it was much shorter than the chiton, its broad, thick folds indicated that it was made out of a heavier material, most likely wool, and thus did not cling to the maiden's form like the chiton. Pinned at the right shoulder, the diagonal mantle had a lower border that was normally shaped like an inverted V. Sometimes this V-shape fell on the stomach of the maiden, while at other times, as with Kore 680, it was draped in a manner that gave it an uneven lower border. The elaborate folds, often ending in what is referred to as "omega pleats," also have the appearance of a swallow's tail in many examples.

Both the chiton and the mantle were frequently, if not always, enlivened by bright patterns and decorated borders. In the case of Kore 680, the painted patterns on both the chiton and mantle consist of crosses and clusters of dots. In addition, the central fold of the chiton carries a continuous meander, which created a stronger distinction between the two garments. In its original state, the color combination would have been extremely bright, with the palette including deep red, yellow, and bright green. Korai from both the Athenian Acropolis and other Greek cities were also frequently shown wearing necklaces and embellished with metal appliqués—earrings, hair ties, and necklaces greatly enlivening the surface of the statue.

Men's Clothing

The depiction of male figures in Archaic art contrasts with that of females. The classic Archaic *kouros* (boy) was defined by its nudity and its focus on the male bodily form and, by extension, its athletic nature. The type embodied several important Greek male characteristics that were also admired in contemporary literature. Chief among these was the aristocratic quality of such beautiful young men, athletic victors and future soldiers; a kouros was *kalos kagathos* ("beautiful and noble"). The culture of male youths was one of the *gymnasium*, where citizens were physically as well as intellectually trained to serve the city-state. As with the korai, emphasis was placed on their elaborate hairstyles, which was a symbol of their beauty. Such hairstyles might also have been sym-

bolic of their status as youths stepping over the threshold of adolescence into adulthood. As men, they would wear their hair shorter, in a more practical style.

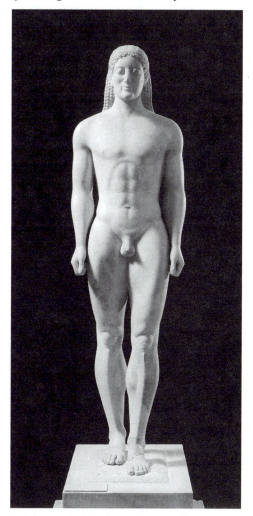

An early example of a kouros is the New York Kouros. He stands frontally with his left leg placed forward, his arms hanging stiffly with his fist clenched at his sides. The pose is strongly reminiscent of Egyptian statues, except that the statue appears to move forward and wears no garments, thus leaving his sexual organs exposed. The hair is long, as with most other *kouroi*, and arranged as thick locks separated into interconnected, beadlike forms, ending in an ornate fringe. The style of this particular hair arrangement is reminiscent, in its wiglike quality, of seventh century BCE figures in the Daedalic style, as are the features of his handsome face. The flat band worn around the head and tied in the back in a Heraklean knot and his necklace are two attributes that are uncharacteristic of later kouroi. These later kouroi have no such decorative accessories, thus placing total emphasis on their nudity. In the case of the New York Kouros, the headband and the necklace could be signifiers that he is a victorious athlete. Kouroi were used in a variety of ways—as funerary markers, votive offerings, or representations of divinities, in particular Apollo. The same is true of their female counterparts.

Complete nudity was considered taboo in all other ancient cultures. As we have seen,

Attic kouros, Kroisos. From Anavysos. Greece, ca. 525 BCE. © Nimatallah / Art Resource, NY.

nudity always carried a particular meaning and should be considered a type of costume indicating a figure's special status. In the Bible, it always signifies death, degradation, slavery, vulnerability, or danger. Conversely the nudity of the goddess in Near Eastern art shows a woman in her full power and glory, and it is an epiphany.

The Greek innovation of male nudity may go back to a special, original costume of a right of passage of kouroi—signifying their transition to adulthood, being allowed to participate in warfare, and becoming full-fledged citizens. In Greek literature, there is reference to the beginning of Greek athletic nudity, which is said to date to the fifteenth Olympiad in 716 BCE. In fact, male nudity in art began around this date. In the Greek world, nudity was directly related to athleticism; males not only exercised in the nude but also participated in athletic competition without clothing. The Greeks considered this custom, along with their language, a marker that distinguished them from barbarians.

In the eastern Greek cities of Ionia, where male nudity was not fully accepted, we find statues of kouroi wearing a mantle or short cape-like garment, which appears to be a large square of woolen fabric. The mantle was normally draped over the left shoulder, leaving the right arm free for easier movement. Most of these statues also show the kouroi wearing a chiton underneath the heavier woolen mantle.

CLASSICAL PERIOD

In contrast to the Archaic period, when city-states were often ruled by tyrants and aristocratic values flourished, Athens in the Classical period introduced a new form of government—democracy. Participation was not open to all inhabitants of the larger region of Attica, but there was no reference to economic class, and those who did partake in governmental affairs did so on a grand scale.

The origin of Athenian democracy stemmed largely from specific influential historical events that marked the beginning of the fifth century BCE. Although Archaic Greece experienced and accepted cultural influence from the East, a strong and consistent rivalry with the Persian Empire, whose influence stretched from the Euphrates River to the coastline of Asia Minor, is noted in the historical record. In 481 BCE, the Persians invaded the city of Athens and desecrated the Acropolis, the holiest area of all of Attica, where the Parthenon—temple of Athena Parthenos—stood. Never had such a grave act occurred on Attic soil. With Athens as its leader, many Greek city-states brought their armies together, soundly defeating the Persians in the battle of Marathon. Aristocratic values and lavish culture were then rejected in Athens and its surrounding territory, replaced by the concept of citizen and a citizen-run city-state.

After this glorious victory over the Persians, great cultural enthusiasm and self-confidence radiated from Athenian art. The Parthenon, which is considered the most important architectural monument from the Classical period and which will be discussed in detail later in this section, expresses the dominant role Athens came to play during this period. The fifth century is thus marked with an air of cultural euphoria like no other in Greek art.

Women's Clothing

Peplos

Although the *peplos* is represented in the visual record well into the Roman period, most scholars consider it the hallmark of Early Classical female dress. The peplos was a decidedly simple garment with a heavy, almost sober appearance that contrasted sharply with the extravagant dress of korai from the preceding period. Rectangular in shape, it was constructed from an untailored piece of woolen fabric that was draped around a female's figure and then pinned at the shoulders. The garment normally had an overfold, or *apoptygma*, that was created by folding over the top part of fabric and could vary greatly in length. Sometimes, it was shown sewn shut on the side, while at other times it was left open along one side. Finally, the garment could be worn ungirded or with a *zone* (belt) either under or on top of the overfold. If the excess of the apoptygma was pulled over the belt, it created a pouch of fabric known as a *kolpos*.

The origin of the peplos has been frequently discussed by modern scholars, perhaps because of its ubiquity during the Classical period, as well as its identification with the goddess Athena, who is almost always depicted wearing some form of it. It should also be pointed out here that the Greek term *peplos* is used in a variety of manners, but modern scholars have come to use it to identify this particular garment; the correct Greek word for this distinctive garment type is not known.

Bronze statue of "figure praying" wearing a peplos from Villa dei Pisoni at Ercolano. © Scala / Art Resource, NY.

Earlier scholarship looked at the peplos as a direct derivation from Daedalic female dress, which as we have seen was also simple in overall form, viewing it as one of the many garment options for females that existed throughout the Archaic period with it simply becoming popular during the Early Classical period. Many scholars argue that most of the women and goddesses represented on the François Vase, for example, which is dated to 570 BCE, wear a very simple version of the peplos. Most are shown with a type of dress that is belted below the apoptygma with very little excess of fabric shown.

The primary literary evidence for the peplos, which is a passage from Herodotus's *Histories,* and which was written in the mid-fifth century BCE, suggests, however, that the peplos may have been banned during most of the Archaic period. At an unknown date, the Athenians attacked the city of Aegina, resulting in a disastrous end to the Athenian army with only

Central scene of the east frieze of the Parthenon, Acropolis, Athens. c. 438–432 BCE. Scene showing a folded cloth thought to be the sacred robe or peplos of Athena that was escorted to the Acropolis by the procession of the Great Panathenaic Festival, held in Athens every four years. © British Museum / Art Resource, NY.

one soldier returning home alive. But this soldier also met an untimely death:

> And even this one man died in the following way. When he came back to Athens, bringing word of the calamity, the wives of the Athenian men who had fought against Aegina were furious that he alone should have survived the slaughter of all the rest. They crowded around him and stabbed him with the brooches with which they fastened their dresses. . . . The Athenians thought this deed even more horrible than the fate of the troops. (Herodotus *History* 5.87–88)

They made the women change their dress, and wear the costume of the Ionians, whose fine linen *chitons* were sewn or buttoned rather than pinned, like the heavier Doric peplos they had been wearing. Described so vividly by Herodotus, the passage is thought to suggest real events that occurred sometime at the beginning of the sixth century BCE, with his story reflecting a real change in dress from the simple pinned style of the Daedalic period to the sewn or buttoned chiton, and the elaborate coverings worn over it in the Archaic period.

The reappearance of pinned garments at the beginning of the Early Classical period, the nascent period of Athenian democracy (480–50 BCE) is thus believed to have occurred in rejection of all things Eastern. After more than a hundred years of direct and open interaction, Athens desired to assert both its political and cultural authority, and one way was through self-presentation. By looking back to traditional nonpolitical, and most importantly indigenous, dress, the peplos became a representation of what was Hellenic or Greek, with the moral, cultural, and social ideology following it. But regardless of when the peplos originated and its meaning, it is perhaps the best-known dress type of ancient Greek women.

Chiton and Himation

By the later Classical period, however, the popularity of the peplos had waned, replaced largely in art (and most likely in real life) by a garment combination that would remain in use by women into the Roman period: the chiton and himation. This form of attire included the familiar chiton, a tubular-shaped garment made of fine linen and sewn or buttoned at the shoulders to create openings for the head and arms. The chiton could be belted in varying styles or left unbelted. Because of the fine material of this garment, the *himation*—a large, square, woolen mantle—was worn over the chiton, particularly outdoors, for warmth. The himation could be draped in many different ways—over either shoulder, over both shoulders, wrapped around a woman covering her completely or tied around the waist for practical rather than iconographic purposes. Women were also shown wearing the himation pulled over their head, most likely connoting a funerary or marital context. The gesture of pulling up the himation as if to place it over the head is the typical gesture of a bride.

On red-figure vases from this period, women depicted in interior scenes were often shown in a much more casual style, either wearing their himations draped loosely around themselves or wearing only the chiton. The informality of these scenes suggests that they were in an area of their home that was reserved mainly for female activities, which might have included working with wool and weaving, toilette scenes that were often related to preparation for the marriage, or quiet female companionship—sometimes even with women reading to one another, dispelling the view that women were illiterate and uneducated.

In *symposium* scenes, women also often appear wearing similar garments, but these are not the wives of the symposiasts. They are hired entertainers that included musicians and *hetairai*, a term used to describe noncitizen women—whose social status ranged all the way from Aspasia, the common-law wife of Pericles, the leading fifth-century BCE Athenian political figure, to musicians and low-class prostitutes. Vase painting is again our richest source of visual evidence regarding hetairai, who can be shown in various stages of dress and undress, sometimes in elaborate chitons that are belted and draped in a variety of provocative manners, sometimes completely naked. In the *tondo* of a vase in the Metropolitan Museum, for example, a *hetaira* reclines with a male, her elaborate chiton with large, billowing sleeves slipping off her shoulders, indicating her social status and the physical interaction that is yet to come.

Greek male nudity distinguished men from respectable women, who were always shown dressed. During both the Archaic and Classical periods, female nudity still carried with it the old meanings of slavery, degradation, danger, or death. In the case of women present at a symposium, their nudity meant that they lived outside the realm of respectable society, functioning in roles that were not considered appropriate for citizens. Female nudity, even for the image of Aphrodite, the goddess of love and sexuality, was not acceptable until after Praxiteles' famous statue of Aphrodite of Cnidus, made in the mid-fourth century BCE. In mythological context, when a woman is shown nude, it was meant to indicate that she was vulnerable and in extreme danger, like the life of a common prostitute.

Perhaps the most famous representation of female dress in the High Classical period (450 BCE) is that of the women in the procession frieze of the Parthenon. The frieze itself represents the presentation of a peplos specially woven for the goddess Athena as a gift to the gods at the climax of the Panathenaic festivals. In contrast to everyday dress, the women here wear what appears to be ritual costume or costume worn only on special occasions.

On the frieze, it is generally agreed that the majority of women represented come from the highest echelons of society and, thus, present themselves in all of their finery with a great diversity of style and dress combinations. While controversy continues to exist over the identification of the individual garment types that the women are depicted wearing, what is most striking is the use of layering. The layering of their clothing can be interpreted as a way to emphasize additional modesty and respect for the goddess being celebrated.

It has been noted that there is a distinction between the costume of married women and the maidens on the frieze. The women who wear a kerchief combined with the chiton and himation have been identified as married women. There may be a hierarchy of dress here similar to wedding iconography, in which the bride is shown already wearing the chiton and himation, while her bridesmaid wears the simpler peplos. Some scholars have also observed that the maidens on the south procession wear chitons under their peploi, whereas those on the north do not.

Men's Clothing

The classical male citizen clothing, like in the archaic period, was the combination of the chiton and himation, the latter draped in a variety of manners to suggest various public activities, such as an oration or addressing a large crowd. If a male was represented standing and holding his himation in place, this could suggest that he was in the act of speaking. A seated male was in a much more relaxed and informal atmosphere and thus did not have to worry about keeping his dress in place.

Older male citizens were sometimes shown without the chiton and with the himation draped over the right shoulder, leaving one arm free. Additionally, komasts, or drunken revelers, could be depicted nude, wearing a simple mantle draped across their shoulders, exposing their lower body, or, a simple *chitoniskos,* which was a short chiton that allowed for easier movement.

As in the time of Shakespeare, all characters in Greek drama were played by male actors, with female roles being filled by young men dressed in female garments. All actors were dressed in long-sleeved garments, perhaps in reference to the royal dress of the Persians, although this could also be to cover the hairy arms of males. Satyrs, creatures of Dionysus and the wild, who were part of Greek drama, wore the perizoma with attached phallus, in a sense using nudity as costume. It should be pointed out that while nude kouroi never have erect phalluses, both satyrs and *herms* were ithyphallic. In the case of satyrs, their erect phalluses indicate distance from the civilized realm. For herms, which functioned as boundary markers, their erect phalluses had a protective function, keeping evil spirits away from the city centers.

Musicians, often accompanying their own singing with musical instruments, wore long white linen chitons, as seen in numerous depictions on Greek vases. We have seen that this costume was a traditional one for musicians from early times (as depicted on the Agia Triada Sarcophagus).

The long white linen chiton worn alone without a mantle was also the traditional special costume of charioteers. The famous life-size bronze statue of the

Charioteer from Delphi, dated to around 470 BCE, wearing such a costume, depicts the victor in the chariot races held in the sanctuary. Depictions of this dress on vase paintings often show the straps that kept the soft material in place so that it would not impede the movement of a competing athlete as he drove his horses to victory. The long, elaborately draped chiton whose fine folds cover the body of a standing male figure on a marble statue of the same date, found at Motya at the eastern end of Sicily, has also been convincingly identified as being worn by a charioteer. Its identification was controversial when it was first discovered because of the close relations between Carthage and Motya, which was originally a Phoenician settlement. Some scholars thought that this might be the ritual costume of Punic, a Carthagian priest.

HELLENISTIC DRESS

After the death of Alexander, his generals carved the empire into kingdoms. The Hellenistic kingdoms embraced three large areas, ruled by three great families: the Antigonids in Macedonia, the Ptolemies in Egypt, and the Seleucids in Asia (Anatolia and Syria). These great powers ignored a fourth that had appeared in the west—Rome, which by the third century BCE had won control of all of Italy and was about to embark on wars against Carthage.

An economic boom brought prosperity, and the new, more international world brought momentous changes in society, art, science, literature, and religion. A person's identity was no longer necessarily tied to his or her citizenship; you belonged to a group, perhaps a profession, and your dress reflected that identity. Everyone spoke Greek, the *koine* or common language of this new, larger world. The ruling, classical culture was no longer Hellenic, but Hellenistic, not so much eclectic but specialized.

As in more modern times, there were many personal choices an artist could make in the style of art. Several choices were available to an individual—the profession he would follow, the dress that proclaimed his choice—although fewer, or perhaps different, choices were available to women. In terms of artistic endeavor and individual identities, this was the most diversified period in terms of types of images, costumes, and artistic styles: we see that romantic, virtuoso, and realistic styles determined the way artists represented both human bodies and the costumes they wore.

Examples of dress are found in sculpture and painting, the latter principally from Pompeii, which predates the eruption of Mount Vesuvius in 79 CE and is thus Roman in date but reflects famous paintings of the Hellenistic period. Many monuments of the period have been lost and are only known, like much of Hellenistic art and literature, from Roman copies of Greek originals. Examples are mostly taken from three-dimensional sculpture, which show the details of dress better than paintings or reliefs and which allowed sculptors to carry out the drapery effects that were so important in the art of this period.

The two basic Greek rectangular garments continued to be worn by both men and women in the Hellenistic period. They were still simple pieces of cloth, woven to order, straight from the loom, uncut and unfitted. But they were made in a dazzling variety of variegated fabrics, differing in textures, colors, borders, patterned decorations, and sizes. They were worn in a similarly striking variety of fashions and are depicted in sculpture and painting with a virtuosity, technical skill, and artistic imagination resulting in a flamboyant style that has been compared to Bernini's. The prosperity and magnificence of much of the art of the Hellenistic period, as well as the far-reaching commerce of the time, were reflected in the dress worn by wealthy men and women; this was the time, for example, when silken garments (*coae vestes*) were introduced, and the complex patterns created by the varieties of textures inspired sculptors and painters to remarkable extremes of effects, visual, emotional, and technical.

Women's Clothing

Much variety can be found in the way women wore the chiton. In art and surely in life, they most often wore it belted high, just below the breasts, like the much later "Empire style," with a wide flat belt or a narrow ribbon, sometimes tied in a knot in front. It is generally represented with many fine pleats, like the earlier fine linen chitons. Sometimes it was kept in place by a shoulder cord, whose appearance in sculpture goes back to the Parthenon pediments. In the statue of Themis, the thinness of the chiton's fine texture is indicated by the representation of her navel, shown as if it were seen through the transparent garment.

A number of statues, however, show a heavier chiton, perhaps woolen, covered by the fine folds of a thin, transparent himation. Artists in this period delighted in the virtuoso rendering of the contrasting effects that the different textures of the garments made possible. One statuette that shows this virtuosity is the so-called Baker Dancer in New York. Only 8 1/4″ (21 cm) high, this beautiful bronze statuette represents a girl wearing heavy robes. She is wearing a full chiton that swirls around her feet, and a fringed or bordered himation, evidently made of fine linen, through which the heavy folds of the chiton can be seen. The himation covers her completely, including her right hand, with which she pulls a fold of the mantle over the lower part of her face. It covers her head, leaving only her eyes peering out from the veil, which hangs from her forehead,

Large marble statue of the goddess Themis from the third century BCE, wearing a himation. The name of the artist, Chairestratos, is engraved on the base. © Erich Lessing / Art Resource, NY.

serving as a mask. She is evidently a professional dancer, dressed for the dance she is executing.

Hellenistic art differs from earlier art in including a wide range of characters, types, and ages—old men and women, children, philosophers, lower-class figures. A number of statues of old people, long held to be genre figures, are today thought to have religious significance. One famous figure represents an Old Drunken Woman, sitting on the ground, clutching a wine jug. Judging from her dress, she is not poor, for she wears earrings and a ring on her left hand, and is probably a participant in a Dionysiac festival. She wears a kerchief on her head, and a special chiton with straps on the shoulders of a type seen also on other statues of women in this period. This kind of chiton would later become a symbolic garment in Roman times.

A special way of wearing the mantle characterized two widely used statue types, known as the Herculaneum Women because examples were found in the decoration of the theater at Herculaneum. They represent an older and a younger woman and were once identified as the statues of Demeter and Kore that written sources attributed to the Greek sculptor Praxiteles (ca. 350 BCE). The older woman, or Larger Herculaneum Woman, has her head covered with her himation, the raised edge of which she pulls across to the opposite side so that it forms a triangular pattern; in her left hand, held close to the body, she often has an attribute such as poppies or wheat. The marble originals had painted borders. The idealized features sometimes depicted a portrait. The Smaller Herculanensis, as she is called, was bareheaded, often wearing her hair divided into neat rows, in the so-called melon hairstyle popular at the end of the fourth century and later. Like the statue of the older woman, she raises her right hand to pull the drapery to the left shoulder, from where it cascades along her body on the left; but her left hand is completely covered by a twisted piece of drapery. Her himation also has a wide border, which was once painted. The replicas of these two types number in the hundreds and were extremely popular in Roman times down to the third century CE in Italy, Greece, Asia, and North Africa.

Though the paint has disappeared from the sculptures, we can get an idea of their brilliant colors from the paintings at Pompeii, which illustrate Greek Classical and Hellenistic, rather than Roman, dress. The splendid woven decoration of some of the textiles is represented in relief on a fragment from Lykosura: such decoration was used in Rome for the *toga picta* of the triumphing general.

While this chapter, like the others, deals with the dress of real women, we see that in art, Greek male nudity, accompanied by nudity for women, had become acceptable in all parts of the Hellenistic world after Praxiteles' nude statue of Aphrodite of Cnidus. An important part of the classical tradition that has come down to our own times, the image of nudity now carried with it new, multiple meanings of beauty, divinization, heroization, and virtue.

Men's Clothing

The youthful, charismatic image of Alexander caught the public imagination and served as a model for representations of rulers, who had themselves represented as heroically nude, youthful, dashing figures, beardless, with the leonine mane of hair, *anastole*, that characterized portraits of the handsome empire builder. This romantic image filtered down to the upper levels of society; a stag-gering number of standing nude male figures remain; mostly, as usual, in Roman copies of Greek originals. By this time, the gymnasiums had been turned into schools, and the ideal of the heroic male nude had changed once more, from athlete, youthful *ephebe*, and Athenian citizen, to a more general, universal divine image, symbol of power and virtue.

For the rest, male garments, like those of the women, were still the basic rec-tangular chitons and himations. Men, however, had a far greater variety of man-tles available, in keeping with the more varied roles they played in the world. The variety of male images reflected in artwork shows how dress identified dif-ferent ideals, as well as different professions, nationalities, religions, and social classes. The philosopher-type wears his mantle directly on his body, without a chiton, and drapes it lower on his body, at waist height, so that he is bare-chested. He is bearded, rather than clean shaven. Not surprisingly, this is how Socrates was represented. The soldier wears a smaller mantle, the *chlamys*, draped over his left shoulder and pinned on his right shoulder, leaving his right, active arm free. Such a chlamys seems to have had a curved border: according to Plutarch's account of the foundation of Alexandria (Plutarch, *Life of Alexander,* 26.3–10), the city plan used Alexander's chlamys as a model and followed the curve of the mantle's border.

Soldiers did not fight naked or wear only this short mantle, however, and Hellenistic realism in art shows them in battle scenes wearing the usual armor, or with the short chiton, or *chitoniskos*, normally worn for active wear. Alexander himself is represented dressed in a variety of costumes. On the Alexander Sar-cophagus, he wears a chitoniskos that, surprisingly, has long sleeves. Long sleeves, like long pants, and fitted clothes in general, were typical barbarian, in this case Oriental, costumes. This detail agrees with the literary sources, which explain that Alexander adopted a mixed Oriental costume, a measure that was much criticized by the Greeks, but evidently was accepted in some areas. It was reflected on this monument, where Persian costumes are depicted with great accuracy.

A number of other foreign costumes came into fashion in this period. Already in Archaic and Classical times, Thracian dress was known, depicted, and some-times worn. With its thick, heavy, patterned woolen mantles and fur hats, it was a practical costume for cold weather. Also known was the Scythian costume, with its colorful, patterned hose, long sleeves, and hat with lappets; this may have served as the "uniform" of the Scythian slaves that functioned as police-men in Athens. The Macedonian felt hat, the *kausia*, was worn by men who also wore the Persian *kaunaka*, a sleeved jacket flung over the shoulders with empty sleeves flying out behind them. They also wore the similarly sleeved *candys*.

Children's Clothing

The statuettes of little girls from the sanctuary at Brauron were evidently votive offerings at the shrine of the goddess, along with statuettes of little boys. The girls' crinkly chitons, worn without a mantle, have shoulder cords holding them in place at the shoulders. Cloth was expensive, and the long, belted overfolds of the chitons of the little girls could be let out as they got older, so that they could grow into them.

FURTHER READING

Bibliography Greek Dress

"Ancient Greek Dress." In *Timeline of Art History*. New York: Department of Greek and Roman Art. The Metropolitan Museum of Art, 2000. http://www.metmuseum.

Barber, E. J. W. *Prehistoric Textiles*. Princeton: Princeton University Press, 1991.

Barletta, Barbara. "The Draped Kouros Type and the Workshop of the Syracuse Youth," *AJA* 91 (1987): 233–46.

Bennett, Michael J. *Belted Heroes and Bound Women: The Myth of the Homeric Warrior-King*. Lanham: Rowman & Littlefield, 1997.

Bieber, Margarete. *Ancient Copies. Contributions to the History of Greek and Roman Art*. New York: New York University Press, 1977.

Boardman, John. *Athenian Black Figure Vases. A Handbook*. London: Thames and Hudson, 1972.

Boardman, John. *Athenian Red Figure Vases: the Archaic Period. A Handbook*. London: Thames and Hudson, 1975.

Boardman, John. *Athenian Red Figure Vases: the Classical Period. A Handbook*. London: Thames and Hudson, 1989.

Bonfante, Larissa. "Introduction." In *Essays on Nudity in Antiquity in Memory of Otto Brendel. Source* 2 (1993): 7–11.

Bonfante, Larissa. "Kleidung." In *Mensch und Landschaft in der Antike. Lexikon der Historischen Geographie*, ed., H. Sonnabend, 257–60. Stuttgart, Weimar: Metzler Verlag, 1999. (skin garments).

Bonfante, Larissa. "The Naked Greek. The Fashion of Nudity in Ancient Greece." *Archaeology* Sept./Oct. 1990: 28–35.

Bonfante, Larissa. "Nudity as Costume in Classical Art." *AJA* 93 (1989): 543–70.

Brinkmann, Vinzenz. *Bunter Götter*. Munich: Staatliche Antikensammlunen und Glyptothek, 2004.

Brinkmann, Vinzenz. *Die Polychromie der archaischen und frühklassischen Skulptur*. Munich: Biering und Brinkmann, 2003.

Coldstream, J. N. *Geometric Greece 900–700 BC*. 2nd ed. London: Routledge, 2003.

Connelly, Joan Breton. "Parthenon and Parthenoi: A Mythological Interpretation of the Parthenon Frieze." *AJA* 100 (1996): 53–80.

Fantham, Elaine, Helene Peet Foley, Natalie Boymel Kampen, Sarah B. Pomeroy, and H. Alan Shapiro, eds. *Women in the Classical World*. New York: Oxford University Press, 1994.

Grossmann, Janet Burnett. *Looking at Greek and Roman Sculpture in Stone: A Guide to Terms, Styles and Techniques*. Los Angeles: The J. Paul Getty Museum, 2003.

Harrison, Evelyn Byrd. "The Dress of Archaic Greek Korai." In Diana Buitron-Oliver, ed. *New Perspectives in Early Greek Art, Studies in the History of Art* 32 (1991): 217–39.

Harrison, Evelyn Byrd. "Notes on Daedalic Dress." *JWaltersArtGal* 36 (1977): 37–48.

Higgins, Reynold. *Minoan and Mycenean Art*. Rev. ed. New York: Oxford University Press, 1981.

Jenkins, Ian. *The Parthenon Frieze*. London: British Museum Press, 1994.

Jones, Bernice. "The Minoan 'Snake Goddess': New Interpretations of Her Costume and Identity." In *POTNIA: Deities and Religion in the Aegean Bronze Age*. Proceedings of the 8th International Aegean Conference. Göteborg University, 12–15 April 2000. *Aegaeum* 22. Robert Laffineur, and Robin Hägg, eds. Austin, TX: University of Texas Press, 2001, pp. 259–69.

Jones, Bernice. "Veils and Mantles: An Investigation of the Construction and Function of the Costumes of the Veiled Dancer from Thera and the Camp Stool Banqueter from Knossos." In *Metron. Measuring the Aegean Bronze Age*. Proceedings of the Ninth

International Aegean Conference. New Haven, Yale University, 18–21, April 2002. Aegaeum 24. Karen Polinger Foster and Robert Laffineur, eds. Austin, TX: University of Texas Press, 2003, pp. 441–50.

Karakasi, Katerina. *Archaic Korai*. Los Angeles: The J. Paul Getty Museum, 2003.

Lee, Mireille. "Constructing Gender in the Feminine Greek Peplos." In *The Clothed Body in the Ancient World*. eds. Liza Cleland, Mary Harlow and Lloyd Llewellyn-Jones, 55–64, Oxford: Oxbow Books, 2005.

Lee, Mireille. *The Myth of the Classical Peplos*. Ann Arbor: University of Michigan dissertation, 2001.

Llewellyn-Jones, ed. *Women's Dress in the Ancient Greek World*. London: Duckworth, and The Classical Press of Wales, 2002.

Marcar, Ariane. "Reconstructing Aegean Bronze Age Fashion." In *The Clothed Body in the Ancient World*, eds. Liza Cleland, Mary Harlow and Lloyd Llewellyn-Jones, 30–43. Oxford: Oxbow Books, 2005.

McDonald, Myles. "The Introduction of Athletic Nudity: Thucydides, Plato and the Vases." *Journal of Hellenic Studies* 111 (1991): 182–93.

Osborne, Robin. "Men without Clothes: Heroic Nakedness and Greek Art." *Gender and History* 9 (1997): 504–28.

Pomeroy, Sarah B. *Goddesses, Whores, Wives and Slaves: Women in Classical Antiquity*. New York: Schocken, 1995.

Rehak, Paul. "Aegean Breechclothes, Kilts and Keftiu Paintings," *American Journal of Archaelogy* 100 (1996): 35–51.

Richter, Gisela Marie Augusta. *Korai. Archaic Greek Maidens. A Study of Development of the Kore Type in Greek Sculpture*. 2nd ed. London: Phaidon, 1968.

Richter, Gisela Marie Augusta. *Kouroi. Archaic Greek Youths: A Study of the Development of the Kouros Type in Greek Sculpture*. 3rd ed. New York: Hacker Books, 1988.

Ridgway, Brunilde S. *The Archaic Style in Greek Sculpture*. 2nd ed. Princeton: Princeton University Press, 1993.

Ridgway, Brunilde S. "The Fashion of the Elgin Kore," *Getty Museum Journal* 12 (1984): 29–58.

Ridgway, Brunilde S. *Fifth Century Styles in Greek Sculpture*. Princeton: Princeton University Press, 1981.

Ridgway, Brunilde S. *Fourth Century Styles in Greek Sculpture*. Madison: University of Wisconsin Press, 1997.

Ridgway, Brunilde S. *Hellenistic Sculpture I. The Styles of ca. 331–200 BC*. Madison: University of Wisconsin Press, 1990.

Ridgway, Brunilde S. *Hellenistic Sculpture II. The Styles of ca. 200–100 BC*. Madison: University of Wisconsin Press, 1995.

Ridgway, Brunilde S. *Hellenistic Sculpture III. The Styles of ca. 100–31 BC*. Madison: University of Wisconsin Press, 2002.

Ridgway, Brunilde S. *The Severe Style in Greek Sculpture*. Princeton: Princeton University Press, 1970.

Roccos, Linda Jones. *Ancient Greek Costume. An Annotated Bibliography, 1784–2005*. Jefferson: McFarland, 2006.

Steingräber, Stephan. *Etruscan Painting*. New York: Johnson Reprints, 1986.

Stewart, Andrew. *Greek Sculpture: an Exploration*. New Haven: Yale University Press, 1990.

Vermeule, Emily. *Greece in the Bronze Age*. Chicago: Chicago University Press, 1964.

WEB RESOURCES

Metropolitan Museum of Art, Department of Greek and Roman Art. "Ancient Greek Dress." *Timeline of Art History*. http://www.metmuseum.org/toah/hd/grdr/hd_grdr.htm.

http://www.mlahanas.de/Greeks/Arts/MinoanFresco.htm, http://www.virtourist.com/europe/crete/12.htm

http://cobalt.rocky.edu/~moakm/archaicsculpt.htm

http://www.stoa.org/gallery/album224/p1010012

http://www.metmuseum.org/toah/hd/god2/ho_28.57.23.htm

http://www.ancient-greece.org/images/museums/parthenon-sculpt/index.htm

http://www.metmuseum.org/store/st_family_viewer.asp/familyID/%7B39023019-80DE-11D3-9367-00902786BF44%7D/FromPage/catSculpture/familyNo/9/catID/%7BEF58F4D2-8B11-11D3-9367-00902786BF44%7D

http://www.scholarsresource.com/browse/work/6128

MOVIES

Alexander (2004)
Damon and Pythias (1962)
The Odyssey (1997)
The 300 Spartans (1962)
Troy (2004)

Etruscan and Roman Clothing

Larissa Bonfante and Jennifer Chi

TIMELINE

1000–750 BCE	Iron Age; Villanovan period; Verucchio rounded wool tebennas; armor in warriors' graves; wool-working for women
753 BCE	Beginning of Roman monarchy; rounded toga
750–600 BCE	Orientalizing period in Etruria; heavy wool, patterned fabrics; women wear long back braid, back mantle; men wear perizoma, chiton
600–450 BCE	Archaic period in Etruria; Etruscan kings bring triumph, luxury, earlier symbols to Rome; painted tombs at Tarquinia; athletic nudity or perizoma; Apollo of Veii; rounded, bordered mantle; pointed shoes
500 BCE	Beginning of Roman Republic
500–100 BCE	Wars in Italy
450–300 BCE	Women wear Ionian dress, or himation over chiton; tassels; himation or rounded tebenna
300–90 BCE	Hellenistic period; Roman expansion into Mediterranean; Eastern luxury; Arringatore; sarcophagus reliefs; Volterra urns
44 BCE	Julius Caesar killed; civil wars
31 BCE	Roman Empire begins; Augustus becomes first Roman emperor (31 BCE–14 CE) and restores republican virtues; dress is symbolic and marks status: stola, toga, calcei
13–9 BCE	Ara Pacis; Principate

ETRUSCAN CULTURE

The Etruscans, who lived in central Italy from the tenth to the first century BCE, were in touch with the Greeks and the Near East, especially the Phoenicians, influenced Rome, and constituted one of the three great classical civilizations of the Mediterranean. The mineral wealth of their land—iron, copper, tin—made them wealthy and attracted the Greeks westward. As with the Greeks, their settlements became more concentrated during the course of the Iron Age (1000–750 BCE) and developed into rich cities in the course of the following Orientalizing period (750–450 BCE), which flourished during the Archaic period (600–450 BCE). In this international period, the influence of the sophisticated Ionian cities was important, and Etruscan kings, traditionally the dynasty of the Tarquins, ruled at Rome from 600 to 510 BCE. In the fifth and fourth centuries, which constituted the Classical period in Greece, the Etruscans were less involved in the Mediterranean. The Hellenistic period (300–50 BCE) saw the inland cities of Chiusi, Perugia, and Volterra prosper.

The Etruscans adopted and adapted the alphabet, mythology, monumental architecture, sculpture, and a narrative style of art from the Greeks. Their literature is almost completely lost, but they have left many artistic monuments that give precious information about their clothing and about their luxurious lifestyle. Because their society remained aristocratic to the end and never developed into a democracy like that of Athens, nor an oligarchy like that of Rome, status symbols were always very important, and great families vied with each other in providing their women with luxurious clothes and jewels, and their ancestors with great tombs that showed off the family's wealth and power.

Women and men of this aristocracy lived much less separate lives than the women of the contemporary Greek world or of the later Romans. Married couples represented the generations of a great family, and wives shared their husbands' lives and attended the family banquets that took the place of the Greek all-male *symposia*. In art, couples were ubiquitous. For these reasons, the costumes of men and women will be treated together, rather than separately. This section also uses mythological figures to illustrate specifically Etruscan clothing, since such images figure prominently in Etruscan art at all times.

The dress worn during the Iron Age (in Etruria, this is known as the Villanovan period, named for the site of Villanova, where it was first recognized) is difficult to identify from the monuments. As in Greece, the figures provide few details. Recent finds of surviving organic material from eighth-century tombs at the northern site of Verucchio, near Rimini, however, include preserved textiles and garments. Most surprising was the discovery of three woolen mantles with rounded borders, the ancestors of the Roman togas, in the grave of an important man. These indicate that already in this early period the shape of garments differed from those of the Greeks, which were always woven as square or rectangular pieces of cloth. It is particularly interesting to find these rounded mantles in the north, since a rounded mantle is also found among the surviving garments in the northern peat bogs, including one from Gerömsberg in Sweden; the form may ultimately derive from the rounded shape of animal skins.

Also preserved at Verucchio is a remarkable, full-size wooden throne decorated with scenes of wool-working carved on its back in a miniature style. The women are distinguished by their long braids; the other figures are male, including a number of armed guards flanking a ritual scene. It is assumed that this seat of honor was made for a woman, since everywhere in Etruria, throughout this period, women's graves are characterized by wool-working equipment—loom weights, spindles, and distaffs. These objects distinguished them from the men, who were provided with the armor and the weapons that identified them as warriors. Thus from very early times, grave goods distinguished the gender of the deceased, just as their manner of dressing identified the living.

By the seventh century BCE, narrative art shows images of men and women and distinguishes their costumes. A painted vase made in the city of Cerveteri shows a man and woman. The woman touches the man's chin in a gesture of affection. Some scholars see the gesture as one of entreaty and identify the figures as derived from Greek mythology, with Helen pleading with Menelaus to spare her at the end of the Trojan War. But their attire is purely Etruscan. The man, evidently a warrior, has greaves on his legs and wears either a short tunic or, more probably, the *perizoma* that men regularly wore in Italy. The Greek innovation of male nudity, sometimes accepted as an image in art, was never adopted in real life. The woman wore a long dress, or tunic, and the characteristic back braid. The patterned weave of the man's kilt or perizoma is carefully shown, as is the texture of both garments, which identifies them as being made of wool.

Typical of Etruscan art, and evidently of Etruscan society, is the importance of couples of men and women like these. In the Archaic period, married couples appear in the brightly colored tomb paintings of Tarquinia. They are fully dressed, in contrast to the naked slaves that serve them. Greek authors take note of the luxurious dress and furnishings of these aristocratic lords and ladies and tell us that in Etruria even the slaves were beautifully dressed.

These images of men and women paired together were not always loving nor always married couples. Mothers and sons often appear together, as in the scene from the highly decorated bronze chariot from Monteleone di Spoleto, recently restored. Here we see a scene from Greek mythology, the goddess Thetis handing to her son Achilles the golden armor made by the god of the forge, Hephaistos. Both wear a woolen shirt or tunic—Achilles a short one appropriate for an active warrior, Thetis a long one, over which she wears a long, bordered mantle or veil that covers her head. The details of all these garments are carefully depicted, down to the fringe on the corner of Thetis's mantle, the ornamental rosettes on her tunic, and the decorated borders of the mantle. Two features of the tunics distinguish them from most Greek Archaic *chitons*: they are made of heavy wool that falls straight down along the body, and they are tailored. The seams of Thetis's long sleeves and Achilles' short sleeves are marked out by same borders as the hems of their tunics and Thetis's mantle.

Other features of the costume of the Archaic period are the pointed shoes and the rounded mantle, or *tebenna*, of the men. The statue of Apollo from the rooftop of the temple at Veii, just across the Tiber from Rome, wears a white tunic and a red-bordered rounded tebenna, made of light wool. The mantle is draped over the left shoulder, leaving the active right arm free; its rounded shape results in graceful folds that cling to the body. His long hair, fashionable for both men and women in this period, falls over his shoulders. The god is

Terracotta statue of Apollo of Veii, sixth century BCE. © Scala / Art Resource, NY.

barefoot. This statue is from the time of the reign of the last Tarquin, who ruled in Rome until the end of the sixth century and was said to have built the great Temple dedicated to Jupiter on the Capitoline Hill in Rome, for which he called in the only Etruscan artist whose name has come down to us, Vulca of Veii. He also celebrated the first triumph. Indeed the influence of Etruscan culture at this period in Rome was considerable and included the manner of dressing and specific types of garments.

Men and women alike are often shown wearing pointed shoes, which are either laced or soft and slipper-like. They were made of leather, dyed black or bright red; bright blue pointed shoes are worn by a young nude Troilos being ambushed by a heavily armed Achilles in the Tomb of the Bulls in Tarquinia. On the Sarcophagus of the Married Couple, from Cerveteri, husband and wife recline as on a blanket, both of them handsomely attired, with long locks and chitons. The bright colors with which they were once painted have disappeared, so we do not know the original color of their hair or of the woman's hat and laced, pointed shoes. We can still see the rounded shape that covers them both, however, symbolizing their married status. After the sixth century BCE, pointed shoes tend to be reserved for women, particularly for goddesses.

In the fifth and fourth centuries, Etruscan art changed from the pointed, lighter forms of the Archaic period to the more solemn forms of the Early Classical period of Athenian art. Many bronze Etruscan mirrors made in this period illustrate figures wearing garments and accessories reflecting new clothing styles, new symbols, and new artistic stylizations. Young men, especially divinities, are represented nude, as in the fourth-century mirror shown with Venus and her young lover, Adonis. Venus (the Etruscan Turan) wears a thin linen chiton with many folds. From each shoulder falls a fringe or braided tassel. Over this, a heavy woolen mantle is draped in such a way that a triangular piece falls in front of her like an apron. This detail clearly had a special significance, since it is shown in art being worn only by goddesses or women of high rank. Shoes usually had lost their pointed shape by this time, like those of Venus on this mirror, though they sometimes appear on goddesses, as on a famous mirror showing Hera nursing the full-grown Heracles.

Women's mantles were always square; women are said to have worn the tebenna (or toga) in the early days, but they were rarely depicted this way. For men, there was an alternation of rectangular *himation* with rounded tebenna that does not seem to be altogether casual. On the side of a sarcophagus from Vulci in the Boston Museum of Fine Arts, for example, the deceased wears a mantle with square corners, contrasting with the rounded tebenna of the musicians who accompany him on his journey to the underworld. The significance of these choices is not always easy to understand. Perhaps it marks his special status as a dead ancestor, who is heroized.

Nudity, always a special "costume," is used in such a way on the lid of a similar sarcophagus from Vulci, on which the husband and wife are lying naked as if in bed. They are covered from the chest down by a blanket whose rounded edges, clearly emphasized, show it to be a man's tebenna; the fact that it covers them is a symbol of marriage. Their parallel nudity, which contrasts so strongly with Greek custom and Greek art, also reflects their status as a married couple with equal status in their aristocratic society, while the nudity itself is the nudity of death, of their heroization, and of the consummation of their marriage.

The art of the Hellenistic period illustrates a dazzling array of costumes. Aside from the normal dress of Etruscan men and women and of divinities, it illustrates the dress of soldiers and triumphing generals, of the theater, of male and female demons, of priests and priestesses, of children, and of ghosts. Some of these hearken back to earlier times, but there is now a concentration of local elements, as if to emphasize an identity that is in danger of being swallowed up by the rising tide of Rome.

Much of the dress worn by men and women is similar to that worn at the same time in Rome: men and women continue to wear the square mantle or the rounded tebenna, musicians wearing the tebenna escort the dead as if in triumphal processions, men are often shown in armor. What is new is the large number of special costumes. Already in the fourth century BCE François Tomb in Vulci, the owner of the ambitious family tomb was depicted wearing the purple decorated triumphal mantle of a victorious general—and not only is he a general but also a priest, for he is reading the omens from the flight of birds, one of which is shown being released by his young assistant.

Indeed the dress of priests and priestesses is featured on a number of artistic monuments. The rituals of divination are depicted with men who wear characteristic priestly hats with a twisted conical top. A number of such hats are illustrated on the figures of priests reclining on the lids of the small ash urns, made of alabaster, stone, or terra-cotta, from the inland cities of Chiusi, Volterra, and Perugia. A number of statuettes of priests are also shown wearing the hat; one of these also wears an animal-skin mantle fastened with a *fibula* or pin of an earlier, traditional shape. Some priests on the lids of urns are shown with their mantles pulled up over their heads, in the later Roman fashion. Another traditional attribute of priests is the curved ceremonial wand or *lituus*. On the lid of a full-size sarcophagus in the British Museum, a priestess of Bacchus is shown with the attributes of a follower of the god: an ivy-topped *thyrsus*, a handled cup or *kantharos*, and a fawn who lies at her side. She is barefoot and richly attired with jewelry and headdress, and from her shoulder hangs the braid or tassel worn by goddesses and elite women of a previous generation.

In general, jewelry includes necklaces with several large locket-shaped pendants, and the twisted necklace or *torque*, once the typical badge of honor of Celtic warriors, but now part of the costume of Etruscan and Roman women and children.

The dress of the theater shown on the ash urns consists of long-sleeved tunics and perhaps a strange garment with detached sleeves. Some traditional costumes, such as the *peplos*, pinned at the shoulders and belted over the over-fold at the waist, were worn by goddesses but were probably not part of normal dress.

Various divinities were distinguished by special costumes. Hades, the King of the Underworld, regularly shown with his consort Persephone, wears a wolfskin hat; a drawing by Michelangelo records one such image from the Renaissance.

Unique to Etruscan mythology and religion were the various groups of demons who populated the afterworld and assisted the dead on their way to join their families in the underworld. Two of these demons, Charu and Vanth, appear frequently (though not always) as a couple, flanking the deceased or a figure who is about to die. The way in which Achilles is represented in the scene of the sacrifice of the Trojan prisoners is a good example. Two figures of Charu, two Vanths, or Charu and Vanth together are depicted at either end of a Greek mythological scene, as if claiming it as Etruscan. Charu, often a horrible, frightening, devil-like demon with a grinning face and bluish skin, regularly wears a short chiton-like garment pinned at the shoulders. The female demon Vanth, who appears only slightly less often than her companion Charu, is often winged and wears a twisted necklace or torque and a chiton, either short or long. There are also groups of Charus, as in the Tomba dei Caronti. Many images of the Etruscan Vanth look like the Furies on southern Italian vases, with bare breasts, between which are crossed straps.

A number of ghosts make their appearance in the Etruscan iconography of the fourth century and later. Agamemnon, in the François Tomb, and two Amazons on a red-figure *crater* from Vulci wear bandages across their chests, indicating the wounds from which they died. Similar bandages worn by Michelangelo's statues of the "Prisoners," or as some scholars have called them, "Souls," seem to have been inspired by such images. In the François Tomb, the ghost of the Greek prophet Teiresias is shown in the underworld leaning on Hermes, with his mantle pulled up over his head, Roman style. On an Etruscan mirror, his blindness, walking stick, and feminine face, dress, and shoes refer to the story that he was struck blind by Hera because, having lived as both a man and a woman, he angered her by reporting that women enjoyed making love one hundred times more than men.

The Etruscan identity ended when the Etruscan cities became Roman, at different times and under different circumstances. Nevertheless, much of Etruscan costume was preserved by the conservative Romans, as if in memory of their kings and in respect for their own past. A number of these images inspired medieval and Renaissance artworks.

BEARDS

Beards were worn at various times, with different connotations. Short, stubbly beards signified seriousness of purpose and disdain of luxury (as depicted in portraits from the Republic and of third-century emperors); longer beards characterized a philosopher-type or an admiration for Greek culture (Marcus Aurelius); and the beardless image had connotations of youthful heroism (Alexander) or of an ageless, Classical ideal (Augustus, Constantine).

ROMAN CULTURE

Rome developed from a primitive eighth-century BCE Iron Age settlement on the Palatine Hill, on the banks of the Tiber River in Latium, whose closest neighbors to the north were the wealthy, sophisticated Etruscan cities. The two stories of Rome's foundation—either by Romulus, a native of the region, or by Aeneas, the Trojan hero who came West after the Trojan War, like Odysseus—reflect the double legacy of the Romans that runs throughout their history: on the one hand, their own native traditions, and on the other, the artistic and cultural ideals of Classical civilization. During the thousand years of its history, Rome changed from being a city of the Seven Hills to a new world, the reality and the symbol of the civilized world of Europe.

While it is said that the Greeks were outstanding in their role as originators in Western history, it is the Romans who can be seen as exceptional organizers, and their quest to make the world "one world" led to colonies being established throughout the Western world like never before, all related in their connections to Rome. Their incredible dominance of the era before the "fall" of Rome has been a fascinating lesson for modern civilizations, but the rise of Rome from one city to its dominance of Europe is equally intriguing. The Romans borrowed heavily from the Greeks in both thought and organization of their people. As the Romans dealt with the Greek colonies, with whom they came into direct contact in their travels, they

"Rome" can mean many things depending on the chronological period it refers to. It can refer to the primitive eighth-century BCE Iron Age settlement on Palatine Hill on the banks of the Tiber River in Latium, whose closest neighbors to the north were the wealthy, sophisticated Etruscan cities. Or, it can refer to the Rome of Julius Caesar, when Roman armies, aristocratic intermarriages, and a variety of treaties had turned all the inhabitants of Italy into Roman citizens and Rome had become the greatest power in the Mediterranean and inherited the Greek culture that had become Classical civilization. The two stories of Rome's foundation, either by Romulus, a native of the region, or by Aeneas, the Trojan hero who came West after the Trojan War, like Odysseus, reflect the double legacy of the Romans that runs throughout their history: on the one hand their own native traditions, and on the other the artistic and cultural ideals of Classical civilization.

The history of Rome is traditionally divided into four periods: The monarchy, which lasted from 753–510 BCE, including the period when the Etruscan dynasty of the Tarquins ruled at Rome, 600–510 BCE; the Republic (510–31 BCE), when Rome became, in fact, all of Italy. The latter part of this period overlapped with the Hellenistic world (300–31 BCE), which brought together the peoples of the Mediterranean, and which Rome soon inherited; the early Empire (known as the Principate), which was established by Augustus, the heir of Julius Caesar; and the Late Empire, from the third to the fourth century CE, which ended with Constantine's foundation of a new Christian capital in Byzantium, renamed Constantinople, and where Christianity became the state religion. Thus, during the thousand years of its history, "Rome" changed from being a city of the Seven Hills to a new world—the reality and the symbol of the civilized world of Europe.

absorbed many of the Greek ideas, recognizing the sophistication with which the Greeks lived.

Originally, Rome was governed by a monarchy. Its kings served as high priests of the state's religion, military commanders, and supreme judges. There was a senate, with a council of advisers from leading families, the *patricians*. Unlike dynastic monarchies, where the crown was handed down to the next generation of men, when a Roman king died, the Senate chose the next king from among its members, and this was then subject to the approval of the Assembly of Clans, made up of male citizens.

The monarchy was abolished around 500 BCE and was replaced with a republic, with executive power lying with two chief magistrates, *consuls*, who were annually elected by an Assembly of Centuries. This guarded against concentration of power and hasty actions that could be the downfall of a sole leader. A dictator, however, could be chosen by the consuls in a time of emergency, with a limited term of six months.

Within both the Roman government and society itself, there were two classes that developed under the Republic: the upper-class patricians and the common citizens, or *plebeians*. The line was sharply drawn as the Republic emerged. The patricians dominated Roman politics in small but powerful numbers, and magistrates could be elected only from the upper class. The Senate was composed of about 300 senators, who were the heads of patrician families and were appointed for life. After much discussion and exercising different forms of resistance, Roman law was finally written down in the Twelve Tablets. The plebeians eventually gained rights though the Assembly of Plebeians, which consisted of elected officials called *tribunes* who originally acted to protect plebeians who they thought were being wrongly treated by patricians. The tribunes later acquired the right to initiate laws as well.

With great military might, the Romans, largely patriot farmer-soldiers, launched numerous campaigns to conquer lands far and wide, including the Gauls, Greeks, and Etruscans. Based on conscription, all men were liable to enter military service at some point. The Romans built their empire by forming friendships with their conquered former enemies, offering to protect them and giving them self-rule. The Romans did not interfere with local affairs or religion and customs; they merely governed their allies' interactions outside their own lands and asked that they provide additional troops for Roman forces. Rome triumphed close to home and across the sea and established colonies, from where ambassadors were sent to report back to the Republic.

The final collapse of the Roman Republic came as a result of discontent among the people. Julius Caesar, a young man from a patrician family, entered politics and identified Rome's problems—the class struggles, the impact all the wars had on the economy and social lives of Rome's citizens, and deep-seated rivalries within military ranks. Struggles especially among the generals meant that civil war endured until Caesar was appointed dictator, at first for ten years, then for life in 44 BCE. Caesar attempted to unify the provinces and settlements; gave Rome great infrastructure such as roads, buildings, and a revived agrarian program; and reformed all the departments of the administrations, thus attempting to make life better for more people. In the same year he made himself lifelong dictator, he was assassinated in an attempt to restore the Republic.

Octavian, Caesar's adopted heir and grandnephew, took over where Caesar had left off and completed the reforms begun by his uncle. He assumed the title *Augustus* ("Revered") and proclaimed himself emperor. Augustus advanced new order at home and in all the settlements close and far away, expanding the empire as far as Africa, Spain, east of the Danube, and Britain. He introduced the concept of the *Pax Romana* (Roman peace). The running of the Roman Empire was relatively smooth for two hundred years after Augustus, with a succession of leaders who gave the Empire great buildings, highways, and the ability for the Empire to exist as one, with the people feeling a part of the whole. There was, compared to earlier times, political and social stability.

Roman cities were complex and well-run entities, often with running water and a sort of plumbing in houses. Wealthy citizens built extravagant villas, and the emperors erected buildings and civic monuments to mark their leadership. The poor, however, lived in wretched apartment tenements.

Roman Architecture

The Romans were architectural geniuses, which is evident from their many ruins scattered throughout Europe, although they learned much from earlier civilizations. They were indebted to the Greeks for their architectural knowledge, as they had already been building for centuries (e.g., the Acropolis dates from the fifth century BCE). In the ninth and eighth centuries BCE, Latium, the area in which Rome was founded, was peppered with small huts, and the towns had no formal organization or public buildings. Early Roman architecture was a mixture of Italian and Greek elements, as well as features of the squat top-heavy-looking buildings of the Etruscans. Starting in the sixth century BCE, the Italians built temples to their gods in public spaces in towns and cities. Early Roman temples were constructed in this way, and a good example is the reconstructed Portonaccio Temple in Veii—an Etruscan city that rivaled Rome early on—originally from about 500 BCE. It is built on a podium and has a series of colonnades that line the deep porch.

More expensive, all-stone buildings—as opposed to wooden buildings with stone foundations—were not common until after 150 BCE when Romans began to develop their own techniques for construction and design that allowed the buildings to combine massive form with Greek elegance. The Romans molded concrete and built buildings quickly. Arches and vaults are commonly known Roman architectural highlights, and using concrete vaults allowed the Romans to build massive buildings on a scale that had not been seen before. Increasingly buildings were more impressive all over the city, as emperors tried to better their predecessors in their contributions to public architecture. All this was happening while most of the population of Rome toiled away in rickety wood apartment buildings in cramped quarters.

As emperor, Augustus inaugurated a style of architecture that synthesized Italic, Etruscan, and Greek elements into a style of Roman classicism that was widely imitated in the provinces. Next to the *forum*—a space built for public business—that Julius Caesar built as Rome's dictator, Augustus built a more magnificent one, the Forum Augustum, which was dedicated in 2 BCE. In addition, Augustus built all kinds of other structures. Before he became emperor, Augustus built a giant mausoleum for himself, shaped like an Etruscan tomb.

He also built Rome's first public baths, thus allowing the Roman public to enjoy baths—which were previously the delight of rich Romans alone, who had private baths. These styles of building spread to the provinces; examples of Roman baths can still be found in the modern city of Bath, England.

In the next two centuries, Roman architecture continued to thrive, and emperors continued to use state funds to finance and construct buildings all throughout the Roman world. The Flavian emperors, following Augustus, had numerous structures built to try to gain favor with the people. The most famous example of their largess is surely the Flavian Amphitheater, which is known to us as the Colosseum. The Flavians built this massive structure to house gladiator contests.

Hadrian's Pantheon was a building that was originally constructed under the auspices of Agrippa but was totally reworked by Hadrian. Because this building served as a Christian temple after 609 CE, it has survived from antiquity and is Rome's best-preserved ancient building. The Pantheon is an interesting combination of shapes and forms. The front of the building presents columns and the facade of a classical Greek temple. Behind this stands a huge domed cylinder, which is the temple proper. The whole building is lighted by a round opening about thirty feet (9 m) in diameter at the dome's top. Due to its height, most of the moisture from rainfall evaporates before reaching the floor. In order to build such a dome, Roman architects had to be masters of the properties of concrete—this is not a building that could have been constructed by fifth-century Greeks. As such, it is one of the greatest examples of Roman innovation in architecture.

Religion and Literature

Romans were polytheists, worshipping many gods. Like the Greeks, they had anthropomorphic gods. Their chief gods were Jupiter, Hera, and Venus, among others and the deities remained closely related to the Roman sense of values; there were personifications of luck (*Fortuna*), success (*Felicitas*), victory (*Victoria*), health (*Salvus*), and peace (*Pax*).

Religion and values or morals were taught to the family by the *paterfamilias* (father), who was in charge of the household's education in religion and otherwise. The Roman family was different than the Greek, with the father, master of the household, involved in the education and devotion of the children. As in Greece, babies were checked for signs of deformities, and if any were found, the babies were ordered abandoned. Girls were more often left to die than boys, who would grow up to be more valuable. Girls were not even given names—they were called simply by their last names—whereas boys were given personal names. Once girls were teenagers, they married and bore children quickly. They had more rights than Greek women and could own property and had greater freedom and respect in society.

In literature, writers such as Virgil, Horace, Ovid, Cicero, and Seneca wrote on a myriad of topics and in poems, speeches, and epigrams. Each emphasized different aspects of Roman culture, and their works allow historians to glean some ideas of what life was like and what was valued by the citizens of this vast empire. Their writing included not only fictional tales but also biographies of the great leaders.

Decline of the Roman Empire

The decline of the Roman Empire set in by the third century CE, when there were particularly unsteady leaders whose competence was questionable. The military became anarchic, with rogue generals working against the Empire. The economy was failing, as were the morals of a once peaceful society. As German tribesmen moved south, taking land and resources, and a separate eastern capital was built in Constantinople (modern-day Istanbul, Turkey), the Western Empire was doomed. Two Roman emperors were named to head up the two capitals in the east and west, which split the Empire along religious and social lines. The Byzantine Empire grew strong and powerful in the east, establishing an influential society, but the west was plagued by invasion from the northern barbarians, which managed to throw the entire region back into a dark age where little progress was made, in great contrast to how life had been during the height of the Roman Empire.

FABRIC PRODUCTION

Like the Greeks, the Romans used both wool and later imported linen and cotton from Egypt in their clothing production. Silk was also imported and used but was precious and expensive, so not widely accessible. Fibers were sometimes blended together to achieve certain drape, sheen, or textures; for example, such expensive fibers as silk could be mixed with less expensive fibers. The Romans produced many varieties and weights of fabrics for use in different styles of togas and cloaks, the most common types of clothing.

Colored fabrics were common, varying from white undecorated fabrics to fabrics with colored borders, such as those dyed purple to represent nobility or certain magistrates (and also worn by young children), to black fabrics used in mourning the dead. Decorative applied design was also part of the fabric production, and threads of gold were found on the fabrics used for special occasions and for people who had in some way distinguished themselves in battle or otherwise. In addition, some fabrics were made in patterns, such as multicolored stripes made from yarn that was dyed before it was woven—it is worth noting that fabrics were woven at this time, as opposed to knitted.

Fabrics were made in various weights. Some were gauze in open weave, allowing a lot of air to pass through the fabric to keep the wearer cool. Others were tightly woven to keep the wearer warm.

Unlike the homespun fabrics of Greece, Roman textile production was on a larger scale, with slaves working the looms and spinning and dyeing the yarns in factory-like settings with multiple workers performing certain tasks. Clothing was also available ready-made, as is evidenced in some of the literature. Marketplaces, for example, stocked clothing that could be bought, rather than made to fit a specific person.

ROMAN DRESS

Perhaps it was the rapid transformations of the culture and a desire for a stable identity that caused the extraordinarily conservative Roman elite to think of their dress as an unchanging, permanent, deeply symbolic uniform or costume that visibly proclaimed their citizenship, rank, status, and gender, distinguishing them from Greeks, foreigners, slaves, and members of other groups, nations, or social classes. This stability and symbolic value was true in theory if not in fact, and its symbolic force was strongly emphasized in the time of Augustus, at the turn of the first century CE.

Evidence of Roman dress comes from literary references and their own artistic representations of human figures. The Romans of the late Republic and Empire made much use of stone, especially marble, and their portrait statues and historical reliefs give important information about the construction and manner of wearing a number of Roman garment types, both male and female. They also provide occasional examples of representations of foreigners. Wall paintings from Pompeii provide us with an idea of the rich color schemes of the costumes, as well. The clothing worn by men and women was surely realistically depicted, and artists were familiar with the costumes they were illustrating, which were so important for the identification of the people who wore them. Images of Greek and Roman divinities, personifications, or mythological characters, on the other hand, were shown wearing their standard costumes with Greek attributes, although there were plenty of Roman additions and modifications.

As with Greek dress, there is difficulty with the terminology. While some ancient names, forms, and color terms mentioned by Roman authors can be connected with actual garments, many clothes, colors, cuts, and draping styles cannot be matched with the images that remain. The importance of ritual garments was such that while the names are recognizable, as are their representations, there are some costumes for which the ancient names are not known.

Most garments in ancient Rome were made of wool, which was woven in a great variety of textures and weights and dyed in many colors. The sturdy dark cloth was worn by slaves, while fine purple wool was used for imperial togas. In the early Republic, clothes were made at home by the women of the household. This idea of the *matrona* or *materfamilias*, the head of the household, was resurrected by Augustus, like so many archaic customs of an idealized time gone by. It was symbolized by the story of Lucretia, the virtuous Roman matron, whose dishonor at the hands of one of the Tarquins led to the expulsion of the Etruscan king and the beginning of the Republic.

Based on findings in cleaning shops in Pompeii, woolen garments were dry-cleaned in the fullers' shops, using chemical components that included sulfur and human urine. These shops also dyed and felted the cloth to order.

Linen, used for ritual purposes, was mostly imported from Egypt. It was usually left in its natural color and could be woven to an extremely fine sheer texture. In the time of Alexander, silk was introduced, but it always remained an extravagant luxury.

Greek, Etruscan, and Roman dress changed very little over time. It basically consisted of rectangular woven pieces of cloth, which varied in size, material, texture, and color, and manner of draping. There were changes in fashions, but by and large the construction of the garments remained the same. Many of the symbols of Roman dress went back to a very early time, as garments and accessories that had once been normal and that had in time become fossilized as ritual costumes, full of symbolic weight. This was important for the Romans, for these clothes and symbols were part of rituals that were intended to communicate with the gods, and so they had to be permanent and unchanged going back to the *mores maiorum*, or ancestral customs.

Many of the rituals and the objects or attributes connected with them were in fact very ancient. A certain sacrifice actually required the use of a knife made of stone (*silex*) rather than iron or bronze, so that it harked back to a time before the use of metal. This archaic aspect of Roman religion, which drew its authority from its connection to the early days of Rome, was emphasized by Augustus and later emperors, under whom the importance of official dress, even more than other distinctions, signaled the social status and rank of freeborn Romans and the public roles of magistrates and priests.

Men's Clothing: The *Togatus*

A number of garments of magistrates and priestly attributes can be traced back to the Iron Age Villanovan period of the tenth and ninth centuries BCE. A surprising and recent discovery has been that of the remarkably well-preserved woolen, purple-bordered tebennas with rounded edges found at the northern Etruscan site of Verucchio. Dating from the eighth century BCE, this find proves beyond a doubt the antiquity of the tebenna, the ancestor of the *toga*, the most symbolic of Roman garments.

The toga's shape was an exception to the earlier rule that garments were made from rectangular pieces of cloth, for it was woven—not cut—in the shape of a large semicircle. This shape resulted in bias folds that draped more gracefully over the body, as can be seen on the Etruscan statue of the Apollo of Veii, in contrast to the more angular, disconnected folds of the rectangular himation, which the Romans called the *pallium*. Like the Greek himation, the toga was draped over the left shoulder, leaving the right arm free. It did not need to be sewn or pinned into place, since the weight and shape of the cloth kept the garment in place.

Togas were much fuller than the earlier rounded tebennas, like that of the Apollo of Veii or the shorter toga of the bronze statue of the Arringatore, who wears the *toga exigua*, or narrow toga. Augustus required citizens to wear the toga in the forum and at formal occasions. The classical form of the toga can be seen on the Ara Pacis, a monument set up in honor of Augustus with relief portraits of the imperial family, attending magistrates, and priests. The manner of draping this larger toga became more elaborate in the course of the Empire and required the assistance of three specialized servants. The costume became more

A detail from the Ara Pacis Augustae of the procession of Augustus's family showing clothing for men, women, and children. © Alinari / Art Resource, NY.

and more a formal costume, until, according to a Roman poet, it was worn only at funerals. The large overfold in the front of the body was called a curve, or *sinus*; part of the material was pulled up and draped over the sinus to form the *umbo*, or "knob." For religious ceremonies, the top of the toga was pulled up over the head in the back, as can be seen on the figure of Tiberius on the Ara Pacis. The heavy, beautifully draped toga made the wearer look dignified and stately, but it was not made for active wear, nor was it practical for traveling or for life in the country—much less for banquets and parties, when Romans wore a garment known with the Greek name of *synthesis*.

The toga was the national garment of Rome and was usually worn over a tunic only by male citizens. Its symbolism was wide ranging. The Romans were said to be the *gens togata*, the "people who wear the toga."[1] The rite of passage that marked a Roman boy's becoming an adult was the ceremony of taking off the toga of childhood and putting on for the first time the *toga virilis*, or man's toga. It was also the symbol of peace: *Cedant arma togae*, "Let war give way to peace." The toga signified civil office, in contrast to the armor of military officials. Statues of Augustus portray him in his various costumes, according to his role: as head of state, he is shown wearing the toga; as commander in chief, he wears a *cuirass*; and when he fulfills his priestly functions as high priest or *pontifex maximus*, he pulls his toga over his head, appearing *capite velato*, "with covered head." The emperor sometimes is portrayed in the guise of a god or a deified hero, with portrait head over a nude or seminude body like a statue of a god such as Jupiter, Hermes, Apollo, or Hercules.

The color and decoration of the toga was significant, marking differences in age and status. Most prestigious was the *toga picta* of the triumph ceremony, worn by a victorious general when he climbed the Capitoline Hill to the Temple of Jupiter to pay the tithe owed to the god. Behind his chariot came the procession of the army with the booty from the campaign and the royal prisoners they had captured, bound in chains. Many details of the ceremony of the triumph were inherited from the Etruscan kings who had ruled at Rome in the sixth century BCE, when they had the great temple and brought aspects of their sophisticated culture to Rome, including the alphabet, musical instruments, insignia of power such as the curved *lituus* and the axe placed in the center of the *fasces*, and the rounded shape of the toga, like their tebenna, as well as special decorated forms that took on a special meaning in Roman symbolism. The sumptuously gold-decorated toga picta took the place of the earlier, simpler *toga purpurea*. From the time of Augustus, only the emperor, as commander in chief, could celebrate triumphs. These togas became an important part of the imperial insignia, and the purple murex color with which they were dyed was eventually reserved by law for imperial use.

The *toga praetexta* with purple border can be clearly seen on the life-size bronze statue known as the Arringatore, or "Public Speaker," because of his gesture. That it is Etruscan can be seen from the Etruscan inscription on the hem of his toga that states his name, Aule Meteli—Aulus Metellius in Latin. But he looks like a Roman. He is dressed in a costume that is indistinguishable from what a Roman citizen wore at this time, the second century BCE, a narrow toga exigua, not yet the fuller toga of imperial times. Its border, clearly set off by a narrow binding, shows it to be a toga praetexta, worn with a tunic whose vertical stripe or *clavus* prolcaimed his status in society. In Rome, the narrow stripe, *augustus clavus*, was the mark of *equites*, or gentlemen outside the senate, while a senator wore a wider stripe, the *latus clavus*.

Footwear

The intricately laced boots worn by the Arringatore and the male figures on the Ara Pacis formed part of the official costume of a Roman citizen: a *togatus* wore the *toga et calcei*, toga and high-topped, laced boots. These clearly distinguished him from a Greek, who wore a rectangular himation mantle with sandals; Roman men wore sandals (*soleae* or *crepidae*) only indoors. Certain forms and colors of calcei marked the wearer's special status, such as the dark red boots (*mullei*) of a patrician or a senator's calcei with black laces and a buckle. The Romans' claim that there was a connection between the form of the Roman calcei and that of early Etruscan shoes is confirmed by archaic Roman monuments, which show the laced, pointed shoes, a purely Etruscan style from around the middle of the sixth century BCE, worn mostly by women. In Rome, it became a symbolic male costume, and as is often the case with Archaic aspects of costume, it acquired a special meaning in later times.

Togas for Special Occasions

The purple-bordered toga praetexta had also became an important symbol in Rome and continued to be used for a man who held one of the most prestigious offices, a *curule magistracy*. Because its purple border was held to have magic power, it was evidently considered an appropriate costume for a boy who had not yet reached adulthood, one that would protect him from harm. Other special togas also carried specific meanings. A man who sought to be elected for office wore a bleached toga to distinguish him from the men in the street wearing plain woolen togas: this bright white *toga candida* marked him out as a candidate for office, or *candidatus*. Mourners wore the dark toga, or *toga pulla*.

The toga was regularly draped over the left shoulder; the same rounded shape was worn, draped in front so that it formed a large semicircular shape. Special forms or ways of draping the basic semicircular toga included the short *trabea*, purple and scarlet, with purple borders, worn by the knights and members of certain priesthoods, such as the Salii. Ritual occasions called for the gesture of covering the head with the edge of the toga, capite velato. For certain military rituals, there was the special draping of the *cinctus gabinus*, a manner of pulling up the toga over the left shoulder and tying it at the waist. Written sources inform us that the early Romans used to gird themselves for battle in this way, to gain freedom of movement and perhaps to provide some protection from enemy weapons.

For warmth, and for travel, a variety of heavy, hooded woolen mantles were worn. These were called the *byrrus*, *cucullus*, *caracalla*, and *sagum*.

Undergarments

Under the toga, men wore a tunic or shirt. The Roman tunic was different from the Greek *chiton* in that it was sewn down each side. Though some tunics do not have real sleeves, other examples of such sleeves exist. Unlike the chiton, where openings for the head and arms were left along the upper edge of the garment, the tunic had openings for the arms at the sides, and there are many examples of added sleeves. It is a further indication of Etruscan influence that Roman tunics, as well as other garments, were sometimes cut and made from complicated patterns with separate pieces stitched together, including tunics with real sleeves. Neither long-sleeved tunics nor the full-length pants of the northern barbarians were worn by Roman citizens until the third or fourth century CE, when the adoption of barbarian clothes marked the end of Classical civilization.

The Romans never accepted the Greek innovation of total male nudity. As an undergarment all year-round, and in the summer directly under the toga, they wore short pants, similar to the Greek *perizoma*. The name of this garment was the *campestre*, because it was what was worn for exercising in the *campus martius*, the exercise ground for the army. It was also called a *subligaculum*.

Short, tight, knee-length pants covering the thighs, worn by Roman soldiers under the tunic in colder climates, are illustrated on Trajan's Column from the early second century CE, which depicts the Dacian campaigns of that emperor. Suetonius's biography of Augustus tells that the emperor, whose health was delicate, wore *feminalia* in the wintertime.[2] *"Feminalia"* is connected to "femur," or thigh-bone. This was a kind of long underwear that covered the upper part of the leg, quite different from the full-length pants of the northern barbarians, which were not worn by self-respecting Roman citizens until the third or fourth century CE.

The baggy pants or *bracae* of certain Gallic tribes marked out the part of Gaul that was least Romanized, known as *Gallia Bracata*. The situations of other parts of Gaul, too, were reflected in their names—*Gallia Comata* was "Long-haired Gaul," and *Gallia Togata* was the more Romanized Cisalpine Gaul.

Foreigners and slaves were easily distinguished from Roman citizens on formal occasions. The slaves' simple, dark tunics and mantles (they received new ones once a year) stood out from the lighter, white togas of the citizens, while foreigners could be picked out by their exotic clothes.

Priestly Costumes

The priests, or *flamines,* on the Ara Pacis wear the *laena*, a rounded garment like the toga, worn draped with the end thrown in back so that the cloth forms a semicircle in front. According to one source, the flamines were *infibulati*, that is, their garments were fastened with fibulas, large safety pins or brooches. These are not visible on the monuments, but several fourth-century BCE bronze statuettes of Etruscan *haruspices* or priests show them to be wearing animal-skin hats and animal-skin mantles fastened with fibulas of a type that were frequent in Villanovan times. We have seen that such an early, often Etruscan origin for ritual garments and accessories of Roman priests is not surprising and in fact is true of the priestly hat the flamines wear with the laena: the *galerus*, a helmet-like head covering made of animal skins or leather. The fact that they have a spike (*apex*) on top of this hat shows that they belong to the highest rank of Roman priesthoods.

Women's Clothing

Roman women wore a linen tunic that was longer and wider than that of the man, but this garment was basically unchanging in shape, being made up of one

Roman relief showing priests and the imperial family led by Marcus Agrippa (south frieze). © Alinari / Art Resource, NY.

or more rectangular pieces of cloth, sewn, buttoned, or pinned at the shoulders, belted at the waist, and draped on the body, creating pleasing folds. The *stola*, which looked much like a slip with thin shoulder straps, was worn over the tunic, from at least the time of Augustus, by the Roman *matrona* or married woman.

The outer garment of women was a rectangular mantle (*palla*). Only very young girls and disreputable women wore the toga. Otherwise, Roman women's clothing did not have the same varieties and distinctions that marked the status of men. A higher class woman depended on the elegance, color, and luxury of her garments, her jewelry, and her hairstyle to set her apart.

The costume and hairstyle of the important public priesthood of the Vestal Virgins resembled that of brides; they also covered their hair with a veil and added woolen fillets.

Footwear

Women's sandals, normally made of leather, had straps arranged in a variety of styles and attached to soles of various heights. They ranged from the sturdy simple styles of working women and slaves to the luxurious, extravagantly decorated footwear of sophisticated Roman ladies.

Undergarments

In Rome, as in Greece, women wore brassieres under their tunics. Whether these linen bands around their breasts were to support or to bind them is unclear. Women athletes and entertainers wore a sports costume consisting of short pants and brassieres; this was probably the usual underwear of women, which was usually not visible through the outergarment.

Children

Babies are regularly shown either swaddled or naked. Children were not distinguished by gender until they reached adolescence; until then, whether slave or freeborn, they all wore simple narrow tunics and sandals. On the Ara Pacis, both boys and girls wear, as formal garb, the rounded toga. One little boy wears a *bulla* or locket meant to keep him safe from evil influences. The bulla was made of a variety of materials, ranging from cheap leather to bronze, silver, or gold, according to the status and wealth of the family. Over the tunic, boys normally wore the characteristic toga praetexta, meant, like the bulla, as a good-luck charm to keep them safe. The rite of passage marking the change from childhood to adulthood took place for a boy sometime between his fifteenth and seventeenth year, at which time he laid aside his bulla and purple-bordered toga and put on the plain white toga virilis of an adult, full-fledged Roman citizen.

The equivalent rite of passage for a girl was the wedding. As for the boys, a formal change of dress marked her initiation into womanhood and her new status as a matrona. Just as the boy laid aside his bulla and toga praetexta, the girl put aside her dolls and toys and her toga before the wedding. Many features of the bride's wedding costume were traditional and symbolic. The night before the wedding, she slept in a narrow white tunic like the boy's, and a yellow hairnet, both of which she had woven herself. Her wedding dress was tied with a square knot, called the Hercules knot. A flame-colored, yellow veil and a wreath of flowers and herbs covered her head, while her hair was ritually dressed in a special, primitive style: it was parted with a spear and twisted on top of the head to form a kind of bun made up of six braids or coils.

NOTES

1. Virgil, *Aeneid* 1.282.
2. Suetonius, biography of Augustus, Aug. 82.

FURTHER READING

Barber, E. J. W. *Prehistoric Textiles*. Princeton: Princeton University Press, 1991.
Bieber, Margarete. *Ancient Copies. Contributions to the History of Greek and Roman Art*. New York: New York University Press, 1977.
Bonfante, Larissa. *Etruscan Dress*. 2nd ed. Baltimore: The Johns Hopkins University Press, 2003.
Bonfante, Larissa. "Introduction." In *Essays on Nudity in Antiquity in Memory of Otto Brendel. Source* 2 (1993): 7–11.
Bonfante, Larissa. "Kleidung." In *Mensch und Landschaft in der Antike. Lexikon der Historischen Geographie*, ed., H. Sonnabend, 257–60. Stuttgart, Weimar: Metzler Verlag, 1999. (skin garments).
Bonfante, Larissa. "Nudity as Costume in Classical Art." *American Journal of Archaelogy*. 93 (1989): 543–70.
Bonfante, Larissa. "Riflessi di arte cretese in Etruria." In *Studi in Onore di Luisa Banti*. 81–87. Rome: L'Erma di Bretschneider 1965. (Daedalic Capelet).
Bonfante, Larissa and Judith Lynne Sebesta, eds. *The World of Roman Costume*. Madison: University of Wisconsin Press, 1994.
Brendel, Otto J. *Etruscan Art*. 2nd ed. New Haven: Yale University Press, 1995.
Fantham, Elaine, Helene Peet Foley, Natalie Boymel Kampen, Sarah B. Pomeroy, and H. Alan Shapiro, eds. *Women in the Classical World*. New York: Oxford University Press, 1994.

Grossmann, Janet Burnett. *Looking at Greek and Roman Sculpture in Stone: A Guide to Terms, Styles and Techniques.* Los Angeles: The J. Paul Getty Museum, 2003.

Haynes, Sybille. *Etruscan Civilization. A Cultural History.* Los Angeles: The J. Paul Getty Museum, 2000.

Llewellyn-Jones, ed. *Women's Dress in the Ancient Greek World.* London: Duckworth, and The Classical Press of Wales, 2002.

Marcar, Ariane. "Reconstructing Aegean Bronze Age Fashion." In *The Clothed Body in the Ancient World*, eds., Liza Cleland, Mary Harlow and Lloyd Llewellyn-Jones, pp. 30–43, Oxford: Oxbow Books. 2005.

Pomeroy, Sarah B. *Goddesses, Whores, Wives and Slaves: Women in Classical Antiquity.* New York: Schocken, 1995.

Smith, R. R. R. et al. *Roman Portrait Statuary from Aphrodisias. Aphrodisias* II. Mainz: von Zabern, 2006.

Torelli, Mario, ed. *The Etruscans.* London: Thames and Hudson, 2000.

Zanker, Paul. *The Power of Images in the Age of Augustus.* Translated by Alan Shapiro. Ann Arbor: University of Michigan Press, 1988.

WEB RESOURCES

Metropolitan Museum of Art, Department of Greek and Roman Art. "Ancient Greek Dress." *Timeline of Art History.* http://www.metmuseum.org/toah/hd/grdr/hd_grdr.htm.

http://www.coh.arizona.edu/classics/inst/clas362/class362slides/etrusc4.jpg

http://en.wikipedia.org/wiki/Image:Colosseum_in_Rome%2C_Italy_-_April_2007.jpggames

http://travel.webshots.com/photo/2476849090100710185gSyyRC

http://www.unc.edu/courses/rometech/public/content/arts_and_crafts/April_Anderson/shoes.html

MOVIES

Caligula (1980)
Cleopatra (1963)
Gladiator (2000)
The Robe (1953)
Rome (HBO, 2005–2007)

Byzantine Clothing

Jennifer Ball

TIMELINE

324 CE	Constantinople founded by Emperor Constantine I
380	Emperor Theodosius declares Orthodoxy the true faith
Fourth century	Sumptuary laws governing clothing use written by Theodosius; Byzantines continue with Roman dress and customs, but speak Greek
Sixth century	Silk imported and produced in Byzantium
Seventh century	Expansion of the silk industry
Eighth century	Control of Egypt ends; empire reaches its height; Byzantines develop exquisite and decorative fashions
Tenth century	*Book of the Prefect* emphasizes the importance of the textile industry
1204	Westerners sack Constantinople in the Fourth Crusade; Eastern Empire enters decline
1453	Fall of the Byzantine Empire to Ottoman Turks

Byzantine clothing, like many other aspects of Byzantine culture, initially continued Roman styles and was virtually indistinguishable from Roman dress. Historians date the beginnings of the Empire to the year 324 CE, when Emperor Constantine I moved his capital from Rome to the city of Byzantium, modern-day Istanbul, Turkey, renaming the city Constantinople. The Empire at its height, having the same borders as its Roman predecessor, stretched from Spain into the Middle East, down across North Africa, and north up to the Danube River and north of the Black Sea. These first citizens of Constantinople called themselves Romans; built and decorated the city with Roman sculpture and architecture; kept the same Roman administrative systems, military, and coinage; and, of course, wore the same types of clothing that they had always worn. Slowly, however, through the fourth, fifth and sixth centuries, a distinct culture emerged, which we now call Byzantine—a word coined by later historians, from the old Greek name of its capital city, Byzantium.

Nevertheless, their culture and their dress are distinguished from Roman society in many ways. Of primary importance, after Constantine legalized the Christian religion in 312 CE and Emperor Theodosius I declared Orthodoxy the true faith in an edict of 380, the Byzantine Empire was officially a Christian Orthodox state, as opposed to the Roman Empire, where many religions continued to be practiced. The citizens of the Empire became largely Greek, rather than Latin, speaking. A new visual culture arose where, for example, Roman floor mosaics were perfected and moved to the walls of Byzantine churches and palaces, which glittered with gold and precious materials. Alongside this cultural shift away from the Roman tradition, new styles of dress came into fashion, seen in the finery of Byzantium's wealthy elite and members of court.

As the Byzantines always thought of themselves as Romans, even centuries after the last vestiges of the Roman state were gone, they continued to refer to their Roman heritage in their dress while forging a distinctly Byzantine style that became the envy of the wider medieval world, particularly those in Western medieval courts. Thus, we find certain garments that recall in both form and function Roman clothing, such as the *loros*, an imperial stole, which resembled the *toga trabea*, a stole worn by Roman consuls. The emperor would wear this garment, referencing his Roman heritage, over a long, brightly colored, brocaded silk tunic, known as a *divetesion*, which had no connection to the Roman past but instead showed the riches of the current administration.

Despite the fact that Byzantium was the leader in fashion and the textile industry for much of its existence, it was influenced by outside styles of dress, especially those from the Islamic world. The nation-state of the Muslims that rose up in the seventh century in the Middle East bordered the Byzantine Empire to its east, and later to its south as well. Islam was unified under a *caliph*—a religious and political leader—but was not a single people ethnically speaking, although the first converts to Islam were Arabs. Styles were passed along the famed Silk Road, which ran from China through Islamic territory into Europe, with the Byzantines controlling much of the route around the Mediterranean. Shifting borders from various conflicts throughout Byzantium's history often meant that populations along the edges of the Empire were culturally mixed, which naturally affected the clothing that was popular in those regions. Georgians, Armenians, Bulgarians, and Normans, in addition to Islamic peoples, all influenced the styles that became popular in the Byzantine world.

Silk, more than any other fabric, made the Byzantines famous for their clothing. They wore precious silks manufactured within the Empire beginning in the sixth century, at a time when the rest of Europe had to rely on Byzantine imports because they had not yet unlocked the secrets of manufacturing silk—and would not until the twelfth century, when the Normans of Sicily began to produce silk. Venetians and Genoese merchants made their way into the markets of Constantinople to acquire the precious Byzantine commodities for export to Italy. Charlemagne, the Holy Roman emperor in ninth-century France, scolded monks and courtiers in his circle for what he saw as their vain desire to wear Byzantine silks. Archaeological digs as far away from the Byzantine Empire as England, China, and Viking territories in Scandinavia have uncovered scraps of Byzantine silks.

Western Europeans wore wool for the most part, while the Byzantines donned not only silk but also fine linen produced from flax grown in Egypt, which was under Byzantine control until the eighth century. Visitors to Byzantium often remarked on how opulently dressed its citizens were. A twelfth-century rabbi from Spain noted that the Byzantines wore silk decorated with gold and precious gems and "[appeared like] princes."[1] During the Fourth Crusade, when Westerners sacked Constantinople in 1204 and set up their own emperor within the Empire, raiding the imperial treasuries of its garments was of primary symbolic importance; the crusaders staged a coronation ceremony, piling the imperial raiment on Baldwin I.[2] Several leaders on the edges of the Empire, such as the Georgian or Norman kings, enviously mimicked Byzantine emperors by wearing the same regalia in official portraits.

The Byzantines themselves were perhaps even fonder of their own manner of dressing than outside admirers. The Byzantines manipulated markets, both local and export economies, so as to keep certain fabrics and colors, especially purple, within its borders. A well-known story of an embassy to Constantinople by Liuprand of Cremona in the tenth century tells of their entourage being stopped at the gates of the city after they had done some shopping. Their belongings were checked and they were told: "Those [garments] that are fit for you shall be marked with a leaden seal and left in your possession; those that are prohibited to all nations, except to us Romans, shall be taken away and their price returned."[3] The Byzantines felt that certain garments were just too precious to be worn by outsiders. Sumptuary laws were written and updated under emperors Theodosius, in the fourth century, and Justinian, in the sixth century, to regulate dress. The tenth-century *Book of the Prefect* contains economic codes for controlling the textile, dye, and clothing markets. These texts highlight the economic force of the textile and clothing industry, which was the largest of any Byzantine market, more precious than gems or gold.

Even more telling are the prescriptive texts that survive for the clothing of courtiers. The *Notitia Dignitatum*, while it does not discuss clothing, lists the offices and depicts many of the emblems of insignia—accessories or badges worn on clothing—for Early Byzantine officials. Other texts are far more detailed: Philotheos's *Kletorologion*, Constantine VII's *Book of Ceremonies*, and Pseudo-Kodinos's *Treatise on the Dignities and Offices* describe hundreds of court ceremonies, from marriages and coronations to diplomatic dinners and exchanges of prisoners between Byzantium and its foes. Significantly, these books detail what should be worn for each occasion, down to the accessories of office, such as batons and embroidered insignia, and colors. What is most remarkable about these books is not that these government officials are told what to wear, but that they are typically ordered to change clothes several times during a particular day's events; in other words, several outfits were required to make it through a single day's work at court. Furthermore, these ceremonies were the primary business of the court and not simply for special events. Merely having a meeting with the emperor or attending church on a feast day, of which there were numerous throughout the year, required special clothing. Courtiers were paid in textiles and garments as well as in gold, so this helped to defray the costs of their wardrobe needs.

Outside of court, while clothing was not prescribed, we find that it carried equal importance. Fictional stories as well as factual histories talk about the lives of Byzantium's private citizens with great attention to the clothing they wore. For example, the fifth-century Pelagia of Antioch is described as being decked out with gold ornaments, pearls, and all sorts of precious stones, resplendent in luxurious and expensive clothes. On her hands and feet she wore armbands, silks, and anklets decorated with all sorts of pearls, while around her neck were necklaces and strings of pendants and pearls. Her beauty stunned those who beheld her, captivating them in their desire for her.[4]

Oftentimes, the details of fabric—brocade, damask, twill, and so on—the type of dye and its source, and even the technique are described by writers, suggesting that the general population had a greater knowledge of how clothes were made than we do today. Byzantine authors describe silkworms as almost magical creatures, and weavers are typically lauded in the written sources.

Dowries and wills provide evidence for the clothing that was passed on to family members. One father complains of the expense of dowries in Byzantium, as he bestowed his daughter's husband with twenty-one garments, many in silk![5] An examination of the surviving wills written by Byzantine citizens suggests that, on average, two or three items of clothing would be bequeathed. Even assuming that most people owned some clothing not worthy of mention in a will, a handful of garments is a small number compared to the extravagant number of garments that were expected to accompany a bride in marriage.

Being properly dressed was a mark of one's wealth, but also of good character. Modesty in dress was often a trope used in describing a virtuous saint, while sound rulers were typically identified as such by their superior garments. Saintly characters in literature sometimes wore as few as one article of clothing per year, giving away their fine silks to the poor. Men gave the clothes off their backs to the beggar on the street, and several pious people are described as wearing goat-hair clothing—presumably a rough and uncomfortable choice—as a way of relinquishing the fine clothes that were presumably the norm. The eleventh-century historian Michael Psellos recounts that Emperor Basil II (R. 976–1025) scorned purple cloaks and extra ornament as a way of demonstrating his sound judgment. Other sources chide Emperor Nikephoros II Phokas (R. 963–969) for dressing crudely, as a way of characterizing him as a usurper who came from military rather than elite ranks.

The literature of the period paints a picture of a fashion-obsessed society where being properly dressed was of primary importance. One story tells of a mother who worried that a particular convent was not right for her daughter because the clothes the nuns wore were not fine enough. The local hospital in Constantinople provided all patients with a new outfit upon release, in addition to cleaning the garments with which they were admitted. Another story recounts a man fretting upon his wife's death that she will not be buried in suitable clothes.

In addition to the literary descriptions of clothing, scholars learn about Byzantine dress through painted images, particularly portraits of the citizens of the Empire. Donor and funerary portraits in churches, in the opening pages of illuminated manuscripts, and on other objects of metalwork and ivory provide numerous examples of complete outfits. Coins, which have portraits of the emperor and empress, also give us lots of information about imperial regalia, because they can be firmly dated and we have multiple examples of what every emperor wore for these portraits. For those not wealthy enough to have their portraits made, we find ordinary folks represented in the background scenes of historical or religious stories.

Unfortunately, what has not survived is the clothing itself, so we are left to rely on depictions of clothing in art and literature to compose a history of Byzantine dress. Garments are not only more susceptible to wear and tear than objects made of sturdier materials, but they also are more likely to succumb to moisture and insects. It was typical for a Byzantine to wear an article of clothing until it was worn out, then to repair it and wear it again or pass it on. This cycle might repeat itself a few times until finally the surviving parts of a garment would be made into something else—a bag, for example—so each piece of clothing was heavily used in its lifetime. Furthermore, while precious garments—such as ecclesiastical vestments kept in church coffers or the items protected in the imperial wardrobe—might have been cared for with greater attention, these were often targets of soldiers looking for booty in times of war. Many precious silks survive in Western treasuries and museums that came from Byzantium during the Crusades. Unfortunately, these textiles were often used to wrap up other significant items of booty, such as icons or books, and rarely retain their original appearance. The occasional seam or fastening suggests that they were once part of an article of clothing, but it was the embroidery of an angel or woven silk griffin that was considered magnificent to Western eyes, and more often than not the beautiful design was cut out, leaving us with little material evidence for the Byzantine costume itself.

Graves are another source for full garments, as people were buried in their clothes and then wrapped in a shroud. Burial in the ground creates hostile conditions for textiles, however, and except for dry climates like Egypt, the clothing rarely survives beyond scraps. Several textile collections around the world own linen tunics found in burials from Byzantine Egypt (from the fourth to seventh centuries). These are mostly undyed and ornamented with embroidery around the neck and shoulders, sometimes with vertical stripes or decoration at the hem. There are a few exceptions, however: a fourteenth-century elite woman was found buried in Mistra, Greece, in a full dress, small crown, and shoes; some fragments of Middle Byzantine (eighth- to twelfth-century) clothing have been found in graves at Amorium, Turkey. For the most part, though, the picture of Byzantine dress must come from the literary and artistic record of the Byzantines.

While a garment-by-garment history of Byzantine dress cannot be reconstructed, it is possible to present an overall framework for how dress worked within Byzantine society. Historians divide the Byzantine Empire into three major periods: the Early Byzantine period, the fourth to seventh centuries; the Middle Byzantine, the eighth to twelfth centuries; and the Late Byzantine, from the thirteenth century until 1453 when the Empire fell to the Ottoman Turks. These periods correspond nicely to three phases of fashion in the Empire. In the Early period, dress followed Roman prototypes to a large degree, not just at court but also in the clothing of everyday citizens. Distinctly Byzantine dress emerges in the Middle period, which can be characterized as the height of Byzantine fashion. Beginning in the twelfth century, as the borders of the Empire begin to shrink, the Byzantines begin to wear more and more styles that came directly from or were influenced by surrounding Western and Islamic cultures.

These changes in fashion, not coincidentally, correspond to major shifts in the textile industry. Just prior to the Middle Byzantine era, in the seventh century, the Byzantines established silk-weaving workshops within the Empire and no longer had to rely on imported silk. At the end of the Middle period, in the twelfth century, they lost their monopoly on silk manufacture in Europe, when the Normans of Sicily began producing silk. It was also around this time that Islam, particularly the Fatimids in Egypt, began to trade textiles directly with Western Europeans, circumventing the Byzantine trade routes that had allowed them to control the markets in Europe. It should be no surprise that fashion trends followed the changes in the textile industry itself.

EARLY BYZANTINE DRESS

Imperial Dress

Perhaps the most famous images of any Byzantine imperial couple are the mosaics of Emperor Justinian and Empress Theodora, with their entourage symbolically bringing gifts to the altar, in the apse at San Vitale, Ravenna, Italy, from around 547. Both Theodora and Justinian wear the marks of the Byzantine imperial office: elaborate, jeweled crowns and the full-length purple cloak known as a *chlamys*. Theodora's chlamys is decorated with a gold-embroidered image of the Three Magi, perhaps a metaphor for her giving a gift to the church. Justinian's cloak is embroidered with a large, gold piece of embroidery—a *tablion*—in the shape of a trapezoid; this is yet another form of insignia, the emperor's tablion being more elaborate than the other male courtiers who also don tablia on their cloaks. Theodora additionally wears a long tunic and Justinian a short one, which was appropriate for men. These tunics are white trimmed at the edges, with embroidery in rich saturated colors. White was a color of political significance in the Roman period and the color of choice for a toga worn for any special occasion. White continued to be a powerful color choice in the Byzantine period, worn by many at court. Each wears additional jewels, Theodora an elaborate collar covering her shoulders and chest, and Justinian a large brooch, a *fibula*, which holds up his cloak. Theodora's shoes are not visible enough to be identified, but Justinian wears jeweled boots known as *kornithoi*.

The garments worn by Justinian and Theodora, while appropriately elaborate for these grand mosaic portraits, are typical of Early Byzantine imperial dress. The emperor and empress have some similar accessories marking their office, usually referred to as insignia, but wear gender-distinct clothing befitting any aristocrat or court official—only with more ornament due to their royal status. Many of the items they wear recall Roman imperial garb, which will be discussed later. Finally, Justinian's clothes are military inspired, which was typical in the Early Byzantine period.

HEADGEAR IN THE BYZANTINE EMPIRE

Women—with the exception of the empress—always wore veils, and men probably wore hats at court as part of their official insignia. Anyone who held an ecclesiastical office also wore a hat or veil of some type, and monks covered their heads as well. Shepherds and others who worked in the sun wore broad-rimmed straw hats. Sailors wore black hats that tied beneath the chin.

Crowns

Many types of crowns existed in the Early period, but the most common stems from a *diadem*, which was worn by both emperor and empress. The diadem dates back to Alexander the Great and was originally a leather headband that was jeweled; it was tied in the back of the head and had fringe that hung down at the sides. Constantine I (*R.* 306–337) adopted this type of headband for his crown, probably to emulate the great Hellenistic leader, and most Byzantine emperors wore a similar crown or one that derived from it, following Constantine's example. The diadem evolved quickly into a more heavily jeweled, sometimes metal, headband. The fringe was replaced with *prependoulia*, the jewels that hang down around the ears of both Justinian and Theodora. Shortly after Constantine's time, the diadem became less a headband than an open crown encircling the head.

According to written descriptions, other types of crowns were sometimes worn, but it is not always clear what images go with these other terms. Some crowns, according to literary accounts, were more like full hats made of metal lined with cloth; others were mounted with crosses. The imperial couple owned multiple crowns, and they were not passed down to the next ruler, which is somewhat unusual when compared with practices in Western kingdoms. Crowns were worn for every public appearance, so having multiple crowns was a necessity. A court eunuch the *praipositos*, was charged with the care of the crowns and other insignia and crowned the emperor and empress during ceremonies.

Fibula and Collar

The fibula was also a significant marker of Justinian's imperial status. While the crown he wears in the mosaic had its origins in ancient Greece, Romans did not wear such crowns. The fibula, however, was a Roman imperial symbol carried on by the Byzantines. A fibula is in essence a large fastening pin, worn more often (but not always) by men, to hold up a cloak. Fibulae were worn by people at all levels of society, with those of lower status wearing bronze examples, while the emperor's was gold and encrusted with gemstones. Many of the courtiers surrounding Justinian and Theodora also wear fibulae, but theirs are simpler, metal examples. It became common practice in the Roman era for the ruler to bestow a fibula on vassal rulers, and this continued in the Early Byzantine period. Its purpose always remained functional, as well as symbolic of status, as cloaks had no other way of being worn and fastened except with a piece of jewelry such as a fibula.

Theodora's imperial status is similarly noted with jewels, but in this case with a jeweled collar. The collar encircles her neck and drapes over her shoulders. Although no examples or exact descriptions survive, it was probably made of leather or heavy fabric, with gems sewn onto it. It may be a descendant of the *torque*, a metal collar worn as a sign of military rank, seen on the guardsmen on the far right of the Justinian panel. The torque dates back to Roman times and was originally Scandinavian. Sometimes they were used by Romans and Byzantines as crowns, referred to as *maniakion* when they were placed on the head. When worn around the neck, the torque became more and more elaborate through time, developing a jeweled or enameled medallion at its center, which may have led to collars like Theodora's. The empress, and later the emperor, was often shown in these jeweled collars, but it is not known what they were called, as they are not clearly described by writers of the day. It may be that it was considered part of the cloak she wears and actually sewn on to it or that it was thought of as a piece of jewelry and not described as a garment.

Chlamys

The chlamys worn by both Justinian and Theodora is also Roman and military in its original use. Justinian wears it like a military man, pinned at the shoulder freeing one arm for brandishing a weapon. Practicality dictated that the military chlamys be short, however, so Justinian's long cloak has been transformed into a silk, gold-encrusted garment that recalls the military and Roman past but also speaks to his imperial status. His tunic remains short (in later periods, long tunics would come into fashion for men), which is again a vestige of military wear that allowed for freedom of movement. Women did not typically wear the chlamys in the Roman or Early Byzantine period; Theodora is one of the first empresses to be seen wearing this article of clothing, which by the Middle Byzantine period became the business attire for both men and women at and outside of court. Theodora, in this image, clearly dons the chlamys as a sign of her rank, asserting her position as empress, although she held little actual power.

Footwear

The imperial boots that Justinian sports, the *kornithoi*, are yet another military-inspired Roman accessory. Boots were the typical footgear of a soldier, but in the mosaic they have been elevated to imperial rank with the application of jewels—making them completely impractical for anything beyond brief moments of standing or walking—and are decorated to communicate the wearer's status and position. Around the foot, the boots are red, a color that signified imperial status, but they are black on his leg, suggesting leather.

SHOES

Byzantine men usually wore laced-up leather boots or dressier silk slippers. Finer boots may also have been made out of silk. *Tzangia* are the red silk boots worn by the emperor. Sandals appear to be shown only on biblical figures, although we may imagine that lower-income people wore sandals or went barefoot. Women's feet are rarely shown in images—from the few depictions that I have seen, I expect that they wore slippers and boots as well.

Color

Purple and gold were imperial colors, dating back to the ancient world as well. Certain types of purple, such as the deep purple seen on both Justinian's and Theodora's *chlamydes*, were restricted to imperial use by sumptuary law. This purple is probably murex purple, made from mollusk shells from the Mediterranean and extremely expensive. The color became synonymous with imperial status, evolving into expressions such as "born to the purple," meaning a legitimate child of a crowned emperor and empress. Purple was a popular color in general for all who could afford it, as it had been in Roman times, but the murex purple, specifically, was reserved for monarchs, to the point that sumptuary laws governed its use.

Every emperor and empress, of course, did not wear the exact outfit modeled here by Justinian and Theodora. Many different types of crowns existed, for example. The marks of office, though—the crowns, footwear, jewels, and embroidered panels—remained fairly consistent throughout the Early Byzantine period. Theodora's clothing signals a shift in at least the symbolic role of the empress as a public figure. By contrast, the empresses of the Theodosian era (late fourth and early fifth centuries) are often depicted wearing clothing without the distinct mark of imperial office. For example, Theodosian empresses wore wide-sleeved tunics called *dalmatica* beneath a *palla*, a type of mantle worn over both shoulders. Coins and weights provide some of the only Early Byzantine portraits of empresses, and typically they are only bust-length, thus not giving much more information. While many empresses wore a diadem, there is little indication that before the sixth century other garments of imperial regalia were worn.

Dress of Courtiers

Courtiers were for the most part men, with wives symbolically carrying the same title as their husbands. The empress had women in her entourage—what might now be called "ladies in waiting"—who were typically relatives of the empress or the spouses of other courtiers. An examination of the Justinian and Theodora panels shows that men wore clothes signifying their rank, and in these images they stand grouped accordingly around the emperor and empress, while the women wear individualized long tunics, probably a dalmatica, underneath a palla. The women cover their heads and a few wear jewelry, which may or may not signify their status in relation to each other.

Conversely, the men wear cloaks and tunics according to rank, often specified by color, patches of embroidery, or whether or not they were secured with a fibula. The two men to Justinian's right and the one to Theodora's left all wear white chlamydes over white tunics, with a large purple tablion. Their dress suggests that they are of the same rank, but the embroidered patches on their shoulders, which differ, may have implied subtle differences in rank. The man on the far left of the Theodora panel is also dressed similarly but wears a gold cloak, suggesting that he is of a different rank. The spear-bearing men in the far left of the Justinian panel are again dressed similarly—each wears a short-sleeved tunic layered over a long-sleeve one, all with short hems, over white boots, and they each have torques around their necks. Their spears and shields should be considered part of their insignia. The different colors they wear may imply different ranks.

There are many terms for cloaks and tunics, some of which may have named the same garment just as today we might say "sportcoat" or "jacket" to refer to the same item of men's clothing generally worn with a dress shirt and tie. It is not possible to tell from depictions of courtiers what specific tunic or cloak is being worn; subtle differences exist in the cut of the hem, embroidered decoration, among other things, but whether a certain cut signified a *colobium* instead of a *himation*, both types of tunics, is not known.

Additionally, many courtiers carried or wore insignia, ranging from accessories such as certain shoes or headgear to symbolic items carried, such as batons, books, or *mappa*—a linen cloth. Because many of these courtiers held military positions, their insignia and dress were often items of armor or weapons, as seen in the Justinian panel. Swords and helmets were very common; even a courtier's horse might have trappings denoting his rank.

Four sports factions existed, dating back to Roman times, who were known by their colors: Blues, Greens, Reds, and Whites. These factions were teams of charioteers and other circus sportsmen, whose support was so strong that certain high-level courtiers incorporated their favorite faction colors into their dress. Thus, there are several officials seen wearing either blue or green denoting their faction. Reds and Whites, it seems, were secondary in popularity to the Blues and Greens and thus did not draw anyone to the wearing of their colors. Beyond this use of color, however, colors were for the most part not fixed for courtiers; descriptions suggest that the same courtier might wear different colors for different occasions and further that this changed over time.

The Clothing of Elites

The clothing of the wealthy was not unlike that of courtiers—the cloak and tunic were staples of the wardrobe, and fine fabrics, especially silk, separated their dress from that of ordinary citizens. Furthermore, like the clothing worn at court, Roman styles influenced Byzantine outfits, but this influence slowly wore away over time. Short, military-inspired tunics and cloaks gave way to longer ones with greater adornment. Additionally, Persian styles imported via the Silk Road from the East were also popular, seen especially in fabrics with griffins and roundels inscribing mounted hunters that arise at the end of the Early Byzantine period.

The dress of men and women did not differ greatly; both wore tunics and cloaks. Men, however, were more likely to wear short styles, as well as tunics with short sleeves; for women, modesty was of greater concern, and women generally covered their arms and legs. Most importantly, women often covered their heads; the *maphorion*, a mantle covering the head and shoulders, was worn, at least for public outings. This is the same garment in which the Virgin Mary is always shown.

Early in the Byzantine period, women followed the Roman custom of wearing elaborate hairstyles pulled up in a coif, which seemed to change with each new group of ruling women, sometimes ornamented with small crowns or jewels. While wearing the hair pulled up continued throughout the Byzantine period, women began to cover their heads (the maphorion is first mentioned in fourth-century texts), so that it is impossible to see their hairstyles for the most part. Empresses seem to be the exception: they are always shown wearing crowns and are therefore left unveiled. Written accounts, especially stories of the lives of saints, indicate that while it was customary for women to cover their heads, it was by no means strictly followed. The occasional mention of a woman putting on a head covering demonstrates that they were not wearing them all the time. Portraits may have shown women with their heads covered because of the formality of such an image. According to literary sources, men wore maphoria covering their heads, too, but more often than not it was a monk, or the occasional courtier, who donned this item of clothing.

The true mark of an elite figure, in terms of dress, was the ornamentation and layering of the garments. While many Byzantines of any class likely layered an undertunic or perhaps a loincloth, which served as underwear, beneath a standard tunic, the elite citizen wore layers that peeked out to display in literal terms the amount of fabric actually worn. Thus, men and women might have worn an undergarment, a full-length simple tunic trimmed with embroidery over that, sometimes a second tunic—sleeveless or short-sleeved so that the first tunic is revealed—and finally a cloak, with women also wearing a maphorion. The cloak was parted at the shoulder for men or in the center for women to display the tunic(s) beneath, giving the effect of being draped in sumptuous fabric. Because fabric was a precious commodity, the more layers a person wore, the wealthier they appeared.

A typical example of elite men's dress can be found in a seventh-century image of Agios Demetrios, patron saint of children, standing with two boys, in the church dedicated to him in Thessaloníki, Greece. He wears a tunic with ornamentation at the shoulder and cuff, beneath a cloak of brocaded fabric with an embroidered panel. A golden fibula and matching belt, used to secure his tunic, are also visible. Finally, he wears shoes, white with a dark blue toe. It is impossible to tell if these are boots or a more elegant shoe, but their decoration suggests a shoe that was more than simply utilitarian.

The procession of virgins at Sant'Apollinare Nuovo in Ravenna, Italy, from around 500, while not portraits of specific women, is a good indicator of Early Byzantine dress for elite females. They each wear several layers, all richly decorated. A long tunic with embroidered stripes is displayed beneath a short-sleeved overtunic cut on a bias to show the longer undertunic. The outer tunic is encrusted with jewels at the collar and hem, and each woman also wears a gemmed belt. Their hair is pulled up in a chignon on top of the head, encircled with more jewels, and covered with a diaphanous veil that falls to the center of the back. Each woman also wears another mantle, draped over one shoulder, which she uses to carry crowns to Christ in the apse (symbolizing the holy nature of the event, the women do not touch the crowns directly with their hands); these mantles are white with embroidered designs near the hem with a beautiful fringe. Their outfits are completed with red silken slippers.

These images of elites demonstrate the importance of layering and using a variety of patterns and ornament. Unlike today's fashions, there was no sense of wearing fabrics that coordinated in terms of color of pattern; rather, the more ornamented the better. Thus, they tended to use ornate techniques, such as brocaded weaves and embroidered panels. It is possible to further imagine that the layers worn and dense fabrics used were heavy and that weight was part of the virtue of a particular outfit.

Nonelite Dress

It is extremely difficult to determine what the average Byzantine wore, as most were not wealthy enough to have their portrait made for a church or manuscript illumination and their clothing was not fine enough for anyone to want to preserve it. Furthermore, Byzantine writers rarely bothered to describe farmers or other working-class laborers. The poor were usually described in hyperbolic terms—naked, wretched, or at least tattered—in a description of a pious saint or emperor helping the destitute soul.

Nevertheless, a few things can be culled from the sources to give us some idea. First, it seems that wool was the standard fabric for a poorer person; the exception may be Byzantine Egypt, where linen tunics are found in all sorts of graves, suggesting that linen may have been affordable at the source where it was made and wool less common in such a hot climate. Regardless of fabric, the clothing of nonelites was likely plain and undyed, as both ornament and color were expensive. Unlike elites, the common people probably wore fewer, if any, layers. Images also suggest a certain practicality in their dress; for example, tunics are tucked up into belts for ease of movement, and high boots, with a more protective function, are worn.

A fourth-century mosaic floor from North Africa depicts various scenes of country life and includes many nonelites herding animals, carrying loads, caring for children, and preparing food outdoors, among other activities. The men uniformly wear short tunics, excepting the two elite men pictured in the scene—on horseback and seated on a throne—who wear the longer tunics in layers. The women wear full-length tunics; probably for reasons of modesty and decorum, it is rare to see a woman depicted in a short tunic. Regardless of the gender of the wearer, the tunics are decorated merely with simple stripes or not at all. Each nonelite figure has only a single layer of clothing visible, perhaps because of the warm climate, but more likely as the artist's way of signifying their nonelite status. The two aristocratic men in the image notably wear multiple layers despite the weather. All of the footwear shown is simple, without ornament or extra fastening, usually in black or brown, suggesting they were made of leather.

At this point, it would be helpful to compare the images of these nonelites with a typical tunic from North Africa in a museum collection, as these are some of the few surviving examples of dress that can actually be compared to the artistic record. The Metropolitan Museum of Art has a typical fifth-century linen tunic found in Egypt. It measures 72 × 53 inches (183 × 135 cm). Its great width suggests that it was belted, and its length on most adults would be full length, so it was probably for an elite person rather than a nonelite. This is further supported by the fact that it is decorated with wool-embroidered stripes and medallions. Along the shoulders and around the neck are panels with images of Dionysiac figures—warriors bearing spears and dancers—surrounded by floral and animal imagery, awaiting the arrival of the god, which was a very popular motif on tunics of this period. The short sleeves have two bands of further, similar ornament, and the hem is trimmed with a band and two square panels, again with this same figural imagery. All of the embroidery is in black on a white background, and the tunic itself is undyed. Tunics of elites tend to survive in far greater numbers from burials, where this one was found, because archaeologists until recently would often throw out textiles that did not have tantalizing decoration on them. This find reinforces suppositions about the clothes of both elites and nonelites. It is easy to imagine this piece layered over another tunic and worn by an elite. This also helps formulate an image of the plainer tunic that was probably worn by nonelites.

In the fourth-century mosaic depicting several nonelites, it should also be noted that there are men wearing pants or leggings beneath their tunics. Pants were generally regarded as coming from "barbarians," the Roman term for any outsider. Byzantine writers make reference to pants as variously "Gothic" or "Hunnic," among other ethnic terms. In general, trousers were looked down upon in Byzantine society; the Theodosian Code even had laws to control the wearing of pants:

> Within the venerable City [Rome or Constantinople] no person shall be allowed to appropriate to himself the use of boots or trousers. But if any man should attempt to contravene this sanction, we command that in accordance with the sentence of the illustrious prefect, the offender shall be stripped of all his resources and delivered into perpetual exile.[6]

In part this was due to the xenophobic nature of the Byzantines, who disliked anything foreign, and in part it may also have been a class issue—that pants were worn for manual labor.

The danger of relying on this type of image to learn about nonelite dress is that this is a mosaic made for the floor of a house of a wealthy man, and the artist likely took license with several factors: he may have codified the clothing of the laborers to quickly point out their class in the image; he may have added stripes to their garments or the occasional splash of color to beautify the mosaic rather than to reflect actual clothing; he likely did not look at real models for these figures but instead relied on images of other artists for inspiration, as was common practice for painters and mosaicists. Thus it is impossible to say for sure that this is what nonelites wore. However, this is how Byzantines *perceived* nonelites and their dress; in other words, what is represented in this mosaic and similar images is a stereotype, which often has some basis in truth.

MIDDLE BYZANTINE DRESS

Many more images and texts describing clothing survive from the Middle Byzantine period than from the earlier era from which to study dress, allowing us to see a picture of Byzantine dress that, while not complete, is more comprehensive. During the Middle period, the Byzantine textile industry and fashion were at their height. A greater variety of fabrics are witnessed in images during this period, although the styles of garments remain similar. The major change in dress is seen in imperial attire, while tunics and cloaks remain the essential Byzantine garments for all others. It is also in this period that greater contact with Islam resulted in the introduction of many Eastern-influenced styles in the Empire, including, for example, turbans and caftans from Persia.

Imperial and Court Dress

In the Middle Byzantine period, of course, the emperor and empress wore special regalia that separated them from their courtiers, as was the case in the Early Byzantine era. However, it seems that the official imperial insignia were only actually worn once or twice a year, although they are pictured in nearly all official portraits of the imperial couple. The insignia were significantly less wearable than what was worn by Early Byzantine emperors and held the status of "crown jewels" instead—of great symbolic importance, but rarely worn. Therefore, it is more appropriate to consider imperial and courtly dress together, because more often than not, the emperor dressed like his courtiers, with just a few accessories—more ornament, special shoes, and a crown—to denote his imperial status.

The Loros

The official imperial insignia consisted of a *loros*, a long, leather stole encrusted with jewels, over a full-length tunic, known as a *divetesion*; a crown; and *tzangia*, red, jeweled, ankle-length booties. Both the emperor and empress wear this regalia, without gender distinction, a shift from the Early period. The empress's role was deemphasized in the first centuries of the Empire, so there was no need for her to wear official insignia. Furthermore, when Early Byzantine empresses did wear some insignia, they certainly would not have dressed like their husbands, as this was not appropriate. Theodora was the first empress to even approach this by donning the chlamys. While the Middle Byzantine empress still held almost no power, there was more of an emphasis on the procreation of a dynasty to succeed the emperor, and thus the empress became more important as the potential bearer of the next emperor. While the loros existed in the Early period and had originally been worn by Roman consuls, it did not become the official imperial insignia until the eighth century. Furthermore, while some emperors wore it in the Early period, empresses never wore it until Empress Irene (*R.* 797–802). Interestingly, Irene is the first empress to rule on her own, following her husband's death and her son's blinding while still in his minority, so it should come as no surprise that she chose to make coins depicting herself in the most important imperial garment, as a justification for her unusual position as sole female ruler.

Roman consuls wore the loros on January 1, when they kicked off their consulship with games in the hippodrome and a ceremonial distribution of largess, throwing coins and other goods to the courtiers beneath him. The distribution-of-largess ceremony was transformed in the Byzantine era to the day that courtiers were paid their salaries, which was Easter Sunday, also the most important date on the church calendar. The emperor and the empress, then, recalling this Roman use of the loros, wore the stole on Easter Sunday, as is illustrated in the imperial mosaic of Empress Zoe and Constantine IX Monomachos in the church of Hagia Sophia. This, it seems, was one of the only days during the year in which the loros was actually worn. On occasion, certain diplomatic visitors from other nations may have prompted the imperial couple to don the loros, but it was mostly relegated to being pictured in official portraits.

In the Hagia Sophia panel, the emperor and empress wear a jewel-studded loros, which (while we cannot see in this seated image) was extremely long, pulled over the head, going head to foot on both the back and front of the body. Another style of loros, more similar to the Roman original, was wound around the body, over the shoulders, and around the back, emerging across the abdomen to be carried over one arm. Both versions must have been extremely heavy, being made of leather and entirely covered with jewels. It was an estimated 12 feet (3.6 m) in length, too, which is probably another reason why it was not usually worn.

Crowns

Empress Zoe and Constantine IX Monomachos also wear crowns in this Hagia Sophia mosaic. Crowns seemed to have changed little since the Early Byzantine period, where there was already a great variety of styles. Crowns derived from the diadem remained the most typical crown type, which is worn by both Zoe and Constantine. Hers has triangular points rising off the top, which is seen only on the crowns of empresses, while Constantine's is straight across the top.

One of the few surviving elements of Byzantine imperial regalia is a crown of Leo VI (*R.* 886–912), which gives an idea of what Zoe and Constantine wore, at least in form. A gold band encircles the head with enameled medallions ringed with pearls and separated by precious stones. The medallions have portraits of apostles, in addition to one of Leo himself. Small rings around the ears must have once held prependoulia, strands of jewels. Because the crown has a portrait of the emperor, it may have been an honorific gift rather than a crown worn by Leo himself; still, its shape and decoration help us to imagine crowns worn by the emperor and empress.

In the twelfth century, there is an emergence of a closed crown, unrelated to the diadem. In some imperial portraits, crowns encircled the head with jewels, as did the crowns previously discussed, but covering the top of the head as well, like an upside-down, shallow bowl. The diadem still remained the crown depicted in coins and on seals, indicating its traditional status, but some portraits exhibit this closed crown. References to different-colored crowns in the sources might refer to the lining of these closed crowns.

Nikephoros III Botaneiates sits with his courtiers in an image from about 1071–1081 wearing a similar open crown to the imperial couple at Hagia Sophia, but, notably, not wearing the loros. There is no question that he is the emperor, not only because of his crown, more heavily ornamented chlamys, gold armbands, and luxurious shoes but also because he is larger in scale than those who flank him and he is enthroned. Nevertheless, he wears essentially the same garments as his courtiers—a chlamys over a long tunic, the divetesion—which was akin to a business suit for the Byzantines by this period.

The Chlamys and Tablia

In the figure to the right, all except the courtier directly to Nikephoros's right wear the chlamys. The courtiers pull theirs over both shoulders, while the emperor wears his slung over one shoulder. Their cloaks are decorated with tablia, the embroidered panels signifying

Nikephoros III Botaneiates and courtiers in the Homilies of John Chrysostom, c. 1071–81. © Giraudon / Art Resource, NY.

rank. The courtiers to his left notably have the same tablia surmounted on their red-and-gold chlamydes with a slightly different pattern. The identical tunics and hats suggest that they are of the same rank, and the inscription across the top of the image confirms that both of these men hold the title of *proedros*. All four courtiers wear unadorned, slipper-like shoes, distinguished from the jeweled, scarlet tzangia allowed only to those of imperial rank.

The courtier to Nikephoros's immediate right, who does not wear a chlamys, instead wears a long tunic with large roundels on it, a fabric type that stems from Persian and later Islamic designs. He also wears a distinct, black scarf. His title was *protovestiarios*, a high-ranking officer in charge of the imperial wardrobe, which perhaps accounts for his unusual dress.

Hats

Each courtier dons a hat, which appears to be of soft material. Hats are rarely mentioned in the Middle Byzantine sources, giving the impression that they were not worn often, but images like this suggest otherwise. It is likely that hats were such a common part of the insignia of courtiers that they were not mentioned separately: a typical description of a courtier would simply say that he wore his proper insignia, of which a hat may be a part. Many surviving images are religious images of obeisance, showing the courtier prostrate before Christ or the Virgin Mary, so it may have been improper to wear a hat in such an image, which would explain why so few are shown.

Women's Dress

As in the Early Byzantine period, with few exceptions women did not hold court titles in their own right but had the title of their husband. Furthermore, courtly women are rarely pictured, so it is difficult to discern what women at court wore. When they are depicted, as in the Theodora panel at Ravenna, the women do not appear to wear clothes implying any rank. Thus we may assume that they wore clothing similar to that of any elite female of the Empire. For women in Constantinople throughout much of the Middle Byzantine period, this outfit would consist of a long tunic, cloak, and maphorion. By the twelfth century, women began to wear dresses elsewhere in the Empire. There is some evidence that a few women at court began to wear these styles very late in the Middle Byzantine period.

Elite Dress

The dress of elites, for both men and women, has a greater variety across the Empire than anything seen to date. In part, this may be a misconception based on the surviving pictorial record compared with the Early Byzantine period: more extant portraits means that more styles are discernible. However, it is also true that expanded textile trade and greater access to neighboring cultures through those economic routes exposed Byzantine elites to a quantity of styles not seen in earlier periods. This trade also meant that the capital city of Constantinople was not the only or even the primary fashion center. In fact, Constantinople with its large population of courtiers tended to exhibit more traditional styles, many of which were prescribed as part of court ceremony. We find, rather, that elites outside of the capital wore fashions that break from tradition and prompted Byzantine writers to comment, sometimes negatively, on these differences in taste. For example, a military governor of Thessaloníki, Greece, the second-largest city in the Empire, was described as wearing

> a brocaded [garment] and sandals of the latest style. He covered his head in the Iberian manner, with a strange red covering. This was a barbarian custom (the barbarians have a special name to designate it), and it was made in this manner: it is formed of many folds which on the flounce fall with little regularity, while in the front it is sufficiently large to protect the face from the sun. Moreover, he did not assume the martial attitude, but he appeared in an effeminate manner in order to escape the rays of the sun.[7]

Here, the writer notes the new styles that the governor wears—the sandals and hat—and emphasizes that these fashions are imported. The "Iberian" hat, for example, comes from Georgia. As Thessaloníki was host to the largest annual textile fair in Europe, it is not surprising that the latest trends in dress would be known there. Finally, the author throws in an insult, calling the governor "effeminate," noting that he did not sit on his horse properly in the "martial attitude."

Byzantine writers are often very disparaging of so-called barbarian dress, that is, any clothing derived from outside the Greco-Roman tradition, the types of items typically worn in the capital. Most of the literary sources come from the capital city—historians of the court and the like. However, when a literary source such as a Romantic tale or story of a saint was written outside the capital, the writer did not often remark on the foreign origin of a particular garment, probably because it was not seen as different. Insulting someone's clothing was also a common Byzantine way of blackening their character, as clothing was so important to them. This above passage goes on to describe how this commander lost Thessaloníki to Norman occupation in 1185, and his being ill dressed, according to the author, is a perfect metaphor for his weakness as a military leader.

Dresses

Once these foreign styles became the norm, however, they eventually made their way to the capital city, and thereafter less attention was paid by writers in the capital to the apparent ethnicity of a particular garment, especially in the Late Byzantine period. Despite the slow reception of these fashions in the capital in the Middle Byzantine period, there are many examples of new styles in other fashion centers that, while they may be foreign derived, are not designated disparagingly as ethnic by the local elites who wore them.

Northern Greece, including Thessaloníki, is one such area. The Normans who briefly conquered the region in the 1180s brought with them dresses for women, with wide sleeves and fitted bodices, as distinct from the free-flowing tunics of earlier centuries. An example of such a dress can be seen in a family portrait in the church of Hagia Anargyroi, of the late twelfth century, in Kastoria, Greece. Here, Anna Radene stands with her husband and son wearing a red dress with a high neck and pointed sleeves with white cuffs, so long that they nearly touch the floor. Over this, she wears a deep purple cloak trimmed with gold fabric decorated in a lozenge design. A glimpse of the luxurious lining of the cloak, with a large pattern of leaves in roundels, is visible.

This dress, and others like it seen on female donor portraits in the area, is significant not only because it is a new style but also because it served to distinguish the dress of men from women far beyond anything that had been seen to date. In the medieval West, gender distinction was very important in dress, while in the Byzantine world it was less pronounced—both genders wore tunics and cloaks and did not wear anything that hugged the body to indicate the sex of the wearer. Dresses for women were, therefore, revolutionary. Likely Anna Radene and other elite women saw these styles during the Norman occupation and began to covet the dress of the powerful who dominated their region of the Empire.

Men's Dress

Men also wore styles derived from beyond Byzantium's borders. Northern Greece became heavily populated with Georgians and Armenians, beginning in the eighth century when many of them fled their homeland due to raids of the Arabs. This population was strong enough to establish Georgian monasteries and acquire substantial lands in the area, and thus it is not surprising that their fashions spread to this region as well. Many of the Georgians and Armenians who relocated to the Byzantine Empire had held princely titles in their homeland and were thus wealthy and powerful, bringing with them riches, including fine clothes. Some men wore a short-sleeved, belted caftan over a tunic, which is the typical garb of Georgian princes seen in Georgian churches of the same era. In the fresco with Anna Radene, her husband, Theodore Lemniotes, wears an open, long blue caftan with a pattern, now indiscernible, fastened at the chest over another blue tunic, and a small black, brown, and red cap. The hat appears to have been repainted, so it is difficult to tell much about how this originally looked. Armenian leaders are depicted on church images of donation wearing similar caftans and probably brought this style with them to the region.

Tiraz

Men wore embroidered armbands, known as *tiraz*, which were originally honorific symbols bestowed by the Islamic caliph to his subjects. Georgian and Armenian princes, who served as vassal leaders to the Abbasid caliphs in Baghdad, were given these tiraz, typically embroidered with the caliph's name and a blessing, along with special robes and turbans, all of which became badges of power and honor. Eventually, the elites started to mimic the wearing of these honorific tiraz, incorporating them into their own clothing for their prestige, although they no longer were markers of caliphal praise and were instead simply decorative.

Why the Georgians and Armenians influenced male dress and not the Normans, and why women picked up on Norman fashions and not Georgian or Armenian fashions, is impossible to say for sure. However, it is likely that the Byzantine elite in these areas were not associating these styles so directly with their ethnic origin; the styles were available and became popular with all elites of various backgrounds living in the area.

Turbans

Looking to another region of the Empire, locally influenced fashions, different from those in northern Greece, were being worn by elites in Cappadocia, an area in central Anatolia, Turkey. This region bordered Armenia, Georgia, and the Islamic caliphate, and Islamic styles, sometimes filtered through Armenia and Georgia, became very popular. Men and women both wore turbans, beginning as early as the ninth century. Turbans had many styles, but in a general sense were always made of cloth wrapped around the head, as opposed to a fitted cap or a hat with some sort of substructure that stiffened it.

Turbans in Islam were originally used to designate who was a Muslim and who was not in their newly conquered lands, but this distinction was long since gone by the ninth century. Turbans had become honorific and were bestowed by the caliph on subjects, sometimes Armenian and Georgian vassals, as a marker of subjugation. These turbans usually had embroidery with the caliph's name and were of a particular color, designated by the caliph. Turbans date back very far in the history of Middle Eastern dress and were worn by pre-Islamic Arabs, as well as Armenians, long before the rise of Islam, so they were worn by all levels of society in this region. To the Cappadocian, then, turbans were extremely common, worn by people of several nations and at varying levels of the social strata.

The Caftan

The staple of the Cappadocian wardrobe for both men and women was the *caftan*—a garment that was worn like a tunic but opened all the way down the front—instead of the tunic-and-cloak ensemble seen in the capital. Caftans were part of the Armenian and Georgian wardrobe, in addition to being common in Islamic lands. Cappadocia was a region in which horse breeding and riding were widespread, so it is no wonder that the caftan, a garment that could be easily worn astride a horse (because it opened), was more popular than the tunics, with no opening, worn by elites in Constantinople.

Elites in the Middle Byzantine period thus wore what was most fashionable in their particular region, so there were many different styles worn throughout the Empire. While courtiers and other elites in the capital tended to wear more traditional clothing, associated with the Roman past or the military elite, those in other regions wore clothes reflecting local influences—resettled populations of Normans or Georgians, for example, or powerful neighboring groups, such as the Abbasid Muslims or Armenians. Not coincidentally, these provincial areas tend to be situated on major textile trade routes: Northern Greece was home to the largest textile fair in Europe, and Cappadocia hosted the major thoroughfares for the famed Silk Road. Elites in these regions had greater access to fine textiles and garments.

Nonelite Dress

As during the Early Byzantine period, scholars are faced with similar problems in determining the dress of nonelites: the pictorial and literary record largely ignores all but the upper echelons of society, making it difficult for scholars to unearth what was worn by the poor and working classes. As in that period, it is safe to say that nonelite clothing was less adorned, worn in fewer layers, and often cut in shorter styles to accommodate the labor in which many nonelites were engaged. What does survive was often based on stereotypical, codified images of nonelites that decorate the background of important scenes in a manuscript or a description in the story of life of a famous saint. It can be assumed that the dress of nonelites likely did not change from the Early to the Middle period and that they did not follow the same changes in fashion the elites did, not having the means to buy or make such clothes. However, because more images and texts survive from the Middle period, we can at least expand our view of nonelite dress further than in the Early Byzantine period. The expanded pictorial evidence suggests some other types of clothing not seen in any early examples, such as the wearing of fur.

Various groups of nonelites are visible in the backgrounds of artworks. For example, soldiers, entertainers, servants, slaves, and even artists, none of whom made a substantial salary nor were considered to hold much status in Byzantine society, are often visible. Laborers such as farmers, vintners, shepherds, builders, and others can be found in numerous manuscript illuminations and, as in the Early Byzantine period, continue to be depicted wearing short tunics with boots, or sometimes sandals, with little or no adornment. A few significant literary mentions of short clothing, however, provide reason for caution before simply accepting this stereotypical outfit for nonelites. *The Book of the Eparch*, a book of economic regulations targeted primarily at the people of the capital, in a rule about the use of purple dye on cloaks, mentions that citizens of all classes wore short cloaks. *The Book of Ceremonies*, a text about court dress, used the term *paganos*, which likely referred to short clothing, to describe several tunics and cloaks. Conversely, there are the occasional glimpses of a nonelite wearing long, rather than short, tunics. For example, the *Cynegetica*, a manual on animals and hunting, shows several men, bird catchers and an ivory carver, for example, in longer styles despite the physicality of their task. It is likely that Byzantines of all classes wore both short and long tunics, with short tunics being more common for nonelites due to the types of occupations that they held.

Fur

Fur is shown being worn in Middle Byzantine images and probably denoted a country dweller who hunted as part of his livelihood. In modern times, we associate fur with wealth—and there were luxurious ermine furs mentioned in the imperial treasury—but fur is often seen depicted on men shown hunting or working with animals. Hunters are depicted in fur caps or garments, for example. These clothes are notably rather shapeless, and the fur is unkempt and looks more like a pelt than a finished piece of fur, befitting the lower status of the wearer.

Servant Uniforms

Servants, who were sometimes slaves, wore a uniform presumably supplied by their employers. In a twelfth-century illuminated manuscript telling the story of a foreign princess being brought to Constantinople to marry the emperor, one image depicts the newly crowned empress enthroned with six ladies-in-waiting wearing identical dresses and hats surrounding her. Because of the prestigious position of these particular servants in the empress's entourage, these women wear stunning clothes, but it nevertheless is clearly a uniform. However, a uniform, in the Byzantine sense, may not always have meant the exact same garment but simply dressing alike in some way, to inform others of their status. Descriptions of some Middle Byzantine court ceremonies mention servants lined up in the same color outfit, for example. Emperor Basil II took a diplomatic envoy to the palace of the Buwayid caliphate in 986 with a group of attendants noted as carrying identical swords and wearing the same girdles, and it is likely that this group had on individualized tunics and cloaks.

Outside of court, there is far less evidence for the dress of servants. One image in a *Book of Job*, from the late 11th century, depicts two servers rushing with plates of food to a banquet table, where the Biblical feast is meant to look as if it is set in a Byzantine aristocratic home; here the servants wear identical short tunics, suggesting that the practice of dressing one's servants in a uniform was common.

Soldiers

Soldiers are another group of nonelite citizens well represented in the Middle Byzantine evidence. However, while soldiers in the Roman and Early Byzantine periods wore simple armor—a *cuirass*, a leather top to protect against arrows, and a *ptergyes*, a fighting skirt also made of leather to protect the groin area, over protective leggings, with boots and a helmet—Byzantine soldiers by the Middle period often had to fend for themselves. Even career soldiers employed full-time by the army were not given uniforms or armed; unless they were of high rank, they procured their own weapons and their protective gear was makeshift. A soldier might simply wear multiple layers to create a protective skin against arrows. Some military treatises recommended garments, "at least a finger thick."[8] Thus when soldiers are depicted in art, as seen in numerous examples of soldiers executing saints in some calendars of saints' days (known as *menologia*), they wear short tunics, tucked up into belts, with leggings and knee-high boots. In the only instances where a soldier is shown in true armor, he is obviously of high rank, such as a cavalryman.

Entertainers

Byzantine entertainers held no celebrity status; society considered them to be low born and often associated performers with various types of immoral behavior. The love of entertainment is nevertheless evident, especially when examining the marginal illustrations of manuscripts, which are frequently adorned with acrobats, musicians, and dancers of all kinds. These entertainers, of course, wear costumes intended as part of their performance, so sometimes what is represented is showy or even eccentric.

Acrobats, wrestlers, and others who performed physical feats for entertainment wore very few clothes and are sometimes shown simply in loincloths. When they wore sleeveless shirts, they often also wore accessories that were secured to the body, such as skullcaps or choker neck rings. The occasional performer was even shown in the nude. Nudity was not typical in this Christian, conservative society, but it seems that some leeway was given to performers. One eleventh-century image shows two snake charmers playing their flutes in the nude for the mesmerized serpents. Perhaps the nudity added to the danger of the potential deadly bite from the snake.

Dancers are shown more covered, probably because dancing was done in circles or lines standing up and was probably not as physically demanding. Dancers are shown in short or long tunics, with heavy ornamentation to add to their glamorous appearance. Often dancers, especially female ones, are shown with long scarves, presumably an accessory used to emphasize the movement of the arms or torso spinning or floating about the body. Dancers also wore other accessories, too—typically headbands and jewelry—to enhance their ensemble.

Musicians generally are shown in long, patterned tunics and seem to always be male. In many cases, they wear hats; several musicians are shown in turbans, for example. More than other entertainers, their dress seems to draw on Islamic sources: turbans and caftans made of Persian/Islamic-looking fabrics. This connection is further made by the fact that, often, musicians are depicted seated with legs in a lotus or half-lotus position, which was typical of Islamic society. In the Byzantine world, those who were shown seated usually sat in chairs or thrones with their feet on the floor, although there is much evidence to show that people also sat on carpets on the floor much as they did in the Islamic world. Perhaps musicians added an exotic element to their songs by dressing in Islamic, or at least foreign-looking, dress.

Nonelites can hardly be characterized as one group, and therefore, of course, they did not dress alike, either. At least in art, the clothing of nonelites was appropriate to their occupation more than anything else, and thus clothing was used by artists as a code for a particular type—a farmer, dancer, hunter, or soldier. It is not possible to say for sure that the short tunic and boots of a laborer was what he always wore in reality—only, again, that this was the stereotype. As in the Early Byzantine, it is easy to imagine that their clothes were plainer than those of people with more money, but anything beyond this is speculative.

LATE BYZANTINE DRESS

The Late Byzantine period witnesses the influx of Western styles into the Empire and the continued influence of Islamic styles, but to a greater degree than in the Middle Byzantine period. The Empire itself was shrinking during this time, with much of its territory in Greece under Venetian control and the majority of its lands in the Middle East, North Africa, and eastern Turkey under Islamic rule. Furthermore, Crusaders had occupied Constantinople itself from 1204 to 1261 during the Fourth Crusade and brought Westerners and their clothing styles permanently to the capital. Despite these influences from beyond Byzantine borders, it is interesting to note that outsiders who describe the Byzantines increasingly remark on the oddity of their clothing—and by "odd," these historians, travelers, and diplomatic envoys mean "foreign." Especially items such as hats stood out to Westerners in their variety and difference from Western styles and were deemed "Greek" or "Oriental," even though their origins may have been otherwise.

A second trend that evolved in the Late Byzantine world was the division between men's and women's dress. During the Middle Byzantine period, women had distinguished themselves with headscarves, and in some parts of the Empire women wore dresses, but for the most part, clothing was not greatly differentiated by the wearer's gender. It was not until the Late Byzantine period that the emperor and empress, for instance, began to wear distinct styles, and courtiers followed suit. Gender-distinct styles continued to spread among elites, who always took the lead in fashion.

A final, more general development occurred in the Late Byzantine period with the emergence of ecclesiastical-inspired garments making their way into lay styles, and vice versa. Elements of sacerdotal dress and imperial dress, in particular, crossed over. In part, this may be due to the growing fluidity between lay and monastic communities; in the Late Byzantine period, it became very common for aristocrats to join monasteries for retirement or with their families, once their children were grown. Their wardrobes and other personal possessions were donated when they joined the community. Monasteries were also typical locales for imperial charity, including many donations of textiles and dress, which were reused and remade into ecclesiastical textiles and vestments.

Imperial Dress

Diadema (Loros)

The greatest change in imperial dress of the Late Byzantine period was in the use of the loros, which continued to appear in imperial portraits. However, the term *loros* falls out of use and is instead replaced by the word *diadema* in prescriptive texts on court ceremony. A diadema was a military belt, and one scholar has suggested that the former loros was simplified in the Late Byzantine period and sewn onto the tunic beneath it to create a stole/belt that was no longer a separate and cumbersome garment. It is impossible to tell for sure if the garment has changed since the Middle Byzantine period or if it was a change in name only. There is no direct evidence that it was sewn on and perhaps the use of the term *diadema* connoted a military connection at a time when the Empire was shrinking and needed to appear strong militarily.

Footwear: Tzangia

Emperors are still shown wearing the *tzangia*, the red imperial footwear, along with the long tunic and crown, as they wore in the Middle Byzantine period. However, with the exception of the shoes, these items had evolved since that time.

Sakkos

The long tunic is nearly always dark purple, blue, or black in the Late Byzantine period. This tunic is known as a *sakkos*, which replaced a similar tunic called a divetesion. This was also long and made of silk but varied in color and pattern. The dark color became fashionable in later centuries, not only in the Byzantine Empire but across the West as well. Dark saturated colors were more expensive, because they required the most dyestuffs to make. Black became the most prestigious color because a true black, as opposed to a very dark brown or purple, was very difficult to achieve. The word *sakkos* was also used to describe a short-sleeved vestment worn by patriarchs, and sometimes also by metropolitans and bishops;

this usage of the same word for the garment worn by the highest officials in both the ecclesiastical and state realms was typical of the Late Byzantine crossover in dress (which will be discussed in the section on ecclesiastical garments).

Crowns

The crown of Manuel II Palaiologos is bulbous, tall, and solid like a hat rather than a headband. This closed crown, seen already in the late twelfth century, became the main crown of Late Byzantine emperors and was commonly used on coins and other significant effigies. It not only was larger than the first examples seen in the twelfth century, but also was usually surmounted by a jewel or sometimes a cross, making it appear even grander.

The diadem crown did not completely disappear, however. As in earlier periods, Byzantine emperors and empresses continued to own and wear many types of crowns. In one portrait, Manuel's youngest child dons a diadem, while the older children appear to wear closed crowns. The oldest child, the heir apparent, not only wears the identical crown to his father, but his entire imperial ensemble is the same as well.

Insignia

In Late Byzantine imperial portraits, the emperor often carries additional insignia not seen as frequently in the Middle Byzantine period, as Manuel II Palaiologos does in one of his portraits. In one hand, he carries an *akakia*, a small pouch containing dust to remind the emperor of his own mortality. In his other hand, the emperor carries a scepter, in this case mounted with a cross, although examples with eagles on top exist as well. His tunic is decorated with jeweled and embroidered armbands. These are obviously descendants of the tiraz worn by the fashionable elite of the Middle Byzantine period. The sources do not mention them as part of his official insignia, although they are commonly depicted, so they probably became a staple accessory for luxurious tunics, imperial and otherwise, and were loosely associated with power and prestige; presumably Byzantine authors found them unworthy of separately naming them.

The empress of Manuel II Palaiologos, Helen Dragas, wears the loros/diadema and crown insignia of the Middle Byzantine empresses, but instead of a divetesion of previous centuries or the sakkos worn by the emperor, she wears a red dress with exceptionally long, pointed cuffs. This style of dress was already worn by elites beginning in the twelfth century, as was shown on Anna Radene in the portrait in the Kastorian church discussed earlier, and was brought from the West. A few Byzantine empresses of Western origins wore dresses like this one as early as the twelfth century. By the early fifteenth century, however, dresses were common for women of all ranks, and this style was fully incorporated into imperial and courtly dress for women, regardless of nationality.

It should be noted that most of the empresses by this time came from Western kingdoms and were not Greek; as the power of the Empire waned, the emperors sought to make alliances through diplomatic marriages. Many Italian and some French, German, Serbian, and Bulgarian women married into the Byzantine Palaiologan family, the last major ruling dynasty of the Empire. These Western-style dresses reflect this, but the style was probably no longer associated with a specifically Western locale as it once had been.

The empress carries a scepter like the emperor. Hers is studded with pearls at the top. She also wears a closed crown, though hers is angular rather than bulbous, a shape reserved for females. Her dress, like the emperor's sakkos, is adorned with decorative armbands, making an interesting blend of Eastern and Western symbols of power in her ensemble.

The wearing of a dress and differing crown by the empress, seen in this and other imperial portraits, served to distinguish the empress from the emperor. This is a departure from Middle Byzantine imperial dress, where often it was difficult to tell the imperial couple apart in images. This may be seen as an influence from surrounding kingdoms, where gendered clothing was more common. In addition, the empress's power was falling off from its zenith in the Middle Byzantine period, which had witnessed the few examples of women ruling in their own right, as well as a great number of women ruling as regents for their sons. In the Late Empire, emperors ruled for shorter and shorter periods, and their children were less likely to succeed them, making the concept of a dynasty practically nonexistent—and thus the power of the empress disappeared. Her dress reflected this and did not match her husband's, although it still clearly connoted her rank.

Male Courtiers

Male courtiers acquired a new staple garment in the Late Byzantine period that, like the dresses of women, had appeared already in the fashions of elites in the Middle era. The caftan, or *kabbadion* as it came to be called in Greek, replaced the ubiquitous chlamys overtunic of earlier centuries for official dress. Theodore Metochites, a Constantinopolitan bureaucrat, wears an example with wide sleeves and a belt in his portrait in the Chora Monastery of 1315–1321. It is made of a brocaded fabric with a pattern of two types of leaves, trimmed with further ornament at the cuffs, hem, neck, and along the front opening. Notably, he accompanies this Eastern style of dress with a turban, striped and voluminous, also typically Eastern. The turban by the Late Byzantine period had made its way to Constantinople from fashionable elites in the provinces and had become part of the insignia of many courtiers. The caftan is depicted in different styles throughout the Empire by this time, short- or long-sleeved, tight or loose at the cuff. The length was almost always to the ankle, but some three-quarter-length versions existed as well. A belt was worn with it in almost all cases.

Cloaks

Cloaks, which were so important in the Middle Byzantine period, seem to have disappeared from court dress. As a caftan was now often worn over a tunic, perhaps an additional layer was impractical. At the very least, it was certainly easier to wear. One put a caftan on like a robe rather than pulling it over the head, and unlike a cloak, it had sleeves that allowed for greater freedom of movement. Furthermore, there was less desire in the Late Byzantine court to reference military dress, of which cloaks were a major part.

Hats

As mentioned earlier, Theodore Metochites dons a large turban in his portrait in the Chora Monastery. There is a virtual explosion in hat wearing in the Late

Byzantine period, if the pictorial record is good evidence. Turbans, structured hats with brims, soft caps, bulbous and pillbox-shaped hats that are worn high off the head all are represented in the visual evidence of the Late Empire. There is little doubt that the custom of covering one's head was important for both genders throughout the Byzantine ages, yet it is not until the Late period that artists began to depict so many varieties of hats for both on men and women. According to Pseudo-Kodinos, who wrote about the dress of courtiers in the fourteenth century, hats became specified for particular ranks at court. Women often followed suit with elaborate hats of their own, although veils still predominated for women.

While some terms for hats survive in the sources—most typically *skiadion* and *skaronikon*—these terms cannot be linked with the pictorial representations to know what these specific hats looked like. A few literary descriptions suggest that the skiadion was striped and angular in shape. Writers mention that the skaronikon was bulbous, and some are described as having an imperial portrait embroidered on them. These descriptions, however, are not uniform, making it difficult to ascertain if all versions of the hat looked like this or not.

Footwear

Like hats, shoes were important for distinguishing courtiers from one another. The imperial tzangia have already been discussed. In the Late Byzantine Empire, it seems that the color of one's shoes was a crucial part of insignia: red and white for the *despotes*, blue and red with eagles for the *sebastokrator*, blue for the *caesar*, green for the *protovestiarios*, yellow for the *panhypersebastos*, and so on. Unfortunately, no shoes survive, nor can we ever see anything but the tips of the toes in the pictorial record. While Pseudo-Kodinos lists the particular shoe color appropriate for each courtier, the color and shoe style does not seem to have been fixed, as other writers mention different shoes for the same courtier. The only thing that is certain is that the color became important. Another literary source suggests that pointy-toed shoes became extremely popular in this period. This would be aligned with Western styles, which is not surprising, as so many styles from foreign courts seem to have permeated the formerly traditional dress of the Byzantine court.

Elite Dress

Many more portraits survive from the Late Byzantine period than from earlier periods. The increase in portraiture is, in part, due to accidents of survival. In addition, however, the Byzantine elite became increasingly interested in commissioning works of art (in and for private churches) and creating manuscripts, both of which would typically contain a portrait of the patron. These portraits reflect what was already seen in the dress worn by courtiers, with a great variety of hats and foreign-inspired dress. Furthermore, the same types of garments—dresses for women and caftans for men—are seen as well.

Because elites lived throughout the Empire, there are noticeable geographically inspired style trends, as was seen in the Middle Byzantine period. In southern Greece, for example, there are more Western-inspired styles from the Venetians and Franks, who brought with them Western styles of dress mimicked by the Byzantine elites that colonized much of this area. In the northern parts of the Empire, Slavic (Bulgarian, Serbian, and Rus') styles influenced the locals. Finally, Seljuk Turks, Armenians, Georgians, and, eventually, Ottoman Turks influenced the clothing of those living near the Empire's eastern borders.

While the caftan is the staple of the Byzantine elite male wardrobe, it is worn differently depending on the location of the wearer. For example, a donor named George in a thirteenth-century Cappadocian church wears a short-sleeved caftan, which is belted over a long- and tight-sleeved tunic. He also wears a turban, befitting the Georgian influence in that area. Conversely, at the church of Pantanassa, in Mistra, Greece, a funerary portrait of a man depicts him wearing a wide-sleeved version with a pointed, brimmed hat denoting Western influence.

With female portraits, we find similar variances based on the locale of the wearer. Tamar, the wife of George in the thirteenth-century Cappadocian church, wears a dress with tight sleeves beneath an outer cloak, and a small turban or cloth cap, again in the Georgian styles. In the western provinces, women tended to wear embroidered veils down over the shoulders instead with their dresses.

Nonelite Dress

Nonelites are pictured and discussed even less often in the Late Byzantine period than in the Middle period. Greater interest in forms of art that generally do not have detailed backgrounds where nonelites might be found and fewer surviving examples of historical manuscripts, where we get the chance look at the lower classes, contribute to this. From the extant evidence, there is a visible trend showing that the styles of the court officials trickled down to the nonelites.

The short tunic for the workingman still prevailed, with generally undecorated simple styles for both men and women. Leggings with utilitarian shoes or boots were worn beneath the tunics. Interestingly, however, many more hats are represented on nonelites than in previous periods. This may be associated with increased wealth, because it is a less than necessary accessory. The hats, of course, are smaller than the very showy hats of the elites and courtiers. Those seen on men might be more properly termed "caps" and often had small points, with the occasional decorative stripe up the middle. The hats worn by women appear to have been simple turbans.

Dresses

One style seen on elites that does not enter the pictorial record for nonelites is the dress for women. Women still appear to wear long, shapeless tunics. One reason for this could be expense. A dress is distinguished from a tunic in the amount of tailoring: bodices or sleeves are fitted in some way; a waistline is evident; necklines are shaped and not mere holes for the head. All of these additions required sewing that was more complicated and therefore more expensive than the simple tunic, thus likely out of financial reach for many nonelite women.

Soldiers

Soldiers should be briefly mentioned in any discussion of Late Byzantine non-elites, even though the standing army shrank dramatically in this period. Most soldiers were not career military men in the Late period but rather were farmers and other peasants called upon by their wealthy landowners in times of strife, of which the Late Byzantine period had plenty. Due to soldiers' even lower status than in the Middle period, only the extremely high-ranking cavalryman or general had body armor—which, when present, notably copied Western and Turkish advancements in armor at this time. Foot soldiers continued to procure their own clothes as they had in the Middle Byzantine era and instead wore thick clothes, treated with mixtures of wine and salt to stiffen the cloth against arrows. The visual record demonstrates that shields imitated Western shapes now and were triangular rather than circular, and with the great number of Crusaders within the borders of the Empire this is to be expected. Archaeological finds indicate almost no usage of chain mail, gauntlets, or greaves so common in the West. These would have been likely to survive due to the metal content, so it suggests that the Byzantine army was simply too poor to provide these styles of armor, and soldiers could not pay for these items themselves.

Entertainers, Servants, and Laborers

The other groups of nonelites discussed in the Middle Byzantine period were hardly depicted in the Late period, which makes it difficult to say anything about entertainers or servants, for example. In the Late Byzantine period, religious scenes more often show servants, laborers, and the like in purposefully archaized dress meant to conjure up biblical times. While this had been done in other periods as well, it is more widespread in the Late Byzantine period, making it harder to find an accurate pictorial record for nonelites. It is likely that their clothing changed far less than the fashion of more elite groups, however. Yet, if the introduction of hats is any indication, some styles of elites influenced nonelites.

ECCLESIASTICAL DRESS

The dress of clerics and monastics in Byzantine society is somewhat easier to parse than the variety of clothing worn by the fashionable laypeople. The clothing of clerics was ceremonial and prescribed and did not change based on location within the empire or the wealth of a particular church. There are five offices that composed the major offices of the Orthodox church: deacon, priest, bishop, metropolitan, and patriarch. While other offices existed in the church, for example, subdeacons, their dress deviated only slightly from the hierarchy set out by the major offices. In addition, nuns and monks in monastic societies had their own style of clothing.

As with lay dress, the Middle Byzantine period is when ecclesiastical dress became canonized, so to speak, and little changed through the period once the official vestments were set, after the period of iconoclasm in the eighth century. Ecclesiastical dress is by nature conservative, so change was less likely to take place, as clerics were presumably less susceptible to the desires that drove changes in the fashions of the general population. Ecclesiastical dress was also cared for differently than lay dress. It was stored when not in use and worn only for weekly or sometimes annual rites, so the vestments tended to be reused for longer periods of time and, in a few cases, have survived, which is not the case with lay dress.

While a relatively slow rate of change in dress when compared with the laity occurs in Byzantine ecclesiastical vestments, it seems clear that a number of changes did take place beginning in the twelfth and thirteenth centuries. Most of the changes affected the dress of the higher offices, from the bishop on up, and involved the ornamentation of already established garments or the addition of embroidered ornamentation to the insignia. Crosses and other types of embroidery were added to garments, and embroidered accessories in their own right were added to the entire ensemble. These changes coincided with the increasing contact with the Latin rite by the Byzantines, and this was certainly no accident. The Latin and Orthodox rites were directly competing against one another and the drama of the liturgy was one battleground for hearts of the laity. Many churches were actually transformed into Latin churches for a period, only sometimes to be converted into Orthodox churches again, so the influence on sacred vestments is significant in the Late Empire.

Byzantine ecclesiastical vestments are outlined below, noting changes that took place between over the history of the Empire.

Deacons

A deacon wore a *sticharion*, a wide, unbelted tunic that was most often made of linen, although the use of silk became more popular in the Late period. It was typically white, but other colors were not unheard of, with two vertical stripes down the front. All vestments were worn over an undertunic and the sticharion is no exception; the undertunic itself is not strictly ecclesiastical and was probably the same type of garment that a layperson wore under his or her outer tunic. The deacon also wore a stole, an *orarion*, which was the unique insignia of his office. It was worn over one shoulder for most of the service, then wrapped around the body and brought over the shoulders at the close of the rite.

Priests

A priest also wore a sticharion, as did the bishops. Theirs was typically plain, however, as they had other accessories to distinguish them. The sticharion of a priest was not cut as widely as the deacon's and had tight sleeves instead. In the Late Byzantine period, the priest added a girdle, known as a *zone*, over his sticharion; it was flat and encircled the hips, usually fastening in back, and contained a cross (or other ornament) in the front center. This was an example of a Latin vestment—derived from a Latin monastic cincture—that was added to the Byzantine repertoire after the Latin occupation, following the Fourth Crusade.

Like the deacon's orarion, the priestly stole—the *epitrachelion*—was the distinguishing mark of his office. It began as a long thin stole, similar to the deacon's, and was worn around the neck with fringed ends. In the Late Empire, the two ends were joined, sometimes with buttons rather than being sewn along their edges. This stole was always embroidered, but it is difficult to know what iconographical program was typical, as it is not visible in images.

An outer *chasuble*, known as a *phelonion*, covered much of what the priest wore. The phelonion was plain and, according to literary descriptions, was a very large garment that was often moved during the service by assistants to free the hands of celebrant.

In the Late Byzantine period, *epimanikia*, or embroidered cuffs, were added to the priestly vestments. In some cases, deacons even began to wear these. The priest's sticharion was tight at the sleeves, so the epimanikia would have been worn easily with this. The deacon's sticharion, on the other hand was wide, and thus the cuffs must not have been attached to it.

Bishops

The bishop's garments were notably more decorated than the priest's or deacon's, although the elements of the outfit remained the same. He wore a sticharion, belted with a *zone* and accented with epimanikia. Additionally, beginning in the twelfth century, bishops could further ornament their vestments with various types of embroidery, such as *potamoi* (red or purple stripes on the body and sleeves), *gammadia* (shaped like the Greek letter *gamma*), and *trigonia* (patches of embroidery affixed to the garment).

The bishop also wore the embroidered epitrachelion stole, probably more decorated than the priestly version from what surviving examples tell us. The epitrachelion was usually adorned with portraits of Christ around the neck, surrounded by the Virgin Mary and St. John the Baptist, with other saints and apostles below. Over this, they wore a phelonion in a variety of solid colors that was virtually indistinguishable from that of a priest.

Many epitrachelia survive, allowing us to see what was typical. For example, Metropolitan Photios (*R.* 1408–1431), when he was a bishop in the late fourteenth or early fifteenth century, is thought to have owned and worn a particularly rich example of an epitrachelion that is today housed in the Kremlin. This stole is more than 60 inches (150 cm) long and about 13 inches (33 cm) wide and is made of silk. It is embroidered with silver-gilt and colored thread but also luxuriously adorned with pearls and small gilt metal plaques. Christ is pictured in a bust portrait on the neck with two full-length images of the Virgin and St. John on the fronts of the shoulders. An additional eighty-eight portraits, in small medallions of saints, form two vertical stripes on each arm of the stole. The stole was buttoned up the center with gold buttons, and the bottom was hemmed with red tassels.

A second stole, the *omophorion*, distinguished the bishop's vestments from that of the priest's. It was worn wrapped over the shoulders and tossed over the left side. The omophorion was decorated with crosses and was typically made of silk.

The epimanikia of the bishop were heavily embroidered, often with figural decoration. These were worn affixed to the cuffs of the sticharion. The bishop wore yet another piece of embroidery: the *encheiron*, a stiff, embroidered kerchief tucked into the *zone*. The *epigonation*, a slightly larger but similar swath of embroidery, began to replace the encheiron in the twelfth century, although we see the encheiron in use until the fourteenth century. In either case, they were decorated with elaborate figural imagery and tucked into the belt.

Metropolitans and Patriarchs

A metropolitan distinguished himself from the bishops by wearing a *polystaurion*, beginning in the eleventh century. This is the same garment as the phelonion but decorated all over with black or dark-colored crosses and gamma shapes on a white background. This garment was also worn by the patriarch. The patriarch, however, wore the polystaurion over a sakkos, the vestment used to distinguish the highest office in the Orthodox Church, rather than over the sticharion. The sakkos should be distinguished from the imperial vestment, although both are T-shaped, because of its short sleeves. It is not clear from where exactly the ecclesiastical sakkos evolved, as it has no Latin ancestor and is unrelated in shape to other Byzantine sacerdotal garments. Given that it is the only T-shaped article of clothing of all of the Byzantine vestments, which were usually circular cuts, it seems likely that it was at least inspired by the imperial garment.

An actual sakkos survives in the treasury of the Vatican and is attributed to fourteenth-century Constantinople or Thessaloníki, Greece. It is $63^3/_4 \times 56^3/_4$ inches (162×144 cm) of embroidered blue silk, containing silver, silver-gilt, and colored threads. The scenes on this garment are splendid, befitting a patriarch or metropolitan. Metropolitans also wore the sakkos rather than the sticharion but generally with less embroidery. The front depicts a large medallion of Christ Emmanuel on a rainbow surrounded by angels and saints. The short sleeves show the communion of the apostles. The back of the sakkos illustrates the transfiguration of Christ on Mt. Tabor. The background of the entire garment is dotted with small crosses and hemmed with an embroidered vine that scrolls around other crosses. This and other surviving ecclesiastical garments demonstrate the theater of the Orthodox rite, which must have been spectacular to see with these resplendent vestments.

Ecclesiastical Headgear

One element of clerical vestments that has not been addressed is headgear. The picture is very murky here, and it seems that most hats, miters, and caps of other sorts were probably not worn in the Middle Byzantine period at all, and if they were worn in the Late period, only as late probably as the fourteenth century. The miter may have been worn by patriarchs but certainly not by lower offices until well after the Byzantine Empire had fallen. The few known miters of patriarchs from literary sources did not arrive until the fourteenth century and had portraits of Christ flanked by angels embroidered on their centers. It has been suggested that, like the sakkos, the miter may have been derived from the hats of high-ranking officials, such as the skaronikon, which was sometimes described as having imperial portraits flanked by angels and also had a high, bulbous shape according to some descriptions. Bishops and other higher clergy may also have worn embroidered hats, but these were a version of a monastic cap, a *koukoulion*.

Monastics

The dress of monks and nuns follows a completely different trajectory from the Byzantine ecclesiastical vestments of clerics because they did not tend to be influenced by Western monasticism, which was notably not imported into the Empire in the way that the Latin rite was. First, monks and nuns dressed very modestly, usually in colors and garment types prescribed by the monastery, but did not wear a uniform that would identify their monastery as was seen in the West. Byzantine monasteries did not ascribe to particular orders (Benedictines, Franciscans, Cistercians, and the like). Rather, individual monasteries and nunneries created their own sets of rules, many of which followed great church fathers such as Basil the Great. A rule per se, such as the Benedictine rule, was not followed. Their dress, then, was usually dictated only in a loose sense.

Monks and nuns dressed modestly, wearing plain, often undyed clothing; such garments would generally appear to be off-white or tan. Their clothing was also sometimes in a somber darker color, a brown of some sort. Both men and women covered their heads. Women wore veils, the *maphoria*, while men wore caps, or koukoulia. The fabrics worn by monastics were naturally rougher than those worn by laity or clergy, usually in wool, coarse linen, or, in extreme cases, scratchy goat-hair, as was dictated by the modest way of life of a monk or nun.

Monastics also owned very few garments. Most charters for monasteries note that monastics were allowed one outfit for cold weather and one for warm weather. These garments were replaced only every year or two. As previously mentioned, many laypeople, especially aristocracy and even emperors and empresses, joined monasteries late in their lives as a way of retiring. Theodore Metochites, whose portrait was examined earlier in a discussion of Late Byzantine courtly dress, is an example of such a person. Significantly, he paid to have his picture put into the monastery, the Chora Monastery in Constantinople, where he retired. He was not wearing monastic garb but the clothing of his courtly office, which was far more beautiful for a mosaic. These aristocratic men and women, who wore rich silks and soft linens in bright colors their entire lives, hardly renounced their sumptuous garments at the moment of joining the monastery. Thus, many monastics were given a little freedom in what they wore; some monastic charters even insisted on it in the rules, probably written personally by an aristocrat at the time a donation was made. It is likely that only those who were of the lower classes and who were lifelong monks or nuns wore the modest garb that is associated with the monastery.

THE CLOTHING INDUSTRY

Cloth and, by extension, clothing were either made within the borders of the Empire or imported, almost always from the East. There were three types of fiber primarily used by the Byzantines: wool, silk, and linen. Wool could be produced anywhere in Europe, although the best wools came from the British Isles, but there is no evidence that the Byzantines imported wool.

All silk was imported from China and Central Asia until the sixth century, after which the Byzantines figured out how to cultivate the larval moths, whose cocoons were unraveled into silk thread. From then on, the Byzantines produced their own silk, although they also still apparently imported beautiful silks from Asia. Silk production seems to have been concentrated in two places: southern Greece and Syria. Both were places where mulberry trees (on which the moths fed) could be easily grown. There is also some evidence for moriculture, the cultivation of mulberry trees, in Italy. By the seventh century, the Byzantines had established imperial silk-making workshops, which produced all sorts of fabrics and garments. These workshops were built in Constantinople.

Linen was a product of Egypt, which was under Byzantine control until the eighth century. Flax, from which linen is made, could be easily grown in the wet delta region of the Nile River. After the eighth century, most linen had to be imported from Islamic Egypt, but this does not seem to have affected the supply.

Cotton was imported into the Empire in a few instances in the Late Byzantine period, but it was largely a product of South Asia and did not make its way into Europe until later. Fur was also worn from time to time, and not only by laborers trying to keep warm. Country dwellers used fur from a variety of animals, but it is ermine, with its white fur and black spots, and miniver, in light gray, that were the most prized furs. These were stored in the imperial treasuries and are described in many Byzantine sources.

After the thread, of whatever type, was spun, it had to be dyed and woven. Most of the dye experts were located in southern Greece, where there is also evidence for weaving workshops. The dyes came from many parts of the Empire: indigo (blue) from the Middle East, saffron (yellow) from Anatolia and Greece, kermes (an insect that produces red) from the eastern Mediterranean, greens from any number of plants, and murex (a purple from crushed mollusk shells) from Greece. The dye centers were located by the sea so they were close to the salt water they needed to set dyes into fabric. Silk held dye the best, and so was often the brightest, most intensely colored, followed by linen and then wool. Weaving was done in many centers throughout the Empire, most notably in southern Greece, around Constantinople, and in Syria.

Once cloth was made, tailors bought it at trade fairs and made it into clothing and other textile goods. All locales had weekly markets where cloth could be purchased either by professional tailors or domestic sewers. Larger markets containing imported as well as locally made goods existed along the major trade routes that traversed the Empire. One had to be licensed to buy and sell at these types of fairs.

While we speak of the famed Silk Road, it was neither a single road nor only for silk. It in fact comprised several routes crisscrossing the Empire from east to west and carried goods of all kinds, not just silk. Silk was the most sought after and precious commodity traded, but all types of textiles and even ready-made clothes were bought and sold along the Silk Road.

This brief overview of the textile industry might suggest that everyone bought his or her tailor-made clothes from this system, but this is not the case. Textiles were also often woven in the home and the clothing itself made at home. There was also a vibrant secondhand clothing market to buy used garments. For the poorest in society, monasteries and churches provided clothing, which was one of the most common items of charitable donation to the poor in the Empire.

Weaving was commonly done in the home, where it was typical to own at least one small loom. Domestic looms were usually vertical looms or small horizontal pit-looms, sometimes with treadles to ease the process of lifting the sheds, which lifted the warp threads so that the weft threads could be passed through to create the design of the cloth. By contrast, the looms of professional weavers were large horizontal looms, operated not only with the help of treadles but also often with an assistant who helped to keep the many colors of the weft design organized. Women of all classes wove in the home, whereas professional weavers were usually men.

Women could also sew clothing from ready-made cloth. Clothes made in the home, even those woven from scratch, were less expensive than items purchased from a tailor. It seems that some clothing was made at home in all levels of society, suggesting the expense of buying garments prohibited many people from buying it.

As previously mentioned, wills and trousseau lists provide a great deal of evidence for the passing on of clothing through the generations. These types of documents also suggest that it was common for wealthier people to leave clothes to their slaves, servants, and freedmen. Presumably many of these inherited garments were recut to fit the new wearer, which would have been done at home and not likely brought to a tailor.

For those who bought clothes, the question becomes how much did they cost and what could one afford. The *Book of Ceremonies* notes that silk tunics cost around twelve *nomismata* (a basic gold coin) and an eleventh-century sources states that a *skaramangion*, a richly embroidered garment with gold thread, was worth twenty nomismata. Marriage contracts of middle-class Jews in the eleventh century show that an embroidered dress cost two gold pieces and two women's dresses were worth one gold piece. Presumably the less expensive dresses were plain, giving a closer approximation of the value of something owned by an ordinary Byzantine.

When these prices are compared with what little we know of wages in the Byzantine Empire, it is clear that even the least expensive garments were beyond the means of the middle and lower classes. For example, a seventh-century merchant in Constantinople made a mere fifteen nomismata annually, putting clothes out of reach because his limited income would have been needed for food and shelter for a family. Builders in Egypt in the eighth century made similar salaries. An examination of wills in the Late Byzantine period demonstrates that in the average middle-class household, the deceased typically left two or three garments to his or her heirs, worth two to six *hyperpyra* each. A twelfth-century servant in Constantinople made only a little more than six hyperpyra, making it impossible for him to purchase such a garment that was worth his annual salary.

This unscientific economic analysis shows a disparity between the cost of clothing and the amount of money that people had to spend on clothes. Clothing had to be prohibitively expensive for many, and therefore the working class must have traded goods and services for clothing, made their own, or obtained secondhand clothing. The sources, however, do not discuss secondhand markets or clothing made in the home, so this must remain speculative.

CONCLUSION

It is difficult to characterize the dress of a people whose Empire lasted for more than 1,200 years and spanned across three continents at its height. In fact, the question should be asked, Is there such a thing as a Byzantine style of dress? The answer is yes; some of the trends discussed can rightly be used to point out some distinctly Byzantine styles and notions about dress.

First, the obvious importance of dress to the Byzantines cannot be overstated—it was a high art form in the Empire, prompting books to be written about how to dress properly and allowing textiles to become the largest of any of the Byzantine economies.

Second, the Byzantines constructed their outfits thoughtfully, imbuing them with the meaning associated with particular garments. Byzantine clothing constantly refers to its origins—Roman, military, ecclesiastical—and to centers of power and cultures outside of the Empire, most notably Islam. Their clothing was thus eclectic, rather than homogenous and nationalistic, which distinguished it from other medieval European peoples. Despite the fact that much of the dress of Byzantines was multicultural, it was not derivative, as the reactions of foreigners to it suggests. Outsiders coveted what they perceived as Byzantine dress, which was notably exotic to them, but they did not see it as a mélange of copied styles from Byzantium's neighbors and neither did the Byzantines themselves. The conglomeration of sources for costume was used to create a sophisticated style of dress, drawing on the best weaving and construction techniques for the garments, that was in touch with cosmopolitan centers of fashion.

In their love of dress, the Byzantines also wore their clothes distinctively. While tunics and cloaks may have existed in other cultures, we find that the Byzantines layered their garments and ornamented them more than surrounding groups. The clothing they wore was brightly colored, and techniques such as embroidery, brocade, and damask were meant to emphasize an abundance of colors and decoration. The outfits of the rich must have been quite heavy and perhaps even hot to wear, but ease of wear is really a modern concept, not at all of interest to the medieval person. The Byzantines seem to have taken this to an extreme where fashion did overtake comfort.

The Byzantines were also modest, which may seem to contradict the seeming flamboyance of these heavily encrusted jeweled outfits seen in representations. Their religious feelings dictated, however, that they by and large be covered up. Thus surrounding cultures took up tighter-fitting clothing such as pants and dresses much earlier than did Byzantium. The body virtually disappears in the Byzantine world until very late in the Empire, so that only hands and face are consistently shown. Of course, Muslims in Islam and Christians in Western European cultures were modest as well, but it does not seem to have permeated their fashions to the degree that it did in Byzantium. In many parts of the Islamic empire, hotter climates would have prompted its citizens to wear fewer layers. In the kingdoms of the medieval West, it seems that modesty instead drove a more severe differentiation between the sexes than in Byzantium, which led to the rise of clothes that illustrated sexual difference.

Class difference was also extremely important to the Byzantines and was carefully demarcated with dress, certainly in depictions in art if not in reality. Again, surrounding cultures also had an interest in identifying people by class but developed other systems to do this. For example, in the medieval West, where patrimony was crucial to the workings of society, the system of heraldry developed whereby coats of arms were inscribed on clothing and other objects to denote not only one's class but also one's specific birthrights. In Byzantium, where birthright was far less of a concern, clothing necessarily had to denote one's profession, rank, and even geographical locale so that one's identity in relation to the rest of society would be known.

These fashions, arguably distinct to the Byzantines, were inextricably linked to the powerful textile industry. As Byzantium's monopolies on certain textiles swelled and then dissipated, fashions notably shifted. As other groups, especially Muslims, entered the European marketplace, Byzantine fashions reflected this sea change. Their obsession with fashion meant that downturns in the textile economy did not adversely affect their dress or diminish what made it distinctly Byzantine, but fashions nevertheless changed with the influx of these new influences. The Byzantines used their dress as a powerful mode of expression, making it the envy of their neighbors and a fascinating subject of study.

NOTES

1. Marcus N. Adler, *The Itinerary of Benjamin of Tudela* (New York: P. Feldheim, 1938), 53–54.
2. Michael F. Hendy, *Catalogue of Byzantine Coins in the Dumbarton Oaks Collection and in the Whittenmore Collection: Alexius I to Michael VIII* (Washington, DC: Dumbarton Oaks Research Library and Collection, 1999), 144.
3. Liuprand of Cremona, *The Embassy to Constantinople, and Other Writings*, trans. F. A. Wright (North Clarendon, VT: Charles E. Tuttle, 1993), 202.
4. Sebastian Brock and Susan Harvey, trans., "Pelagia of Antioch," in *Holy Women of the Syrian Orient* (Berkeley: University of California Press, 1998), 42.
5. Michael F. Hendy, *Studies in the Byzantine Monetary Economy, 300–1450* (Cambridge: Cambridge University Press, 1985), 213.
6. Clyde Pharr, *The Theodosian Code and Novels, and the Sirmondian Constitutions* (New York: Greenwood Press, 1969), 415.
7. Deno John Geanakoplos, *Byzantium: Church, Society, and Civilization Seen through Contemporary Eyes* (Chicago: University of Chicago Press, 1984), 309.
8. George T. Dennis, *Three Byzantine Military Treatises* (Washington, DC: Dumbarton Oaks Research Library and Collection, 1985), 55.

FURTHER READING

Ball, Jennifer L. *Byzantine Dress: Representations of Secular Dress in Eighth- to Twelfth-Century Byzantine Painting.* New York: Palgrave, 2005.
Houston, Mary. *Ancient Greek, Roman and Byzantine Costume and Decoration.* London: Adam and Charles Black, 1959.
Kazhdan, Alexander P., ed. *The Oxford Dictionary of Byzantium.* 3 vols. Oxford: Oxford University Press, 1991.
Muthesius, Anna. *Byzantine Silk Weaving, AD 400 to AD 1200.* Vienna: Verlag Fassbaender, 1997.
Parani, Maria. *Reconstructing the Reality of Images: Byzantine Material Culture and Religious Iconography (11th–15th Centuries).* Leiden: E. J. Brill, 2003.
Piltz, Elisabeth. "Middle Byzantine Court Costume." In *Byzantine Court Culture from 829 to 1204*, ed. H. Maguire, 39–51. Washington, DC: Dumbarton Oaks Research Library and Collection, 1997.
Woodfin, Warren. "Liturgical Textiles." In *Byzantium: Faith and Power*, ed. Helen C. Evans, 295–98. New York: Metropolitan Museum of Art, 2004.

WEB RESOURCES

McGinnis, Tara. *The Costumer's Manifesto.* http://www.costumes.org/history/100pages/byzantinelinks.htm.
Vukson-Van Beek, Dawn. *The Basics of Byzantine Dress, c. 1000 AD.* http://www.gryph.com/byzantine/dress.htm.
http://www.metmuseum.org/special/Byzantium/g5_pop_2.L.asp?altView=0

Medieval Clothing

Marie Botkin

TIMELINE

800   Charlemagne crowned as Holy Roman emperor
851   Danish Vikings sack England
1066   William the Conqueror takes over England
1070   Bayeux Tapestry commissioned by Bishop Odo of Bayeux
1095   First Crusade announced by Pope Urban in France
1140   First Gothic cathedral built at St. Denis
1170   Thomas Becket murdered in England
1186   Courts of love flourish in France under the direction of Eleanor of Aquitaine
1202   Middle Eastern clothing styles are brought to Europe after the looting of Constantinople during the Fourth Crusade
1300   Sumptuary laws related to clothing are decreed in Spain, Portugal, Italy, France, and England
1309   Avignonese Papacy
1340   Beginning of fashion is noted by chroniclers in France, Italy, and Spain
1347   Black Death
1350   Textile guilds develop at full force in Italy, France, and Belgium
1431   Joan of Arc burned at the stake
1450   Movable type invented by Johannes Gutenberg in Germany
1490   Spanish Inquisition
1492   Christopher Columbus sails to America
1495   Unicorn Tapestries woven in France

THE EARLY MIDDLE AGES (800–1300)

When many people think of the Middle Ages, they think of princesses, knights in shining armor on horses, and castles tucked away in deep forests. These symbols from the past are representative of the era but present only a very small part of the greater picture of the age. For much of the medieval period, the majority of the population spent most of its energy simply trying to survive. The romance of the period is counterbalanced by ignorance, violence, and cruelty, which were everyday occurrences during some periods. On the other hand, the medieval period formed some of the great cities of Europe, many of them based on textile manufacture and trade. In no other period of history has religion taken such an enormous part of the culture of society. Many medieval people, both wealthy and very poor, were devout believers, and this lent a great force of cohesion to society. This unity made it possible for them to build some of the world's most exquisite cathedrals and churches. The Middle Ages were also a period of great expansion, in which the blueprint for modern Europe would be drawn, and during which the great routes of trade connecting East to West would open up, bringing silks, spices, and fabrics into the markets across Europe. The Middle Ages witnessed the creation of thriving urban centers, the rising power of a middle class, and the birth of what we know today as fashion.

During the Middle Ages, the continent of Europe was divided up very differently than it is today. In the early medieval period, France, Germany, and England did not exist. Instead, the most populated and advanced civilization was located in the southern part of the continent, in the city of Rome, which was the center of the West for hundreds of years and held its place until the fall of Rome in 476. After this epic event, the locus of power moved to Constantinople, which was located to the east of Europe in modern-day Turkey. Constantinople had many connections to Middle Eastern countries, which proved to be beneficial in terms of trade and dangerous in terms of fighting off Muslim invaders. The rest of Europe was more or less unsettled. While Rome was still the center of Western Christianity and had a large population, much of the energy that would shape the continent was dispersed in northern lands that would later become the powerful countries that constitute the geographical divisions of Europe today.

In the twelfth century, loose approximations of the countries we see on the map today began to form. The entire continent of Europe was considered to be part of the Holy Roman Empire, and rather than countries, the main divisions were the kingdoms of France, Germany, Italy, Castile (modern-day Spain), Denmark, Norway, and Portugal. Rulers would battle over the specific boundaries of their lands for centuries, and these disputes constituted some of the greatest wars in medieval history.

Historical Background

The main cultural forces responsible for the shaping of early medieval Europe were the Classical heritage inherited from Greece and preserved by Rome, the religion of Christianity, and the barbarian tribes, who were in part responsible for the destruction of Rome. Europe was in great confusion during the period after the fall of Rome until the ninth century, so much so that this era has sometimes been called the "Dark Ages" by historians. The city of Rome provided a center and model to aspire to for the rest of the continent, whose settlements were far behind in civic development. Aside from housing the pope and providing the spiritual center of Christianity to the Western world, Rome was a hub of learning and great artistic achievement. And in terms of practical living, Rome presented some of the most advanced systems of its time, including organized agriculture, aqueducts to supply water to the city, and early trade routes.

The history of early medieval Europe after the fall of Rome is shrouded in darkness; there are few written records or artworks from this time that would indicate any type of cultural development. As a result of the near-disappearance of many of these advancements and the isolation of the Germanic tribes that had settled throughout Europe, the quality of everyday life declined considerably. Education for the average citizen virtually vanished, the common culture that Rome had afforded along with it. Instead, with the breakdown of public administration, the structure of society in early Europe was based on a smaller model of community—the kingdom—which was frequently headed by a Germanic tribe leader.

Life in early medieval kingdoms or estates was centered on defense and sustenance. The earliest types of settlement for the Germanic tribes such as the Franks and the Goths housed several generations under one roof, which sometimes sheltered the animals as well. Social organization was based on the kin group, which promised to take responsibility for all its members. After the defeat of Rome by the Goths, many tribes, attracted by the standard of living once known in Rome, settled nearby. The newcomers adapted some of the ways of the Romans, converted to Christianity, and intermarried with Roman women. This combination of cultures, Germanic and Roman, would later be the most influential force in shaping medieval Europe.

Many of the early Germanic kingdoms that were scattered throughout Europe as far north as Belgium were rendered powerless through constant warfare with neighboring kingdoms. However, the kingdom of the Franks, led by Clovis from 471 to 511, survived to found the Merovingian dynasty. The Merovingians were soon overthrown by the mayor of the palace, Pepin the Short, who founded the Carolingian dynasty. This dynasty became increasingly powerful and later would produce one of the most powerful rulers of the Middle Ages, Charles the Great, better known as Charlemagne.

Charlemagne was the great force of civilization in the early Middle Ages. He influenced every facet of medieval life and brought order to a chaotic world that had lost many of its civilized features of daily life. He revived the Roman ideal of an empire; designed the currency system of pounds, shillings, and pence that was used until 1970 in Great Britain; and supported the preservation of the Classical works from ancient Rome and Greece. Charlemagne was above all a great warrior, and he commanded his army with great charisma and bravery. According to his tomb remains, he was a tall man of six foot four (1.93 m), and in the records of Einhard, his secretary, he is described as a "tall, well-built man with large piercing eyes. Like many great men, he had a big nose. At the end of his life his hair was white, but abundant. His manner was impressive though affable, and held both authority and dignity."

In addition to his bravery on the battlefield, Charlemagne was also profoundly concerned with education, both his own and that of his people. He spent many hours trying to learn to write, invited scholars to his court, and started schools for his children and other youths of the aristocracy. He believed strongly in a solid work ethic, and this extended to all of his subjects, including his own family. He encouraged his daughters to learn weaving and spinning so they would not become idle, and he admired the gold embroideries and handwork done by skilled princesses and abbesses. Charlemagne also established the custom of requiring his men to swear an oath of loyalty to him, which would be the basis of the feudal system developed in later medieval times. These men were bound to serve him on the battlefield and were rewarded with land, so they might establish estates of their own.

The climax of Charlemagne's rule was the day he was crowned the "Emperor of the Romans" on Christmas Day in 800. Crowned by Pope Leo III—as a way to guarantee his own security in Rome—Charlemagne represented one of the most powerful leaders in history that was able to fuse the institutions of Church and State. At this point in history, he had command over Rome and all the rest of the territories reaching up into northern Europe.

Charlemagne brought organization and order to all aspects of life. His court was the most sophisticated in Europe, and along with scholars who had traveled long distances to join the court came singers, musicians, and poets who sang of the beauty of Charlemagne's wife and daughters. However, Charlemagne did not stay in one palace for long. Instead, he moved from residence to residence to oversee the goings-on throughout his lands. Each royal residence, or *vill*, was completely self-supporting. Managed by the king's stewards, there were carpenters, blacksmiths, silversmiths, weavers, shoemakers, brewers, bakers, and soap makers. Food was harvested in plenty, and each vill kept careful records of all that was produced on his estates, down to each egg. Charlemagne did not neglect the poor or downtrodden, either, and created regulations for the education of female orphans and the prevention of serfs dying from starvation.

After the death of Charlemagne in 814, Europe fell into chaos again. Without the leadership of one powerful ruler who could oversee the workings of his empire throughout the continent, smaller individual groups started to fight each other. Vikings from northern Europe wrought havoc throughout the continent, sailing their long ships along the coastlines of modern-day England, Ireland, and Scotland and down into the ports of France, Spain, and Portugal. They were merciless warriors and did not hesitate to rob sacred chapels, slay unarmed monks, or destroy libraries that held ancient documents. What they could not carry out of a village, they burned.

The Vikings were part of the barbarian forces from the north that shaped the early medieval world. They had their own system of beliefs, based on a pagan religion that worshiped Odin, king of the gods; Thor, the god of war; and Frey, the goddess of peace and pleasure. Among their early rituals were sacrificial offerings, and every nine years they would sacrifice nine males of every species to placate their gods.

However, with time, their customs and beliefs were gradually modified. Many descendants of the early Vikings converted to Christianity with hopes of gaining power and support from the Church in Rome. In addition, many of the Germanic tribes also converted to Christianity, swayed in part by the pagan beliefs combined with and replaced by Christian holidays. Yet even conversion to the same religion did not prevent battles being fought between neighboring lords. The early Middle Ages were marked with a constant struggle for power between kingdoms and peoples of different heritage within the continent, until the advent of the Crusades.

The Crusades were the most significant events in the history of the early Middle Ages. After centuries of being uncomfortable neighbors, the two cultures of Christianity and Islam resorted to a series of wars that would last for more than two hundred years. The initial causes of the Crusades have been attributed to the several factors. The first was the aggressive actions of the Turks in Jerusalem against Christians. Previously, Muslims and Christians had lived peacefully together in the holy city, but when the Turks took over in 1070, pilgrims brought back accounts of the oppression of Christians and desecration of their holy sites. The second cause was the diminishing power of the Byzantine Empire. That great empire, seated at the intersection of Europe and Asia, was under attack from both sides. Leaders of the West were greatly concerned that, should Constantinople fall, Muslim invaders would continue to move up through Europe in their quest for domination. The third cause of the Crusades was the desire of Italian merchants to expand their commercial activities across the Mediterranean. The potential fortune to be made in trade was phenomenal, and merchants from Pisa, Genoa, and Venice were anxious to export their goods to the Eastern markets.

After an appeal from Emperor Alexius for help to defend Constantinople, Pope Urban II announced the First Crusade in 1095. He implored the people of France to cease the disputes and bloodshed among themselves and to become soldiers of Christ to defeat the infidels who were closing in on the continent of Europe from all sides. Pope Urban's demands were met with great enthusiasm from the populace, and word spread throughout the country. With conflict between the Muslims and the Christians reaching as far back as the battles of Charles Martel, the father of Charlemagne, the fervor to preserve Christian Europe was a strong drive in the early medieval man's heart. Europe was united as never before in the fight to defend Christianity.

News of the First Crusade spread through medieval Europe via the passionate speeches of many who had attended the meeting in France. Serfs were freed from their indentured status, prisoners were released, and citizens were exempted from paying their taxes in the name of the Crusade. Preparations for the endeavor began on both sides; in Europe, leaders started to assemble their armies and Emperor Alexius in Constantinople prepared for their arrival. The pope instructed that those who committed themselves to the crusade wear a symbol of their status that could be seen by all. A cross was attached to their chests or to their brows to announce their pledge.

The main army of Crusaders was made up of four major factions. Their leaders were powerful men, including some dukes with large estates, but there were no kings among them. The first large army to depart was led by a German duke, Godfrey of Bouillon, who despite his German background spoke mainly French. He and his army traveled through Europe through Hungary and arrived in Constantinople without any major setbacks in December 1096. The second group was led by Bohemond, who was a Norman from Italy. He was known for his ferocity and skill in war and was keen to make a profit on the spoils of war in the East. The third faction was the largest and was led by Raymond IV, Count of Toulouse. He was the most politically prominent of the leaders of the Crusade forces and hoped to become the leader of the entire effort. Raymond led his knights and other followers across northern Italy and southward into the capital of Constantinople in April 1097. The fourth army to arrive in Constantinople was led by Robert of Flanders, who crossed the Adriatic Sea from Italy with his troops.

In total, there were approximately four thousand knights and twenty-five thousand soldiers who arrived in Constantinople to wage the Holy War against the pagans at the end of April 1097. In addition to the official Crusaders following the dukes and princes, there were other groups of knights and peasants who keenly felt the desire to defeat the infidel and journeyed independently into the East. These smaller bands were less organized and came to be known as the People's Crusade.

Emperor Alexius of Constantinople was somewhat overwhelmed by the arrival of these massive forces. By coercing the leaders to swear an oath of loyalty to him, he strove to protect his own interests and regain the lands that had previously been lost to the Muslims. After the emperor had extracted promises of allegiance from the Western Crusaders, they departed for their ultimate destination of Jerusalem, defeating the city of Nicaea at their first stop.

The Christian forces advanced with some difficulty through mountainous Anatolia to the great citadel of Antioch, which was bulwarked with enormous walls and hundreds of towers. The battle at Antioch proved much more difficult than Nicaea. Many Crusaders died of disease and starvation, and some were so disheartened that they deserted and left to return home. One of the deserters Stephen of Blois met with Emperor Alexius on his journey back to Europe and told such a convincing tale of the impending defeat of the Crusaders that Alexius took his reinforcement troops, turned around, and went back to Constantinople. This move had dire results for the emperor, because as soon as he had deserted the effort, many of the European leaders of the Crusade believed that they were entitled to take possession of their winnings.

After a long and arduous battle with the Turks, the Christian Crusaders moved victorious to claim the citadel of Antioch. Thus, reduced considerably in number but triumphant, they continued on to their goal of Jerusalem, led by Raymond of Poitiers. In June 1099, the Crusaders stopped before the city of Jerusalem to set up camp and wait for an influx of supplies. As soon as the supplies arrived and were unloaded, the Crusader army began its attack by building siege towers that were set up against the walls encircling the city of Jerusalem. The leaders entered and the Muslim governor surrendered on the condition that his people would remain safe in the mosque. The leaders duly ordered their troops to leave the civilians alone, but their orders were not followed by the Crusaders, and hundreds of innocent men, women, and children were slaughtered. The Europeans then ignored the oaths they had sworn to the emperor of Byzantium and moved in to claim the lands they had won though battle. This was the beginning of the creation of Crusader states, which were ruled by the most powerful leaders of the First Crusade.

Women who traveled and stayed in the East with their husbands or families were quick to adopt the styles of the local people. They wore long gowns with flared sleeves constructed of elaborate silks, and many costume historians believe that this is one of the main channels that circulated Islamic styles and textiles back into Western Europe.

The highly improbable success of the First Crusade was to be held up as an example and inspiration to later generations of Crusaders. Against the odds, the struggling Christian army had managed to attain its goal that it had set out with from Europe: to reclaim the cities taken by the Muslims in three years. European men and women of the medieval era believed firmly that the success of the Crusades was due to the divine intervention of God himself, who protected his knights with a series of miracles.

The Second Crusade was again issued by a pope. In 1145 Pope Eugenius III called for Christians of Europe to defend the city of Edessa, which had been captured a year earlier by a Muslim leader. Again, the call from the pope was met with great enthusiasm throughout Europe. The Second Crusade was promoted by the powerful St. Bernard of Clairvaux, who told his audiences that joining the Crusade would wash them clean of the earthly sins and provide a blessed way to salvation in Christ. When Bernard ran out of the crosses prepared for those ready to enlist, he tore his robe to pieces and handed them out to the eager crowds for additional symbols of their commitment.

As in the First Crusade, many peasants and pilgrims responded to the call to defend their faith and territories against the infidels. However, the Second Crusade was different from the First in that it was led by two powerful European rulers, Emperor Conrad III of Germany and King Louis VII of France.

Conrad III left for Edessa in May 1147, flanked with many German nobles, the kings of Poland and Bohemia, and the future emperor, his nephew Frederick of Swabia. Ignoring advice from Constantinople, he marched his army directly through Nicaea to Anatolia, where his army met a bad end. Conrad was forced to retreat with a few survivors to Nicaea to await reinforcements.

Louis VII, accompanied by his wife, Queen Eleanor of Aquitaine, marched with his armies to Constantinople in October 1147. There he met with the emperor, Manuel, and like his predecessors from the First Crusade, swore an oath to restore back to the emperor the lands that had previously been a part of the Byzantine Empire. When Louis arrived in Nicaea, he joined forces with Conrad and headed toward the city of Antioch. Unlike during the First Crusade, however, which had been greatly desired by the ruler of Constantinople, this time the people of neighboring cities in the empire were hostile toward the Crusaders, fearing that they would take over their lands, as they had done with Antioch and Jerusalem after Emperor Alexius had failed to reinforce the First Crusaders.

At the time of the Second Crusade, Antioch was under the rule of Prince Raymond of Poitiers, who was the uncle of Queen Eleanor of France. When the Crusaders finally arrived in Antioch, many of the troops had been slain during the journey by Greeks and Turks defending their cities. At this point, the French had spent more time fighting Christians than Muslims. When Eleanor met up with her uncle Raymond, there were great celebrations, and she soon espoused his plan to attack Aleppo, the center of power in Edessa. King Louis was dissatisfied with his queen's enthusiasm for the plan of her uncle, though, and forced her to move on with his army of Crusaders to Jerusalem.

Once the French Crusaders had met up in Jerusalem, which was ruled at the time by Queen Melisende, the councils decided that the next move would be to attack the city of Damascus. However, the Crusaders from Western Europe and the rulers of Jerusalem did not necessarily share the same motives. Melisende wanted to expand her empire, while Louis clearly remembered his oath to the Byzantine emperor to return his former lands. The divergence in interests led to a weakly planned attack on Damascus. The large crusading army led by Louis, Conrad, and the barons of the Crusader states was overwhelmed by the large armies of the Muslim leader Nur al-Din.

The Second Crusade ended in defeat, and the kings who led it returned to Europe in great disappointment and anger. In particular, King Louis changed his mind about the motivations of Constantinople and joined the king of Sicily against the Byzantine emperor in exchange for ships to bring him and what was left of his army home. The collapse of the Second Crusade caused great sorrow in Europe, as many hopes were pinned to the knights of Christ. Bernard of Clairvaux preached that the reasons behind the failure of the Crusade were linked to the sinfulness of Europe, and he condemned the knights for their vanity, which he claimed was evident in the way they decorated their armor with plumes and wore their hair as long as women. He recommended purification rites for all men and women of Europe to restore the favor of God to his knights.

The following six Crusades followed the pattern of the Second Crusade and were largely unsuccessful, to the great sorrow of Christian Europe. The Third Crusade was led in 1189 by King Richard I of England, the son of Eleanor of Aquitaine, and earned him his sobriquet of "Lion Heart." He fought bravely, fiercely, and cruelly, but in the end was no match for the genteel and brilliant ruler Saladin. Richard had managed to win over the city of Acre for Christendom, but during the three years of the crusade, the German king Frederick Barbarossa drowned and the French king Philip Augustus left in the middle due to illness.

The pride of Europe suffered under these results, but in 1202 Pope Innocent III called for another crusade despite a general lack of enthusiasm. The shameful end result of the Fourth Crusade was due to an initial shortage of funds. When the French Crusaders arrived in Venice, they began their journey short of soldiers and money to fund the campaign. In the meantime, the Venetians had invested enormously to prepare for the arrival of the French. Furious with their inability to pay for what they had initially requested in terms of transport and supplies, the Venetians demanded that the Crusaders invade the town of Zadar to recompense their losses. The Crusaders were thus forced to abandon the spiritual goals set forth by the pope to satisfy their material needs. They took the city, and were scolded by the Pope, whose veto had been ignored.

After their success against Zadar, the participants of the Fourth Crusade continued on to Constantinople after receiving an offer for huge monetary reward from Alexius, the Byzantine prince. When Alexius was subsequently unable to produce the reward he had promised to the Crusaders who had toppled an empire for him, they revolted. The Crusaders declared war on Constantinople and sacked the city; they took all spoils they could lay their hands on, raped women, destroyed holy places, and burned libraries filled with ancient manuscripts. Some costume historians attribute the taste for luxurious silks and furs in Europe in the thirteenth century to the silks and furs brought back from the looting of Constantinople. Meanwhile, the city was ruined and would never return to its former glory.

Europe continued to produce generations of leaders, aristocrats, and peasants willing to set out on a crusade despite their declining reputation. The Fifth Crusade was led in 1217 by King Andrew of Hungary, who initially won the war at Damietta in Egypt and secured the release of Christian prisoners. However, the victory was short lived, and when reinforcements failed to appear in 1221, the Crusaders were again defeated and evacuated Egypt. This failure was partially blamed on Frederick II, the ruler of Italy and Germany, who had not kept the promise he made at his coronation two years earlier to go on Crusade.

After years of preparation and illness, Frederick II embarked on the Sixth Crusade in 1228, only after being excommunicated by the pope for failing to do so earlier. Frederick, fluent in Arabic and extremely knowledgeable in Arab history and culture, succeeded in resolving many of the issues that were fought for so hardily in earlier Crusades. He signed a treaty with the Muslim ruler al-Kamil which gave the cities of Acre, Jaffa, Nazareth, Bethlehem, and Jerusalem over to Christendom. Christians across the East rejoiced, but the pope denounced the treaty, and the success that Frederick had been able to achieve through intelligence and diplomacy disappeared into thin air. Soon after, Jerusalem fell to a Turkish invasion and eluded Christian rule again. The Seventh and Eighth Crusades were organized by the religious king Louis IX of France, who would be canonized as a saint after his death. In 1248 he took the cross, pledging to regain Jerusalem as a Christian state. Both of his efforts ultimately failed. At the onset of the Eighth Crusade, many believed he was unreasonable in his plans and refused to join him. He traveled down to Egypt toward the city of Jerusalem, where he fell sick and died.

In the end, the goals for which the kings, gallant knights, and peasants of the early Middle Ages left their families and their homes were never met despite two hundred years of crusading. But many changes ensued as a result of the Crusades. The social structure of feudalism suffered greatly after so many years of crusading: Many serfs had taken advantage of the opportunity to leave their lords and never returned to their manors. Knights had bankrupted themselves, selling their lands to fund their exploits, and returned to a lifestyle that was less luxurious than they had known in the earlier periods of feudalism. The crucial social institution of the era, the Christian Church, was also significantly weakened. After so many failures and the sack of Constantinople by the Turks, the prestige of the Church was considerably lessened.

On the other hand, continued exposure to Eastern culture brought an influx of new ideas and products to the attention of Europeans. Many Crusaders were shocked at the level of material and intellectual sophistication at the Arab courts. Elaborate textiles, exotic fashions, and a taste for spices were carried back to Europe with the returning armies or given as gifts from leaders in the East. The Muslim leader Saladin presented Count Henri of Champagne with a luxurious silk tunic and turban, both of which he wore in his court in France. Inventions such as gunpowder and the compass were also introduced to Western culture, with dire results in the following wars. Trade with the Middle East exploded, and silks, rugs, velvets, perfumes, cloves, cinnamon, and ginger were made available in abundance throughout Europe. Italy capitalized on the new trade goods available, and the expansion of commerce exchanged throughout the Mediterranean was unprecedented.

European Leaders in the Early Middle Ages

Aside from the powerful presence of the Church, the development of laws, customs, and beliefs were also very much influenced by the kings, queens, and nobility of early Europe. They were the greatest consumers of fashion and spent huge amounts of money on textiles, furs, and jewels to impress their superior status upon their people. Many of the rulers of the Middle Ages showed great courage, intelligence, and innovation. Some inspired great loyalty, and others were disliked or feared by their people. Otto I developed a system of government that brought peace and stability to his kingdom by appointing religious clerics rather than nobles as guardians of the developing cities. Eleanor of Aquitaine organized elaborate courts of love, which raised the status of women to a new level in society. Louis IX was known for his just acts and became one of the only kings in history to become a saint. In effect, many of the actions of the rulers of medieval Europe shaped the world in which they lived profoundly and would contribute to the evolution of Western culture as we know it today.

One of the most powerful and influential rulers of the Middle Ages after Charlemagne was Otto I of Saxony. The Saxon Empire was smaller than the area that had been ruled by Charlemagne and located farther north, extending across the greater part of Germany and Italy. It was, in fact, predominantly German and is considered by German historians to be the first of their three empires, the First Reich. However, it is important to keep in mind that, although the geographical area ruled by Otto is now indeed part of modern Germany, the people of the tenth century did not consider themselves German. Instead the people of his realm belonged to groups who called themselves Franks, Saxons, Bavarians, and Swabians.

Otto I succeeded his father Henry I to become king. In an election where he had to be chosen by the dukes, counts, and knights of the realm, he was crowned in a double ceremony. The ceremonies took place at Aachen in the chapel of Charlemagne, and after the nobility swore loyalty to him, lifting him onto the throne, he was sworn in by the clergy. When the archbishop led him to the central space of the chapel, he proclaimed him as chosen by God to rule and asked the people to agree to his election by raising their right hands. After this part of the ritual was performed, Otto was given the regalia appropriate to the king, including a tightly fitted tunic called a *bliaut*, a cape, a sword, a scepter, and a crown.

Otto proved his worth later in battle against the Hungarians in 955. At the time, the Hungarians were considered the scourge of Europe and invaded only to destroy everything in their paths. After this great victory, he attained the name Otto the Great and was known throughout Europe as the leader who had preserved Christendom from the heathen Hungarians. However, even after such success in preserving his kingdom, Otto was seriously troubled by the unrest in his own regions, and this is where he used boldly innovative ideas to stabilize his rule. His main problems were related to the constant fighting between the duchies. He experimented by appointing his brother, Bruno, an archbishop, to take over the duchy of Lotharingia. There were many positive aspects to his decision. First, a member of the clergy would not produce any heirs, so the land did not have to be divided among the sons nor would there be the beginning of a potentially powerful dynasty. Second, by granting the clergy immunity from the control of dukes and other members of the nobility, Otto was able to gain willing administrators who were conscientious and loyal to him. What began with appointment of his brother became his modus operandi; Otto soon appointed several clergymen to take responsibility for the various lands in his kingdom, forming what was to become the Ottonian System of Government.

The Ottonian System had many benefits. It gave the king control over his lands through his appointed administrators of the clergy and resulted in a strong, peaceful government. Another remarkable effect of Otto's system was a revival of arts and letters. Because many of the clergy members appointed by

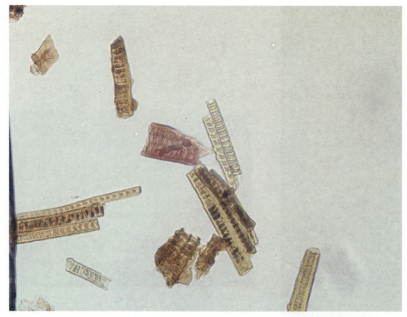

Prehistoric fragments of Carbonized textiles. Courtesy of C. and M. Baldia.

Detail of a wallpainting from the Tomb of Tutankhamen in Egypt showing collars, kilts, shenti, headdresses, and crowns, 18th Dynasty, c. 1357–1349 BCE. © E. Strouhal / Werner Forman / Art Resource, NY.

A gold plaque showing a Persian man wearing Median costume, from the Oxus treasure, Achaemenid Persian, Fifth–Fourth century BCE. © HIP / Art Resource, NY.

Fragment of Persian enamelled tile showing two feet with sandals turned to the right. From Susa, Sixth–Fifth century BCE. © Erich Lessing / Art Resource, NY.

An undated hand-colored print of Babylonian leader and Persians. © North Wind / North Wind Picture Archives.

Detail from the Greek Francois Vase: Calydonian Boar Hunt; Chariot race at the funeral games of Patroklos; Gods arrriving after the wedding of Peleus and Thetis, c. 570 BCE. © Scala / Art Resource, NY.

"The Roman Bride from the Villa of the Mysteries." Courtesy of Laetitia La Follette.

Brass statuette of the Serpent Goddess of Knossos shows the bared chest, flounced skirt, and rounded apron (1600 BCE). © Nimatallah / Art Resource, NY.

A mosiac showing Christ flanked by Emperor Constantine IX and his wife the Empress Zoe, Hagia Sophia, Istanbul, Turkey. © Erich Lessing / Art Resource, NY.

Mosaic panel of Theodora and Attendants, San Vitale, Ravenna, c. 547, shows a variety of ornate cloaks and headdresses. © Cameraphoto Arte, Venice / Art Resource, NY.

Mosaic panel of the procession of virgins in Byzantine dress, S. Apollinare Nuovo, Ravenna, c. 500. © Scala / Art Resource, NY.

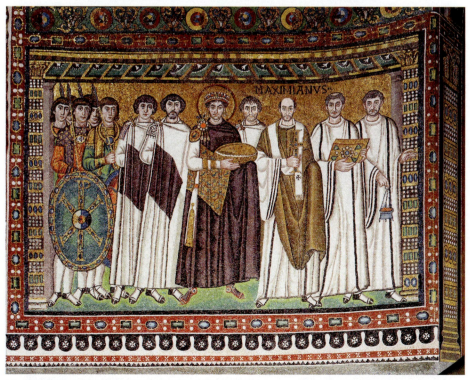

Mosaic panel of Justinian and Attendants, San Vitale, Ravenna, c. 547, showing Byzantine religious clothing and military dress. © Cameraphoto Arte, Venice / Art Resource, NY.

Manuel II Palaiologos with his wife and three children, 1403–5, shows both Byzantine adult and children's dress. © Réunion des Musées Nationaux / Art Resource, NY.

Mosaic panel of Theodore Metochites kneeling before Christ, in Byzantine headdress and garments. © Erich Lessing / Art Resource, NY.

A scene from the Bayeux Tapestry showing Norman soldiers in medieval military garments. © The Art Archive / Musée de la Tapisserie Bayeux / Gianni Dagli Orti.

A scene from the Bayeux Tapestry showing a medieval messenger reaching William Duke of Normandy. © The Art Archive / Musée de la Tapisserie Bayeux / Gianni Dagli Orti.

"The Working Class. The Four Estates of Society," fifteenth century, shows a working man wearing a chemise (his undergarments showing) and a woman in a simple gown with a low v-neck and plain tubular sleeves with turned back cuffs. Both are wearing simple head coverings. Tempera on panel, by Jean Bourdichon [1457–1521]. © Bibliothèque de l'École des Beaux-Arts, Paris, France / Bridgeman-Giraudon / Art Resource, NY.

Otto were well versed in history and scholarly writings, their new power allowed them to expand their knowledge and interests into projects that ultimately benefited the kingdom as a whole.

Bruno, Otto's brother, collected classical manuscripts, knew Greek, and was highly interested in reforming the monasteries. He spent a great deal of his energy in the school that would train future clergy in grammar, geometry, music, and astronomy. Bruno also brought into the curriculum Classical studies of Roman art and more practical subjects such as city planning and controlling markets. He was determined to bring the great ideals of Rome to the Germans, who were still counted among the barbarians. These developments in culture were known as the Ottonian Renaissance.

As Otto's governmental system grew and flourished, problems appeared that were similar to the problems that had surfaced when the provinces were controlled by dukes and other nobility, and Otto was obliged to devise a mechanism in his system that would check the power of the clergy. He solved the problem with regard to a very large and rich province that was in danger of becoming too powerful. In order to control its growing power, which was a result of its success in defeating neighboring lands and absorbing their territories, the king sought the support of the pope to divide it into two provinces. Otto's successful relationship with the papal power in Rome would later be of great advantage to him.

In 959, Pope John XII turned to Otto for help in fending off attacks against Rome by one of Otto's enemies. Otto dutifully led an expedition with his troops to Italy, defeated the pope's enemies, and, with the legacy of Charlemagne in mind, asked to be crowned Holy Roman emperor. Pope John rewarded Otto for his aid in battle, and Otto the Great was crowned emperor in 962. However, this great honor was soon to be darkened by disagreements with the pope, who was not eager to assume a role of dependency to the emperor. John soon regretted his decision, turned on Otto, and invoked the help of his earlier enemy, the Byzantine army, and the Hungarians. This move was treasonous and with the help of the bishops, Otto was able to get John deposed from the papacy. As John had not lived a model life during his papacy, the archbishops were not against his deposal. Before his connection to Otto, John XII had been accused of turning his palace into a brothel, invoking the aid of Jupiter while playing dice, and castrating a cardinal. In 963, John was deposed and replaced with Leo VIII, who was handpicked by Otto to serve as the pope. At this point in history, Otto had regained the supreme power once held by Charlemagne and presided over the pope in all matters.

Meanwhile, farther westward in the area of modern France, a dynasty that would last more than three hundred years began with the rule of Hugh Capet in 987. The Capetian dynasty was to yield thirteen kings, each succeeding in a direct line from father to son until 1328. The rule of Hugh Capet was much different from that of Otto I, for his direct influence was limited to the domain closest to his own domicile, near Paris. The rest of the French kingdom was under the control of powerful members of the nobility. Hugh's successors gradually expanded their power and domain through conquests and exploiting their rights over lands not under their direct authority.

However, one of the most extraordinary men of the Middle Ages was not a Capetian king, but a duke who ruled under them. William the Conqueror, born an illegitimate heir to the Duke of Normandy, became the most powerful feudal lord in France and changed the course of history by taking over the throne of England. Normandy was located west of Paris and was named after the "north men," the Vikings who had settled there from Denmark and Sweden. When William's father died, he became Duke of Normandy at the age of seven, thereafter surviving many dangerous years during which three of his guardians died violent deaths. At fifteen, William was knighted and began to take part in the administration of his duchy. He learned to fight in battle at an early age and was later known for his strength and shrewd strategic skills that made him one of the greatest warriors of his age. He won the approval and fear of his countrymen by moderating the exploitation of the peasants by nobility, was imbued with a devout sense of his religious duties, and when necessary, used extreme violence to quell his enemies. When the town of Alençon mocked his grandfather's trade as a tanner by hanging hides in their windows, for example, he cut off the hands and feet of his prisoners, gouged out their eyes, and catapulted the body parts back into the center of town.

In 1066, William, at thirty-nine years of age, set out to conquer England. He had earlier procured a promise for the throne of England from the English king Edward. In return for protection in Normandy, King Edward had promised to bestow the crown of England on William. However, before his death, he either forgot or changed his mind and instead named one of his men, Harold, to succeed him. William had a counterargument for the crowning of Harold and claimed that Harold had sworn an oath of loyalty to him, when William had knighted him in France. As the oath of loyalty was taken very seriously as part of the foundation for feudal society, William took the matter to a higher court. He appealed to the Pope, Alexander II, who condemned Harold as a usurper and excommunicated him. The pope blessed William's invasion and sent him a diamond ring that was believed to contain a hair of St. Peter's head within it.

William invaded England in September 1066, taking a fleet of 1,400 ships from Normandy and convincing the brother of Harold to become his ally. Tostig, Harold's brother, proved to be a devious ally, because at the same time he agreed to fight on the side of William, he also promised the throne of England to King Harald of Norway, who joined him in battle. Tostig and Harald invaded England and the people of York surrendered to them without a fight. Harald of Norway was then crowned king of England, but Harold, named by the dead king as successor to the throne, rushed up to defend his claim; he defeated them, and both Harald of Norway and Tostig were killed in battle. In the meantime, William was pillaging and burning the southern areas of England, and Harold rushed down to defend his country against this new threat. In a battle that lasted nine hours, Harold was shot in the eye with an arrow and dismembered by the Norman knights that were in the service of William. The battle for England had been won, and its conqueror was crowned King William I of England on Christmas Day 1066. The tale of William the Conqueror and his conquest of England is immortalized in the Bayeux Tapestry, a textile that measures 77 yards (70 m) and is embroidered with the scenes of William's valor.

After William's reign, the kingdoms of France and England continued to flourish and took active parts in the Crusades. The Capetian dynasty was ruled in the twelfth century by Louis VII, the pious king that led the Second Crusade alongside the German emperor Conrad. Louis VII was the son of Louis VI and had ascended to the throne only by default: Louis VII, as the second son, was destined from birth to become an archbishop, but when his elder brother Philip died in a horse-riding accident, he found himself in direct line to be king of France. However, the emphasis on religious training that he experienced in his youth was to have a formative effect on him for the rest of his life.

One of the great trials of Louis's life was his marriage to Eleanor of Aquitaine. Louis and Eleanor were married as teenagers, with great ceremonies celebrated in the southwest of France, Eleanor's birthright, as well as in Paris, which was the center of government and Louis's home. Their journey through the countryside of France was filled with signs of joy at their marriage; streets were decorated with tree boughs and tapestries, and their marriage caravan was preceded through the streets of the towns by musicians and banners. Initially their marriage was strong, but Eleanor, raised in glorious, sun-filled lands overabundant in golden grains and wine, soon tired of the dingy, dark castle in Paris.

Eleanor of Aquitaine was one of the most powerful and influential women of the Middle Ages. She had been raised in the courts of Aquitaine, which, partly because of its sunny climate and fruitful lands, was prone to rearing vigorous, lively progeny. The court that she grew up in was much influenced by her grandfather, Guillaume, a famous troubadour, who sung of the beauty of women and joys of love in his poems. Eleanor was the heiress to one of the richest duchies of the medieval world, one that was larger and more beautiful than that owned by the king himself. Even as a young duchess, she was acutely aware of her own value and prestige, and in the tradition of her forefathers, she devoted herself to the enjoyment of life. Her court was filled with musicians, merchant princes, bishops, entertainers, and poets who sang of her graces. With the love of adventure firmly implanted in her spirit and eager to escape the dinginess of Paris, Eleanor insisted on accompanying Louis on the Second Crusade.

As described earlier, the Second Crusade proved to be disastrous, not only for Europe but also for the young royal couple that had set out from Paris in 1147 with glory in their eyes. While the Crusade was falling to pieces around them, Eleanor and Louis grew apart. Louis, who had been deeply influenced by the preaching of St. Bernard of Clairvaux, did not entirely approve of Eleanor's method of travel. She had brought many of her relatives from Aquitaine along with her on the long journey, as well as several trunks full of colorful clothing and cosmetics. Many historians attribute the falling out between King Louis and Queen Eleanor to the relationship that developed between Eleanor and her uncle Raymond of Poitiers, who was then the leader of Antioch. When Eleanor arrived in the foreign lands of the East, she found a warm reception and the evidence of a fascinating new culture.

For Eleanor, the dreary, dilapidated castle and days filled with pious observations under the influence of Louis's bishops in Paris were a sad comparison to the lifestyle and splendor in Antioch. She found that as the queen of France and key to Raymond's plan of action to expand and fortify Antioch, she became the center of attention. Raymond, with charm characteristic of his upbringing, used all the seduction of his riches to prevail upon his guests. He brought the French royalty and barons all the spoils of the East he could muster up from the great bazaars of Antioch and served them wines cooled with mountain snows, rare fruits and spices, and great feasts. However, the Franks, including King Louis, were mistrustful of his motives.

Louis perceived quickly after his arrival in Antioch that the holy Crusade he had embarked upon in the name of the Cross was, in Raymond's eyes, merely troops sent to fortify his city. The king was shocked and displeased with the manner of government in Antioch, where Raymond had left a large statue of the pagan Greek god Apollo, and citizens were as likely to wear long Eastern dress and turbans as they were European dress. Eleanor, on the other hand, charmed by her uncle's success and the sensual panorama of culture around her, fully supported Raymond's plans. When Louis refused to commit himself and his troops to the welfare of Antioch, Eleanor demanded a divorce from the king and revealed her plan to return to her native land of Aquitaine. Disagreeing on the ultimate goals of the Crusade, the young king and queen found a distance between them that would never be remedied. Louis, after hearing the advice of his councilors, feared losing his wife, as well as her great expanse of lands. He swept the furious queen away in the middle of the night and moved on to Jerusalem, losing the majority of his troops to Muslim invaders en route. He returned to France after making pilgrimages to sacred shrines with defeat in his heart.

On return to France, the divorce that was so fervently desired by Eleanor was granted on the basis of her claim that her marriage to Louis VII was unlawful due to the fact that they were related by blood. In 1152, after the birth of her second female child, the bishops saw no reason to insist upon the marriage. Because she had failed to produce a male heir to the throne, Louis and Eleanor were divorced, and she returned to her beloved golden lands of Aquitaine. But the story of Eleanor of Aquitaine did not stop with her divorce from the king of the Franks. Her attractiveness as a potential wife was demonstrated immediately after her divorce. En route to her home, she was accosted in two separate attacks by enterprising dukes eager to kidnap her person and gain ownership of the fertile duchy of Aquitaine. However, her escorts protected her, and she arrived safely home. Her status as Duchess of Aquitaine did not last long. Despite her colorful past, she married Henry Plantagenet, Duke of Normandy, scarcely two months after her divorce.

The second stage of her adventurous life was to begin with the marriage to Henry II, who was much more like the people of Aquitaine in character than her previous husband had been. Henry Plantagenet was the picture of health, strength, and ambition when Eleanor married him. Twelve years her junior, Henry had been educated by his mother Matilda for a great destiny. Leaving Eleanor behind to oversee the courts of Rouen under the tutelage of Matilda, Henry left to claim the throne of England. His most serious rival to the crown of England had died choking on a plate of eels, and the future looked bright indeed for the young Plantagenet whose power had grown exponentially in his young lifetime. In 1154 Eleanor was summoned by Henry from her court in Rouen to claim the crown of England at his side. Eleanor of Aquitaine, who was once the queen of France, stepped up two years later to be crowned the queen of England.

However, life as queen of England did not flow as harmoniously as Eleanor would have liked. Although the court in England was far more interesting and less prone to religious duty than the one in Paris, Eleanor continued to miss her homeland and the joyous life filled with poetry and gallantry that she had led. Her longings for the courts of Aquitaine were exacerbated when Thomas Becket appeared in the royal household to serve as chancellor. Becket became the favorite of King Henry and took an active part in the administration of the court. Eleanor was relegated to taking care of her sons and keeping company with the female relatives in the royal family. Yet Henry, with all his practical inclinations, supported the development of the arts and letters that were a long tradition in the courts of Aquitaine. During his reign there was a flowering in the crafts of poetry, much of it devoted to the fair Queen Eleanor. The legend of King Arthur had such success that many knights were schooled with the etiquette and chivalric virtues exemplified in the tale. Eleanor kept busy, arranging matters of court and acting as a great patroness of the arts. She also gave birth to seven more children.

While Henry Plantagenet at first prized Becket as his right-hand man, he later changed his mind with great regret. Eventually, Becket became one of the most powerful men in England. Henry could no longer control him, because he had moved out of political circles into the one place that was more powerful: the Church. The drama that unfolded as a result of their relationship jeopardized the status of the king and became one of the most well-known historical tales of the English Middle Ages.

Thomas Becket had risen quickly through the ranks as a brilliant young man. He was born in London in 1118 to a wealthy bourgeois family that was able to give him an education. Like many ambitious men born outside the aristocracy, Becket was obliged to make his rise to power through the Church, even though he was more inclined toward a diplomatic career. His success during his studies was such that he became the archdeacon of Canterbury on return from Bologna, where he had studied canonical law. Through his successful works, he caught the eye of Theobald, the archbishop of Canterbury. He showed such promise in his administrative skills that, at the age of thirty-seven, he moved to state governance as secretary of state with a recommendation from the archbishop.

King Henry and Becket got along splendidly. Becket planned war campaigns, led armies of knights into battle, and fought in combat. Henry was extremely pleased with the handsome young man who performed his work so brilliantly and therefore rewarded him with riches and respect. Becket was quickly taken into the fold in the king's daily activities. They hunted together as friends, and Becket gave banquets that were almost equal to those of the royal household. Indeed, the king held Becket in such high regard that he entrusted him with the education of his son and namesake, Henry. The practice of sending noble children to be brought up and trained in the arts of war in other noble households was a common occurrence in the medieval period.

Becket made his transition from clergyman to secular statesman with grace and acumen. He became an extravagant courtier and was well respected and appreciated by his peers. He also followed his orders from the king without hesitation, staunchly adhering to the hierarchy set before him in his career and life. This meant that he went against some of the clergymen, earlier his colleagues, at the wishes of Henry. Henry had set out with incredible determination and energy to diminish the power the Church had over his rule of England. His main desire was to subvert the power of the Church to his will, so he would rule supreme over England. Becket duly helped Henry in his goals by enforcing the *danegeld* taxes, which required all landowners—including the Church and its parishes—to pay taxes to the state. This created tensions between Becket and the clergymen of England, who resented their diminished funds and political power.

However, Becket's secular career would not continue, despite his success with the king. In 1161, when Archbishop Theobald died, Becket was elected by King Henry to replace him. This became the great turning point in their relationship, and Henry would regret it the rest of his life. As soon as Becket received the nomination and went through the ceremony for his new position as archbishop, he completely changed his life and habits. Instead of the ideal courtier and statesman, he metamorphosed into a model archbishop. He rid his closets of silks and brightly colored costumes, donning instead a hair shirt next to his skin and plain, simple garments to show his dedication to a spiritual ideal. Becket, knowing himself well, had begged the king not to appoint him as archbishop. He told Henry directly that he could never serve two masters. However, Henry, much to his own chagrin later, never imagined that his most trusted friend and right-hand man would change so completely in his role as archbishop of Canterbury.

As he assumed his new role, one of the first things Becket did was to set out to destroy the laws he had helped Henry create to diminish the power of the Church. His goals were to exempt the Church from civil jurisdiction and to separate the property of the Church from that of the secular world to avoid any taxation. Becket also worked to make the clergy immune to any laws set forth by the government, which meant they were not required to go through a trial, even if they had committed a crime.

King Henry became livid and immediately began to work on plans to subvert the new policies set in motion by Becket. In 1164 he called an assembly of knights and bishops of England at Clarendon to pass the Constitution of Clarendon, a document that ended the immunities of the clergy. The members gathered in Clarendon were inclined to yield to the king's wishes, but Becket refused to give in. He agreed to sign the constitution only if it contained a disclaimer that ensured the independence of the Church. In effect, his objections undermined the premise of the constitution and provoked Henry to such a degree that he left the assembly in anger.

Henry did not yield to the will of Becket without a fight, however. The king called another assembly at Clarendon to revisit his earlier plans, again attempting to eradicate the immunity of the Church. All parties involved agreed, including Becket, but when it came time to sign the actual document at the assembly, Becket staunchly refused. Henry retaliated by holding him in contempt of royal authority and summoned him to appear before a council to answer for his crimes. Becket, citing the exact policies he was trying to protect, claimed that the king had no authority over him and went into voluntary exile.

Immediately after the summons from the king, Becket sailed to France for protection, leaving England in disguise and traveling in a small fishing boat. Once in France, the archbishop met up with Pope Alexander in the city of Sens. When Henry heard of the whereabouts of Becket, he appealed to the pope to deliver him back to England, but Pope Alexander, who had been a longtime friend of Becket, refused, thus frustrating the efforts of the king even more. As a result, Becket spent six years in self-imposed exile in France under the protection of Louis VII, living at a Cistercian abbey until threats from Henry forced him to move back to Sens.

In the meantime, Henry tried every possible way to mandate the return of Becket to England to face his demands. The furious king issued several edicts that were aimed at Becket and his supporters, including banishing all of Becket's relatives from England. Becket appealed again to Pope Alexander to counterattack with counteredicts and ultimately excommunication. While the pope was supportive of Becket's position, he did not want to take such drastic measures, preferring instead to patch up the misunderstanding between the king and the archbishop in a peaceful manner. Finally, with the intervention of the French king, Alexander gave in to the wishes of Becket and threatened Henry with excommunication. Henry saw the imminent danger in these developments and realized the precariousness of his position.

At this point, Henry promised the pope he would reach an agreement with the stubborn archbishop. They met up in Avranches, France, and Henry agreed to listen to the demands of Becket on return to England. As soon as they reached Canterbury, Becket repeated his excommunication of all the bishops who had opposed him earlier. The English bishops were infuriated and immediately went to complain to the king, who in turn became enraged himself. Henry is often quoted as saying, "Shall a man who has eaten my bread insult the king and all the kingdom ... and not one of the loathsome vipers whom I nourish at my table does me right for such an affront." His words incited his men at arms to form a plot against the miscreant archbishop. Reginald Fitzurse, William de Tracy, Hugh de Moreville, and Richard le Breton were among the men that carried out the plan. In December 1170, they were successful, murdering Becket at the altar of Canterbury Cathedral.

All across Europe, Christians shrank back in horror at the horrible deed, and Henry was summarily excommunicated. The English king retired to his chambers and did not eat for three days, and when he finally appeared, he ordered the arrest of the assassins. He also sent emissaries to the pope, proclaiming his innocence and stating that, despite any culpability, he was prepared to perform any penance required. Many historians agree that Henry was not, in fact, guilty of the crime, as he had never ordered the murder of Becket outright. He also gave up on the Constitution of Clarendon and returned all of the privileges and property to the Church. Ultimately, although he lost his life in the process, Becket was victorious in the end.

In 1172, Becket was canonized as a saint, and the pope proclaimed that many miracles had occurred at his tomb, which soon afterward became a pilgrimage destination. In penance, King Henry walked three miles to Canterbury in bare feet, stopping at the entrance to allow the monks to flog him.

His luck had changed considerably with the turn of events precipitated by the battle of wills with Becket. Queen Eleanor of Aquitaine, who had been banished and imprisoned so Henry could take another mistress, used her considerable influence to turn his sons against him. His eldest, Henry, led revolts against his father and died at an early age. The younger Henry had never been resistant to objecting to his father's rule; he had long considered Becket to be a kinder, more just father figure than the king and resented his father for his connection to the murder. His other sons, Richard the Lion Heart and John Lackland, joined forces with King Philip of France. Henry II, once the wealthy and power-ful king of England who had married the richest and most brilliant woman in Europe, died cursing the sons that had betrayed him.

The events that passed as a result of the feud between Becket and Henry con-tinued to influence the culture and political systems of England well beyond the time that they occurred. Chaucer's *Canterbury Tales*, one of the greatest pieces of literature to come out of England in the medieval period, recounted the sto-ries of people on a pilgrimage to visit the tomb of St. Thomas Becket. In addi-tion, many legends of the powers of Becket circulated as folktales in England. Some claimed that when he didn't like the taste of the water in Kent, he struck the ground to create a well of spring water. In Oxford, it was said that the ab-sence of the melodic song of the nightingale was also due to the temporary presence of Becket; according to legend, the sounds of the nightingale disturbed him so much during his praying that he commanded them to never to sing again in the part of town where he was staying. Politically, the history of Eng-land never forgot the havoc created by the disagreement. While Becket had been victorious in his own time, the lesson was learned by the next generations. English courts forever afterward made it a point to liberate the secular govern-ment from clerical influence and thus paved the way to the modern world, free of the powerful influence of the Church.

While her husband suffered the effects of the rise of Becket in the Church, Queen Eleanor had her own worries to consider. Much to her chagrin, she was not to retire gracefully in England watching her brood of beautiful children mature and scatter across Europe as kings, queens, and great dukes. Henry made the grave mistake of flaunting his mistress Rosamund to the courts of England in such a way that Eleanor could not forgive him. Infuriated, Eleanor waited until the time was right and then left England to return to Poitiers. There, she was determined to cut herself away from feudal kings and establish rule of her own making, while securing strategic success for her children. This break was to be the beginning of the great court of Poitiers, which brought civi-lization to new heights and was in particular a realm where feminine graces and taste ruled.

The courts of love that were formed under Eleanor's rule soon overflowed with travelers, troubadours, and poets, who wrote that she was to them "what dawn is to birds." Her eldest daughter, Marie, left her father Louis in Paris and was soon installed in the castle of Poitiers. Marie took great initiative in the courts of love, and with the help of a clerk named Andre, wrote a treatise on love, emphasizing that in matters of love, woman is the mistress, and the man her vassal in service. Eleanor took great pleasures in her court and had great plans for the paths her children would take. Her third son Richard, her favorite, was installed in Poitiers as duke, which marked him for a great future. But her husband Henry was not pleased with the state of affairs later, when his sons moved against him. He fought their rebellion with a swift hand and captured his entire family, Eleanor included, and brought them all back to England.

When he returned to his court, Henry was perplexed as to what to do with his queen. He did not want to divorce her, because he knew that she would return to France, only to find another man to join forces against him. He did not want to keep her in custody forever, either, because that would make it impossible for him to marry again. He resolved finally to both divorce her and imprison her, and the imperial Queen Eleanor, at the age of fifty-three, was imprisoned in the Abbey of Fontevrault in France.

The home of the Plantagenet family saw many quarrels among the sons and their father, especially after the death of Henry, the second son of Eleanor and Henry Plantagenet. The heir to the throne thus became Richard, who after refusing to give up his dukedom of Aquitaine, signed up to serve in the Third Crusade—while Europe was feuding, Jerusalem had been captured by Saladin. Although Henry was angry that Richard had not consulted with him before he took the cross, he could not deny the need to defend Christendom from its invaders and signed up to join the Crusade himself. Fleeing the fury of his son, Henry crossed paths with one of his former subjects, William Marshall. Instead of killing the king, he struck down his horse and left him to his own devices. King Henry died soon afterward, leaving his kingdom to Richard I.

Richard soon freed his mother Eleanor and prepared his realm for his departure on crusade. He left England with 114 ships and arrived in Messina, only to find that his sister Joanna had been widowed and imprisoned. He overthrew the city quickly, and his sister and her dowry were handed over to him. He continued on to Palestine, arriving near the port in 1191. Richard fought fiercely alongside his knights despite the fact that he had contracted ague fever on the journey. Wrapped in silk blankets, he had his men carry him within range of the largest tower so he could join the crossbowmen in shooting at the enemy. It was during these battles that he attained his reputation for incredible bravery and became known as Richard the Lion Heart.

The city of Acre was conquered by Richard and his men, and they pressed forward to Jerusalem. However, Jerusalem was in the hands of Saladin, who was well prepared to defend the city against the Crusaders. Frustrated that he could not free it from Muslim rule, a chronicler of the time quotes Richard as crying to the heavens, "Fair Lord God, I pray Thee that Thou suffer me not to behold Thy Holy City since I cannot deliver it from the hands of Thine enemies."

Richard returned from Palestine and in disguise crept through the countryside of Austria to reach his homelands. However, he was soon discovered and imprisoned by Leopold of Austria, whom he had offended during battle at Acre. The rumor that the heroic king was in captivity spread like wildfire to England and, ever the skillful ruler, his mother Eleanor came to Richard's rescue. At seventy years of age, Eleanor took it upon herself to free her favorite son, writing the pope to enlist his help. She raised the enormous sum of 100,000 silver marks—more than a year's worth of revenues from England and Normandy—and brought Richard back to a hero's welcome in England. He spent the rest of his rule trying to regain financial stability in England, which had been bled dry to supply the Third Crusade.

In 1199, Richard was shot down on horseback by a crossbowman in revenge for the deaths of his father and brothers. Displaying the virtues of chivalry that were sung by the troubadours, Richard forgave the offender and died in his mother's arms. Eleanor continued to exercise her skills in statecraft and was able to preserve Richard's realm for her youngest son, John. However, in 1204 as King Philip of France stormed the chateau while John remained idle, Eleanor passed on, having lived as queen of two countries and mother of two kings.

One of the most remarkable rulers of the Capetian dynasty had none of the ambition characteristic of the mighty Henry II or Richard the Lion Heart. Louis

IX was an entirely different sort of king, ruling from the heart. Louis was brought up in the tradition of Paris, under the tutelage of his beautiful, wise, and devout mother Blanche. Known in France as the "Good Queen" and "Good Mother," Blanche was the granddaughter of Henry II and Eleanor of Aquitaine. She was raised in Spain but married into the Capetian dynasty and moved to Paris to become queen of France and mother of eleven children. Her husband Louis VIII died when she was thirty-eight and Louis IX was twelve years old. For nine years while her son was too young to rule, Blanche took over and proved to be a generous, beneficent queen and role model for her son. During her rule, she freed many serfs on the royal estates, provided dowries for poverty-stricken girls, and helped to finance the building of Chartres Cathedral. In 1225, when Louis IX inherited the kingdom, France was peaceful and prosperous.

As a young man, Louis was tall, blond, and handsome and had elegant tastes. He did not have the soul of a scholar; rather he was fond of falconry and games and liked colorful clothing and luxurious furniture. In the *Life of St. Louis*, the biography written by Jean Sire de Joinville, the writer tells of an incident when the young Louis was criticized because his clothing was more elaborate than that of the king. His habits became less ostentatious when his mother found him a wife, however, and Louis became a model of conjugal fidelity. His wife bore him eleven children, and he conscientiously took part in their education and upbringing. As he grew older, his taste for luxuries waned. Joinville states that Louis later wore a simple black cloak in his everyday life, and when he returned from the Crusades, he refused to wear any furs except inexpensive lamb- or hareskin. He became more and more concerned with affairs of state and the just administration of his government. Louis governed with a just hand that took account of the welfare of all classes. While he respected the rights of the nobles, he would not tolerate abuse on their side to the men and women who served them.

The reign of Louis IX corresponded with the beginning of French dominance in Europe, which was to last for five centuries. He was the epitome of a Christian king and the answer to the prayers of many medieval churchmen. His conception of the role of the monarchy was as an office that would secure national unity and as a means to protect the poor and weak from the more powerful. He became a model of virtue and fair-mindedness such that his reputation as an arbiter was superior than that of the pope. He founded and contributed to monasteries, hospitals, asylums, a home for the blind, and a home for redeemed prostitutes. Whenever he traveled throughout his provinces, he held a dinner for 120 poor people and selected three to dine with him. He waited on these three, ensuring that they were blindfolded so they did not know they were being waited upon by the king, and washed their feet himself. He felt the burden of his flesh heavily and wore a hair shirt underneath his kingly raiment and practiced acts of self-mortification with chains. However, Louis's saintly demeanor and popularity in Europe did not preclude acts of violence that were used to protect the Church and his kingdom. He once punished a man for blasphemy by burning his nose and lips and was largely responsible for the organization of the Inquisition in France in 1233. His kindliness and just nature did not extend to those who held different religious beliefs.

The reigning passion of Louis IX in his later life became the desire to return the city of Jerusalem to Christian rule. In 1248 he set off on his first Crusade, leaving France in the capable hands of his mother, Blanche. Initially victorious in several battles, Louis, his queen, and their newborn son were captured by Muslim invaders in the city of Damietta in 1250. The captives were held until their ransom was paid, and despite the advice of his councilors, Louis stayed until he could negotiate the release of as many of his men as possible. He returned to France and again showed his intractable sense of duty and fairness when he insisted that the full ransom, which had not been delivered to his captors, be paid.

He set out on his second Crusade in 1270 when news traveled from Constantinople that the Muslim invaders were becoming increasingly successful in gaining territory in the East. When Louis and his troops landed in North Africa, disease struck the French crusaders and took the lives of both Louis and his son John Tristan. The Crusade ended in tragedy, for the loss of the just king was mourned throughout Europe. Louis IX was known and loved by his people for his sense of justice and his ability to rule wisely, and his piety and devotion to God were ultimately rewarded in 1297 when he was canonized as St. Louis, the only European to be both a king and a saint.

The thirteenth century was also host to a completely different sort of king, Frederick II, who provided many points of direct contrast to the saintly doings of Louis IX. Frederick was born in 1194 and crowned king of Sicily when he was four years old. Unfortunately, his mother died a year later and left him in the care of Pope Innocent III, who did all he could to undermine the union of Sicily with Germany that Frederick's father had worked so hard to achieve. As a child, Frederick grew up in neglect and was left to run free in the streets of Palermo, sometimes having to be fed by kindly strangers. He was not given a traditional education, either, but he learned much about the world around him through observation and experience. By virtue of his inborn intellect, he managed to learn Arabic and Greek, and he read many history books. Despite his lack of systematic education, he soon made a reputation for himself as a wonder of learning and was much admired throughout his life for the extent of his knowledge.

Frederick began his career in 1211 and managed, with luck and support from the pope, to be crowned emperor of the Holy Roman Empire at Aachen in a splendid ceremony seated in the marble throne of Charlemagne. At his coronation, he promised the Germans that he would defend all Christendom, punish any heretics, and take the sign of the cross on crusade. However, Germany did not compare in his eyes to the splendor of Italy. He soon left Germany and was absent from its borders for forty-eight of the fifty-six years of his rule. After his first wife died, the new pope Honorius persuaded Frederick to marry Isabella, the heiress to the lost kingdom of Jerusalem, and he added the title of King of Jerusalem to his name. Frederick built his capital in Italy at Foggia and maintained a strict rule over his empire. He revered the Roman Empire as the model upon which he would build his state and had coins minted that bore the image of the Roman eagle, encircled with his name. Frederick believed strongly in the supreme rule of his office, and he ingrained in his administration and subjects that his status was close to the Son of God. He proved to be skilled in the management of his economy and nationalized the production of iron, steel, salt, hemp, tar, dyed fabrics, and silks. Foreign trade was by and large managed by the government, carried in ships owned by the state.

Amidst the orderly direction of the state, Frederick also ran a court that was to rival any in intrigue and interest. He kept a large number of slaves of different races to administer to his every need, as well as a harem and a large collection of exotic animals. Included in his collection were leopards, apes, bears led on chains, panthers, and a giraffe that was a gift from the sultan of Egypt. His harem and zoo would often travel with him, so that his caravan provided a strange and fearsome sight as it rambled through his countryside. His interest in animals became scientific, and he conducted many experiments on the behavior of animals to add to his great store of knowledge. He kept a zoo expressly for learning about animals' breeding habits and as a result later enforced laws on hunting that allowed the procreation of each species in peace. Experts were summoned from Egypt to test out the possibility of hatching eggs by the heat of the sun. Frederick later wrote and illustrated a book on birds, entitled *About the Art of Hunting and Falconry*, which displays an acute attention to detail that could only have been accomplished after many hours of observation.

Whereas St. Louis turned to religion as he grew older, Frederick turned more and more to science and philosophy. He filled his court with learned men from many places: mathematicians from Egypt, poets from Aquitaine, and scientists of both Jewish and Muslim heritage. He had all the scientific classics of Greece and Islam translated into Latin, and in 1224 he established the University of Naples without an ecclesiastical affiliation. Frederick paid scholars of all arts and sciences high salaries and set up funds to make it possible for poor students to attend. He himself read spoke nine languages and wrote seven, frequently corresponding in Arabic with al-Kamil. His scientific curiosity was so profound that he took part in the dissection of cadavers and amazed his court physicians with his knowledge of anatomy. In one case, Frederick is said to have invited two men to a luxurious dinner, sent one to bed and one to hunt, only to have them disemboweled afterwards to see which one had better digested his food.

Unfortunately, Frederick's love for knowledge took him into realms that were unacceptable to the pope and sometimes feared by his people. With his love of science came a pointed skepticism toward religious matters. As Frederick had been raised in southern Italy, a crossroads of different cultures, languages, and customs, he was disinclined to view the Muslim faith as unquestionably evil. He became known for his religious skepticism and took great satisfaction in uttering blasphemies without any regard to who was listening. He is said to have publicly claimed that the world had been "deceived by three men: Jesus, Moses, and Mohammed," shocking Christians and Muslims alike. His antireligious reputation soon spread all over Europe and he was dubbed the Antichrist for his blasphemies. The sight of him and his traveling caravan of Muslim bodyguards, harem girls, and collection of exotic animals convinced the common people who happened upon this fantastical sight to believe these accusations, as he appeared to them as not unlike the beast in the Book of Revelation.

For these sins, Frederick paid a heavy price. Pope Gregory IX excommunicated him in 1239, unleashing the fury of the emperor. When the pope summoned a council to Rome in hopes of deposing of Frederick permanently, Frederick retaliated by sending his navy to capture the ship that held a hundred prelates and two cardinals. Frederick marched into Rome to use his power of persuasion to revoke his excommunication, but in the process, Pope Gregory died of old age at ninety. Frederick rushed to secure a candidate for the papacy that would be sympathetic to his cause but was ultimately unsuccessful. Innocent IX initially promised allegiance to Frederick but, once he was enthroned, turned on him and met with a large group of churchmen and bishops in Lyons to proceed with the deposition of Frederick. Frederick's army marched out to stop the ceremony but was ultimately defeated in 1248.

Frederick, tired and discouraged, retired to his private castle and died in 1250. His empire was soon dissipated, and the goals he had worked for all his life were lost with him, but Frederick continued to inspire admiration after his death. He foreshadowed the ideals and new scientific attitudes that would characterize the Renaissance.

The Social Fabric of the Early Middle Ages

Feudalism

After the century of invasions and calamities that took place following the death of Charlemagne, the social system that evolved and ultimately provided some security to many members of the medieval population was *feudalism*. Brutal men battled over power and riches. Few kings could exercise the power wielded by Charlemagne, and they needed the support of other men to defend their interests in their kingdoms. Because the Merovingian kings also lacked money, the reward they offered for loyalty and protection was land. Men who proved their worth as warriors or advisers were given large areas of land, or *fiefs*, and thus a hierarchical system was born. The king needed loyalty and warriors, and the lord or knight who was rewarded with land needed other men to fight for him as well as people to work the land and tend to the everyday needs of his estate. Peasants and artisans who were landless needed protection as much as, if not more than, the king. They in turn would work or fight alongside the lords of the manor for food, shelter, and protection.

Vassalage

The bond between the kings and the lords was called *vassalage*. When a man was chosen to become a vassal of the king and received a large gift of land, there was a symbolic ceremony that continued throughout the Middle Ages. In 1127 a chronicler described the ceremony where the vassals of a murdered count would swear loyalty to his successor: The vassals verbally state their intention that they are willing to serve the new count, and this statement is sealed with a kiss between the new vassal and his lord. After the kiss, the vassal swears his loyalty to his new lord on the relics of saints. The kiss demonstrated that both the lord and the vassal were on the same level of familiarity, but it was not used everywhere in Europe; in Germany in particular, some of the most powerful kings refused to acknowledge the equality of their vassals to themselves, and their ceremonies did not include a kiss. The homage ceremony was one of the most significant rites performed during the period, and the tie between the vassal and his lord was considered almost as strong as blood. The people of the Middle Ages were largely illiterate, and written contracts were rarely forged. The ceremony was a method of legitimizing an act, in front of others as witnesses, that made it binding to both parties present.

Knights

One of the foundations of the feudal system was the medieval knight. In most cases, the knight was a person of aristocratic birth, born into a landowner's family. The aspiring noble had to endure a long apprenticeship to become a knight. At age seven, he became a page, and at fourteen, a squire who worked in service to a lord. At the same time, the youth trained in the arts of war, learned to handle a horse, and practiced with swords and lances as soon as he was able to manage them.

When the apprenticeship was finished, he went through a ceremony that was even more sacred than the homage ceremony. The first step was a bath, symbolic of purification, and gave the name "Knight of the Bath" to those who had undergone the ceremony. The candidate was then clothed in a white tunic, a red robe, and a black coat, colors that symbolized purity, blood, and death, respectively. He fasted, confessed his sins, attended a Mass designed to remind him of the moral and religious duties of a knight, and was finally blessed by a priest. He then changed into a costume more suitable for a knight with a breastplate, gauntlets, and a sword and was knighted by the lord with three slaps of the sword on his neck or shoulder. Gold spurs were attached to his boots to symbolize his knightly status. After the dubbing ceremony, he received a lance, a helmet, and a horse and threw a feast for his friends. Knights were also made without this lengthy ceremony, however; if a man showed extraordinary valor and bravery on the battlefield, he could be dubbed a "Knight of the Sword."

The medieval knight was expected to serve under his lord and defend the estate he represented, although when the Crusades began, many medieval knights left their estates for the higher call to defend Christendom and defeat the infidel. When there weren't any battles to wage, the main occupation of the knight was to engage in tournaments, which served the purpose of amusement as well as preparation for battle. The tradition of tournaments began in the tenth century and, to a certain degree, sublimated the passions and energies that had in previous centuries caused so much disruption in society. Before there were tournaments, fights broke out frequently among the knights, who were forever jockeying to prove their superiority on the battlefields. Some of the knights, bored without any battles to fight, would raid their neighbors on a whim, take whatever they could get their hands on, and ravage the peasants' crops. Even though the jousting games were heartily disapproved of by some religious men, tournaments distracted the aggressive urges and flourished particularly in France.

The sons of Eleanor of Aquitaine were great supporters of tournaments in the twelfth century, and they developed a following that could reach three thousand participants and spectators, who would take over the town chosen as the location of the tournament. Aside from the knights and spectators, there would be horse dealers, musicians, haberdashers, fortune-tellers, acrobats, troubadours, women of high birth, and women of loose morals attending the event. The tournament was far from just a spectator sport; it was a colorful festival that included song and dance, love trysts, and gambling.

The code of conduct followed by the knights of the Middle Ages was marked by the chivalrous behavior. *Chivalry* began in the tenth century and reached its zenith in the thirteenth after the courts of love of Eleanor of Aquitaine. According to the rules of chivalry, the knight was ideally supposed to be both hero and saint. When he was knighted, he pledged to defend the Church, protect the less fortunate, always speak the truth, and pursue the infidel. He was to protect women and their chastity, be courteous to other knights, and if he took prisoners, treat them as guests. But few knights ever measured up to the high standards set forth for them. Indeed, during the Crusades, many Arabs were surprised at the brutality of the Crusaders. One event that illustrates the ruthlessness and vulgarity practiced by the Crusaders was when Bohemond, leader of the First Crusade, sent the Greek emperor a shipment of sliced-off noses and thumbs. Nevertheless, the ideals of chivalry left their mark on medieval society. The courts of love so carefully developed by Eleanor and her daughter Marie of Champagne influenced the cultivation of manners, and this moved throughout the courts and the rest of society in the Middle Ages. In essence, modern manners are a product of medieval chivalry. Education was likewise highly influenced by chivalry. The orders of knighthood, which grew in numbers throughout the period, later combined the chivalric ideal with liberal education.

Peasants and Serfs

Peasants were fated to an entirely different destiny than that of the celebrated knights of the Middle Ages. Early medieval society is often said to have been divided into three groups: the warriors, the priests, and the laborers. The last group was generally held in little esteem, particularly by the nobility. Work with the hands was regarded as part of the curse inflicted on humankind due to the sins of Adam. Nonetheless, many peasants forfeited their freedom willingly to a stronger and richer man. The danger of trying to survive alone was such that the guarantee of food and shelter in exchange for labor was worthwhile, if not desirable. Peasants worked every day, apart from saint's days, but this was preferable to starvation, which was a common threat during the Middle Ages because of frequent famines. One chronicler of the twelfth century notes that in a bad famine year, there was human flesh on sale in the market.

These men and women, the serfs of the Middle Ages, contributed to the harmony and stability of society as much as the knights who defended the estate did. Without the labor done by serfs on the land, the entire system would have collapsed. They provided the foodstuffs and raw materials for the everyday implements of the entire estate. More skilled men and women worked as artisans on the feudal estates and cooked, baked, made textiles and clothing, cobbled shoes, made soap and candles, and in general produced all the needed amenities for a higher-quality lifestyle for the lords of the manor.

Women

Women in the early Middle Ages seem to have suffered and rejoiced alongside their men. The quality of women's lives depended to a great degree on their station in life. Working women of the medieval period were skilled in many crafts, particularly in those related to the upkeep of the home. Medieval women of the working and peasant classes baked bread and pies, made soap and candles, brewed beer and concocted herbal medicines, made yarns with the distaff or spinning wheel, and wove, constructed, and decorated the clothing for herself and her family. Food in the Middle Ages was usually prepared by women, and as soon as spices were made available through trade, they were generously used to flavor many recipes. Pepper, cloves, garlic, cinnamon, and wine were common ingredients used in the preparation of foods. Aside from performing the domestic arts, women of the Middle Ages helped cultivate crops, took care of the animals, sheared sheep, and helped keep the buildings in good repair.

The aristocratic woman's situation differed considerably from that of a merchant's wife, and even more from the wife of a serf or peasant. Aristocratic women were educated to be demure, practice their embroidery, prepare for marriage and children, and run their households. The art of dress was one of the chief interests of medieval women, particularly those with the income to spend on it. Aside from the feminine interests of fashion and family, there are accounts that tell us that noble women of the medieval period learned to read, played chess, attended tournaments, and hunted along with their menfolk. In the *Taymouth Hours* manuscript from 1330, there are several illustrations of upper-class young women riding and shooting at deer and rabbits without male chaperones. In the twelfth century, John of Salisbury reproached the practice of hunting by women and criticized the fervor with which women joined in the sport.

Yet, despite the fact that women may have taken part in some of the activities enjoyed by men, most men believed they were inferior beings. Included in this belief was the assumption of the right to inflict corporal punishment on them. In a handbook written to instruct his daughters, the Knight of Latour Landry tells them of a well-born woman who dared to criticize her husband in public; in reaction, he "smote her down with his fist down to the earth, then with his foot he kicked her face and broke her nose." Peasant women who nagged their husbands could be publicly humiliated by being doused in the village pond.

Women in the medieval period had a dual reputation to contend with, being at one moment attributed with the beneficence and grace of the Virgin Mary, and condemned to burn in hell as an evil temptress in the next. The Church was by and large staunchly mistrustful of women, and priests, monks, and clergy preached the dangers of the woman, as well as her inferiority to man. They never forgave her for the sins of Eve, which were evoked time and time again. This attitude was tempered by the efforts of the courts of love under Eleanor of Aquitaine, where the cult of the Virgin Mary found an earthly counterpart in noblewomen during the age of chivalry. Women were held up to be the mistresses of men and expected the brave knights to court them and obey their wishes in return for their favor.

It was decided in the courts of love in the twelfth century that love could not occur in marriage. Highborn women were expected both to marry and to take a lover. Because most aristocratic marriages were arranged by parents and guardians with the ultimate purpose of gaining wealth and land, this was the first occasion women could choose the object of their affection. Indeed, the taking of a lover was as highly organized as feudalism. When a lover was accepted by a lady, a formal ceremony took place in the court, similar to the act of homage between a vassal and his lord. The admirer knelt at his lady's feet and swore a lifetime of service to her. In addition, the chosen lover was expected to write poems that celebrated his mistress's charms, meet for secret trysts, and take a lively part in court life with her.

Less ethereal pleasures of everyday life in the medieval period for classes outside the nobility included visits to the alehouse. Working women exchanged gossip and told stories at the establishment, which was frequently run by a woman who brewed the ale. Entertainment was also provided at fairs and tournaments by traveling actors and musicians. Other activities included visits to the public bath. After the Crusades, hot steam baths were reintroduced to the main cities of Europe. They served as a type of social club for men and women but were condemned vehemently by the Church as dens of sin.

It is easy to look at the age of feudalism as a period marked by exploitation, violence, indentured servitude, and ignorance. However, the feudal picture also includes the brave and vigorous men who sang of the beauty of women and defended their lord with their lives, knights seeking adventure rather than comfort and security, and women praying to the Virgin and running their households in spite of the difficulties they faced. While feudalism may not appear to the modern reader as the ideal system of social organization, it nonetheless restored economic and political order to a society that had previously been under the thrall of barbarians and invaders.

European Expansion and Feudal Collapse

In the eleventh century, in part due to the relatively peaceful political climate and the growing power of kings, an unprecedented expansion took place in Europe. In the early part of feudal Europe, the lord's manor was an isolated unit of self-sufficiency. Everything needed by the lord, his vassals, and his serfs was produced and consumed by them. Surplus goods rotted away or were devoured by rodents. But in the latter part of the Middle Ages, the system changed. With a rise in the population of towns, there was a new demand for products, and the lord could dispose of his surplus food as well as wares produced on the estate. For the first time in the medieval period, the lords of the manors began to feel capitalistic urges.

The feudal structure crumbled with the opportunities of town life beckoning, and a widespread urban migration took place. The lord of the manor began to replace the labor charge of his serfs with a money rent and hired more farm hands to cultivate crops that would bring him profits in the market. These changes gave new opportunities to the serf to escape his servitude; some purchased more land to become free farmers, and some moved into the thriving towns themselves to seek a better life. Many went into the thriving textile industry to become weavers and later formed powerful guild systems. In addition to specialized artisans, the textile industry was also partly responsible for the new class of townspeople, the most powerful of which was the merchant class.

The main agent for this change was the improvement in trade. In the feudal period, merchants were heavily taxed as they made their journeys from the south to the north. Aside from the taxes levied on the sale of goods imported into the region, there were also toll stations located on bridges, along roads, and in ports. The route on the Loire River alone had 74 toll stations. Many of the tolls were exacted in exchange for the protection of the traveling merchant, who was easy prey to the robbers and pirates who lurked in forests and sailed the high seas. While he undoubtedly needed the protection, his efforts were not well rewarded; after the journey, the merchant was lucky to have 40 percent of the value of his cargo left.

By the eleventh century, this situation began to change. The growing power of the monarchy diminished banditry, removed some of the tolls, and established a fair system of weights and measures. Trade flourished and was partly responsible for the growth of towns. Great fairs developed that displayed products from countries all throughout Europe. Important fairs were held in Paris, London, Lyons, Frankfurt, Bruges, and Geneva and could last six or seven weeks. With the road relatively clear of thieves, merchants flocked to the markets from Africa, Byzantium, China, India, and the Far East. They carried elaborate textiles for the wealthy, and spices that could not be found on the European continent. One fourteenth-century treatise included some 288 products that were imported into Europe, including almonds, cinnamon, cloves, coconuts, elephant's tusks, ginger, indigo, licorice, musk, pepper, pearls, and sandalwood. Many of the products that came from the Mediterranean commanded great prices in northern Europe.

Trade and Technological Developments

The expansion of trade in the eleventh century was facilitated by technological developments in the production of textiles. Some of the new inventions made the fabrication of cloth faster and simpler, so that the value of textiles went down on the market and made them available to a larger portion of the population. Waterpower was harnessed for the process of fulling fabrics, which made them denser and of a much higher quality. Water mills were already in use for several tasks, including grinding grain, pressing olives, polishing armor, and tanning leather. Before the use of the water mill, fulling was performed by several people who trampled the fabric or beat it with a fulling bat, methods that dated back to antiquity. The water mill substituted wooden hammers that were driven by the movement of water over the wheel. The use of this innovation cut down on labor considerably. Initially used in Italy, the water mill spread throughout Europe in the twelfth century and was quickly adopted in the north, where the production of wool fabrics constituted one of the main industries of the area.

Another invention that dramatically impacted the production of textiles was the spinning wheel. The spinning wheel originated in India and was invented between the fifth and eighth centuries, and its design was improved upon by the Chinese, who added a treadle to the frame. It was initially used in Spain, where many Muslims of the Middle East resided. In the thirteenth century, the spinning wheel was adopted in Paris, doubling the output of yarn. In addition to speeding up of the process of spinning yarn, the yarn spun on the spinning wheel was of a better quality, smoother and more uniform.

Other industries witnessed progress as well: fine glass was produced for cathedrals from the eleventh century on, a paper mill was opened in Germany in 1190, and the use and knowledge of the manufacture of perfume trickled in through the ports of Italy from the East. New products adopted by the Europeans included the compass and gunpowder, which were brought back as novelties from the exploits of the Crusaders. The use of gunpowder was rare in the early Middle Ages but would change warfare considerably in the latter part of the period.

Religion

While improvements in trade and technology were critical factors in the economic development of the Middle Ages, the force that lent the most social unity to the people of Europe was religion. From the time of Charlemagne, who was blessed by the pope as the Holy Roman emperor, Christianity and the future administration of Europe were wedded. Otto I enhanced these ties when he turned over the management of his duchies to religious clerics rather than to members of the nobility. Kings and nobles rose and fell according to the favor or disfavor shown them by the medieval Church. But more than anything, at a time when violence and disorder touched the lives of thousands on a daily basis, Christianity provided a moral code of behavior and promised that rewards, so fleeting in this life, were waiting in the next one. Christianity balanced tribulation with hope and softened the harsh realities of disease, hard labor, and misfortune with the solace that came from the belief that there was meaning in the universe.

While Christianity was ubiquitous on the continent of Europe during the Middle Ages, there were small groups of people of different faiths among the numerous Christians. Many Jews settled into Christian communities during the Middle Ages, bringing their highly valued skills in textile manufacture with them. Kings and popes alike facilitated their entry into western Europe for the simple fact that their knowledge was valuable to the economic success of their countries. This, however, did not mean they were welcomed as comrades among the Christians. In 1215, the Lateran Council ordered bishops to organize an effort that would provide an identifying mark for those of the Jewish faith, citing a need to prevent intermarriage between Jews and Christians. Jews were required in many cities to wear a piece of cloth, frequently yellow, attached to their exterior garments. These practices enraged many of the Jews that were forced to follow them, and in some cases they were able to purchase exemption from them for small groups and individuals.

Christianity and its beliefs dominated the lives of the people of the Middle Ages. While some Christians envisioned the shiny gates of heaven, many more feared the threat of hell. Preachers and reformists addressed crowds of onlookers at every chance to warn them of the fires of hell that waited for them if they did not reform before it was too late. Monks and clergymen gave colorful descriptions of the terrors that awaited sinners in the pits of hell. For example, in the twelfth century, the monk Tundale reported that the Devil was bound to a burning grate by red-hot chains and would seize the damned and stuff them into his mouth, which was filled with burning flames. Satan was accompanied by assistant demons, which plunged the bodies of the damned in fire and water, sliced them with a saw, hung them by the tongue, or boiled them and strained them through a cloth. Screams of agony resonated throughout the fiery chamber, which reeked of sulfur.

The Christian Church itself gave no description or location of hell, but the imaginations and superstitions of men and women of the medieval period were nonetheless filled with images supplied elsewhere. Indeed, medieval people believed heartily that the Devil existed in the flesh and could turn up at any moment. He lurked everywhere and had temptations in mind for any weak soul he could find. He could be averted with the sign of the cross or a splash of holy water, but the scent of sulfur lingered even after he left.

The Middle Ages were also filled with tales of supernatural events, and news of the miracles spread like wildfire throughout the towns. The Madonna was sighted and churches were built, or offerings to statues produced unforeseen results. One tale involved the offering of bread to Christ in the Nativity by a child; Christ thanked him, invited him to Paradise, and three days later the child died. Another story told of a Flemish monk who, in the midst of painting the walls of his abbey, was visited by the Devil himself and tempted into painting him as a young handsome man; when the angry Devil pulled the scaffolding out from under the monk's feet, he was caught in the arms of a statue of the Virgin Mary. The stories that told of the wonders of the power of God were not only town gossip: Pope Gregory I wrote many of these types of stories down for posterity in his works, and Pope Leo IX claimed that after he returned to Rome from his visit to France and Germany, a river divided like the Red Sea to let him pass.

One way for a sinner in the Middle Ages to escape the fiery pit of hell was to travel to the holy sites where saints' relics rested. The act of pilgrimage had existed since the fourth century, when Christians traveled to the cities of Jerusalem and Rome to visit the great churches, and by the eleventh century, Santiago (St. James) de Compostela, Spain, was equally as famous. Reasons for the long journeys over land varied from the hope of forgiveness of sin, of entry into paradise, or of the healing of a sick loved one to, for some, simply an escape from the boredom of daily life. For some criminals, a pilgrimage meant freedom from prison. For most Christians en route to Jerusalem, the journey meant the possibility to worship God in the place where He had spoken. Many Christians risked terrible weather, exhaustion, danger of attack, and death to visit the lands where Jesus had spoken. Rome, which housed the relics of St. Peter, was another holy destination, and Pope Boniface VIII declared a jubilee for the year 1300. It was estimated that every day of that year there were 200,000 foreigners in the city of Rome, and two priests with rakes had to be stationed near the tomb of St. Peter to clear away the coins deposited there as offerings.

The saints and members of the family of Christ were important figures in the lives of the people of the Middle Ages. Many churches were built around a specific saint and held relics that were purportedly genuine effects—belongings or body parts—of that saint. The popular pilgrimage destination of the church of St. James at Compostela claimed to house the bones of that apostle, and the Sainte-Chapelle gothic masterpiece, built by St. Louis in Paris, housed relics he had gathered on the Crusades, including a piece of the True Cross. In 1290 the Archbishop of Genoa collected all the stories of the saints into a collection called *The Golden Legend*, which told of the great deeds accomplished by them. Some of the stories bore more of a resemblance to myth than fact. In popular culture, St. Christopher was an 18-foot-tall (6 m) giant who dedicated himself to Jesus Christ, and St. George saved a princess from the dragon. Nonetheless, the people of the Middle Ages loved the stories of the saints and celebrated each saint's day with great reverence.

The Virgin Mary was a particularly significant religious figure during the Middle Ages. Many historians believe that the figure of Mary in early Christianity absorbed some of the attributes of pagan goddesses. One fact that lends credence to these claims is that the feast day of Mary's Assumption into heaven is celebrated the same day as the ancient festival of the Greek goddess Artemis. During the twelfth and thirteenth centuries, she became an all-important part of the everyday lives of people who turned to her for help and guidance. In an era where God was believed to be omnipotent and inclined to damning weak sinners to the fires of hell, Mary represented a merciful, gentler side of the Christian Church.

All classes joined in worship of the Blessed Virgin. Knights made vows of service to her, bourgeois families saw in her the model for motherhood and family, peasants prayed to her for good crops, and even such grand characters as Abélard bowed his head in silence before her image. Her popularity was such that her followers were sometimes classed as followers of the Cult of the Virgin Mary. The Church, which did not encourage a distraction from the Holy Trinity, was nevertheless powerless in the face of the great popular sentiment for the Virgin. Images of the Virgin were everywhere, on street corners as well as in the fields. Mary became, in essence, the symbol for the Church itself and several cathedrals were devoted in her name. She acquired many alternative devotional names, such as "Mother of Mercy" and "Star of the Sea." Many stories were written of her divine influence in the lives of medieval people, and sightings were common. The Church absorbed this pure love and adoration of the Mother of God and celebrated festivals related to the important events in her life. The worship of Mary was a crucial element in the evolution of Christianity and changed it from a religion of trepidation and fear into a religion of mercy, at the same time elevating the status of the feminine sex in the eyes of men.

While the figure of the Virgin Mary did much to soften the harsh mandates of the Church, the brutal side of its dominance did not entirely fade away. The Catholic Church in all of its power and glory throughout much of the medieval period was not above fearing loss of popularity. One of the most severe declarations the Church could pronounce on people was heresy. Individuals like Abélard and Frederick II were publicly denounced, excommunicated, or in the most dramatic cases, tortured. Ironically, while priests and monks preached "Thou shalt not kill," the Church systematically attacked those who did not follow its precepts or posed a threat to the dominance of Christianity in medieval society.

The most ruthless of these acts were inflicted upon a religious group called the Cathari or Cathars. Cathari, named for the Greek word for "pure," formed a sect that called themselves Christians but held some beliefs that were very different than those of the Roman Catholic Church. The Cathar religion flourished in the south of France in the cities of Marseille, Montpellier, and Narbonne. Some scholars believed the concentration of Cathari in this area was due to the facts that these cities were near other religious groups such as Muslims and Jews and that the inhabitants regularly socialized with an influx of merchants from Bulgaria and Italy, which were also centers of Cathar sects. Another place that was particularly influenced by the Cathar religion was the small town of Albi, where there was such a large number of Cathari living that the sect is alternately called the Albigensians.

The Cathari believed in two principles, Good and Evil, which were similar to God and the Devil. All earthly things were considered evil, and they credited the creation of the visible world of matter to the Devil. The Cathari practiced ceremonies but did not have priests. Instead, the sect was divided up into ordinary believers and the Elect, a small group of people who led ascetic lives. Some of the beliefs held by the Cathari were extremely different from those of mainstream Christianity. They believed that each soul would enter into Paradise as soon as it was pure, but that this process sometimes took several lifetimes, thus making their faith similar to Eastern religions that believe in reincarnation. In order to ensure purity at death, members of the Cathar sects were given a special ceremony before their passing, similar to the Last Rites of Christianity. If the person receiving their last rite somehow did not die, however, it was considered to be a great misfortune. The member of the Elect who performed the ceremony tried various ways to avoid this spiritual calamity. Some who had received the last rite and lived were convinced to starve themselves, and others were smothered on their deathbed with the consent of the sufferer.

Some of the beliefs held by the Cathari were surprisingly modern. They believed that men and women were equals and that sex for pleasure was better than procreative sex. They did not object to suicide, euthanasia, or contraception. Also, the Cathari did not eat meat. While the Catholic Church did not initially worry about the growing popularity of the sect or its alternative practices, the Cathari drew a significant amount of attention to themselves when they began to openly criticize the belief structure of the Christian Church. They objected to the materialism of the Church and claimed that the papacy did not deserve the authority accorded to it. The Cathari claimed that St. Peter had never journeyed to Rome and that the wealth enjoyed by the succession of popes was against the core beliefs of Jesus, who was penniless and never owned anything.

During the twelfth century, the Cathari became more and more insulting to the Church. They compared the rich bishops, monks, and pope to the Pharisees that killed Jesus and openly called the Roman Church the "Whore of Babylon" and the pope the Antichrist. One story of the Cathari even recounts the fabrication of a statue of the Virgin Mary that was ugly and one-eyed, which they used to perform miracles, only to reveal the hoax soon afterward. Their heretical antics were broadcast far and wide by the troubadours of southern France. The famed poets and singers of the courts of love in Aquitaine were not necessarily devoted members of the sect but nonetheless shared their mistrust of the Church and considered many of its officials to be liars and hypocrites.

However, not all of the criticism of the Church was spiritually or morally motivated. Nobles in the South of France who had lost their fortunes eyed the lands and riches held by the Church with envy in their hearts. They began to seize property and stage acts of deliberate offense to the grounds held by the Christian Church. The Count of Foix chased the abbot and monks from the monastery in Pamiers and then allowed his horses to eat oats at the chapel altar while his men practiced their marksmanship on the statue of Jesus. Later, Count Raymond VI of Toulouse destroyed several church buildings, persecuted the monks, and was excommunicated for his actions in 1196. These acts were outside the realm of the Cathar beliefs, which were staunchly against material gain, but the nobles were either members of the sect or tolerant of it and so facilitated the connection between the blasphemous acts and the religious sect.

In 1198, when Pope Innocent III ascended to the papacy, he became alarmed and dismayed at the growing number of assaults on the Church by the groups associated with the Cathari. He saw the Cathar beliefs that discouraged having children, allowed suicide, and forbade the ownership of property as threatening the very fabric of society. The new pope wrote to the bishops of the towns in France most affected by the Cathar movement, expressing his concerns over the popularity and actions of the sect. Significantly, he included instructions that allowed for the use of violence to destroy the heretical group. When his orders were received without much enthusiasm, he enlisted the head of the Cistercian monks, Arnaud, to persuade the French king and nobles to act against the Cathari.

Again Innocent's desire to thwart the sect was met with a lukewarm reception, even though he increased the stakes and intensity of his demands. He offered the king all the lands of those who refused to enlist in the fight against the Cathari. Count Raymond of Toulouse agreed to the abolishment of the group but refused to use violence, and Pope Innocent excommunicated him for his refusal. Raymond finally agreed to the pope's wishes to avoid excommunication but still did not act against the Cathari, creating even more frustration for Innocent.

Throughout France, the sentiments toward the Cathari were very tolerant, and many nobles and knights pointed out that the group was made up of people they knew and had grown up with rather than foreign infidels. But Innocent would not be persuaded by these arguments, and after ten years of waiting for action on the part of the Christians against the Cathari he took extreme measures. He tired of the antics of Raymond and excommunicated him yet again. In addition, Innocent made a decree that the lands belonging to Raymond and his associates were now open to ownership by any Christian that could seize them. Raymond appealed for forgiveness and joined in the fight against the heretics. In a final and ultimately disastrous gesture, Innocent summoned all Christians across Europe to a holy war against the Cathari or Albigensians. The effort to root out the religious sect came to be known as the Albigensian Crusade.

Many of the people of southern France believed that the crusade was more deeply motivated by the desire of many to own their fertile lands, so even the non-Cathari among them fought off the attacks from the outsiders. However, their efforts to resist the crusaders came to a frightful end in the city of Beziers. In 1211 the crusaders arrived at the city gates and demanded the surrender of all of the Albigensians. When the town leaders refused to turn them over, the Christian army attacked the city and killed more than 20,000 men, women, and children in a bloody massacre. The fight against Cathar heresy lasted for four years, and the crusaders marched throughout the southwest of France, demanding oaths of loyalty to the Christian faith and the pope. Those who resisted were sentenced to death and killed. In 1215, the city of Toulouse surrendered to the crusaders and was taken over by their leader, Simon de Montfort.

While Pope Innocent was glad the heretics were being duly punished, he was alarmed when he heard of the brutality and bloodthirstiness of the crusaders. He took mercy on Raymond of Toulouse and promised to protect the heritage of his son. When Raymond VII came of age, he conquered his father's duchy, and the crusade lost its momentum. In 1218, Innocent died, and much of the fervor against the heretics faded with him. Although most of them had been slaughtered or recanted their beliefs to save their lives, some Cathari reemerged to practice their faith in the city of Toulouse.

The Inquisition

The papal Inquisition issued by Pope Gregory IX in 1231 developed out of the inefficiency of the official efforts previously made by the dioceses and the growing mistrust and anger in the Christian Church against similar heretical movements. It was more effective than the earlier efforts that had been enforced by the individual archbishops in their parishes. The papal Inquisition was more methodical, and the pope saw to it that there were several men, mostly from the Dominican Order, that were specially trained for the role of inquisitor. These men traveled from city to city and held public trials to root out the heretics in each city and town.

The process of the papal Inquisition was thorough and deliberate. When the inquisitor arrived in a town or city, he would hold a town meeting where attendance was voluntary—except that not attending the meeting constituted immediate grounds for suspicion, so most people would attend. The first step the inquisitor took was to allow any heretic to admit his guilt at this early stage of the process and be sentenced with a lesser punishment. Like a detective, the inquisitor also used this opportunity to question any person who stepped forward at this time about other heretics in their community.

When evidence had been gathered against a suspected heretic, that person was sentenced to a trial. The inquisitors allowed defendants to have a lawyer, although this practice was rarely carried out; if the lawyer lost the case, he was never allowed to practice again. The trials were severely biased against the accused. The inquisitors first seized all the property of the defendant and then held a secret trial where the accused was alone against the inquisitors and their clerks, who took copious notes of the proceedings. The accused heretic was expected to confess, although often enough he did not know his crime. Any testimony against the accused individual was accepted, whether from upstanding citizens or criminals. Family members were also expected to testify against their kin. If an inquisitor was not satisfied with the evidence he had accumulated against a defendant, he could keep the suspect in prison for years while working on the case. On the other hand, the accused was protected at one stage of the trial. In order to avoid allowing the trials to become entrenched in local feuds, the defendant was allowed to name any persons who held a serious grudge against him before the trial began. If the accuser was named, the defendant was set free and the accuser potentially faced a sentence of life imprisonment.

Torture was introduced later into the inquisition process. In 1252 Pope Innocent IV issued a decree that gave the inquisitors the right to torture accused heretics as part of the trial process. A common practice of torture enacted by the inquisitors was to bind the hands behind the back and suspend the accused, thereby dislocating the joints in the shoulders. Other methods included flogging, solitary imprisonment, or the rack. While torture was an accepted part of the medieval justice system, the methods practiced by inquisitors were considerably less harsh than those allowed in secular courts. The inquisitors could not mutilate or kill the accused, and as the offense was intimately connected to the failure of the individual to accept the Christian faith, the ultimate goal was to convert the lost soul back to Christendom. However, there were some inquisitors who took the authority granted to them by the Church as a free pass to enact horrible judgments upon the accused heretics. Some were known for particularly horrendous acts; "Robert the Dominican" sent 180 accused heretics to the stake at one time in 1239.

Punishment for heretics that were convicted ranged in severity. Some cases took years to be judged, and the offenders were required to stay in prison until their sentences were made public. Inquisitors could wait to announce the verdicts en masse to strike fear into the hearts of those who would stray from the flock. Sentences for those who had been deemed guilty of heresy included making a pilgrimage to the Holy Land, wearing a yellow cross across the front of one's clothing, banishment, or imprisonment. Death sentences for heretics were rare, as the Church did not want to be perceived as unmerciful. Historians cite the example of Bernard Gui, an inquisitor who served in Toulouse, condemning forty-two persons to death out of the 930 he had found guilty in his career of fifteen years. In such cases, the Church itself would not carry out the death sentence, instead turning the heretical offender over to secular authorities for hanging or burning at the stake, clinging to its age-old motto "The Church shrinks from blood."

Other punishments included the confiscation of property by the Church and the State, which many saw as a corrupt motivation for condemnation. In Italy, one-third of the seized goods were given to the person who acted as the informer. In France, the State claimed everything, which at the end of the thirteenth century resulted in the addition of almost all of the rich lands of Aquitaine to the French Crown. Once these rules had been set forth by the pope, many individuals and members of the French court were highly motivated to join in the efforts of the inquisitors. Sometimes trials were held against persons already deceased, with the express intent of gaining their lands and possessions. Practices motivated by greed and brutality were denounced by several popes and sovereigns without much effect. However, the suffering would be worse still in the later Middle Ages with the Spanish Inquisition.

Monks and Nuns

Religion also influenced the medieval world for the good and provided many support systems to the people. Monasteries and nunneries were the refuge of those inclined to more extreme acts of devotion. Thousands of men and women chose to flee "from the world, the flesh, and the devil." While the devotion of these men and women is not necessarily under question, it is important to understand the practical elements of the decision to commit oneself to a monastery or convent. Life in these communities provided order, security, and protection from the violence of the medieval world.

Some of the communities were attached to the local church, and some were created because of the leadership of a holy man. When one man—or in some cases, woman—was followed by a group of people influenced by his acts of charity and faith who were ready to commit to a community led by him, the man would go to the pope and ask for acknowledgment of the Order in the Christian Church. This is the case of St. Francis, one of the most well-known and beloved saints of the Middle Ages. In 1223, Francis asked the permission of Pope Honorius III to form his Order. All those who entered the Franciscan Order took vows of poverty and pledged to take care of the poor, ill, and weak.

Education

Christians of the Middle Ages considered the services rendered by monks and priests to be of vital importance in their lives. The Church gave them the means to worship God in the Mass, interpreted the gospels, ensured their spiritual progress through the sacraments, and taught them what they had to do to save their souls. In order to fulfill these duties, the church was required to provide some kind of education for the men that staffed its monasteries and churches. For much of the medieval period, the learning that was provided by the Church was the only education that existed. Monks collected and copied Classical manuscripts, and it is largely due to them that that knowledge has been preserved and handed down to us. Although the monasteries in the time of Charlemagne were far fewer, we owe to his enthusiasm for Classical knowledge the continuity of ideas into the Middle Ages and beyond.

Most of the population believed that "book learning" was useless and instead favored training in war, practical activities, and moral education. Aristocratic children received more education than children of the lower classes, but for the most part they were also schooled in the arts of war or running a household. It was a fairly common practice for young upper-class children to be sent to another household to be trained.

Schools existed mainly for young men that were fated to become monks in the monasteries. The subjects studied by these young men were the seven liberal arts: grammar, rhetoric, dialectic, arithmetic, geometry, astronomy, and music. However, by far the most emphasis was put on the study of Latin grammar. Students would study the Roman writers such as Ovid, Virgil, and Cicero. Discipline was severe and physical punishment common. The Winchester School in England frankly advertised its attitude toward the act of learning with a sign that read "Learn or depart; a third alternative is to be flogged."

The economic revolution that occurred in the thirteenth century influenced the growth and evolution of education in the Middle Ages. With the migration of thousands to the cities and the increase in industry and commerce, many business owners felt the need for employees with more education. Despite the arguments of the clergy against the separation of education from the Church, secular schools appeared. Lay teachers were paid salaries by the parents of young students hoping to make careers as statesmen and in business. In 1283, the chronicler Villani recorded 1,100 students registered in the abacus schools that prepared them with an adequate knowledge of mathematics for a business career. Across Europe, the secularization of education continued to surface. Schools outside the Church appeared in Flanders in the twelfth century, and in 1292 there are documents that record the opening of a private school in Paris.

The first institutions of higher learning in Western culture appeared in the Middle Ages. The oldest university in Europe was founded in the ninth century in Salerno, Italy. Initially a medical school, the University of Salerno had many brilliant scholars that attracted students from all over Europe. Basing their curriculum alternately on liberal arts, medicine, law, and classical studies, universities flourished throughout Europe. Aside from Salerno, universities were founded in Italy in Rome, Padua, and Florence in the thirteenth and fourteenth centuries. Spain opened a university in Salamanca in 1218, Czechoslovakia established one in Prague in 1348, and Germany founded the University of Vienna in 1365. However, France was to lead the continent in the dissemination of knowledge in the medieval period. Universities were founded in Montpellier, Aix-en-Provence, Orleans, Chartres, Angers, Toulouse, and Paris.

The University of Paris became the most prestigious intellectual institution of the Middle Ages. Great scholars such as Thomas Aquinas, Abélard, John of Salisbury, and Roger Bacon came to Paris to engage in debate and teach the large numbers of students eager to listen to the masters. The curriculum began with the seven liberal arts. Many students then continued their education with professional studies in law, medicine, or theology. In an effort to identify their status, professors and students wore specific academic dress that was frequently regulated by the universities. The typical costume worn by a scholar was a *cope*, or long-sleeved gown, that was frequently trimmed with fur. In the fourteenth century, the scholars and students at the University of Paris wore colored copes according to their field of study. Those that studied liberal arts wore black or brown robes, law students wore scarlet, and the theologians wore the color sanctified by their Order.

Pierre Abélard was one of the most famous scholars of the Middle Ages. He was a major contributor to the founding of the University of Paris and a brilliant teacher and speaker. However, he is best known for his relationship with Héloïse, and together they lived one of the most legendary romances in the history of the West.

Abélard was born in 1079 near Nantes, in the west of France, and received a solid education, which impassioned him to such an extent that he gave up the rights to his property to his brothers. He spent the early part of his career traveling through France and studied under William of Champeaux at the school of Notre Dame in Paris. He began to defeat the arguments of his teacher and soon afterward started teaching himself, initially at schools outside of Paris at Melun and Mont Sainte-Geneviève.

The main issue that fueled the great debate that lasted for years between Abélard and his teacher was based on Abélard's refutation of the concept of universals. William believed and taught that universal ideas were as real as individual people and things, a concept that was rooted in Plato's writings and that Abélard laughed away. When William claimed that all of humanity was present in Socrates or Alexander, Abélard countered by saying that along William's line of logic, Alexander would thus be present in Socrates. Abélard's arguments became popular with the younger students in Paris, and William was forced to amend his philosophy, a step that considerably lessened his prestige.

Abélard proved to be a hero among his students, and he soon overtook the place at Notre Dame previously held by William. He was well loved by his students, made a lot of money as a teacher, and had eager young men arriving from twelve different countries to hear his lectures. His success was so great that he and many of his contemporaries envisioned a brilliant career in the Church where Abélard would be nominated bishop and perhaps would even reach the ultimate goal of winning the papacy. However, this was not to be. At the height of his power, with all of Paris clamoring for his words, Abélard experienced something unexpected. He fell in love with a young woman named Héloïse, an event that would entirely change his course of destiny.

Héloïse was a young woman who had been orphaned at an early age and raised in a convent. Early in her life, she showed great interest and talent in studying and became the brightest pupil in the convent. When she was sixteen, she was taken in by her uncle, Fulbert, who was proud of the extent of her learning. Abélard, desiring the beauty of the young woman, agreed to tutor her for room and board and a small sum, with the express intention of seducing her. His goal was quickly realized, and they fell passionately in love, all the while living in the house of her uncle. Héloïse became pregnant soon afterward, and Abélard took her away in secret to be hidden at his sister's house. To placate her furious uncle, he offered to take her hand in marriage, as long as Fulbert kept the marriage a secret. The reason he wanted to hide their marriage was because, as a married man, he would have to sacrifice his ambition, because the Church accepted only unmarried men to climb in office and prestige.

Héloïse, however, did not wish to be a pawn in the destiny of her loved one. She refused to get married, because she wanted Abélard to rise in the Church and continue his brilliant career. She proclaimed that she wished to remain his mistress and did not want to "rob the Church of so shining a light." Nevertheless, they married to satisfy her uncle Fulbert and then returned to Paris to live separately to keep their relationship secret. But Fulbert, who was not satisfied with this arrangement because of his niece's fall from grace and his own diminished status, revealed the fact that Abélard and Héloïse were married. Héloïse fought back, denying it to the people her uncle told, and her uncle beat her for it.

Abélard, still very much in love with Héloïse, could not stand for his wife to be abused and again stole her away from her uncle's house. He sent her to the convent at Argenteuil, where she put on the costume of the nuns but did not take the vows. Fulbert and his friends were enraged and believed that Abélard was trying to escape from his commitment to Héloïse. Fulbert forged a plan for revenge, hired some thugs, and bribed the servant of Abélard to locate him in his lodgings. The revenge of Fulbert constituted one of the most bizarre and horrible punishments a man could endure. Abélard was castrated, losing his manhood as well as his chances to rise in the Church.

After this horrible turn of events, all of Paris had great sympathy for Abélard, and the men who committed the violent act were punished. The men hired by Fulbert were themselves castrated and had their eyes gouged out. Fulbert fled, and the bishop confiscated his property. Yet Abélard was in despair; his career was ruined, and any prospect of living a normal life with Héloïse was blotted out by the revenge Fulbert had taken on his person. He retreated to St. Denis to take the vows of a monk and advised Héloïse to commit herself to a religious life as a nun at the convent where she had grown up.

The story of Abélard and Héloïse did not end at this juncture. Their relationship would continue, even though Héloïse rose to the rank of prioress at the convent and Abélard resumed his writing and teaching. It is from this period in their relationship that we have been handed down some of the most beautiful love letters ever written. While the ill-fated couple did not see each other frequently, their letters bear witness to the depth of their passion for one another. In the following excerpt, Héloïse expresses her feelings to Abélard with profound words of love that have rarely been equaled.

> Thou knowest, dearest—all men know—what I have lost in thee....Obeying thy command, I changed both my habit and my heart, that I might show thee to be the possessor of both my body and my mind....Not for the pledge of matrimony, not for a dowry, did I look.... And if the name of wife appears more sacred and valid, sweeter to me is ever the word friend, or, if thou not be ashamed, concubine or whore.... I call God to witness, if Augustus, ruling over the whole world, were to deem me worthy of the honor of marriage, and to confirm the whole world to me, to be ruled by me forever, dearer to me and of greater dignity would it seem to be called thy strumpet than his empress....
>
> For who among kings or philosophers could equal thee in fame? What kingdom or city or village did not burn to see thee? Who, I ask, did not hasten to

gaze upon thee when thou appearedst in public? … What wife, what maiden did not yearn for thee in thine absence, not burn in thy presence? What queen or powerful lady did not envy me my joys and my bed?

Some historians believe that the letters of Héloïse are fakes, claiming that the language used is too graphic for a woman that was a highly esteemed prioress of a convent. Others state that the language used in them has a pedantic style, which also does not match up with the character of the pious woman. The matter has not been resolved, but historians have concluded that they are either genuine or some of the most romantic and brilliant forgeries ever composed.

Abélard responded to Héloïse in letters that encouraged her to give herself over to God and to wait until they could be reunited in Heaven. He continued his writing with great vigor and published various works, including a book that focused on his theological lectures. Despite his ruination, Abélard continued to provoke others with his dialectics and arguments. He had no fear and was ultimately charged with heresy for his writings that contradicted the beliefs of the Church. He spent the latter part of his life fighting for his freedom to argue his viewpoint, while St. Bernard of Clairvaux made it a point to see that Abélard was punished for his dissent. Bernard appealed to the authority of the papacy in Rome, where he was able to secure a condemnation of Abélard and his writings. Abélard, holding fast to his ideals, set off to Rome to defend his cause but stopped at the monastery of Cluny in Burgundy. Partially because of old age and fatigue, he stayed there, swayed by the arguments of the abbot, who convinced him he would never persuade the pope to act against Bernard. Soon afterward Abélard died, at the age of sixty-three. Héloïse lived until she was almost the same age, and when she died she was buried next to him in the gardens of the Paraclete, where Abélard had planned his grave.

While Abélard was a world-class scholar and brought great attention to the development of thought in the Middle Ages, the growth of science developed at a slower pace. The medieval environment was much different from earlier civilizations, which had proudly held up the achievements of the most brilliant members of society. Greece had paved the way for Western civilizations with the early discoveries of the pre-Socratic philosophers. Aristotle categorized animals and plant life, among his many other scientific forays. Rome had valued applied science but let many of the achievements of Greece be forgotten, and the early discoveries of some of the finest minds of history lay hidden away in the libraries of Constantinople. Some historians believe that the greatest accomplishments in science in the early medieval period took place in the Middle East, which had been open to the ideas that filtered through the ports of Greece into Syria and Persia. Indeed, many inventions that were later adopted by Western Europe in the medieval period had originated in the East, including the spinning wheel and gunpowder.

Instead of embracing science from Greece, early medieval Europe was dominated by superstitious and magical belief systems that were combined with the influence of the Church. Many members of medieval society believed in otherworldly beings and the power of witchcraft. The various tribes of barbarians throughout the continent each contributed their own versions of the order of the universe. Trolls, elves, fairies, banshees, dragons, and giants all had their place in the folk beliefs of medieval people.

Because they did not have any real knowledge of how the natural world functioned, superstitions explained away the mystery of a hostile world they did not understand. In order to combat the evils of potential devils and to bring luck, many people wore or carried amulets, specific stones or jewels, or sachets stuffed with special herbs. Some of these beliefs have been carried down to our time, although they are not taken with the same grave concern for the wearer's well-being as they were historically. For example, the horseshoe was a common good-luck charm and was frequently hung over doors to influence the spirits present in the room. In medieval times, the shape was associated with the crescent moon, which had previously been a goddess and thus represented good fortune. In the same vein, garlic was used to ward off vampires. This tradition has been carried on in modern society through vampire novels and around Halloween for fun.

The Church for the most part fought against the belief systems it considered pagan and barbarian, although it was no easy matter to eradicate the practices and beliefs of superstition in the populace. Some practices, such as black magic, were punishable by the Church, although many practiced it in secret. "Black magic," the practice of harnessing demons to influence events, was popular enough to have a text written on its basic precepts. The *Book of Damnation* gave a list of the demons and their special powers. Black magic was practiced by men, often members of the nobility or clergy, who wanted to tap into the souls of the dead to use their unspent energy. Graveyards were common places to practice, and parts of a corpse were sometimes used as charms.

Women practiced as witches and were believed to be able to cast spells of enchantment, cause storms, cast the evil eye, or ensure a healthy baby. A minister of Philip IV of France was accused of enlisting the aid of a witch to make a wax figure of the king to torture him, which she did by poking needles into it. Witches were punished by the Church, most notably during the medieval Inquisition, when many were burned at the stake.

While the methods of necromancers and witches lay well outside the realm of Christianity, medieval people often confused the practices of magic and religion. The idea of prayer was not so different from magical incantations—both were used to summon help from an invisible power to remedy problems such as illness, bad fortune, and famine.

Medicine

The use of magic was also prevalent with the realm of medicine. Lack of scientific knowledge caused educated and uneducated people alike to believe that the causes and cures of illness were related to spiritual attacks. Sick people often thought they were possessed by demons, and as figures such as Thomas Aquinas and Martin Luther agreed, it was not surprising. The Black Plague was credited to the wrath of God rather than to the fleas that carried the disease. Physicians advised their patients to pray and wear amulets, and the Santa Maria della Salute church was built in Venice to appease an angry God and to avoid the plague.

Much of the early medicine or healing arts were practiced by women who used herbal combinations, midwives, and physicians who were not always qualified. Like education and architecture, a lot of early medieval medicine was also practiced in monasteries. The monks who attended to the sick were able to preserve accrued knowledge and had space for gardens devoted to the cultivation of medicinal plants. Nuns could also be known for their skills in healing. Hildegarde, the abbess of Bingen, wrote a book on medicine in 1150 that was filled with useful remedies for the ill and ailing. Similar to the role played by our modern nursing homes, some elderly people chose to retire to convents or monasteries for the medical attention and support. However, like the other trades, the practice of medicine in convents or monasteries shifted to the secular realm, and the healing arts practiced in religious institutions disappeared.

In the early thirteenth century, medicine became an important part of the university curriculum. The University of Salerno in southern Italy was the dominant educational institution that trained men as physicians and women as nurses and midwives as early as the twelfth century. Later, the graduates of Salerno spread throughout Europe to form schools of medicine through Italy and in Paris, Montpellier, and Oxford.

Knowledge was also accrued in less systematic circumstances. With the expansion of trade, pilgrimages to Jerusalem, and frequent Crusades into the East, travel became more common. Marco Polo delighted the imaginations of the European medieval mind with the accounts of his travels to China, Japan, and India. In 1271 he set out with his father and his uncle on a journey across the deserts of Asia that lasted three and a half years. He greatly impressed Kublai Khan, who enlisted him in his diplomatic service. Polo traveled on missions to Indochina, Burma, and South China in this role. He did not return to Europe until 1295. Imprisoned in 1298 as a prisoner of war, Polo made the best of his circumstances, dictating his memoirs while he was in prison. He described all that he had encountered in his travels: geography, religion, government, animals, inventions, plants, and garment styles. The result, entitled *The Travels of Marco Polo*, became one of the most popular books of his time, appealing in particular to merchants eager to trade in spices and foreign goods.

Art and Architecture

The most breathtaking cultural achievement in the Middle Ages was in the realm of art. Architecture, sculpture, and painting were all dominated by the ideals of the Christian Church. The main purpose of every work of art was to illustrate the beliefs of the Church, whether it was the facade of Chartres Cathedral or a small Book of Hours. The ideals of humility, suffering, and compassion were illustrated in sculpture and painting to instruct the largely illiterate population on the virtues and the vices of life. Another characteristic of art in the Middle Ages was its propensity to be applied art. Paintings of portraits or landscapes were unknown; painting was used to illustrate the glories of God and the lives of the saints in medieval manuscripts, and sculpture was carved into the side of church walls. It was not until the period just before the Renaissance that artworks that stood alone became popular.

The early medieval period was characterized by a style in architecture that was closely related to its Roman ancestors. Romanesque architecture was distinguished by heavy solid geometric forms such as the cube and the cylinder. It used arches and vaulting techniques in its doorways, windows, and interiors more than the Imperial Roman style did. By the ninth century, the Romanesque style had traveled from the south and become well established in the north. Decorative sculpture that graced the walls of the churches showed the influence of the Middle East, which at this early period is thought to be a result of the communications between the court of Charlemagne and leaders in Baghdad.

The early architects of the Middle Ages were monks, because they were the only members of the population that had enough mathematical knowledge to understand building construction. By the thirteenth century, laypeople had taken over the role of monks in building, church sculpture, and painting. However, these artisans were not free to choose the subjects they depicted in stone or paint. In 787, the Church decreed that the design of religious images was not to be left to the imagination of the artist and had to be composed in concert with principles agreed upon by the Church and religious tradition. Indeed, in 1306, when an artisan made a crucifix that displeased the clergy of the parish where he was working, they demanded he refund the money he was paid for the job and that he remove the offensive sculpture secretly, under cover of the night, into another diocese. Many of the subjects that became popular in church sculpture focused on daily life and provided illustrations of the right way of life. Biblical events, calendars that portrayed each month and the appropriate activity, and the seven liberal arts personified as women were common motifs.

While the Romanesque style held sway throughout the early centuries of the Middle Ages, the style of architecture for which the period is best known is Gothic. The use of the term *Gothic* is difficult to trace, because the Goths were a nomadic barbarian tribe from Scandinavia that did not develop any particular style in architecture. Some historians credit the use of the term to Italian scholars of the Renaissance, who believed everything north of the Alps was as barbarian as the Goths. In truth, the Gothic style was far removed from any barbarian influence. It arose out of the desires of the Christian Church to build houses of God that reached as far as possible into the heavens.

The origins of the Gothic style can be attributed to an unknown stonemason who rebuilt the choir of the abbey of St. Denis in 1140. But his task would not have been possible without his main patron, Abbot Suger, who made it his life's work to create a magnificent structure that was worthy of the splendor of God. As soon as he was elected abbot of the Church of St. Denis, Suger began raising money to rebuild the abbey. When it was time to begin the project, he carefully chose the stonemasons and artisans and was intimately involved in all areas of decision making in the construction process. His memoirs tell of an

Dream of the Magi, a sculpture of three crowned figures at the Cathedral of Autun, c. 1125, is a good example of Romanesque architectural sculpture. © Scala / Art Resource, NY.

instance when the builders were unable to find trees tall enough to provide timbers for the roof. At sixty years of age, he took it upon himself to venture into the forests alongside the carpenters to struggle through the thickets and brambles to find the twelve necessary trees tall enough to meet the needs of the new roof.

The difference between the Romanesque and Gothic styles was marked. Romanesque buildings were characterized by heavy, solid structures that had small windows to let in the light. In contrast, the new Gothic buildings appeared to be delicate, emphasized verticality rather than bulk, and had huge stained-glass windows that filled the interior with light. Masterpieces in the art of stained glass contributed greatly to the otherworldly experience of the Gothic cathedrals.

Many of the features of the Gothic style represented huge leaps forward in building design and technology. The height of the buildings was achieved with new methods of building support, including flying buttresses, pointed arches, and the pointed cross vault. The load in Romanesque buildings is supported by arches on the interior, so the move to exterior supports made it possible to build much taller and more elaborate structures. The upward movement that is the visual effect experienced in the interiors of these great structures is enhanced by the fact that the viewer cannot see the structure that bears the great majority of the weight. This innovation also took the load off of the walls, so that they could be inlaid with larger windows.

As soon as the Gothic style appeared outside of Paris at St. Denis, it quickly spread throughout Europe. In 1174, the English cathedral of Canterbury was begun, followed by several others, including Lincoln Cathedral in 1192 and Westminster Abbey in 1245. The Germans, Spanish, and Italians were also inspired by the French Gothic style and combined it with elements of their own local architectural styles.

Soon after St. Denis was completed, the city of Chartres began the task of constructing its cathedral, which would become one of the world's crowning achievements in architecture. The church hosts more than ten thousand carved images of men and women. Inspired by the Bishop Theodoric, the whole town of Chartres engaged in the preparation and building of the new cathedral. The building of a Gothic cathedral inspired the entire community in the labors of God, and Western civilization has not ever again experienced that type of unified effort geared toward the glorification of God.

Music

The medieval period is also known for its distinct musical styles, both secular and sacred. Music, like the visual arts, was very important in the Church because it touched the emotions of the largely illiterate populace. Unfortunately, there is not much written music that has been preserved, because, as in the case of books, it was very expensive to produce. Parchment paper was costly and difficult to come by, and it took many hours for a scribe to copy down the notations. Well-funded monasteries were generally the only institutions that could afford the luxury of copying music.

Early sacred music was characterized by its monodic structure, which meant that no matter how many people sang in the congregation, they all sang the same note, with women and boys typically singing in a higher octave. This style is generally accepted by historians as the Gregorian chant, which was created under Pope Gregory the Great. Gregory I held the papal office in the seventh century, and the music that he nurtured was to become the customary style for the next six centuries. In 1011, the Catholic Church standardized the Mass, and Gregorian chants were heard in dioceses across the continent, with the exception of Milan, which held fast to the tradition of its Ambrosian chants.

While the plain Gregorian chants nearly monopolized church music for several centuries, many musically inclined monks put their talents to writing more complicated arrangements with words for their own amusement. This practice was the impetus for the liturgical drama, which took place on feast days such as Christmas and Easter. Religious dramas included speaking, singing, and some instrumental accompaniment. Initially the liturgical dramas were a part of the Mass and told stories from the Bible or the lives of the saints in Latin. In the twelfth century, the songs were written to include the use of French vernacular, and a new form was born. One example of these dramatizations that has continued to the present day is the staging of the Nativity with the Christ Child. St. Francis first popularized the Nativity by acting out the scene with real animals at Christmas.

The second major development in Western music in the medieval period occurred in tandem with the Gothic Renaissance. Several important changes ensued and created the blueprint for musical structure as we know it today. One of the big changes was in the notation of music. The previous method of writing down music, which had been in use since ancient Greece, specified only the notes being played and did not indicate any part of the rhythm of the song. The idea for rhythmic notation is attributed to the priest and mathematician Franco of Cologne, who wrote a treatise on music theory in the eleventh century. Franco laid the groundwork for our present system of musical notation, which indicates both the individual notes as well as their duration.

The development of rhythmic notation laid open the potential for more complicated musical pieces that included polyphonic arrangements. The use of polyphony allowed the composers, musicians, and singers to create pieces that had more than one melody, or harmonies. By the thirteenth century, up to six different voices were sometimes interwoven in musical compositions that equaled in intricacy the delicate and complicated structures of the Gothic cathedrals. Indeed, the center of the development of polyphonic music was located inside of a cathedral, Notre Dame in Paris.

Music was also a part of the secular culture, although it was rarely written down. It survived instead by being passed down in an oral tradition. Music was played for weddings, funerals, and feast days and during fairs. Edward I of England was said to have hired 426 singers for his daughter Margaret's wedding. Many of the early lyrics and songs that have been handed down to us were written by the troubadours, the poets of southern France. Their subject of choice was love, and the Church preached in vain against their songs. Music of all kinds was popular in the more sophisticated courts of the Middle Ages, and there were many traveling minstrels who wandered the countryside and into the towns to find work and appreciative ears for their music.

The instruments used to play medieval music are structural ancestors of many that are used to make contemporary music. They included woodwinds, strings, and percussion instruments. The wind instruments that were most popular during the Middle Ages were flutes, bagpipes, trumpets, horns, and recorders. Some early wind instruments were made of materials different from those used today to fabricate instruments; trumpets could be made of ivory and flutes of wood, for example. Certain instruments had origins reaching back to ancient Greece, including the pan flute, a series of tubes of different lengths bound together. String instruments such as the lute and the mandolin strongly resemble the modern guitar, and the harp used in the medieval period was not much different from those played in our own time. The early version of the violin was called a hurdy-gurdy and had a mechanical crank that controlled bowing. Percussion instruments included bells, cymbals, the triangle, and drums of various sizes.

Music was much appreciated by the members of medieval society and for the most part symbolized joy and religious devotion. However, there were also songs used to rouse men in war, as well as songs of grief. During the Black Death, songs of penitence became popular in Germany. Groups of flagellants sang songs to appease the wrath of God while wandering through the cities and towns while they practiced acts of self-mortification.

Other art forms of the early medieval period included painting, poetry, and textile arts. Illuminated manuscripts were an art form that flourished in the Middle Ages. Movable type was not invented until 1450, and thus the only method of reproducing books was to copy them by hand. This developed into an art, which included illustrations that were often placed strategically on the page of text and at the bottom of the page. These manuscripts provide some of the main sources of evidence for historic costume in the medieval period. However, early manuscripts from the ninth century often portray figures draped in the costumes of Romans. Later examples provide more information on Western European costume.

Poetry and Literature

Poetry and literature were rare in the early medieval period, for the most part because the ability to write was confined to the monasteries and cathedral schools. Many of the books copied by monks were Classical works handed down to them. Illuminated manuscripts were for the most part religious in nature, illustrating the lives of the saints and instructing their readers in prayer. Other writing was largely confined to recording history, and chroniclers kept busy from the time of Charlemagne onward keeping account of the deeds of men and governments.

The art of poetry developed at the end of the eleventh century in the southwestern area of France that would later be the birthplace of Eleanor of Aquitaine. Eleanor's grandfather, William IX, Count of Poitou and Duke of Aquitaine, was the originator of the troubadour style of poetry. While much of the writing of the period is colored by the religious ardor of the Crusades, William of Aquitaine's poetry was by and large love poetry that sang of the triumph of women over the burden laid upon them by the Fall of Eve. His poems were the first signs of the power of women, and the ideas expressed in them came to fruition later in the courts of love presided over by his granddaughter Eleanor.

Another major literary work of the early Middle Ages was *The Romance of the Rose*. The first section was written by William of the Loire in the early thirteenth century and consisted of four thousand lines of prose. After the death of William in 1237, his work was taken up by Jean de Meun forty years later. The plot is based on a young man who struggles to attain the love of his dreams, symbolized by a perfect rose. The only human in the story is the narrator; all the other characters are abstract personifications of emotions and human character such as Hope, Generosity, Evil-Tongue, Courtesy, and Beauty. The section written by William is generally favored for its delicacy and aristocratic tone. The remainder of the work by de Meun is less poetic and contains many negative comments on society. De Meun slanders political figures and women in his work, which grew to be eighteen thousand lines. Despite the marked contrast of the authors' styles, *The Romance of the Rose* was enormously popular, quoted by the clergy and later translated into Middle English and German.

The increase of leisure time in the later part of the early Middle Ages helped develop the taste for literary works. Women during this period looked to books for ideas on fashion and how to best show their graces. Details included in the writings were mimicked by ladies, who were eager to wear the most elegant shoes and the most ornate embroidered belts. Gestures described in books of the period were also taken seriously, and many women took up the practice of swaying their hips while they walked as a result. Historians believe this capricious custom began around 1240.

Textiles in the Early Middle Ages

The textile industry flourished throughout the Middle Ages. Intricate weaves and embroidered fabrics were admired throughout Europe, and exquisite examples of handwork graced the altars of churches and clothed the wealthy and powerful. Tapestries are mentioned as early as the tenth century, but the art of tapestry weaving was not fully developed until the 1300s. One important example of textile art of the early Middle Ages is the Bayeux Tapestry, which was created in the last half of the eleventh century. Although its title bears the word "tapestry," the textile is technically not a tapestry but rather has figures created out of embroidery stitches. Constructed on a strip of linen that measures 19 inches (48 cm) tall and 71 yards (65 m) long, the Bayeux Tapestry tells the story of William the Conqueror's conquest of England. While the figures in the tapestry indicate costumes of the early medieval period, they are not indicative of much detail.

However, most textiles that were produced were not meant as art objects, but rather as functional materials for the construction of garments and household linens. Textiles were an important part of everyday life for many people. Weaving and textile manufacture became one of the most vital economic forces in Europe, building great cities on the basis of their textile trade. Charlemagne began the fashion for royalty clothed in elegantly woven and embroidered textiles when he was crowned Holy Roman emperor. Through the influence of the Crusades, Eastern techniques were introduced and adapted in Europe. Other influences in the design of textiles came from the rich traditions of the Vikings, who were skilled in tablet and tapestry weaving.

The main fibers used for clothing most of the population in the Middle Ages were wool, flax, silk, and cotton. Wool was the primary fiber adopted after the Merovingians gave up the animal skins, and linen, although it was introduced as a luxury fiber, became more available as time passed. Silk was a luxury fiber and an important element of costume for aristocracy in the great Byzantine Empire. It continued to be held at high values throughout the Middle Ages. Cotton was gradually introduced into European textile manufacture from Spain and the East, but like silk was mostly worn by the upper classes.

Wool

Wool was undoubtedly the most important fiber in medieval Europe. Warm, strong, long wearing, and resistant to unpredictable weather, it was worn by both peasants and the aristocracy. Like the previous generations of Roman women, women of the early medieval world were responsible for the production of textiles. Many women worked at home, and some worked in specialized workshops that produced textiles for sale. Wool was sheared, washed, combed with thistles, and spun into yarn. The yarn was then woven into cloth and dyed, usually in blue or a shade of red. Wool fibers could range from very coarse to very fine, and it was this distinction in quality that determined which class could afford it. Peasants wore rougher textiles that were either undyed or dyed with blue woad, one of the less expensive dyes. Wealthier customers wore the finer, softer wools, dyed a deep rich crimson red, green, or blue. As the textile industry grew more sophisticated, wool was finished by a process called *fulling*, using heat and water to shrink the textile into a denser fabric of a much higher quality.

Initially, wool was produced across the continent for the small-scale producers, but later it became a specialized import that had a large impact on the economy of the country that produced it. In the High Middle Ages, England produced most of the wool for northern Europe; the quality of English wool gave it a near monopoly on the market. Many historians believe that the wet, rainy climate of England proved to be ideal for producing fine wools. Raw wool in bulk was shipped to Flanders, which became the wool cloth-making center of Europe, and through this crucial economic relationship, the two countries became inextricably wedded in political policy.

Linen and Cotton

Flax, the second most common fiber in the Middle Ages, comes from a bast plant. Early medieval women harvested the plant, soaked it in water to remove the outer part of the stem, and removed the fiber to be processed and spun into yarn. After the linen fabric was woven, it was frequently used for undergarments, because it is much softer worn next to the skin than wool. Cotton, which has shorter fibers than flax, was generally imported into Europe in the earlier Middle Ages. It was grown and harvested in Spain and gradually spread in use throughout the continent.

Silk

The use of silk textiles in medieval times was a practice directly linked to the legacy of the Byzantine Empire. Silk industries were initially established in the region most closely located geographically to Byzantium in southern Italy and Sicily. The manufacture of silk was a jealously kept secret in Byzantium, but little by little artisans who had the skills and knowledge to produce and weave silk moved and brought with them their knowledge to Italy. By the fourteenth century, many Italian cities thrived in the production and trading of silks, including Florence, Genoa, Venice, Lucca, and Bologna.

Silk was worn chiefly by members of the nobility, powerful men of the church, and royal figures. We have records of the silk robes worn by Charlemagne, and although he was inclined to dress in all the luxuries his power allowed for ceremonies, he did not consider it an important part of daily life. In one story that comes down to us, Charlemagne mocks his courtiers that have just returned from Italy wearing luxurious silk garments; when they arrive at his court wearing beautiful new silken ensembles, he takes them on a hunt, so that their clothing is immediately ruined by rain and torn by thorns. On the other hand, silk garments were so valued that they were frequently gifts between rulers, and silken fabrics and garments from Baghdad and Byzantium were especially prized. Records from aristocratic wills and inventories of church treasuries indicate the importance and richness of silk textiles found in the Middle Ages.

Leather and Fur

In addition to the main fibers used for garments, furs and animal skins were equally popular commodities, particularly in the colder climates in northern Europe. Leather from cattle, deer, and sheep was treated by artisans in tanneries for shoes, boots, purses, gloves, and belts. Leather was cut, stamped, embroidered, and even painted for decoration.

Furs were used for warmth and decoration and lined the cloaks of the nobility, royalty, and later the bourgeoisie. Sheepskin, mole, otter, and beaver fur were popular and sometimes were imported from as far away as the Black Sea. Ermine, a white fur with black spots on it, was used exclusively by royalty and appears in manuscript illuminations in the depiction of kings and queens.

Fabric Production

Weaving became increasingly sophisticated and organized throughout the Middle Ages. Warp-weighted looms that go all the way back to ancient Greece were used initially by the women who wove. Textiles that have been excavated from archaeological sites from this period show diamond and chevron patterns in the construction. Weaving was done primarily in the home in the earlier periods, but women who were especially skilled in the craft could sell their work at local fairs. Large settlements that were headed by kings and nobility generally had their own weavers that were responsible for producing the cloth that was worn by all members of the household. However, cloth making was an industry that began relatively early; Charlemagne established textile centers in Lyons and Rouen in 768 and specialized cloth fairs that were held throughout Europe a few years later.

After the Viking invasions, when medieval society was developing smoothly, the horizontal treadle loom became more common in homes and weaving workshops. The treadle loom allows the weaver to control the weaving process with the feet and made the construction process three times as fast. The adoption of the treadle loom was a critical step in the development of the weaving industry which would later dominate the economies of several European countries. The draw loom, which made it possible for the weaver to produce intricately patterned textiles, was likewise adopted from the East.

Techniques in weaving spread with the migration of skilled textile workers across Europe, and many distinct weaves took on specific names. Many of the fabric names of today betray their origins through etymological traces related to their geographic beginnings. For example, *muslin* is named after Mosul in modern-day Iraq, damask after the city Damascus in India, and denim after the French city Nîmes.

Embroidery was the most common way of embellishing cloth and was both a craft practiced in the home and a profession; printed fabrics were unknown in Europe until the seventeenth century. Embroidery was especially popular in the early Middle Ages because the textile industry was not yet sophisticated enough to produce many fabrics with patterns in the weave. It was sometimes done by women of the upper classes in the early Middle Ages, as well as in convents and workshops that specialized in it. Embroidered cloth was used for clothing, furnishings, and decoration for noble families and the Church. However, almost all of the surviving pieces from the early medieval period are examples that have been preserved by the Church.

The amount of care and labor that went into some of the textiles embroidered for the Church is astounding. "The Creation," an embroidered wall-hanging from Girona Cathedral in Spain measures 12 by 15 feet (3.6 × 4.5 m) and is entirely covered with embroidery stitches. It is dated from the eleventh century and illustrates the various scenes of the Creation, with a large circular portrait of Jesus at the center. The Star Mantle of the Holy Roman emperors is a silk textile that was embroidered with silk and metal threads. Other amazing examples from the early Middle Ages include the *opus Anglicanum*, which was a style from England in which the entire textile was covered with gold thread embroidery. Examples of these works can still be seen in the Victoria and Albert Museum in London.

Color

The colors of cloth in medieval times could be bright and vibrant and frequently indicated social status. Purple, which had from ancient times been the signature color of royalty, continued to be used to clothe kings and queens. The color purple was expensive because it took so much labor to create the dye, and the materials required were available only in certain places. Purple dye was fabricated from a shellfish called murex that was native to the Mediterranean. Hundreds of shellfish were used to produce one piece of cloth, and archaeologists continue to find evidence of their use with piles of shells found on excavation sites.

Some of the other most expensive woolen textiles of the medieval period were named after their color and were called scarlets. Scarlets ranged in intensity of hue and could appear in shades of red from light rose to a dark red. Scarlets designated a finely constructed textile that had undergone many finishing processes, including fulling, brushing, and shearing. The most expensive scarlets were colored with a dye called *kermes*, which was made from crushed beetles. Kermes could also be used to dye silks, and some of the most luxurious fabrics made in Europe were dyed with scarlet.

Other less expensive dyes included madder and woad. Madder, which comes from the root of an herbaceous plant, was grown on Charlemagne's estate and in Paris. The plant served a dual purpose: as well as its red dye, the leaves of the plant were used to feed cattle (a curious side effect of this practice was that it turned the cow's milk slightly red). Woad was the principal dyestuff of the medieval world. The plant's leaves were crushed and fermented to produce mainly blue colors, but in different concentrations it could also yield black or green-toned fabrics. Woad was so readily available that by the thirteenth century even peasants owned blue garments. Combined with madder dye, a purplish tint could be achieved. Later woad was replaced with indigo, which was a stronger blue dye. However, this did not happen without many rebellions in France, where woad was cultivated throughout the countryside and was an important product for the economy.

Saffron produced yellow hues and had been in use as a spice, medicine, cosmetic, and dye since ancient Greece. Aside from producing beautiful yellow fabrics, it was also used in combination with woad to produce vibrant greens and with madder to produce orange fabrics. The use of saffron as a dye entered into medieval Europe through Spain in the tenth century, when Arab culture flourished and shared its traditional secrets with Europeans.

Guilds

The medieval industrial revolution began in the ninth century. The production, finishing, and dyeing of cloth gradually moved out of the realm of the home to become a specialized industry. While the cloth trade was initially conducted in outdoor fairs like the rest of the goods for sale, late in the tenth century northern cities in Flanders set up more permanent places of trade, with indoor cloth halls in Bruges, Ghent, and Ypres.

One of the most important organizational innovations of the Middle Ages was the guild system. Textile guilds appeared as early as 925 in Germany and paved the way for a labor system that would dominate the rest of the period. The medieval guild was an organization that was developed to protect the rights of its members and to regulate prices of raw materials and finished products. The guild regulated the number of workers allowed in each trade and provided an apprenticeship system for new recruits. The leaders of the guilds kept a close eye on the quality and measurements of goods, thus ensuring that neither buyer nor seller would be cheated. Each guild organization would frequently have its own hall, where officers would settle disputes and hold meetings. As a member of a guild, an artisan could rely on his fellow members for help if he was ill, and funerals of members were sometimes paid for by the guild treasury. Powerful merchants arose from the well-oiled guild system, and great fortunes were made by men who were otherwise considered outside the nobility. However, although the guilds served as a powerful protective organization for many artisans, some were excluded to suffer a more difficult path.

In the thirteenth century dyers were excluded from the guild system. Then known as "blue-nails" because of the dye stains on their hands, the dyers were told they were unable to join the system unless they agreed to get rid of all their tools of trade. As a result, the dyers formed a lower-class proletariat and were forced to float from city to city in search of work. In Florence, tailors did not enter the guild system until the sixteenth century because they did not own the materials for the construction of garments. The labor to construct a garment was cheap, and customers brought the fabric of their choice to the tailor. Towns of the Middle Ages were filled with shops that hosted artisans such as drapers, cobblers, hosiers, dressmakers, hat makers, and embroiderers. While royalty and aristocratic families employed their own tailors and furriers, the majority of the population brought cloth to the tailor, was measured for fit, and returned to pick up the finished garment. Tailors charged only for sewing and thread costs.

Overall, the importance of the textile industry in Northern Europe cannot be underestimated. It is probable that approximately half of the population in the textile centers such as Bruges, Ghent, and Ypres was employed in the business. The merchants in the north were responsible for importing wool from England, shipping it across the channel to Bruges, where it was woven and dyed. Each merchant supplied wool to workers, who sorted it and washed it to remove the lanolin. After it was dried, women carded it and spun the fiber into yarn.

For the first part of the Middle Ages, spinning was done with a distaff, a hand-held tool that could be carried anywhere. Traveling through the countryside in the early medieval period, it would be a common sight to see women spinning yarn with their distaffs while they were herding their sheep. Later the spinning wheel was introduced, and yarn production was increased significantly.

The yarns were then delivered to individual weavers, who ran small shops with one or two looms. The weavers in turn would hire dyers to produce colored lengths of cloth. Fulling, the process of slightly shrinking the woolen fabric so that it was more tightly constructed, was initially done with human labor. A regulation in the city of Arras required that at least three men work to full a single length of cloth because the task was strenuous and required "great pain and exertion of the limbs and body." After the cloth was fulled, it was brushed with teasels, or thistles, to raise the fibers on the fabric. The raised fibers would then be cut or sheared by workers with special shears to create a smooth finish. The scissors were so highly valued as tools that they were frequently bequeathed in wills.

One of the important issues to consider in the study of textiles in the medieval period was the change in the organization and division of labor between the sexes. In the early Middle Ages, women performed all of the tasks relating to making cloth—shearing, cleaning the fibers, spinning, weaving, dyeing, and finishing. By 1300, men had taken over the weaving and dyeing, while women continued to do the preparatory tasks for weaving. Historians have attributed this change to several factors. As the Middle Ages progressed, the feudal ties that were the basis of organization in the early medieval period waned, and peasants had more freedom to move around geographically and seek better lifestyles. This increased the population in towns, where men who previously worked the land were forced to find new occupations. The towns became concentrated centers of industry, and organizations such as the guild structure provided support for men to prosper in their trades, while excluding women from this practice. In addition, capital for large industry was required with the advent of technological advances. Large looms and water mills were not within the reach of a woman with a small cottage industry run in her home. Women did, however, continue to weave. Some women wove cloth in the home for their own use, but the majority of women who were involved in the weaving process were connected in some way to a man that was protected by the guild system.

During the eighth and ninth centuries, *sericulture*, the cultivation of silk-worms, was introduced by Arab artisans and tradesmen in Spain and Italy. In 1147 King Roger II of Sicily imported Greek and Jewish silk weavers and housed them in a palace. Their descendants were responsible for the spread of sericul-ture throughout Italy. Under Frederick II, dyeing was controlled mainly by Jewish immigrants, as was silk weaving. Foreign influence can likewise be attrib-uted to the development of brocaded silk and velvet weaving in Italy.

With the decree of the Pax Mongolica, an alliance formed in 1260 by the pope to moderate the power of Islamic rulers, silk production techniques from India and China made their way to Italy. Although sericulture and silk weaving were by far the most developed in Italy, the lucrative industry spread to other countries, including Portugal and France. In 1147, the first mulberry trees, essential for feeding silkworms, were transported from Syria to be planted in France.

In the late twelfth century, Italy began to compete with the northern cloth centers in Flanders. While they could not compete with the quality of wool that was available in England, many Italian cities got around this by importing unfinished cloth and dyeing it themselves at great profit. The guild system in Italy also developed and formed a powerful establishment. In Florence, there were twenty-one guilds, seven of which were called the "Greater Guilds." Three of these important guilds were related to the textile industry: the cloth finishers, the silk merchants, and the woolen merchants. The guilds had great benefits for their members and wielded a lot of political power as well. Men with any political aspirations in medieval Florence were inclined to join one of the guilds to gain support.

Clothing of the Early Middle Ages

Knowledge of costume history from the medieval period comes from various sources. Unfortunately, actual garments, especially from the earlier centuries of the Middle Ages, are extremely rare. The only garments that were preserved were religious vestments, either kept by the Church or exhumed from the cof-fins of powerful Church leaders. They do not tell much about clothing worn by everyday people of the period but do give some indications of the textiles used, their construction techniques, and decorative preferences.

Works of art, including statues and manuscript illuminations of the period, are the best forms of visual evidence, but it is important to consider that the accuracy and detail of garments in these representations are inherently related to the stylistic components of the art of the time. Dating styles in clothing can be problematic with regard to some artworks. In particular, funerary sculpture does not always indicate the style of clothing worn when the person died, because the sculptures were frequently commissioned many years in advance.

Other sources of evidence that tell about the types of clothing people wore, how many garments they owned, and what the medieval people themselves thought of the current clothing practices of the day are the documents written by chroniclers and records kept by clerks of the church or royal households. These are valuable social documents but must also be considered carefully.

The vocabulary used to describe medieval dress is inherently complex and differs in use text by text. Costume historians do not have precise dates for the change in usage of terms, and terms for the same garment may differ from place to place or could be picked up in one geographical location to be used in another.

Men's Clothing

From the evidence that does exist, it is clear that the early Middle Ages were fairly static in terms of changes in clothing styles. In the age of Charlemagne, Men wore simple T-shaped tunics that reached to below the knee, or to the ground for ceremonial occasions. Most tunics were plain, and if they were decorated for the nobility and kings, they had decorative bands attached to the neckline and sleeves in the manner of Byzantine dress. Class differentiation was seen in the length of the tunic: aristocrats wore long tunics, and working-class people wore shorter versions of the same garment. Peasants of this era wore tunics made of rougher cloth, and the outer tunic was frequently sleeveless to save on the expense of additional cloth. For freedom of movement in their work, peasants' tunics were frequently slit on either side of the hem. Outerwear for the upper classes included cloaks that fastened over one shoulder in the style of a Greek *chlamys*, and hooded capes were common among laborers and peasants. Carolingian men wore their hair cut below the ear and had beards. Footwear included leather boots or shoes. We do not have any direct evidence from this period regarding underclothes.

In the tenth and eleventh centuries, the styles were very similar to the clothing worn in the Carolingian empire. Men wore two tunics, an outer tunic and an undertunic, later known as a *surcote* and a *cote*. The fabrics used were most commonly linen and wool. These garments were worn belted at the waist and could be short or long in length. The necklines were either round or square, and the sleeves could be tight fitting or cut loose to show the sleeve of the undertunic. Underclothing of this period included undershirts and drawers, called *braies*. Undershirts, which were also called *chemises*, were typically short-sleeved and made of linen. Braies were loose breeches of varying lengths that were fastened at the waist with a belt. If worn long, the braies were worn bound up with strips of fabrics so they fit tightly to the leg. Outerwear was similar to earlier periods, but cloaks or mantles could be worn either attached at one side or cut from a rectangular piece of cloth with a hole in the center to slip over the head. Hair was cut to the nape of the neck and worn parted in the middle, and older men continued to wear beards, while younger men shaved. Men who wore knee-length tunics covered their legs with long braies or with hose that were cut and sewn to fit the leg. Footwear, as in earlier periods, consisted of boots, sometimes made of decorated leather, and shoes. High heels were not worn in this period.

Dress for men in the twelfth century had some significant changes. Both the undertunic and the overtunic continued to be worn as the main element of clothing, but there were changes in the cut of the garment. Instead of being cut from one piece of cloth from shoulder to knee or shoulder to ankle, the tunics of the twelfth century had separate pieces for the upper and lower part of the garment. The bodice and sleeves were close fitting and were frequently laced at the side to ensure individual fit. Joined to the upper part of the garment was a skirt that was full to allow ease of movement. Sleeves also had more variation in style and could be elbow length or bell-shaped or have decorative, turned-back cuffs. Some stylistic changes in the tunic worn by men were influenced by the garments and textiles brought back from the East by European Crusaders. Fine silks and garments were cherished as gifts between rulers. Other facets of costume were adopted in the style of the tunic, including the slit opening at the neck, which was a detail taken from Eastern garb.

The undertunic worn at this time was most frequently made of linen, because it was softer against the skin than wool. Men also wore hose, or *chausses*, to cover their legs, particularly in the colder regions of Europe. Hose were generally tailored, or cut and sewn to fit the leg tightly, and could be fabricated of brightly colored wool. Hose for men could reach thigh length but varied according to the length of their tunic. Another innovative garment that appeared at this time was the *bliaut*, a long overgown that was limited in wear to men of the upper class and royalty. The bliaut of the twelfth century was made of luxurious fabrics such as satin, velvet, and silk and was decorated with gold embroidery and precious stones. It fit its wearer tightly at the bodice with lacing and could be covered in chain mail or lined with fur. The bliaut is elegantly represented in the magnificent cathedral sculptures of kings and queens on the facade of Chartres Cathedral.

Shoes for the wealthy also went through a stylistic transformation, changing from a rounded toe to a pointed toe. This change is documented in the writings of Orderic Vitalis, a monk writing in the early twelfth century who strongly disapproved of such vanity. He writes of the style being started by a man named Count Fulk of France, who had shoes made to fit his bunions. The new pointed shape of the toes was then adopted by other courtiers, and later adapted again by turning up the pointed toes. Orderic Vitalis associated these changes with corrupt morals and claimed the new fashion in shoes resembled the tails of serpents. In England, men began to wear their hair long, and sometimes curled it with hot irons. This practice was equally condemned by chroniclers and clerics. In 1102, after hearing a sermon preached against the vanity of long hair, King Henry I of England allowed a bishop to cut his hair short. This began a new fashion, and many of his courtiers soon followed suit.

The evolution of style in the thirteenth century continued to move along at a slow pace. When St. Louis IX was king of France, court styles became simpler, as vain display was disapproved of by the modest king. Overall, thirteenth-century men's dress was similar to that of the twelfth century, although class distinction was made more evident through the length of the surcote. Upper-class men wore long cotes and working-class men shorter garments. The two types of sleeves that are represented most frequently in the visual sources of evidence are either long and tightly fitted or cut full under the arm and tapered at the wrist. The surcote or overtunic could be worn sleeveless, with three-quarter-length sleeves, or with long sleeves cut loose at the shoulder for ease of movement.

The cut of outerwear in the thirteenth century became more sophisticated. Cloaks that were fastened at the shoulder with chains or elaborate ribbons continued to be symbolic of high status. The *garnache* appeared, which was a long cloak with big roomy sleeves, and was lined or trimmed with fur. Fur was a valuable commodity in the thirteenth century; King John of England spent exorbitant amounts of money on sable furs to line his cloaks. The *herigaut* was a full-length outer garment that had long wide sleeves and slits beneath the shoulder, so that the wearer could extend his arm and move it freely. The *tabard* was a short, loose outer garment with short sleeves worn mainly by monks or workingmen. Sometimes the tabard was decorated with the symbols or coat of arms of the lord of the manor.

Hairstyles worn by men of the thirteenth century varied by age group; younger men wore their hair shorter than their elders. Beards, if worn, were cut close to the face because the new military helmets demanded by more sophisticated weaponry made full beards uncomfortable. For headwear, men wore hoods, which were either attached to their outer garment or a separate piece of clothing. At the end of the century, hoods were more closely fitted to the head. Some hoods had a decorative feature called a *liripipe*, a long tube of fabric attached at the back of the crown of the head.

Footwear became more complex, and new closures were added that could be decorated to show status, including buckles and lacings. Men continued to wear hose, and some examples of this time show that they were cut to include the foot, like socks.

Warfare was an unavoidable and highly significant part of the lives of medieval men. Kings and nobles made their reputations and fortunes through ferocity and skill at battle. As a result, protective garments worn in battle took on a particular importance. From the earliest part of the Middle Ages, men wore leather to protect themselves from sword blows, and this custom was gradually replaced with the use of metal. There is very little direct evidence of armor from the early Middle Ages, and as the Carolingian empire was based on wood, there were not many capable blacksmiths that could produce arms and armor. The blacksmith in medieval times was among the most important of the artisans, because it was he who ensured the warriors a powerful weapon and protective clothing for battle.

Up to the fourteenth century, armor changed little. The knights of the twelfth and thirteenth centuries were dressed in much the same way as the horsemen of fifth- and sixth-century Europe, with minor differences. Their basic protective wear was helmets and mail shirts, although the Vikings from Northern Europe wore costumes unique to their tribes.

Mail was relatively comfortable to wear because it was flexible and lightweight in comparison to the later plate armor worn by knights. It offered excellent protection against sword cuts but could not protect the wearer from heavy, bone-breaking blows. Thickly padded undergarments were worn both to cushion the body against the rubbing of the mail rings and as a shock absorber. Producing mail took the skill of a master craftsman. The entire process was done by hand, beginning with a piece of iron that was hammered into a flat plate. The plate was cut into thin strips and hammered until it was thin enough to work with. Then the strips were wrapped around an iron bar, so that it would be shaped into a long spring. Each loop of the spring was cut and hammered flat, and a hole was bored into the end of it. The loops were then linked to one another and fastened with a rivet that went through the holes at the end of the loop.

The protection that mail offered lessened with the technological advances in weaponry, however. As the longbow and crossbow became more powerful, the arrows shot by these weapons could punch through the mail rings. Blacksmiths attempted to solve this problem by making the mail rings smaller and using double layers of mail. The most successful innovation was to add small plates to the mail shirts at critical places to defect blows and arrows.

To identify one another on the battlefield, armor was frequently marked with a heraldic symbol or coat of arms. As early as the First Crusade, European nobles mimicked the practice of the Arabs by engraving or painting their heralds on their garments, horses, and armor.

Women's Clothing

Women's costume of the early Middle Ages did not differ much from men's costume. Like men, women in the age of Charlemagne wore under- and outer tunics, although they were without exception worn long by all classes. Statues from eighth-century Italy show women in long tunics that exhibit a marked Byzantine influence with decorative strips of cloth at the neckline and hemline. As outerwear, women wore shawls in the style of a Greek *palla*, draping them over their heads to cover their hair.

In the tenth and eleventh centuries, women continued to wear two layers of tunics. The undertunic was decorated with embroidery on the sleeves and hemlines, and the outer tunic was frequently manipulated in design and worn to show the details of the undertunic. For example, the overtunic could be cut with wide sleeves to show the design on the tight-fitting, decorated sleeves of the undertunic, and the hem of the overtunic could be pulled up and belted to reveal the designs of the hem of the undertunic. Women also wore a linen chemise, an undergarment similar to that of men of the period, although it was longer in length. Women of the working classes often wore an apron to cover the lower half of their tunics. For outerwear, women wore mantles that could be open at the front or slipped over the head. Some examples of the period were elaborate enough to have linings with contrasting colors or fur.

Women of the early medieval period wore hairstyles appropriate to their age. Young women wore their hair long and flowing, and married women covered their hair with a shawl or a veil. The quality of the head wraps varied with social status; wealthy women wore veils of silk or fine linen, while lower-class women covered their hair with wool or coarse linen shawls.

In terms of jewelry, we know from written records that wealthy women wore gold head circlets, necklaces, bracelets, rings, and earrings. Shoes from this time period were similar to those worn by men. Women also wore hose that tied around the knee, and wooden clogs to protect their shoes and long dresses from dirt and mud.

In the twelfth century, women's dress evolved in ways similar to the changes in men's dress of the time. The influence of the Crusades on clothing styles becomes evident and is most apparent in the adoption of lavish textiles of silk that were intricately woven. Most of the changes were related to the fit of the tunic, and only the upper classes who could afford skilled tailors wore the new fitted garment. The fit was achieved with cut and lacing, usually on the side of the garment. Other variations of the tunic included sleeves that were cut exaggeratedly long or had bell-shaped cuffs.

Noble and royal women of the twelfth century, like men, wore the bliaut. It was made of sumptuous materials that could have been imported from Italy or the Far East and was tightly fitted. Some versions of the bliaut have especially elaborate cuts for the time, including inset pieces that were used to ensure a tight fit at the hips. Decorations for the bliaut for women included jewels and embroidery, and the seams of the garment could be covered by pieces of decorative tape that was sewn onto the garment.

Another garment worn by women at this time was called a *chainse*. The chainse differed from the typical tunics of the period in that it was usually made of a light fabric, usually linen, and had pleats on the skirt. Some costume historians believe it was worn as a summer garment or as a house dress.

Outer garments of the twelfth century worn by women included cloaks or mantles that fastened at the front. Some of the cloaks worn by upper-class women were very lavishly decorated. Collars, linings, and clasps could be made of expensive furs or imported fabric from as far as India and adorned with jewels. A cloak that was lined or trimmed with fur was called a *pelicon* or *pelice*. Women in the working classes typically did not own a coat in the early Middle Ages and instead used shawls to wrap around themselves to keep warm.

Wealthy women of this period braided their hair in two braids and let them hang down on either side of the face. However, most women continued to cover their hair with shawls and veils so that only the face was visible. Other more elaborate headdresses of this period included the barbette, filet, and wimple, which were worn to cover the neck and support a veil. The filet was a crownlike linen band that was worn to support a veil. The barbette was a band of linen that wrapped under the chin, reached from one temple to the other, and was worn with the filet. The wimple was a linen scarf that covered the neck.

Makeup was generally disapproved of, but some women resorted to it to enhance their allure. In Italy around 1100, there was a book written about techniques to enhance beauty, and it suggested the application of leeches to the cheeks to remove redness.

During the thirteenth century, women's dress did not change much. Under the rule of Louis IX, women were encouraged to wear loosely fitting tunics, although after his reign, women returned to wearing more tightly fitted garments. The undertunics had sleeves that were either tightly fitted or cut loose under the arms,

A manuscript illumination from the *Codex Manesse,* c. 1305, shows lovers dressed in loose fitting tonics. © Foto Marburg / Art Resource, NY.

and the outer tunics were sleeveless or had long sleeves. The sleeves on a cote could be fitted by being sewn tightly to the arm on a daily basis. This practice led to unique color variations and could be used as symbols of identity for court ladies to give to their lovers. The hand-sewn cuffs were picked apart by the young women who wore them and given to their chosen knight, who wore the sleeve remnant fixed to their helmets or shields in tournaments. Sleeveless outer tunics were often cut with large armholes, so that the undertunic was clearly visible. Women continued to wear cloaks ornamented according to their status, which were hooded in the colder areas of Europe.

Hairstyles changed so that the braids worn in the twelfth century went out of fashion. In 1278, the Church ordered all women in the Italian city of Parma to wear veils. The women were initially distraught at hiding their beauty but found a way to circumvent the decree: They had veils woven with gold filament, so they attracted more attention than if they had gone bareheaded. Young women frequently wore their hair uncovered, and married and older women continued to wear a veil or a hairnet. The barbette, filet, and wimple continued to be worn in the thirteenth century.

Women who were geographically close to Eastern culture, either in one of the Crusader states or in Spain and Italy, were quick to adopt the fashions worn by Muslim ladies. In Sicily, there were many textile factories set up by Muslims, and one chronicler of the time wrote that Sicilian women mimicked exactly the fashions of the Muslims, in wearing gold silken gowns for Christmas and in the way they wore their veils. Melisende, who lived in Jerusalem with her brother Count Tripoli, had a trousseau of many silken gowns that reflected Eastern fashion when she married the emperor of Constantinople in 1161.

Accessories of the early medieval period included gloves, jewelry, and purses. Gloves were worn only by the nobility and clergy. Evidence shows that gloves could be worn either elbow or wrist length and decorated with jewels. Jewelry is rarely depicted in the visual sources of the Middle Ages, but written accounts verify its existence. Men and women wore rings and belts, which could be made of precious metals and inlaid with jewels. Clasps for cloaks could also be made of gold and set with jewels. Another piece of jewelry from the period was a *fermail* or *afiche*, a brooch used to fasten the outer tunic. Purses were made of both leather and cloth and were frequently worn attached around the waist. One existing example of a medieval purse from the Chelles Reliquary in France shows embroidered figures of a man and a woman and has a drawstring closure. Cosmetics included perfumes and oils that were imported from the Middle East and became popular after the Crusades. Also, there is some evidence that women of the upper classes in England wore rouge on their cheeks, used face creams, and dyed their hair.

Religious Clothing

The power of the Christian Church throughout the Middle Ages demanded appropriate vestments for the princes of the Church and its clergymen. Originally, priests did not wear special garments and dressed in clothing similar to that worn by ordinary people. They were more frequently identified by their haircut, or *tonsure*. The tonsure was a haircut that required that the head be shaved, either in the center of the head so the head only had a fringe of hair circling it, or from side to side in the front of the scalp. However, in the sixth century, a special costume was designated because the ordinary clothing of the period was heavily influenced by the barbarians who had infiltrated Europe. Because the Church saw the conversion of barbarians into Christians as an important part of its duty in the medieval world, it wanted to define itself against them.

The basic pieces of the ensemble worn by priests from the Age of Charlemagne onward were the *alb* and the *chasuble*. The alb was a white tunic with sleeves that was decorated in a style that went back to Byzantium, featuring a patterned vertical band that ran over the shoulders and decorative medallions. The chasuble was a large circular cloak that had a hole in the center and was pulled over the head. Other garments worn with this ensemble had their origins in clothing first worn in ancient Rome and included the maniple and the stole. The maniple was a strip of fabric that was held in the hand and later wrapped to the wrist. The stole was a long scarf worn under the alb and reached to the ground.

Bishops were more dramatically attired and had special accoutrements that symbolized their high rank in the church. They wore basic garments similar to that of the priest but also accessories such as the miter, the cross-staff, and gloves. On top of the alb, bishops wore the *dalmatic*, which was cut with wide sleeves to symbolize the Angel of the Annunciation. The miter is the characteristic three-pointed headdress of the bishop, which changed in ornamentation throughout the Middle Ages. Some miters were made of plain white linen, others were embroidered with gold thread, and still others had jewels inlaid on them. The cross-staff, carried in the right hand of an archbishop, and was a long pole with a cross at the top. It could be very ornate and fabricated in costly metal with engravings on it. Bishops carried a similar accessory, but instead of a cross at the top, it had a crook, symbolizing the pastoral staff.

Monasteries and convents, communities of people who had renounced the world, had been around since the fourth century. A vow of poverty and disregard of earthly possessions were often required of those who chose to live the life of a monk or nun. Thus the costume of the religious orders was simple and modest in style and drab in coloring. Both monks and nuns wore a loose-fitting tunic with long wide sleeves that reached to the ground and was belted at the waist. For headwear, monks typically wore a cowl, which was a hood that detached from the tunic. In cold weather, they wore a tabard or a cloak, and like the tunics they wore, these garments were made of plain fabrics.

Nuns wore veils and, as a rule, covered their hair. Later when modesty became a part of everyday women's wardrobes with the introduction of the wimple, nuns adapted this style and have kept it in some cases to the present day. Certain Orders took on specific colors for the habits of their nuns, as in the case of the Order of the Servites in Florence, founded in the thirteenth century. The nuns who served there wore black tunics with white veils and wimples. The use of color became symbolic in the church. Red was associated with the blood of Christ, and white recalled the light of divinity. Black was symbolic for mourning, although princesses could wear purple in place of black. However, the symbolic importance attached to certain colors was not always motivated by spiritual aims. In 1467, Pope Paul II introduced scarlet as the color of the cardinals' robes, because the availability of purple dyes had been cut off with the fall of Constantinople to the Turks.

Thanks to the custom of giving power to the Church as a way of maintaining rule over individual fiefdoms, which had been enacted in the reign of Otto I of Germany, large churches had substantial incomes. The bishops and high-ranking clergymen were therefore able to purchase luxurious silks from Italy and have them embellished with jewels and highly complex embroidery. Many such garments still exist in church treasuries and prove that religious dress was more sumptuous than the clothing worn by royalty. The examples preserved by the Church give important clues to the history of dress overall and reveal the sophistication of fabric construction, ornamentation, and various techniques employed by the artisans that served some of the most powerful people in the Middle Ages.

THE LATE MIDDLE AGES (1300–1500)

The late Middle Ages were a time of continued expansion in the bustling city centers, accompanied by devastating wars, famine, and disease. Many institutions of the earlier centuries had been weakened by changes in values, external events, and technological advances. The feudal system that characterized the early Middle Ages slowly dissipated. Kings of the late medieval period succeeded in centralizing their governments, and the influence of knights and nobles lessened considerably. Many kings had switched to gaining their revenue through the taxation of cities and towns, which allowed them to pay men to fight for them rather than to serve them due to their oath of homage. Serfs also gradually vanished, and workers were paid in money rather than with protection and board. They became free peasants and were required to pay rent. The freedom granted to the men previously chained to indentured servitude allowed the peasants much more mobility, and they were able to seek their fortunes in the cities. Cities built enormous, ethereal Gothic churches, individuals with talent and intelligence could climb the social ladder, and the agricultural system became so well organized that food was plentiful and cheap. The new system flourished in the fourteenth century to such an extent that the peasant could afford to furnish his house in a manner that was not so different from today.

Major Events of the Late Middle Ages

The state of prosperity in the thirteenth and early fourteenth centuries that was enjoyed by the aristocracy, the new bourgeoisie, and the peasant class in France ended with the advent of the Hundred Years' War. The war that began in 1337 and dragged on until 1453 was caused by a feud over the ownership of land in France. England, which was not faring as well economically as France in this period, believed that the rightful ownership of part of southwestern France belonged to them. This was the province of Aquitaine, the huge expanse of land that Henry II of England had once ruled by virtue of his marriage to Queen Eleanor. The reasons the war lasted such a long time are attributed to mistakes made by the French, who were undoubtedly the more powerful in the war. The French were unable to drive the English out of France and lost three major battles that they should have won. Overconfidence, strategic blunders, and the success of the English longbowmen contributed to their defeats. In the *Grandes*

Chroniques de France, the great historical work that records the history of France in the Middle Ages, one of the reasons given for the defeat of the French was their passion for fashionable clothing. The author complained that the new styles were too revealing and were so tight that when the wearer was undressing, he looked as if he were being skinned like an animal. He claimed that their losses in battle were a just punishment from God for the excesses of fashion and pride.

Changes in warfare had a ripple effect on medieval society in general. Just as the shift from foot soldiers to cavalry in the ninth century had created the noble knight, who was the only one who could afford the expensive education, horses, and later suits of armor, so the changes in warfare in the late Middle Ages changed the definition of a soldier. Many changes were due to the introduction of a new weapon, the longbow. The English found the longbow in Wales, and because of its incredible improvement in performance over the typical bow, English kings initially hired Welsh bowmen to fight in their armies. An arrow from a longbow could penetrate an oak door nearly 2 inches (5 cm) thick and could travel a distance of 300 feet (90 m). By the fourteenth century, the English had learned how to handle the longbow themselves and were producing as many of them as they could. English longbows were more than 6 feet (2 m) long and made of yew wood with a hemp or silk string. The popularity of the longbow was such that yew wood became scarce because so many bows were fabricated.

The crossbow appeared around the same time as the longbow. European Crusaders discovered it already in use in the East and brought it back to Europe when they returned, along with many other inventions. The earliest crossbows were made of a thick piece of wood. Later versions were made of whalebone or horn, and in the fourteenth century they were made of steel. The crossbow could outshoot the longbow by more than a hundred yards (90 m) and was capable of piercing plate armor at close range. However, it was more difficult to load, and therefore much slower, than the longbow.

Thus, the most threatening soldiers of the late medieval period needed only a longbow or a crossbow to devastate the enemy army. The use of the new weapons was exacerbated by the introduction of gunpowder to military battle. Gunpowder was said to be in use in the Middle East in the twelfth century but did not appear in Europe until the fourteenth. Cannons employing gunpowder made it possible for soldiers to destroy structures from long distances, and the necessity of mounted knights became even less important. The knight in shining armor became a thing of the past because he was an easy, awkward target who lacked the stability needed to shoot arrows or the mobility to escape them. The economic backing previously needed to become a knight was no longer necessary, and the kings, who were already busily creating self-sufficient monarchies based on tax revenues, were not dependent anymore on the nobility for bodily protection. The knight, no longer needed for Crusades and powerless against the new technology, disappeared. Sadly, he took many of the practices of chivalry along with him.

The Hundred Years' War, while it left few traces in England, devastated France. The countryside was plundered, towns were burned, and the roads were taken over by highwaymen and Englishmen. The elaborate trade system that had evolved in the early Middle Ages was ruined; few foreign merchants stayed in the country, and the great fairs established at Champagne, Lyons, and St. Denis were closed down.

During the battle at Poitiers in 1356, King John II of France was captured, and France was forced to sign a treaty that acknowledged England's claim on France. Much of the northern part of France was transferred to the ownership of the English. However, when John died in captivity, his son Charles V retracted the agreements made with England, and the war began anew. In the meantime, a civil war in France broke out between the Armagnacs and the Burgundians, who sided with the English.

With so much unrest in France, Henry V of England reopened the conflict between France and England when he made claims for the French crown in 1413. It was not until 1453 that the war would finally end. England, earlier victorious in many of the battles, became weakened by the War of the Roses.

The great legend that has come out of the Hundred Years' War is that of Joan of Arc. Also known as the "Maid of Orleans," Joan was a sixteen-year-old girl who claimed that she spoke with the saints. They gave her the mission to save France from the English, and with the strength of her visions, she left the small town of Domrémy to seek the cooperation of the king. The voices of St. Catherine, St. Margaret, and St. Michael told her to save Orleans from the English invaders and to ensure the coronation of Charles VII. After she was ridiculed by an official in a nearby town, she donned men's clothing, acquired a horse from the Duke of Lorraine, and set out to Chinon, where Charles held court. She arrived to find him disguised and picked him out of the crowd, telling of her message from the King of Heaven.

With the initial support of Charles, Joan marched into battle wearing a suit of armor. She was victorious at the Battle of Orleans and then moved on to her next goal, to crown Charles VII at Rheims. Charles was reluctant to acknowledge his debt to the mysterious young woman, who had proved to be a fierce opponent against the English, and instead of allowing her to return to her village, he encouraged her to continue in battle. This time, Joan was captured by the Burgundians and sold to the English. The English clergy kept her imprisoned and wanted to erase the legend of her bravery from French consciousness. They put her on trial for witchcraft, questioned her for five months, and ultimately sentenced her to be burned at the stake. At nineteen years old, Joan was burned alive on charges of heresy in 1431. Legend has it that her heart did not burn and had to be thrown into the River Seine. While temporarily forgotten in the throes of war, Joan of Arc became a national symbol of France and was canonized a saint in 1920.

The devastating battles of the Hundred Years' War were not the only tragedy to strike the continent of Europe in the fourteenth century. In 1347 fatal diseases entered through the ports of the Mediterranean and spread northward like wildfire. The Black Death, named after the physical effects wherein the body turns a purplish-black before death, was the worst catastrophe to occur in the history of Europe. It is estimated that a third of the population of Europe perished from the plague, approximately twenty-five million people. The disease spread through rats, fleas, and the humans that were infected with the disease. Due to limited scientific knowledge, the disease was largely untreatable. Contagion spread quickly, and often whole families died together.

Although the English had been spared devastation of their properties during the Hundred Years' War, the plight of disease was not to be escaped. By 1400, historians estimate that half the population of England had died from the disease, and many villages were left entirely unpopulated. The outbreaks were so severe that not even the wealthy and powerful escaped the plague. Queen Eleanor of Aragon, Princess Joan of England, and King Alfonso of Castile all perished from the disease.

Europe, especially France and England, were ravaged after so many years of war and the effects of the plague, and many institutions that were the hallmarks of the feudal period disappeared. The universities that had grown and flourished with many brilliant minds in the twelfth century were left almost empty, landowners were ruined because of the shortage of available laborers, and trade had stopped in an attempt to isolate the people in cities that had survived the plague from potentially disease-carrying travelers. But with each new generation, energy returned and men and women returned to their daily lives, while some soared to new heights.

The end of the Middle Ages in Europe is marked by events in which the spirit of the Renaissance are already manifest. The last great event of the Middle Ages, which would change history like few others, was the journey made by the adventurer and ally of Queen Isabella of Spain, Christopher Columbus.

European Leaders of the Late Middle Ages

The leaders of the late Middle Ages, like the earlier kings and queens of the medieval period, had their strengths and weaknesses, and much had changed around them. The power of the monarchy had increased substantially. Kings were no longer dependent on the protection of knights because they could hire soldiers and pay them instead with revenues gained in taxation. These significant changes made some of the kings even hungrier for power. Great battles were waged for the glorious, fruitful lands of southwestern France. Some historians believe that if the fourteenth century had not been rife with war and disease, the French crown would have achieved the power of absolutism that did not take place until the sixteenth century.

In the early fourteenth century, France was ruled by Philip IV. At the time of his coronation, France was well organized, prosperous, and peaceful after the rule of St. Louis IX. In 1285, Philip was heir to the most powerful kingdom in Europe, and he spent his life attempting to make it stronger still, disregarding moral and legal propriety. He was called Philip the Fair for his handsome face and elegant bearing rather than for his subtle methods of government. Philip enlisted the services of corrupt lawyers well schooled in the precepts of Roman law, rather than the clergy, to run his government and had glorious visions of the future of France under his reign. His ambitions were without bound: he wanted to bring all French citizens, including the nobility and clergy, under his control; to extend the boundaries of France to the Mediterranean, the Atlantic, the Alps, and the Rhine; and to change the French economy so that it was based on commerce and trade rather than agriculture. He was determined to change the feudal state into a money economy and was so devoted to this idea that he freed the serfs on the royal domain early in the fourteenth century.

During his reign, Philip IV succeeded in some of these pursuits and failed in others. He was able to bring under his control the vast lands of Champagne, Navarre, and Brie by marriage and bought Chartres, Lyons, and part of the Lorraine. Many of his pursuits required a lot of money, and he spent much of his time devising methods of procuring money through taxation and other means. He instigated heavy taxes on imports, exports, and sales and managed to bring about a system that taxed the wealth of the church.

In 1307, Philip had his eye on the treasury of the Order of the Knights Templar. With the recalcitrant cooperation of the pope, Philip arrested all the Templars for blasphemy, suppressed the Order, and confiscated its treasury. The Knights Templar were tortured into confessions, and many were burned at the stake for heresy. Philip's actions had several effects on the future of French government. His methods betrayed the corruption of his administration and the barbarity of criminal procedure in France. In destroying one of the most distinguished orders of knights, he also dealt a heavy blow to the early medieval tradition of chivalry. When Pope Boniface VIII died, weary of the struggles with the tyrannical French king, Philip managed to secure the election of a Frenchman, Clement V, as the next pope. There had never before been such a great victory of a royal personage over the Church. As a crowning achievement, Philip moved the papacy to the south of France in Avignon, which continued to house the papacy for another sixty-eight years.

In the meantime across the Channel, England was not faring as well as France at the dawn of the fourteenth century. The country was in a period of what would unfortunately be a series of periods of poverty—which some historians consider to be the cause of the Hundred Years' War. The first aggressive moves were made by Edward III of England, who had been crowned king of England in 1327 at the age of fifteen. His early coronation was not due to the death of his father Edward II, but rather was part of a political coup led by his mother, Isabella. Isabella, the French-born queen of England, mobilized the nobles against Edward II, who was deposed and charged with incompetence. Thus, Edward became king at an early age, although he did not rule until three years later. After Edward II had been deposed, Isabella took a lover named Roger Mortimer, who became her coconspirator and helped rule England while Edward III was just a youth. The boy soon resented the role dealt to him by his mother and her lover and seized the royal throne for himself in 1330. He waited until the castle was empty, entered the castle through a subterranean passage under the cover of night, took Mortimer prisoner, and executed him.

Once Edward III had full control of the throne of England, he devised a plan to enrich his kingdom by taking control of the duchy of Aquitaine. This was not a move that was undertaken out of the blue, but rather an obvious next move for the ambitious young king. He had been named Duke of Aquitaine through his mother's influence in 1325, on the condition that he acknowledged his vassalage to the king of France. However, the French king was hesitant to give up the rich lands of Aquitaine, which enraged Edward to the extent that he then claimed the French crown. In 1337 he attacked France to claim the crown and began the Hundred Years' War.

Edward III won several battles during the long duration of the war, but was consistently short on resources that would make it possible for him to enforce rule in Aquitaine. The greatest victory of the English during the Hundred

Years' War would belong to his son, rather than to the king. The son, also named Edward and known as the Black Prince for his suit of black armor, managed to capture the king of France in 1355. After John II was confined in England, the prince negotiated with the French and came up with the Treaty of Calais, in which his father relinquished his claim to the crown of France, Prince Edward was named Prince of Aquitaine, and France was required to pay England three million gold crowns for the safe return of their king.

Prince Edward, eager to expand his influence throughout Europe, continued to build an impressive military resume and forged an alliance with Pedro the Cruel, king of Castile. While the French and English were battling over property in France, Spain was going to war against the Muslims. Edward was victorious in Spain and restored Pedro to the throne. However, these efforts bankrupted the treasury of England and again the English were left without resources to take over the area of Aquitaine in France. The people of England were tired of heavy taxes, Edward IV had strained relationships with his bishops and the nobles of the English court, and England was not in much better standing than when it initially started the fight for the French crown. The only reward that has stood the test of time was a large jewel presented to Black Edward by Pedro of Castile in gratitude for his aid in battle against the Muslims; the Ruby of the Black Prince is now a part of the magnificent Crown Jewels of England.

France was overconfident in the battles of the Hundred Years' War, and if it had taken the threat more seriously could have easily quelled the efforts of the English kings. Charles V was king of France at the time of the first attacks by the English. He was named Charles the Wise both for his love of study and for his victories—although not ultimately triumphant—against the English in the battles for France. He was known for surrounding himself with luxury and educated men, and he built a huge section in the Louvre to house his extensive library.

When Charles was seventeen and his father King John II was captured by Edward the Black Prince, Charles was left to devise a method of raising the exorbitant ransom fee. While his father was imprisoned in England, Charles decreed that no man or woman in France was allowed to wear gold, silver, pearls, or miniver—or any extravagant dress whatsoever—until the king was returned. Charles met many difficulties with French councilors, who were not fond of the idea of handing over the entire French treasury to the English. One powerful merchant, Etienne Marcel, refused Charles's taxation and to frighten him he had two of Charles's councilors murdered in his presence. Charles left Paris to raise an army and garner support, returning a year later, after which Marcel was assassinated.

When his father died in captivity in 1364, Charles was crowned the king of France. He retracted the treaty agreements he had made with the English while they held his father, and another round of battles over the ownership of Aquitaine began. Charles won some French victories during this time, but while the pace of the attacks by the English had slowed down due to lack of resources on their part, the Hundred Years' War continued on after the death of Charles V.

Charles VI was crowned king at age eleven in 1388 and demanded to rule alone with the help of his father's advisers. By 1392, he had achieved the sobriquet of Charles the Mad, as he suffered from prolonged fits of madness. It is estimated that throughout his lifetime, he had more than forty-four attacks of madness, each lasting from three to nine months. Because of the obvious weakness of the French king during the reign of Charles VI, the dukes of Burgundy and Orleans began to vie for power. They allied themselves with Henry V of England, and by 1422 the country of France was divided between areas in the north that were under the influence of the Burgundians and the areas in the south that were loyal to the French king; this second group was called the Armagnacs. Charles VI, in the midst of his bouts of madness, signed the Treaty of Troyes, which gave his daughter Catherine to Henry in marriage and named the English king heir to the French throne. This move completely alienated his son, Charles VII, the rightful heir to the throne.

Charles VII, as was discussed earlier, succeeded partly due to the aid of Joan of Arc. With her influence, the spirit of the army was revived, and France was able to defeat the English. The Hundred Years' War was ended during the reign of Richard II in England. Richard had none of the expansive enthusiasm of his forbears and fell to minding his own kingdom, which was rife with unrest due to peasant revolts against the throne. In 1453, he returned Aquitaine permanently to France, after it had been associated with England since the twelfth century when Eleanor of Aquitaine had married Henry Plantagenet.

After the war, Charles VII proved to be a capable ruler and is largely responsible for rebuilding the economy of France. Charles reestablished the fairs in Champagne, Lyons, and Paris as soon as the English and bands of predatory mercenaries were driven out of the country. He also lent his ear to a man named Jacques Coeur, a commercial genius. Coeur was the son of a tanner from Bourges who rose through his own efforts to the highest ranks of the bourgeoisie. His motto was "Nothing is impossible for the valiant heart." His skills in commerce earned him the position of king's treasurer, and with this authority, Coeur was able to revive the almost nonexistent French trade after the disastrous years of the Hundred Years' War and the Black Plague. He organized fleets of ships to import perfumes from the Middle East, furs from the North, and carpets from Persia. He also worked within France to revitalize domestic industry. Coeur established paper mills and dyeworks in France and reopened French mines to attain metals to produce household utensils.

Thus, after the difficult years of the thirteenth and fourteenth centuries, Charles VII brought back some stability to France. The boundaries of the nations of France and England were finally determined in a division similar to the one we know today. England gave up its claim on the continent and focused its energies on the administration of government within the British Isles. Spain had driven out the Muslims and become a Christian nation, as it remains to this day.

The Social Fabric of the Late Middle Ages

The social ties that held medieval society together in the early Middle Ages weakened considerably in the fourteenth and fifteenth centuries. The great expansion and increasingly organized commerce that had marked the twelfth century affected the class structure permanently. Feudalism waned and was completely replaced with paid wages by the end of the fifteenth century. A new class rose out of the wealth accrued in commerce, neither noble nor peasant: the bourgeoisie. The rise of the bourgeoisie is frequently associated with the beginning of the phenomenon of fashion, where clothing styles begin to change rapidly as a result of demand and status seeking. The Church, as a result of the concentrated power of the monarchies in many countries, went through dramatic shifts and lost much of its influence. There were changes in the realm of art as well. Although the building of great cathedrals halted, we have many more great works of literature that have survived the years from the late Middle Ages than from the earlier periods. In addition, textile arts flourished in the last part of the fifteenth century, and France produced some of most refined tapestries ever created.

The Bourgeoisie and the Beginning of Fashion

One of the social phenomena that was indicative of the widespread changes in social organization during the late Middle Ages was the beginning of fashion, or the introduction of quickly changing styles of clothing in the marketplace. Many costume historians agree that the beginning of fashion took place around 1340, and according to chroniclers in many different countries, it happened in many places around the same time. Disapproving observers attributed it to foreign influence. The Italians believed it was due to the influence of the Spanish or the French, the English believed it came from Flanders, and the French complained about it but didn't find anyone to blame.

The new styles for both men and women were significantly different. Men's dress changed the most and the knee- or floor-length tunic that was worn for many centuries evolved into a short jacket and hose. The other significant change that occurred in both men's and women's dress was the fit. The loose tunics of the early Middle Ages disappeared, and the jackets worn by men and gowns worn by women were tightly fitted around the arms for the first time in history. The changes in dress were partially due to advancements in tailoring. Previously, tunics had been fabricated out of one large piece of cloth, so that the sleeves had just one seam, underneath the arms. In the 1340s, the new fashions show the growth of the skill of the tailors, with the separation of the bodice and the sleeve pattern pieces. This allows the fit of the garment to be much closer around the shoulders and arms and creates a silhouette that is much shapelier on its wearer. Some costume historians attribute these changes in fit to advancements in military garments. With the advent of armor, tailors were required to create undergarments for knights that were fitted yet allowed movement for the knight to wear them under the already fitted suits of armor.

Another reason for the changes in fashion is the rise of the bourgeoisie and their newly accrued wealth, which was poured into dress and self-presentation and aroused resentment in the social hierarchy. This resentment was so severe that laws were made to prevent certain classes from wearing clothing and other status symbols reserved for nobility. *Sumptuary laws* began in the thirteenth century with the initial successes of the bourgeoisie in several European countries. In 1244 peasants were required by law to cut their hair short and wear gray clothing in Germany. By 1300 there were laws against the extravagant display of clothing by classes other than the nobility in Spain, Portugal, Italy, France, and England.

In 1337, women in the Italian city of Lucca were forbidden to wear pearls on their headdresses, golden fringe, and gold belts as accessories. Alphonso XI of Spain banned the use of jewels, gold and silver embroidery, and enamel for decoration on men's and women's garments and directed that only the heir to the throne was permitted to wear cloth of silk or gold. In 1351 Pedro the Cruel specified that women companions of the clergy were required by law to use striped fabric for their gowns and wear red headbands around their veils. In England, laws regulated the amount of money artisans, grooms, and servants were allowed to spend on clothing, and France regulated the height of the headdresses worn at the court of Burgundy according to social rank.

In 1430 in Germany, the Duke of Savoy created a document entitled *The Statutes of Savoy*. In this elaborate system, he declared that there were thirty-nine different social categories and determined the proper dress for each group. In his laws, scarlet-colored cloth was forbidden to the bourgeoisie, artisans were prohibited from wearing pointed shoes, and peasants were barred from wearing garments that were made of more than one type of fabric.

These laws often spurred a brand of creativity in which the people who were not allowed to wear certain garments and ornamentations came up with new ways to decorate their garments and draw attention to their dress anyway. Due to a combination of these factors, the period of popularity for any given style grew shorter and shorter. In earlier periods of costume history such as the Ancient Greek period, the Egyptian period, and the Roman period, clothing styles lasted for centuries, if not for thousands of years. It was not until the late Middle Ages that styles changed such a rate as to create clothing *fashions* rather than styles.

Increasing widespread wealth and the rise of the bourgeoisie were certainly part of the reasons behind the creation of sumptuary laws. The social structure shifted significantly during the late Middle Ages, and the new class of wealthy merchants became avid consumers of new fashions and products. In the early centuries of the medieval period, the peasant class had made up four-fifths of the population; by the twelfth century, those who had trades that were valued or showed extraordinary skills in the marketplace were able to make a much better life for themselves.

In addition to the increasing opportunities in the new urban centers, the existing social structure was profoundly affected by the increasing centralization of authority in the monarchy. The kings of late medieval Europe were set on freeing themselves from dependence on the nobility, who proved to be greedy for power and uncertain in loyalty. The growing merchant class provided medieval kings with new revenue that would replace the kings' armies of noble knights with paid soldiers. In essence, taxation of imports, exports, and sales gave prosperous merchants freedom on the market and the king independence.

In the fifteenth century, the line between the bourgeoisie and nobility was less definite. Successful merchants and landowners were the nouveaux riches and became avid social climbers. The wealthier members of the new class of the bourgeoisie bought large tracts of land and patents of nobility and hurried to marry their sons and daughters to nobles who had met some unfortunate turn of fate. Charles V opened the doors of possibility to especially ambitious bourgeois and conferred nobility on mayors and royal officers. Later, he sold titles to anyone who could afford to pay one hundred *livres* (pounds) and allowed members of the bourgeoisie in Paris to wear the golden spurs previously worn only by knights.

The rise of the bourgeoisie proved to be alarming for the nobility. The structure of Europe in the late Middle Ages demonstrated the growing power of the monarch and the shrinking influence of the nobility. The life of privilege, once exclusive by birthright, was no longer guaranteed by a noble birth. Just as there were bourgeois who rose to the noble class by means of service to the king, through marriage, or by sheer purchasing power, so there were also nobles who lost their fortunes. Some, unable to run their manors without the labor of serfs, were forced to sell their homes to the wealthier bourgeoisie. There is evidence of nobles, who, having lost their lands or their fortunes in the difficult years of the Hundred Years' War and the plague, were forced to seek gainful employment. Some became merchants themselves or country gentlemen who sought to make a living through gainful agriculture. Others became doctors, and there is a story of a relative of the Duke of Burgundy who kept an inn.

The nobles reacted to the changing social structure by creating more exclusive traditions attached to their status. The class of nobles became more competitive in their attempts to show up the bourgeoisie. Sumptuary laws were one way to ensure that noblemen and their ladies were the only ones allowed to dress in splendid finery.

In 1430, Philip III of Burgundy established the Order of the Golden Fleece in an attempt to restore some of the traditions of chivalry, emphasizing loyalty to the lord. The order was open only to members of the aristocracy who were of ancient noble families.

However, despite the changes in the social hierarchy, life for many members of the aristocracy continued to be filled with elaborate dress, feasts, and patronage of the arts. This was more evident in the court of Burgundy than anywhere else.

After the capture of King John II, Paris became a center of military activity and Charles V spent most of his time raising the ransom to secure the safe return of his father. During his preoccupation, his younger brother John was to develop one of the most brilliant courts of the late Middle Ages in the area east of Paris called Burgundy.

Some of the most sumptuous, ornate, and exaggerated styles of garments of the late Middle Ages were worn in the courts of Burgundy. They are well documented in some of the finest manuscript illuminations ever created, as well as in the records kept by clerks of the noble households. In their ambition to outshine the bourgeoisie and rival the power of the king, the dukes spent a considerable amount of their revenue on personal luxury, and this included costume. In Paris, members of the royal families each had their own staff for the creation their wardrobes. The tailors, furriers, and embroiderers in the service of the king lived in homes that were paid for by the king and oftentimes lived lives that were similar to the lifestyles of the aristocracy. Their surroundings and experiences were far different from that of the artisans, who toiled to make a living with their labors.

Burgundy was ideally situated geographically to gain economically from the thriving textile industry in Bruges and Ypres—and likewise to consume the exquisite products of the skilled weavers and artisans that worked there. Both men and women of the nobility wore incredibly lavishly embroidered and bejeweled garments. When Philip the Brave, Duke of Burgundy, attended the reception of Queen Isabeau in Paris, he wore four different gowns of velvet decorated with flowers in gold and gems and a jacket with forty lambs and swans created out of pearls. Philip also started the fashion for black clothing, because it set off his jewels to a great effect.

Clothing was even used literally to communicate between the dukes. In the fifteenth century, when the King Charles VI of France was suffering from fits of madness, the Duke of Burgundy and the Duke of Orleans feuded to claim the seat of power in France. Orleans decorated his clothing with an image of a wooden club and the words "I challenge you" embroidered on them. Burgundy responded by wearing clothing that had small carpenters' saws, symbolizing the destruction of the wooden club, and the words "I accept the challenge" embroidered on his garments.

Women's fashions at the court of Burgundy were equally ornate, particularly the headdresses. The pointed-cone headdress, synonymous with the upper-class woman of the medieval period, was worn most frequently there.

While the aristocrats at the courts of Burgundy were careful to preserve the right to wear lavishly ornate garment only for themselves, they were not miserly when it came to outfitting their servants and dependents. During the fourteenth and fifteenth centuries, the lord of the manor would frequently distribute sets of clothing to all the members of his household. This clothing came to be known as "livery" and signified a type of uniform for the servants of the manor. Sometimes the garments were constructed of specific colors to symbolize the heraldry of the coat of arms that belonged to the lord.

The Peasantry

Peasants, while they were not likely to climb the social ladder up to the ranks of nobility, nonetheless enjoyed new privileges in the late Middle Ages. They were freed from the lifetime of indentured servitude that had characterized the status of so many during the age of feudalism. They were free to embrace their new-found mobility, and this new freedom of movement granted to the peasant class contributed significantly to the urban expansion of the thirteenth century. As serfs, they had worked the fields or provided the necessary products with which to run the manor, including cloth, shoes, weapons, soap, candles, and other household products. These skilled artisans were now able to move into the new commerce-based economy seamlessly, offering their trade skills for pay rather than room and board. A few, like Jacques Coeur, who was the son of a tanner, were able to become enormously successful businessmen.

However, the trying times of the fourteenth century hit the peasant class harder than any other. During the Hundred Years' War, peasants were particularly vulnerable to the violence that spread through France and southward into Italy. Although they had won their freedom during the dissipation of feudalism, they also lost their protection. On hearing of the arrival of soldiers in their villages, many peasants would gather together their families and food supplies and rush to the nearest walled town. But these warnings did not always come in time, and many peasants were attacked in the fields, their wives and daughters taken captive and their homes burned.

The Black Death was no less devastating for the peasant class. Millions died and were heaped into the enormous mass graves dug without any ceremony whatsoever. On the other hand, after the plague had passed, the enormous decline in the population of many countries in Europe gave the surviving peasants a marked advantage. With the dramatic labor shortage that resulted from the peasants' high mortality rate, they were able to demand higher wages from their landlords.

While this state of affairs served the interest of the peasants in the years directly following the Black Plague, the lot of the peasants did not ultimately improve much. Much of this was due to the increased taxation of the kings and nobles, many of whom were merciless in their desire to raise funds for the royal treasury. Groups of peasants in both England and France rallied together to form the Peasant Revolts of 1381.

The Christian Church

Like the economies and changes in the general social structure of the late Middle Ages, the role of the Christian Church was to be considerably different than in previous centuries. The late medieval church suffered such upheaval that chroniclers of the time feared for the survival of the institution. When Philip IV removed the papacy from Rome to Avignon in his quest for absolute power, the reputation of the Church suffered greatly.

Regarded as a tool of the French king, Pope Clement V felt his safety threatened and in 1309 moved to Avignon, in the south of France. A great palace was built for the pope, which still stands today in the city. The sacred nature of the office of the pope was seriously damaged by Clement's continuous decisions in favor of the French king. Clement reversed the decrees made by his predecessor that forbade the clergy to pay subsidies to lay authorities, proclaimed the pope's supreme authority, and allowed Philip to destroy the Order of the Golden Fleece and steal its treasury. He was also charged with selling ecclesiastical offices to anyone who could pay the fees. Dante Alighieri, the most renowned author of the fourteenth century, wrote of Clement with great distaste, and the pope appears in his famous *Inferno*.

The papal seat remained in Avignon for sixty-eight years, and this period became known as the Babylonian Captivity of the Popes. The corruption of the pope alienated much of Christendom, and in particular England and Germany ceased to regard the office as supreme. The events that followed the move to Avignon only compounded the weakening of the Church. The Great Schism of the late Middle Ages was the most dangerous upheaval in the history of the Church.

In 1378, a year after he ended the Babylonian Captivity and returned to Rome, Pope Gregory XI died. The cardinals in Rome chose Urban VI as his successor after mobs called for the appointment of an Italian. However, this decision was retracted by several French cardinals who claimed they had been forced into their decision. Their choice, Robert of Geneva, who became Clement VII, rode off to Avignon to take the office in the Palace of the Popes. Thus, at the end of the fourteenth century, Europe had two popes, neither of which would step down from the office. Each called upon his supporters to depose the other, claiming his enemy was the Antichrist and demanding his removal. Europe divided its loyalties between the two popes for almost forty years, during which there was great confusion and, despite the many disagreements, most people wanted an end to the disaster more than anything. It was not until the next century that the papacy was restored to Rome in relative peace.

The dissolution of the Christian Church was followed by the breakdown of the religious Orders. The followers of the great leaders of the Orders of the twelfth century lost much of their devotion after the deaths of their leaders.

Before his death, St. Francis warned many of the members of his Order of the dangers of wealth, which poured into the Order from donations. His foresight proved prophetic when many Franciscans later renounced their vows of poverty and began the building of great organizations. Monks and friars, as portrayed in the works of Chaucer, became associated with avarice, and some of them sold their spiritual services.

However, not all holy men were corrupted. The brothers who adhered to the practices held sacred by St. Francis were called the Spirituals and were subjected to torture for their unwillingness to conform to the times in the fourteenth century. They begged the pope for permission to found an Order of their own but were refused the blessing of the Church. When they asserted that the teachings of St. Francis were identical to Christ's Gospel, four Spirituals were burned at the stake in 1318 in Marseilles.

St. Bernardino of Siena was another figure of the late Medieval period who continued the tradition of St. Francis and drew thousands to hear his sermons. He was tried three times for heresy and finally absolved by the pope, who realized the true value of his teachings and pureness of heart.

When St. Bernardino died in 1444, Europe was on the threshold of a new era. The Church suffered from the Avignon residence and the Great Schism. The spiritual integrity that had characterized the twelfth century and inspired pilgrimage, crusade, and supranational devotion was replaced with a sectarian institution that was swayed by the rising power of the monarchy and was not above trafficking in spiritual rewards. The loss of power of the Church at the end of the Middle Ages was replaced with a new spirit, where nation-states became more dominant and, most importantly, the study of Classical texts became the most significant cultural influence. Preserved by early monks since the time of Charlemagne, Greek thought infused the universities and courts of the late medieval period and heralded the beginning of the Renaissance. Ultimate dependence on God and the Church became a thing of the past.

There was another dark chapter yet to unfold, however. Following in the tradition of the earlier Inquisitions that had essentially wiped out the heretical sects of the Albigensians in France, the Spanish Inquisition made a resolute effort to rid Spain of heretics, Muslims, and Jews. In the fifteenth century, Spain was the most pluralistic country in Europe. Throughout the Middle Ages, Muslims and Jews had traveled from Africa and Middle Eastern countries to settle in Spain. They were responsible for the architectural masterpieces that meld together Islamic and Western styles, as is demonstrated in the Alhambra and other buildings in cities such as Seville and Granada. As members of the literate and professional classes, these groups became wealthy through their contributions to the development of the country and thus provoked a lot of envy among the Christians. The rulers of Spain, Ferdinand and Isabella, who perceived these anti-Semitic sentiments, were determined to create a unified Catholic country, and in 1478 they induced Pope Sixtus IV to authorize the Spanish Inquisition.

The reasons behind the Spanish Inquisition also included racism. At that time in Spain, there were approximately 300,000 converted Jews called *Conversos* or *Marranos*. However, some of those who had converted had done so only superficially and continued to practice the Jewish religion in secret. The Christian population became fearful of their influence and wished to preserve what they believed was the ancestral heritage of Spain. This became known as the Spanish cult of *sangre limpia*, "pure blood," and referred to those of white Christian ancestry. The nobility became obsessed with the idea of pure blood, and while intermarriage between religious groups had been a common practice for centuries, many went to any limit to prove their family's pedigree.

From the beginning, the Spanish inquisitors proved to be more brutal and severe than the earlier Dominican inquisitors in France had been. Every man, woman, and child in Spain was affected by the fear and cruel acts performed by the inquisitors. Marranos and heretics were the main targets of the Inquisition, but anyone who objected to the practices of the inquisitors became suspect.

In fact, the intensity of the Spanish Inquisition was to a great degree due to one man's efforts to rid the country of Jews. Tomás de Torquemada was initially a Dominican and served as the personal confessor of Isabella when she was a young girl. When she matured to take the throne, Torquemada convinced her it was her Christian duty to rid the country of all Jews. He was soon promoted to the position of General Inquisitor and spent the rest of his life trying to abolish Jews from Spain. Ironically, his lineage included Jewish descent.

Torquemada made it his personal mission to rid the country of the Marranos. He began his procedures with processes and punishments similar to those used by the earlier inquisitors in France. The accused, who were often Marranos, were first required to surrender their property to the state. Then they were publicly humiliated and required to walk through their town naked from the waist down wearing only a yellow shirt with crosses on it. They were then given the opportunity to swear their allegiance to the Christian faith. If the accused failed to do so, they were burned at the stake with slow-burning green wood. Burning at the stake usually took place at a grand public ceremony called the *auto-da-fé*, or act of faith, which Torquemada used to increase public fear of the inquisitors.

Torquemada used all means available to enforce his will. He and his associates frequently employed torture to extract confessions from the accused, which were used as evidence in the trials against them. He was a master of manipulating the people, as well as his protectors, and carefully crafted his image. Torquemada demanded the burning of all religious books that were not the Bible. Throughout the countryside, as he stopped in each city, he traveled with 50 mounted guards and 250 armed men.

In 1490, Torquemada staged a trial that would ultimately have dire effects for the entire Jewish population of Spain. The trial, called the LaGuardia Trial, indicted eight Jews and Marranos for the crucifixion of a Christian child, despite the fact that no child had been reported missing and no body was ever found. All of the defendants were tortured for their confessions, which were in turn used as evidence, and they were burned at the stake for their crime. Torquemada used the results of the trial to spread the belief of the evildoings of the Jews and falsely converted Marranos.

At the end of the fifteenth century, Torquemada cited the LaGuardia Trial as proof to convince Ferdinand and Isabella that the kingdom was endangered by the presence of the Jews and persuaded them to throw all the Jews out of Spain. Two wealthy Jewish members of the community tried in vain to convince the king and queen to allow the Jews to stay by offering 30,000 ducats, an offer which appealed to them because they had spent so much of the royal treasury on expeditions. However, when Torquemada accused them of selling out Jesus Christ as Judas had done, they sought to follow his directions.

In 1492, Ferdinand and Isabella issued a formal Edict of Expulsion, which required all Jews in Spain to leave the country within three months or be killed. Many fled to Africa or Portugal; others accompanied explorer Christopher Columbus on his ships. A few remained to worship in secret, and the Secret Jews continue to exist in Spain up to this day. After the expulsion, Torquemada retired, believing he had finished his life's work of ridding Spain of the Jews. He went to live in a monastery, where he spent the rest of his life in fear of being poisoned. While he eventually died a natural death, he kept a "unicorn horn" at his side as a poison antidote for the rest of his days.

Architecture and Art

The nature of medieval art changed along with the zeitgeist. While the pinnacle of art and culture of the High Middle Ages was the Gothic cathedral, the late medieval period saw little development in construction. The Hundred Years' War and the Black Death had exhausted France and England financially, and the social unity that characterized the twelfth century and made it possible to build the enormous, costly cathedrals had disappeared with the dreadful intrusions of war and disease. Most of the revenues gained by taxation in the fourteenth and fifteenth centuries were used for military exploits or hoarded by the kings and nobles. There were very few new churches begun, and many of the grand cathedrals that had been started in the twelfth and thirteenth centuries were abandoned altogether. The delicate, vertical style of Gothic cathedrals was ultimately replaced by the growing interest in Classical influences that were picked up in Italy and were the inspiration for the great architects of the Renaissance such as Brunelleschi.

While the age of the great cathedrals had ended, there was continuing interest in the art of sculpture, in which figures would gradually came to stand on their own rather than being attached to the walls of the church. One artist in particular, Claus Sluter, proves to be a striking example of late medieval sculpture. Sluter worked at the court of Burgundy and produced some of the most lifelike figures in the history of art since the Classical era. His work foreshadows the creations of the great sculptors of the Renaissance such as Donatello and Michelangelo.

In addition to sculpture, the court of Burgundy commissioned several illuminated manuscripts, including the world famous *Très Riches Heures du Duc de Berry*. This illuminated manuscript was commissioned by Jean de Berry, one of the greatest patrons of the arts in the late medieval period. One of the most popular forms of books of the late Middle Ages was the *Book of Hours*, a small devotional prayer book that was created for the use of an individual or family and contained a series of prayers to the Virgin Mary that were said at times specified by the Church throughout the day. Wealthy members of late medieval society commissioned the creation of these books from artists who decorated the pages with images of biblical figures or scenes from daily life. The *Très Riches Heures du Duc de Berry* has a calendar preceding the text, with scenes of each month gracing the pages of the book, as well as scenes of religious nature. At the top of each illustration is the sign of the zodiac, complete with precise astronomical information for the time of year.

Painted by the Limbourg brothers in the first decade of the fifteenth century, the illuminations of the *Très Riches Heures* are a valuable source of costume information for the period. The figures of the calendar are modeled after the lords and ladies of the court of Burgundy and are delicately painted wearing colorful, fitted gowns; *houppelandes* made of sumptuous patterned textiles; and the elaborate headdresses worn by both men and women of the fifteenth century. Peasants are also represented in plainer costume, in scenes that illustrate their occupations, such as harvesting in October and huddling around a fire in December. The *Très Riches Heures du Duc de Berry* also represents a crucial step in the development of art history. The Limbourg brothers portray the castles, trees, and surrounding landscape with incredible detail, thus foreshadowing the explosion of naturalism that was to surface in Dutch painting with Van Eyck and later Vermeer.

In addition to manuscript illuminations, the individual portrait appeared in the fourteenth century. In the early Middle Ages, most depictions of a figure were religious in subject matter. With the waning of the Church and rising power of the monarchy, however, many kings and queens now desired to have large-scale portraits created in their image. The bourgeoisie emulated the royal figures in this practice in the fifteenth century, and portraits became more popular than ever. These paintings provide much better visual representations of dress, as they are large enough to include significant detail of the garment styles. The realistic painting style that became popular was so precise that the viewer is able to see the pins tucked in the headdress of a woman subject. However, it is important to remember that the garments worn in the portraits would have been the best the sitter owned and were not representative of everyday life.

Tapestry

The other art form that blossomed at the courts of Burgundy was tapestry. Records show that tapestries with simple decorative motifs were woven in Paris as early as 1300, and by the middle of the century this art form expanded rapidly. Members of the nobility became enthusiastic about tapestry both for its decoration and its functional qualities. King Philip IV had a building specially designed for the conservation of tapestry in the Louvre in Paris. Tapestries were a reliable means to announce one's status in society, as they required a considerable amount of time and therefore labor power to produce. They were also easy to move around and were frequently rolled up to travel along with their owners on visits to their many estates. The other practical benefit of tapestry was its insulating qualities. The castles that the nobility lived in during the medieval period were huge, unheated blocks of cold stone. A large woolen tapestry hanging on the wall was an effective method of keeping the heat of the fireplace within the limits of the room.

For these reasons and for their decorative qualities, tapestries became one of the favored art forms of the court of Burgundy. Expense accounts from the fifteenth century record the huge sums spent by members of the nobility to accrue them. The sheer number of tapestries created at this period demonstrates how much the people of the late Middle Ages revered them. They became acknowledged as an art form in themselves, and the northern cities of Paris, Brussels, Tournai, and Arras competed to create the most exquisite designs. Unfortunately, because wool is extremely susceptible to the agents of light, mold, and insects, many early tapestries have not survived. In addition to the problems related to natural decomposition, tapestries with golden thread were burned to remove the precious metal.

The Apocalypse Tapestries, created in a seven-year period after 1373 in Arras, show a series of figure compositions heralding the Apocalypse. Like the advances made in manuscript illumination in the fourteenth and fifteenth centuries, tapestries became more complicated in design and more sophisticated in the depiction of figures.

However, the crowning achievement of the art of tapestry did not appear until the end of the fifteenth century: the Unicorn Tapestries are some of the most exquisite textiles ever fabricated. The Hunt of the Unicorn, a popular legend throughout the Middle Ages, is portrayed in seven tapestries that portray different scenes from the story. Many people in the medieval period genuinely believed in the existence of the unicorn, and it was also used as an allegorical figure that symbolized Jesus Christ, who like the unicorn was captured and put to death despite his innocence and purity. The tapestries are 12 feet (3.7 m) in height and range from 8 to 14 feet (2.4–4.3 m) in width. The figures in the tapestries have many color hues and show refined facial expressions and shading techniques to indicate three-dimensionality. The animals and human figures that portray the action of the scene are set against a background of trees and flowers, which gives the series of tapestries their other name of *Mille Fleurs* or "Thousand Flowers." The exquisite detail used in the depiction of the flowers in several of the tapestries is unrivaled. More than a hundred different plants are represented in them, and the majority have been identified by botanists.

Literature

Cultural development in the late Middle Ages was focused in the area of literature. The first stirrings of humanism are evident in the writings of Dante, Petrarch, and Chaucer. Dante, the most acclaimed, was born in 1265 into an upper-class family and enjoyed a privileged upbringing in Florence that was later ruined by his involvement in politics. Taking the side of the losing rebels, Dante was threatened with the punishment of death for his opinions and therefore spent most of his mature life in exile. Inspired by the style of the Provençal troubadours, Dante's great work *The Divine Comedy* became an instant classic and opened up the realm of literature with an allegorical treatment of contemporary problems.

Set in the three realms of Hell, Purgatory, and Heaven, Dante's poem discusses the fates of Classical figures as well as medieval persons as he makes his journey through them. *The Divine Comedy* was groundbreaking not only in the sophistication of its content but also as the first great work to be written in Italian rather than in Latin. Its popularity swept across Europe, and by 1400, twelve commentaries had been written to explain its meaning. *The Divine Comedy* was also the first contemporary work that was included in university curriculum alongside the ancient classics of Greece and Rome.

Petrarch was the most famous scholar of the late Middle Ages and was considered to be one of the founders of humanism. Born in Italy in 1304, he traveled throughout his life, seeking out the works of Classical authors in monastic libraries throughout Europe. He wrote many poems devoted to an idealized woman, Laura, whom he had seen in church. Petrarch's ideas and writings synthesized classical culture and the divine aspirations of medieval scholars and pointed to the new value system that would come into being in during the Italian Renaissance.

In England, the English language reached new heights in the writings of Geoffrey Chaucer. Like Dante, Chaucer wrote a work of such universal appeal that it is still commonly studied by university students today. *The Canterbury Tales* by Chaucer is a collection of stories told by a group of people joined together on a pilgrimage journey. Chaucer writes with exceptional insight, humor, and knowledge of the human spirit in his tales, which are told by such varied members of the social hierarchy as the knight, the cook, the monk, and the wife of Bath. Chaucer served three kings in England as a diplomat and civil servant but is best known for his huge contribution to English literature.

Very few records of writings by women in the late Middle Ages have survived. However, one woman writer of note from the late Middle Ages was Christine de Pizan. De Pizan was the daughter of the astrologer to Charles V and spent her childhood in Paris studying under the tutelage of her father. At fifteen, she married a clerk of the court, and at twenty-five she was widowed. In order to support herself and her three young children, she took up the pen, initially writing poems that bemoaned the loss of her husband. These met with success, and she continued throughout the rest of her life to write poems and works that defended women's roles in the Middle Ages. Her first large work was called *The City of Women*, which was followed by another book called *The Treasure*.

The Treasure is an allegorical poem that involves a dialogue between Christine and the personified characters of Reason, Rectitude, and Justice. The principal aim of the book is the education of women, and it is divided into three parts: part 1 is directed toward queens and princesses, part 2 is for aristocratic ladies, and the third part is for middle- and lower-class women. There are many points made about the dangers of dressing incorrectly for women. De Pizan strongly advises against attempting to rise above one's status by wearing garments that are designated for a higher class, and she also cautions against accumulating large debts for the sake of wearing fashionable clothing. Furthermore, de Pizan warns her readers against wearing their gowns too tight; this fashion, she believed, could make men think that the wearer was trying to provoke desire and attentions.

In addition to the development of literature in the late Middle Ages, there were drastic improvements in the practical aspects of manufacturing books, and the dissemination of printed materials was changed forever. In 1450 a German silversmith named Johannes Gutenberg invented movable type, creating the first printed book known in history. Before the invention of movable type, the only books available in the medieval period were manuscripts that had been copied by hand. Historians estimate that the total number of books in Europe could be counted in the thousands before the advent of printing. By 1500, there were more than nine million books in Europe. Begun in Germany, printing spread immediately to Venice and Paris, where Bibles, Classical texts, and Books of Hours were printed for the larger public.

Textiles in the Late Middle Ages

The textile industry in the late Middle Ages continued to expand with the solid and efficient organization of production and trade. Wool remained the most important fiber in medieval society, and the process of weaving wool into fine cloth was mastered at the highest level in Flanders. Flemish wool clothed Germans, the French, the Portuguese, Norwegians, Italians, Spaniards, the English, and sometimes Greeks and Muslims. Merchants from the north would travel by ship to Bruges and those from the south of Europe would go to the fairs held in Champagne. However, many other cities wove woolen fabrics as well. Florence became a leading producer of woolen textiles and by 1306 hosted three hundred textile factories. The textile merchants in Florence imported wool from England to weave into cloth or imported unfinished cloth from Flanders to dye and finish in Florence. In the latter part of the fourteenth century, England, known for producing the highest quality wool fiber, began to export cloth as well.

Linen continued to be used for undergarments and veils and became less expensive because of improvements in technology. There is some evidence that there were attempts to create a waterproof fabric by waxing linen fabrics. The waxed fabric was used for window blinds and later for constructing early versions of rainwear to protect the wearer from the wet climate in England.

Cotton remained a marginal fiber in comparison to linen. It was still a relative rarity in the late medieval period. On the other hand, because cotton possesses unique insulating qualities that linen does not, it was commonly used for wadding in quilted fabrics and garments. Linings for doublets and other padded garments that were popular from the thirteenth to fifteenth centuries were frequently stuffed with unspun cotton.

Silk was still the principal luxury fiber. It became more available, and as a result the members of the aristocracy tried to ban its use by wealthy members of the bourgeoisie. From the thirteenth century on, Italy produced silks that rivaled the creations of Byzantium. Later developments made Italian silks among the most luxurious ever created in history.

With the unification of the Mongol Empire due to the efforts of Genghis Khan, trade with the Eastern countries from China to Persia was much more common. The impact of the influx of the fabrics that came from the East cannot be underestimated. Fabrics from the Far East had different design schemes and greatly influenced European textile design. Initially, balanced rounded patterns inspired by Islamic designs dominated in the manufacture of luxurious silk fabrics in Italy. However, after seeing the textiles imported from farther east, Italian weavers were inspired to create brocade designs that were asymmetrical. Patterns that had animals in their designs were rearranged in diagonal relationships, creating a more dynamic aesthetic.

The most opulent silk textile of the late Middle Ages was velvet, which could be patterned and multicolored. Solid-colored velvet had been produced in Italy since the thirteenth century. Then, in the fourteenth century, velvets were woven in stripes and checks, which later evolved into highly ornate patterns that included animals and fruits incorporated into the designs.

In the fifteenth century, the most popular silk textile designs included the pomegranate and related motifs such as pinecones and pineapples. During this period, Florence, Genoa, and Lucca were the most important textile centers.

France also began the manufacture of silk, which from the thirteenth century onward was produced in southern cities such as Avignon, Montpellier, and Nîmes. However, as they were unable to compete with the highly evolved silk trade and manufacture in Italy, the French silk weavers limited their products to small things such as ribbons and trims. In 1450 the emerging silk trade in France was centered in Lyons after a mandate by the French king.

The dyeing industry also became much more advanced. With increasing trade throughout the continent of Europe, more raw materials became available to dyers. The dye artisans used vegetable, animal, and mineral materials to produce more saturated colors, which quickly became fashionable. Dark-hued colors such as dark blues, greens, and violets were in great demand throughout the courts of Europe. Black became the preferred color of the elite in the latter part of the fourteenth century; in Italy, many decrees were announced to limit the use of the color black in clothing exclusively to the aristocracy. A deep dark black was produced by dipping the fabric in successive baths of woad and indigo. Along these same lines, the desire for light colors in furs such as ermine declined. Royalty and members of the nobility preferred dark furs at the end of the fourteenth century, although this was more common for male nobles than female aristocrats, who continued to wear white furs.

Dress in the Late Middle Ages

The Evidence in Costume History

Sources of evidence that depict and describe costume for the late Middle Ages are much more plentiful than before. Many books were illustrated with manuscript illuminations showing men and women, rich and poor, in the clothing of the period. Individual portrait paintings that better display garments appear in the fifteenth century. Sculpture of the period also provides visual references to clothing, although almost all sculpture except funerary sculpture depicted religious figures that were idealized and frequently wore garments from earlier times. Inventories from royal households in England and France have also survived and give us a very precise indication of what their inhabitants wore, how much the garments cost, and how many garments were owned by individuals. While these are valuable documents for understanding the clothing consumption of the medieval period, they can prove to be problematic because the terms used to describe garments can be difficult to discern.

Other written sources of evidence include literary works that refer to clothing in the text, and the writing of chroniclers. The testimony of chroniclers of the period contributes substantially to understanding the effect of the new fashion as perceived through conventional wisdom of the period. Some costume historians claim the writings of chroniclers are the strongest evidence of the dramatic changes in fashion that take place in the mid-fourteenth century.

The earliest reactions to the changes in fashion documented were those of two Italians, the Dominican monk Galvano della Flamma and the chronicler Giovanni Villani. The first was recorded in 1340 by della Flamma, who attributed the new clothing styles for men to Spanish influence. Villani also notes the drastic change in the clothing styles in his native city of Florence, although he blames the French for bringing the new fashions to Italy. The descriptions of the changes in fashion of their times of both della Flamma and Villani are strikingly similar; both mention the short, tight fashions and beards worn by civilian men, as well as the extravagance of the new fashions in women's dress. Both commentaries also reflect a distressed, moralistic tone and an opinion that the sudden changes in fashion represented the corruption of society. The two present strong evidence, aside from their matching descriptions, that the changes in fashion in 1340 were of a dramatic nature by the vehemence with which they express themselves.

Men's Clothing

The most important change in styles of the late Middle Ages involved the dress worn by upper-class men. The new costume for men was inspired by military costume, specifically the quilted garment worn under armor for comfort. This garment, which evolved to be worn as an outer garment by men, was a short, fitted costume called a *pourpoint* that reached to the hips. The word *pourpoint* has a functional origin, meaning "pour les points," or in English, "for points." The points were the metal tips on laces that attached the hose to the pourpoint. We are fortunate to have an existing artifact to represent the garment: the pourpoint worn by Charles de Blois, which is dated before 1364. This pourpoint demonstrates several details. First, it is intricately quilted throughout the garment, with round seams at the armholes. Second, it has small buttons running up the front and sleeves. And third, it is obviously cut to cinch in at the waist and hips. The strange cut of the two front pieces of Charles de Blois's pourpoint may suggest as well a fit tailored to a large padded chest. According to some costume historians, this was the first time in Western dress that buttons had been set in a line down the front of the garment. Another feature of the pourpoint was that it was so tightly fitted that it required assistance to get dressed.

The new shorter garment exposed the leg and demanded new designs for hose. The newer versions of hose were made to measure and fastened in the back and the sides as well as in front to ensure better coverage. Variations in design included fur-lined hose and soled hose to replace shoes. Some writers of the period complain of the exposure of the nether parts of men when they bowed to their lord. Later innovations in the design of hose resulted from this need for modest dress and created a new garment. The *chausses à plain frond* was an innovation that sewed the two legs of the hose together and added a triangle of cloth at the crotch to cover the opening. This piece was removable, fastened with eyelets, and was the precursor of the codpiece that would appear as a highly decorated part of men's costume in the sixteenth century. The appearance of short costume thus instigated the development of a staple of modern man's wardrobe: pants. These changes in style are extremely important in the overall evolution of men's clothing. The pourpoint and chausses à plain frond may be considered a prototype for modern man's suit, consisting of a suit coat and pants.

Other garments that appeared in the fourteenth century include the *cote-hardie*, which was a variation of the outer tunic. The knee-length cote-hardie was worn fitted to the waist with buttons and had a full skirt attached that was usually open at the front. The sleeves were a distinguishing feature of the costume; they were cut shorter in the front and long in the back so the fabric hung down to the knees. The cote-hardie is shown in visual evidence from both

English and Italian sources to be worn with a belt at the hips. Lower-class people wore a variation of the garment that had a looser cut and no buttons.

Later in the fourteenth century, an outer garment that had exaggerated bell-shaped sleeves called a *houppelande* was introduced. The houppelande was fitted at the shoulder, widened into large pleats of fabric, and was worn with a belt. It could be designed in several lengths, reaching to the thighs, midcalf, or ankles. The collar of the houppelande may have been influenced by Middle Eastern styles and was cut like a high mandarin collar. Its wide sleeves could be decorated with cut shapes on the edges, which were called *dagging*.

Some outerwear designs were directly influenced by Eastern garments. The *caban* was a Western version of the caftan that had long sleeves and a hood and was often worn belted. It is believed to be the first outer garment with a fitted back, and the earliest precursor of the garment we know today as the coat. Other outerwear worn by men included a garment called a *housse*, which was a wide overcoat with winged cape sleeves and two tongue-shaped lapels at the neck. Simple designs for outerwear continued to be worn, as well, including the corset, or round cape, that closed at the center. New designs for capes included the option of buttons running down the front instead of the traditional ribbon tie or chain.

Along with the short pourpoint, headdresses for men also evolved into new styles. The characteristic headdress for men in the fourteenth century continued to be the *chaperon*, which had been worn since the twelfth century. The chaperon is a hood with a short cape, but many men who were trying to vie for attention among their peers in hopes of securing a lucrative position wore incredibly extravagant designs. The new styles of hats could be made of luxurious brocade fabric and decorated with peacock feathers or other plumes. Some showed the influence of the Middle East and were wrapped like turbans. One Italian man wore such outlandish creations that they had objects placed on top of the hat as part of the design, including a small silver sword and a dove made entirely of pearls.

At the end of the fourteenth century, the fashion for pointed shoes returned. Chroniclers and clerics continued to criticize this style. A 1388 poem pointed out humorously that men could not kneel in church wearing them. These shoes, called *poulaines* or *krackowes* after the Polish city Krakow, had points that could extend 6 or more inches (15+ cm) from the toe. The poulaine style was worn as a badge of rank and implied by its design that the wearer did not perform any physical labor. In 1396, at the battle of Necropolis, French knights found that they had to cut off the points of their shoes if they were to be effective in combat.

Other accessories became more widespread in use at this time. For example, gloves were made of fine leathers and embroidered for the upper classes.

In the fifteenth century, the pourpoint continued to evolve in design, although there were still efforts made to stop the spread of its popularity. In 1430, there were sumptuary laws created in Florence to stop the shortening of the pourpoint. The decrees were ineffectual, however, and the style spread throughout Italy. The pourpoint was also adopted by the English, who called it a *doublet*. It became shorter still and had to be worn with joined hose for the sake of modesty. After 1410, it was worn mostly as a layering piece, so that only the collar and the arms were visible. The standing collar design that was popular at the end of the previous century became more exaggerated and rose to ear level in the fifteenth century; this specific design became known as the *carcaille*. Because the pourpoint was no longer worn as an outer layer, it could be constructed with different fabrics; plain for the bodice, with elaborately decorated textiles for the arms and collar.

The houppelande continued to be worn by men and women, and in England was called a *robe*. Sleeve designs for the garment were wide funnel shapes or straight, worn with turned-back cuffs to display colorful linings. Other sleeve designs included the bagpipe sleeve, which was a full design that tapered at the wrist. Houppelandes could be made of luxurious fabric, trimmed with dagging, and embroidered for the wealthier classes.

The cote-hardie was gradually replaced by a new garment called the *jacket*, which was worn over the pourpoint or doublet as an outer layer. The jacket was constructed of a bodice, sleeves, and a separate skirt that could be worn to the thigh or to the hips. Sleeve shapes varied, with similar designs to those used on the houppelande. At the end of the century, slashes were added to the jacket to show the fabric on the pourpoint worn underneath.

Another outer garment worn in the fifteenth century was the *huke*, which originated in military dress. It was similar to a tabard and was slipped over the head and worn open at the sides.

Headdress continued to take on dramatic shapes and sometimes even took on symbolic value; in 1462, Philip the Good wore a cap covered with teardrops, which symbolized the strained relationship he had with his son. Hoods went out of fashion, and large hats were worn decorated with feathers or in the style of a turban.

Hairstyles also changed with the fashion of the day and included a short cropped style for men that showed the ears and neck. Some costume historians believe the short bowl cut came into fashion because of the high collars in style in the fifteenth century. It stayed in fashion until around 1450 and was immortalized by the fact that it was the chosen hairstyle of Joan of Arc, who was chastised for wearing the garments and haircut of a man at her trial.

Hose, which were now a more visible part of men's costume than ever, had more elaborate designs. Some were laced with leather that had ornate points added on the end, and some were designed with feet. Colors for hose grew more distinct, with some designs using different colors for each leg. This design was called *parti-colored* and is traditionally associated with the costume of a court jester. The costume for the jester integrated many colors, often had diamond or checkered designs and was clearly identifiable with the special hat worn exclusively by these performers. The hat evolved into a three-pointed cap with bells attached to the points in the fourteenth century. However, parti-colored garments were also worn by royalty, members of the upper classes, and musicians. The Count of Artois particularly loved flamboyant color combinations and is recorded to have worn ensembles that combined peach with scarlet-colored wool and yellow with blue- and red-striped fabric.

Shoes continued to have long pointed toes, which were sometimes stuffed or worn rolled up. Boots could reach thigh high and were laced or had buckles.

Accessories included gloves, and belts, which took on a symbolic meaning. Belts could be made of leather or hinged metal and could be lavishly decorated with jewels and etching. Throughout the later Middle Ages, there were sumptuary laws that unsuccessfully attempted to outlaw gold plate on belts and belt buckles to protect the customers from fraud. The belt was worn with money purses and daggers attached to it, so that to take a man's belt away from him was an act of humiliation.

With the technological advancements in weaponry, in particular the adoption of the longbow from Wales and the crossbow from the Middle East, the fundamental design of military costume changed drastically. The only way for the knights to defend themselves against these more powerful weapons was by wearing plates of armor rather than the chain-link mail. The process of adding plates to mail began during the thirteenth century, and by the beginning of the fifteenth century, entire suits of armor were commonplace.

The manufacturing of plate armor was a complicated task that demanded the collaboration of a number of skilled craftsmen. The armorer, or a specialized blacksmith, forged the plates; the polisher polished the shaped plates; and the finisher was responsible for the final assembly. Decorative artists, including etchers, gilders, and painters, would add designs to the assembled suit of armor. The process began with the development of a pattern, like a dress pattern, that would fit its wearer exactly. Rough iron sheets from the hammer mill were marked out from the patterns and cut to size with chisels and shears. The pieces of the suit were then shaped to a three-dimensional metal form with a hammer. The pieces were polished, assembled into a suit, and decorated. The finished suit of armor had to fit perfectly or it would not be useful and might even be dangerous. It had to fit the contours of the body to be effective on the battlefield. And although the weight of it was greater than the earlier mail shirts, a well-fitted suit of armor could be comfortable. The precision of fit also indicated status. If a knight did not own a well-fitted suit, it was a sign that he was too poor to afford his own and had taken his suit off a slain enemy in battle.

Different styles of armor developed, and just as there was fashion in clothing, there was fashion in armor. Among the countries of western Europe, Germany and Italy were known for their characteristic styles, which were copied by other countries. The Italians liked plump, rounded shapes with curved edges and smooth surfaces, while the Germans liked slimmer lines with spiked or pointed edges. Armor even followed the fashions of everyday dress to a certain degree. Some of the suits were made with pointed toes called *pikes*, which imitated the poulaine. The tips of the shoes were extended out beyond the toe in a pointed shape to indicate status.

Women's Clothing

One of the significant elements of the changes in men's dress in the late Middle Ages was that the new fashions established a striking distinction between men's and women's garments. Previously, both sexes were clothed in loose, robe-like garments that reached to the knees or the ankles. With the design of the pourpoint and chausses à plain frond, men revealed their legs entirely and had more freedom of movement. Women's garments did not alter as dramatically as men's. However, there were changes around 1340 that were related to fit, the cut of the neckline, and the general line of the silhouette.

The basic garment worn by women changed in name from *cote* to *gown*. It was fitted tightly to the upper part of the body and revealed the shapeliness of its wearer from the shoulders and bust to the curve of the hips. Other modifications on the gowns of the fourteenth century included low-cut neck-lines and elbow-length sleeves. Aristocratic women wore trains, so that the extra draped fabric extended the overall long slender line of the silhouette, mimicking the verticality of Gothic sculpture. While the aesthetic appeal of the trains must have been powerful, it was not a practical addition to the design and women had to lift their skirts when walking. Chroniclers of the fourteenth century complained equally about the new styles worn by women, claiming that the close-cut gowns were cut too low and were tight enough to strangle them. In addition, these writers claimed that the new fashions were accompanied by new attitudes unbecoming to the female sex. The new breed of women in the four-teenth century was seen by her contemporary critics as "tough and hard-hearted as men-at-arms." Lower-class and peasant women probably never wore a train, both because it made the garment more expensive and because of its impracticality in working conditions.

The surcote continued to be worn over the gown and was worn either with sleeves or without, as was the case during the early Middle Ages, but the cut improved, so it was fitted to the body like the gown. The sideless surcote evolved into a garment that was associated exclusively with royalty. Evidence for the design includes an actual garment from the excavation of the tomb of Leo-nor of Castile, queen of Spain. The gown found in her tomb is a floor-length sideless surcote that is wide enough to span the width of an ordinary door. Later manuscript illuminations show Queen Isabelle of England wearing a sideless surcote that had a stiffened panel called a *plastron* that ended at the hips. The plastron is most frequently represented in works of art with a row of brooches or buttons running up the center. After 1387, women adopted the houppelande. Other outerwear garments included capes and mantles that were fur lined for warmth. The type of fur used was regulated by law in the fourteenth century, and only women of the nobility were permitted to wear the white ermine fur.

Women wore their hair piled up over the temples or braided and coiled around the ears. Adult women covered their hair with veils or tucked it inside hairnets. At the end of the fourteenth century, a veil style called a *huve* appeared; this was a linen veil decorated with *ruching* (fine pleating) and held in position with long pins, forming a sort of canopy jutting out from the head. Veils were also commonly worn with a fillet or band of metal that encircled the head. Overall, women did not hide their hair as much as in previous centuries, and the elaborate linen wrappings of the barbette and wimple went out of style. Only widows and nuns continued to wear the wimple.

Shoes for women changed to incorporate the poulaine style worn by men, but they never had points that were as exaggeratedly long. Jewelry for women was mostly restricted to the upper classes and included rings, necklaces, bracelets, earrings, and jeweled belts. Cosmetic practices of this period include the surpris-ing practice of plucking the hair around the face to achieve the semblance of a high forehead. Many paintings and other visual representations of the time show the broad high forehead on the women of the nobility. Other practices included plucking eyebrows and dyeing the hair. Blonde was the most desired hair color of the Middle Ages, and although the practice was not common, some women attempted to achieve the ideal beauty of the time in this manner.

Women's dress in the fifteenth century continued to evolve gradually. Excel-lent depictions of gowns and clothing throughout the seasons can be seen in the series of illuminations by the Limbourg brothers in the *Très Riches Heures du Duc de Berry*. The woman's gown was the basic garment worn by women of all classes, although women with more resources at their disposal invariably had gowns that had more elaborate cuts, fit better, and had more ornamentation. The styles of gowns continued to feature the stylistic element of the previous century. They had low-cut bodices and long, tight sleeves or funnel-shaped sleeves, and they reached to the floor with long trains. Women in Italy, perhaps due to the hotter climate, were faster to adopt the low-cut gown than their northern neighbors. Some gowns in England had long streamers attached to the end of elbow-length sleeves that were called *tippets*. In the second half of the century, the neckline changed to a deep V-cut, which was worn with a filler. There was also a fashion for protuberant stomachs, which appears in many paintings of women of the fifteenth century. If the woman did not naturally have a rounded belly, it was achieved with the insertion of a small bag stuffed with cotton.

Additional full-length garments worn by women included the *roc* and the houppelande. The roc was a garment that was unique to the fifteenth century. Depicted most frequently in Flemish paintings, it was a loose gown with a round neck that was worn with either short or long sleeves. The houppelande continued to be worn by women, and it developed into a more feminine version of the originally masculine garment. The houppelandes worn by women were always long. The waistline moved to just below the bust and was delineated with a belt. The necklines were either round or V-shaped, and high collars like the styles worn on the male houppelande were common as well. The sleeves of the houppelande varied and could be straight with turned-back cuffs, funnel-shaped, or bagpipe style.

Women's shoes of the fifteenth century continued to have pointed toes, and wooden *pattens*, or platforms that strapped onto the shoes, were worn in bad weather. Accessories for women included jewelry, gloves, purses, and belts.

Young unmarried women wore their hair long and loose. Married women continued to pluck their hair at the hairline, and the extravagant headdresses that mark the fifteenth century were worn to set off a high, bare forehead.

Dress for special occasions varied with status. Unlike in contemporary culture, there were no specific costumes worn by a bride and bridegroom. Rather, each couple wore their best ensembles according to what they could afford. Veils were not associated with bridal wear, and the color of the gowns was not dictated by tradition, although there are indications that red gowns were preferred for weddings in the Mediterranean countries. There was some specially designed jewelry that is thought to be associated with wedding ceremonies. Records from inventories in the late Middle Ages show entries that specify a bridal clasp, and belts sometimes had lovers engraved in metal for the ceremony. Wedding rings were also exchanged by the couple, regardless of their status. Archaeologists have found simple rings forged in bronze or copper that are believed to have belonged to persons of humble status.

Another important event in the life of a woman was the first time she attended church after the birth of a child. Women generally wore their best clothing, and if they were wealthy enough, they ordered new garments constructed especially for this event. In 1330 there are records indicating that the queen of England wore five garments of purple velvet after her child was born;

the exterior garment was embroidered with designs of squirrels created with golden thread.

Some of the most elaborate fashions from the entire Middle Ages were the women's headdresses that appeared in the fifteenth century. During the first half of the century, the headdresses worn were wide and used the hair, which was braided in two coils at either side of the face, as a support. The coils of hair were covered with a *caul*, which was a similar to a hairnet. Various supports were added to the hairstyle, so that a veil could be draped around it to different effects. One striking style added a support called a *bourrelet*, which was a crown-like roll worn on top of the hair, producing an effect not unlike butterfly wings. In northern Italy, women wore a tall hairstyle called the *balzo*, in which the hair was drawn back from the face into a large sphere.

In the second half of the fifteenth century, women's headdresses grew taller. The first vertical style that was worn was the *toque*, a cylindrical hat that was approximately 5 inches (13 cm) tall and had a flat top. In France and Burgundy, this style evolved into a cone-shaped headdress called a *hennin*, which is commonly associated with the costume of princesses today. The hennin could reach as tall as a yard (1 m) high and was worn with finely woven diaphanous veils made of silk pinned at the tip. The height of the hennin, like many other extreme fashions of the medieval period, was regulated by sumptuary laws. Royal princesses could wear a hennin that was as tall as a yard, and noblewomen were limited to headdresses 2 feet (60 cm) high.

As such outrageous fashions were inclined to do during the medieval period, these extravagant headdresses provoked the wrath of religious men. In 1417, the chronicler Juvenal des Ursins recorded that the outraged preachers denounced the butterfly headdress as being similar to the horns of a devil and claimed that the rolls used to create it must have been stuffed with "the hair of dead women who may well be in hell." Some costume historians believe that the hennin could have been named after insults hurled at the elegant women wearing the tall pointed hats. The Bishop of Paris recruited people to shout at any woman wearing a hennin *"Hurte, belin!"* which means roughly, "Nanny goat, use your horns!" This insult was adapted to *"Au hennin"* by another preacher, who promised rewards to children who would insult the women wearing the tall hats whenever they saw them. However controversial the headdress styles were at the time, they also indicate the movements of the zeitgeist; the tall pointed forms suggest the same ethereal verticality that appeared in the Gothic cathedral structures.

Children's Clothing

Evidence for children's costume of the Middle Ages is more difficult to locate than any other type of clothing. Children are rarely depicted in any type of visual art. Babies were swaddled in blankets, whether they were aristocratic heirs to the throne or peasant stock. It was generally accepted among medieval people that swaddling the baby tightly was good for its health. The difference between the blankets used to swaddle different classes of babies was in the quality of fabric used and the ties used to fix the blankets in place. The infants of wealthy families were wrapped with fine white linen that was tied with red braids, because, again, it was believed that the color red was good for their health. Poor children were wrapped with fabric made of grayish-colored hemp.

When the child was a few months old, its arms were released from the swaddling clothes if the weather was warm enough. Wealthy children had alternative garments for this purpose and were often dressed in a small vest. They also had more elaborate headwear; linen bonnets were worn by aristocratic babies, sometimes with luxurious ruffles. More common headwear included knitted caps and cotton bonnets.

When the child began to walk, it was common for their mothers to place a bourrelet, a stuffed roll similar in design to the bourrelet used to construct the headdresses of fifteenth-century women, around their heads to protect them from falls. Toddlers were clothed in short dresses, made of fabric that was easy to wash.

The early clothing for children was the same for both sexes until the age of seven, when boys received a tunic and girls received a long gown. From this age onward, children wore clothing similar to the styles worn by their parents, and their social status was reflected in the quality of the textiles used, the cut of their garments, and the decorations applied. Colors of the clothing worn by young medieval people also reflected their social status—red and green being preferred by the wealthy classes, and blue or undyed woolens worn by the lower classes. Green was particularly favored, as it was believed to be symbolic of spring. Unlike their parents, medieval children did not cover their heads or wear hats very often.

CONCLUSION

The Middle Ages began with a rural society centered on the individual manor or kingdom and ended with a highly organized civilization that had many urban centers in which industry and trade thrived. The early Middle Ages were characterized by the feudal system, which allowed protection for weaker members of society in a period marked by chaos and violence. While indentured servitude cannot not be seen as a mark of progress to our modern eyes, it nonetheless provided enough constancy for social and economic development and led to more democratic systems of social structure that emerged in the later medieval era. Religion also provided stability and moral guidance to the people of the early Middle Ages and was to a great degree responsible for the unification of culture in Europe.

Increased sophistication in the social structure of the thirteenth century created an entirely new social class that has survived to this day: the bourgeoisie or middle class. During the early medieval period, historians estimate that 90 percent of the population was peasantry. With the development of industry and trade, men who had not been born into wealth or privilege were able to amass great fortunes. Many were able to live comfortable lives, and with their new discretionary incomes came a desire to show their wealth—which manifested itself particularly through display in fine clothing. This was one of the impetuses behind the increasingly rapid changing of styles that characterizes the phenomenon of fashion.

The new shorter and more fitted styles were also indicative of advances in tailoring and provoked many unfavorable responses from the clergy and critics of the period. In addition to criticism, the new desire for fashion provoked the territorial instincts of the aristocratic classes, which manifested themselves in the creation of sumptuary laws. Laws were passed across the continent in an effort to keep luxurious clothing in the exclusive domain of the upper classes. Many costume historians believe these restrictions spurred on new styles to circumvent the decrees as much as they hindered newly wealthy members of society from wearing elaborate clothing.

Improvements in textile manufacture also contributed to the rising consumption of cloth and clothing. Innovations that were introduced during the Middle Ages included the horizontal loom, the spinning wheel, and the use of water power for finishing textiles. These all sped up the process of making cloth and thus made it less expensive for the consumer. Other improvements in the textile industry were related to dye chemistry and the opening of trade routes with the East.

While frequently overshadowed by the triumphs of ancient Greek culture and the humanism of the Renaissance, the Middle Ages were host to many of the great achievements of humankind. Among the many accomplishments of the people of the Middle Ages are the design and construction of Gothic cathedrals, the development of universities, knowledge of far places accrued through extensive travel into the East, the fabrication of intricate tapestries, gracious codes of conduct in chivalry, and the elevation of women in the courts of love ruled by Eleanor of Aquitaine. These achievements stand as monuments to the creativity, intelligence, and curiosity with which the medieval people confronted their world.

FURTHER READING

Artz, Frederick B. *The Mind of the Middle Ages*. New York: Knopf, 1953.

Avril, François. *Manuscript Painting at the Court of France: The Fourteenth Century, 1310–1380*. New York: Braziller, 1978.

Boucher, François. *20,000 Years of Fashion: The History of Costume and Personal Adornment*. Expanded ed. New York: H. N. Abrams, 1987.

Calmette, Joseph. *The Golden Age of Burgundy: The Magnificent Dukes and Their Courts*. Trans. Doreen Weightman. New York: Norton, 1963.

Cantor, Norman F. *Medieval Lives: Eight Charismatic Men and Women of the Middle Ages*. New York: HarperCollins, 1994.

Cunnington, Phillis. *Medieval and Tudor Costume*. Boston: Plays, 1969.

Dahmus, Joseph. *The Middle Ages: A Popular History*. New York: Doubleday, 1968.

Davis, R. H. C. *A History of Medieval Europe: From Constantine to Saint Louis*. 2nd ed. New York: Longman, 1988.

Durant, Will. *The Story of Civilization: The Age of Faith*. New York: Simon & Schuster, 1950.

Evans, Joan. *Life in Medieval France*. London: Phaidon, 1957.

Gozzoli, Maria Christina. *How to Recognize Gothic Art*. New York: Penguin, 1979.

Heller, Sarah-Grace. "Limiting Yardage and Changes of Clothes: Sumptuary Legislation in Thirteenth-Century France, Languedoc, and Italy." In *Medieval Fabrications: Dress, Textiles, Clothwork, and Other Cultural Imagings*, ed. E. Jane Burns. New York: Palgrave Macmillan, 2004.

Houston, Mary G. *Medieval Costume in England and France: The 13th, 14th, and 15th Centuries*. New York: Dover, 1996.

Karras, Ruth Mazo. "This Skill in a Woman Is by No Means to Be Despised: Weaving and the Gender Division of Labor in the Middle Ages." In *Medieval Fabrications: Dress, Textiles, Clothwork, and Other Cultural Imagings*, ed. E. Jane Burns. New York: Palgrave Macmillan, 2004.

Kelly, Amy. *Eleanor of Aquitaine and the Four Kings*. Cambridge, MA: Harvard University Press, 1950.

Monnas, Lisa. "Italian Silks (1300–1500)." In *Textiles, 5,000 Years: An International History and Illustrated Survey*, ed. Jennifer Harris. New York: H. N. Abrams, 1993.

Nevinson, John L. "The Costumes." In *The Bayeux Tapestry*, ed. Frank Stenton. Greenwich: Phaidon, 1965.

Newton, Stella Mary. *Fashion in the Age of the Black Prince: A Study of the Years 1340–1365*. Woodbridge: Boydell Press, 1980.

Piponnier, Françoise, and Perrine Mane. *Dress in the Middle Ages*. Trans. Caroline Beamish. New Haven: Yale University Press, 1997.

Riché, Pierre. *Daily Life in the World of Charlemagne*. Trans. Jo Ann McNamara. Philadelphia: University of Pennsylvania Press, 1978.

Rowling, Marjorie. *Everyday Life in Medieval Times*. New York: Dorset Press, 1987.

Santangelo, Antonino. *A Treasury of Great Italian Textiles*. New York: H. N. Abrams, 1964.

Schoeser, Mary. *World Textiles: A Concise History*. London: Thames & Hudson, 2003.

Scott, Margaret. *Medieval Clothing and Costumes: Displaying Wealth and Class in Medieval Times*. New York: Rosen, 2004.

Tarrant, Naomi. *The Development of Costume*. London: Routledge, 1994.

Tortora, Phyllis, and Keith Eubanks. *Survey of Historic Costume*. 3rd ed. New York: Fairchild, 1999.

Tuchscherer, Jean-Michel. "Woven Textiles." In *French Textiles: From the Middle Ages through the Second Empire*, eds. Marianne Carlano and Larry Salmon. Hartford: Wadsworth Atheneum, 1985.

Weibel, Adele Coulin. *Two Thousand Years of Textiles: The Figured Textiles of Europe and the Near East*. New York: Pantheon Books, 1952.

Wilson, Kax. *A History of Textiles*. Boulder: Westview Press, 1979.

WEB RESOURCES

The Labyrinth: Resources for Medieval Studies. Georgetown University. http://labyrinth.georgetown.edu.

"Medieval Costume: 100–1499 AD." Costume Gallery. http://www.costumegallery.com/medieval.htm.

"Medieval History: Medieval Clothing and Fabrics." About.com. http://historymedren.about.com/od/clothingandfabric/medieval_clothing_and_fabrics.htm.

http://www.wga.hu/frames-e.html?/html/l/limbourg/index.html

http://en.wikipedia.org/wiki/Image:Morgan_Bible_10r.jpg

http://www.kbr.be/images/collections/manuscrits/ms_9242_2fr.jpg

MOVIES

The Adventures of Robin Hood (1938)
Becket (1964)
Braveheart (1995)
Henry V (1989)
The Hunchback of Notre Dame (1939)
Jabberwocky (1977)

Joan of Arc: A Portrait of a Legend (1954)
Kingdom of Heaven (2005)
Ladyhawke (1985)
The Lion in Winter (1968)
The Messenger: The Story of Joan of Arc (1999)
Monty Python and the Holy Grail (1975)
The Name of the Rose (1986)
The Passion of Joan of Arc (1928)
The Princess Bride (1987)
Robin Hood: Prince of Thieves (1991)
The Seventh Seal (1957)
Stealing Heaven (1988)
The Virgin Spring (1960)
Willow (1988)

Glossary

à la jardinière A dress with one or more frills on the shoulder, and a wristband, ruching, or plaiting at the hand, with the fullness caught at the shoulder and/or wrist with gathering or pleating.

acetate Generic term for a manufactured fiber composed of acetylated cellulose used since the 1950s.

acid dyes Class of dyes used primarily for protein and nylon fibers.

aiglet Decorative metal tip applied to ribbons and other ties used to fasten clothing.

alpaca Long, fine, natural protein hair fiber obtained from the domesticated South American alpaca, a member of the camel family; a wool variant.

altobasso Velvets characterized by a sculpted effect given by the juxtaposition of two (or more) heights of the velvet pile cut with velvet irons in Renaissance clothing.

anaxyrides or braka Pants, which were rare in Byzantium. *Braka* is a German term for pants. Many images in Byzantine art show the Persian's wearing pants, but they do not seem to be a part of Byzantine dress until the 12th century. The exception may be the pants (or stockings) shown throughout the Menologian of Basil II, worn by soldiers.

angora Goat native to Turkey from which the natural protein fiber, mohair, is obtained; a wool variant.

animal fiber General term for natural protein fiber of animal origin, such as wool (sheep) or silk (silkworm).

apoptygma Overfold of the peplos, formed by folding the top part of the fabric over and below the shoulders. It could be unbelted, or belted, either under or over the overfold; the excess of the *apoptygma* pulled over the belt created a pouch of fabric known as a *kolpos*.

Ara Pacis The marble *Ara Pacis Augustae*, "Altar of Augustan Peace (13 BCE), celebrated the peace established in the Empire after

Augustus's victories in Gaul and Spain. Its elaborate relief decoration represented the actual procession that took place on the occasion of the triumph, with the realistic portraits of the priests, attendants, and members of the family of Augustus, dressed in their official costumes.

armcye
The part of the shirt or sleeved jacket where the top of the sleeve is sewn or attached.

attifet
A heart-shaped wired headdress that sat atop the hair that was brushed aside into two rolls and sat with its point just touching the forehead.

baion
A scepter held by a Byzantine empress.

baltadin
A belt with precious stones, insignia for certain offices in the Ninth–Tenth centuries.

Banyan
Eighteenth-century long robe worn as outerwear by men.

barathea
Twill variation with a broken rib weave on one side and a pebbly texture on the other.

bark cloth
A roughly woven drapery fabric with a bark-like texture, or a nonwoven material made from soaked and beaten inner bark of tropical trees such as tapa.

bast fibers
Woody fibers from the stems of plants such as flax, jute, and hemp.

batik
Resist print in which wax is drawn or blocked onto a fabric before dyeing so the color does not penetrate in the waxed area.

batiste
Fine, sheer, plain-woven cloth of combed and carded long-staple cotton.

bavolet
A loose fitting cap with a flap on the nape of the neck worn primarily by French peasant women. A large ruffle around the band helped keep sun off the face and neck.

beater
Movable frame on a loom that holds the reed and packs the filling yarns into place.

bias
Invisible diagonal line at a 45-degree angle to the grain of a fabric, popular in the 1930s.

binyeo
Long bobbin-headed hair pin.

bionda
A homemade bleaching mixture composed mostly of lemon juice, ammonia, and urine: the combined effect of the *bionda* and of the sun exposure bleached the hair to the signature Venetian blonde in the Italian Renaissance.

blackwork (or Spanish work)
A type of embroidery that creates geometric, lace-like patterns in black silk thread worked on white linen or silk, usually seen on cuffs, collars, and sleeves of shirts and chemises.

blanket
A textile sample showing a series of patterns or colors all on the same warp.

bleaching
Basic finishing process to whiten untreated fabrics (greige goods).

bleeding	A fault in which dye runs from one pattern area into another.
blend	Yarn of two or more staple fiber types spun together, or fabric containing blended yarns in the warp and filling directions.
block printing	General term for a hand-printing process using wood or other solid material blocks into which patterns have been cut.
blotch printing	Open-screen roller-printing process by which the plain background of a printed fabric can be colored.
bobbin lace	Single-element construction, originally handmade on a pillow with numerous threads.
bodice	A close-fitting woman's garment worn over the stays (later, corsets), sometimes with detachable sleeves. The bodice also describes the upper part of a one-piece gown.
bolt	An entire length of fabric, usually rolled full-width on a tube; sometimes folded before rolling.
bombasina	Cotton fabric in the Italian Renaissance.
bombazine	A mixture of silk and wool.
borzacchini	Leather ankle boots worn by people in the Italian Renaissance.
brache	Italian Renaissance trousers.
braghetta	Italian renaissance codpiece. A fabric triangle, originally created to cover the male groin area.
braid	Flat or round, woven or plaited fabric used for trimming.
breeches (or Upper Stocks)	Men's short (usually knee-length) trousers. The style of these changed drastically from period to period and were either close-fitted hose or very elaborately puffed, slashed, and structured.
broadcloth	Tightly woven, lustrous cotton fabric in a plain weave with a fine crosswise rib, or wool fabric with a close twill weave, brushed and sheared to give a uniform, slightly felted, smooth appearance. Originally describes a finely woven wool cloth used for better grades of clothing. At 29-inches wide, it was broader than most woven fabrics of the early American Colonial era.
brocade	Jacquard-woven fabric with a supplementary warp and/or filling which creates an all-over design: background is satin or twill weave.
brushing	Finishing process in which fibers are raised to obscure the construction of the fabric.
buckram	Plain-woven cotton fabric stiffened with sizing.
bulla	An amulet worn by Etruscan children as a good-luck charm, by young men on bracelets on their upper arms, and on horse trappings; or the locket worn by Roman male children as the sign of their free-born status. They were made of leather, bronze, silver, or gold, and were dedicated to the gods when the boys put on the *toga virilis*, or man's toga, around the age of fifteen, signifying the end of their childhood.

burlap	Plain-woven cloth of retted, single-ply jute.
busk	A piece of wood, metal, or bone that slid into the center front of the female dress bodice to provide stiffness and structure.
busun	Padded/quilted sock, made from specially shaped forms with a heal, thick ankle and pointy curled-up toe.
calashes	Very large hoods worn in eighteenth-century France and the colonies to fit over the large piled hairstyles. These were pulled over the towering hairstyles with specially made devices that the woman could manipulate to reach high enough to come over the hair.
calcagnini	Typically Venetian footwear that could reach the height of 50 centimeters. Fashionable in the late fifteenth–early sixteenth century in Italy.
calcei	The high-topped, laced boots that a Roman citizen wore with the toga in public; indoors he wore sandals. A patrician's calcei were dark red (mullei), the Senator's calcei had black laces and a buckle. Their basic form derived from the laced, pointed shoes represented on Etruscan monuments of the Archaic period, though the Roman calcei were not pointed.
calendering	Standard finishing process in which cloth is pressed heavily and/or repeatedly under steel rollers to produce a polished surface also used to emboss fabrics.
calico	Ancient, basic woven cotton cloth.
calze solate (or calzebraghe)	Tight-fitting footed hoses made in wool cloth with a central seam in the back. Used in the fifteenth and early sixteenth centuries in Italy.
camel hair	Natural protein fiber obtained from the undercoat of the Asiatic camel.
camise (or camicia)	Shirts, sometimes ruffled at the cuffs and neck, in which the ruffles were gathered in a short collar decorated with embroidery worn during the Renaissance period.
cammellotti (or ciambellotti, zambellotti)	Very warm wool cloth used for winter clothing in Renaissance Italy. Originally, probably made with camel hair, hence the name.
cammino	A textile pattern characterized by a horizontal sequence of lobed Italian Renaissance motifs framing the "Italian artichoke," a pomegranate, or a pinecone.
camora	A petticoat skirt worn as a feminine gown in the Renaissance. It was known in Italy under various names, according to different regions: *gamurra* or *camurra* in Florence; *camora, socha,* or *zupa* in northern Italy; and *Gonna, gonnella,* or *sottana* in the south.
candys	A long under-tunic thought to be the precursor to the caftan, developed from the Sumerian shawl.
canion	Men's leggings worn over hose and attached to the culots. Very short breeches were laced to the culots and usually came to just below the knee. They were a close fit, but not tight.

capelet	Upper part of the Greek female dress of Daedalic figures; a tightly fitting tubular dress cinched in tightly at the waist.
capigliara	Elaborate hairstyle fashionable in sixteenth century Italy that mixed the hair with postiches, ribbons, bows, jewels, and pearls.
carded yarn	Yarn spun from a carded sliver of fibers.
carding process	Used for all natural fibers, in which they are separated and brought into general alignment prior to spinning.
carrick	A long coat usually of wool broadcloth with buttons down the front and a many-tiered capelet topped by a conventional collar.
cashmere	Fine, extremely soft natural protein fiber obtained from the undercoat of the Himalayan Kashmir goat.
casque à la Minerve	A small, plumed hat styled to look like the one worn by the Roman goddess of wisdom.
casso, busto	Corset, often made with wood or metal busks in Renaissance clothing.
cassock	Long, front-buttoning gowns worn by various clergy.
caul	Hairstyle tied up in a netted *caul* and topped with a flat, very wide-brimmed hat.
ceinture fleshée	Multicolored woven belt worn by the coureurs des bois in Canada.
cellulose	Organic fibrous substance found in all vegetation that is the basic constituent of both natural and manufactured fabrics such as cotton.
cellulosic fibers	Such as cotton, linen, jute, and rayon.
chōnin	The townsmen and merchants, the lowest class in Japan's inflexible class system and the fashion leaders of the urban, cash-based society of Edo Japan.
ch'ma	High-waisted full skirt worn in Korea, with narrow shoulder straps that wrapped to overlap in the back and flowed in slight pleats to the ankles.
ch'ma-chogori	Top and bottom of Korean hanbok.
chang-ot	Outercloak/veil in Korean dress.
chatelaine	A heavy hook with a collection of small thimbles, scissors, needle-cases, scent cases, seals, patch-boxes, toothpick cases, keys, and watches.
cheesecloth	Cotton in loose, plain weave with a very low thread count, originally used to wrap cheese.
chemise dress	A simple straight shift dress made of cotton or light silk, sashed at the waist and adorned at the neckline and hem with a deep ruffle.
chemisette	An underlayer of sheer white fabric made into a sleeveless tunic; the lace decoration around the neckline was often worn to peak over the neckline of the main gown.

chiffon	Sheer fabric, made usually of silk.
chinoiserie	Objects made in Europe in imitation of Chinese styles.
chintz	A plain woven fabric, usually made of cotton, printed with colorful lively patterns such as flowers.
chiton	A Greek rectangular garment used as a basic shirt by both men and women in all periods, made from a single piece of cloth, uncut and unfitted, woven to order, straight from the loom. Its length varied. A long chiton was worn by women, old men, charioteers, and musicians. Active men wore a short or three-quarter length chiton. Also, a tunic worn by middle-rank courtiers in the early Byzantine period. Biblical figures are illustrated wearing the *chiton* throughout the history of the Byzantine empire.
chlamys	A short or long cloak fastened over the right shoulder with a *fibula* (pin). When worn for military purposes the chlamys was left plain and was usually made of felt. The civilian chlamys is decorated with a *tablion*, a trapezoidal or rectangular embroidered panel sewn onto the front and back, along the side of its opening in the knee area. By the sixth century the chlamys became part of the dress for the emperor and began to slowly lose its military connotation. It could be made out of luxury fabrics like silk or wool with embroidered decoration of high quality. By the sixth century, the empress also wore the chlamys.
chogori	Top jacket or blouse with long curved sleeves, *sohme*, that evolved to a short bolero length for women that is overlapped to close right of center front and ties above the bust line with two long sashes, *korum*, in a large loop. Men's chogori length has remained more static overtime, reaching to just below the waist.
choli	Indian woman's short, tight-fitting blouse.
city-states	Athens, Sparta, Corinth, and others, were independent Greek cities, each with its surrounding territory, characterized by different political systems, social customs, and artistic specialties but bound together by language and religion.
clavus (i)	Vertical stripes of embroidery on a tunic, usually two stripes (clavi).
cleaning	**Dry**: immersion of fabric in petroleum or synthetic solvents to remove oil or grease. **Wet**: removal of waterborne soil or stains by a soap or detergent and water process, done usually on a flat surface with a brush, not to be confused with laundering by immersion.
cloth count	*See* thread count.
cloth	General term used for any pliable material whether woven, knitted, felted, knotted, or extruded.
coazzone	Typically fifteenth-century northern Italian ponytail wrapped in ribbons and trimmed with jewels.
codpiece	A man's accessory used to connect the two legs of the breeches and cover the opening at the center front. Codpieces could be a

plain patch of cloth or very decorative, stuffed, and ornamental, often considered risqué.

coir	Coarse and extremely durable fiber obtained from the outer husks of coconuts.
colobium	A sleeveless or short-sleeved tunic.
color	A hue, as contrasted with white, black, or gray.
color abrasion	Loss of color, particularly in pigment prints or from poor dye penetration.
colorfast	Term applied to fabrics colored in such a way as to prevent color fading from light or cleaning.
combing	The process of making carded fibers parallel and removing impurities and short fibers before spinning.
corsaletti	Upper body armor made of steel plates, worn in the Renaissance.
cotton	Natural vegetable fiber from the cotton plant, grown in the southern United States, Egypt, Russia, and China.
coureurs des bois (or Voyageurs)	French fur trappers of the seventeenth and eighteenth century who traveled and hunted with Native American groups in the Great Lakes and Hudson Bay area of North America. They often trapped the beaver used for fashionable hats in the seventeenth century.
courtesans	Prostitutes.
courtiers	The privileged who frequently attended the royal courts of Europe.
couturiers	High-fashion designers.
cravat	A scarf or band of fabric worn by men around the neck as a tie.
crease	A line in a fabric caused by a fold, usually along the front of trouser legs.
crêpe	Yarn that is overtwisted to create a crinkled profile and stretchy resilience; fabric woven of crepe yarn, which has a matte surface texture and slight stretch.
crewel	A hand embroidery technique from Kashmir in which fine, loosely twisted two-ply yarn is stitched onto a cotton base.
cuirasse	Named after the ancient piece of armor formed of leather that protected the upper torso. These long, figure-hugging bodices emphasized a woman's hourglass figure, created by the very heavily boned corsets of the day. By 1878 the cuirasse bodices had reached the thighs. The cuirasse bodice was corset-like-and dipped even deeper in both front and back, extending well down the hips creating the look of a body encased in armor.
culots	Very short breeches often worn with canions, but could be worn only with hose. Culots were so short that they appear in contemporary images as just a band of puffed fabric around the hips.

cuoietto, coletto   Upper body garment worn in the Renaissance made of leather, hence the name.

daedalic style   An artistic style typical of the seventh-century Orientalizing period in Greece, featuring a frontal stance, flat surfaces, a triangular face with triangular, almond-shaped eyes, and a wig-like, layered hairstyle.

daimyo   The top class in Japan's strict four class system. This military class included the elite military leaders and *samurai*.

dalmatic   A wide short or long-sleeved unbelted robe or tunic, with sleeves usually cut on a diagonal and decorated with clavi (lengthwise stripes). This is an older Roman term which may have gone out of use, but this is unclear.

damask   Woven pattern based upon contrasting warp-face and filling-face cloths.

darbar   Term referring to the Mughal court. Paintings of *darbar* scenes are major records of clothing worn at the Mughal court.

ddidon   Fastener for precious metal pendants to the top of an outfit or at the waist or belt section, then a *juche* or knot, and finished with one tassel *yuso*, or three.

decating   (decatizing) Basic finishing process that includes light scouring and single calendering.

degumming   Removal of natural gums from silk yarn or fabric by boiling in a mild alkaline solution.

denim   Yarn-dyed cotton cloth woven in a warp-faced twill, usually with a dyed warp and a natural filling.

density   The measure of the set of a cloth—the total number of ends and picks.

deshabille   A type of "undress" for both men and women such as a dressing gown with often quite extravagant decoration worn among the upper classes in the eighteenth century.

Dionysos   God of wine and drama: in the fifth century Greek drama was presented at Athens at his festivals. As god of the wild, he had a retinue of maenads and ithyphallic satyrs.

direct printing   General term for a process in which color is applied directly onto the fabric.

discharge printing   Process in which pattern is obtained by bleaching portions of already dyed cloth. It may be left white or dyed another color.

disperse dyeing   Process for coloring acetate, acrylic, nylon, and polyester in which a slightly water-soluble dye is dispersed in the fiber solution. Sometimes subject to fume-fading and sublimation.

divetesion   A ceremonial, long, silk tunic usually worn in the Byzantine era over another tunic and belted. The emperor wore this tunic under a *chlamys, loros,* or *sagion,* depending on the time period.

dopo dooroomakee	Korean overcoat that had wider sleeves and collar than chogori, and were generally considered as more formal; the *dopo's* tie position was adjusted above that of the *chogori's* in order that the two ties would not overlap on a man's chest.
double cloth	Compound cloth based on two sets each of warp or filling yarns held together at regular intervals by a warp or filling thread passing from one fabric to the other.
double crown	Emblematic of both upper and lower Egypt (the red and white crowns are combined) with the white crown (symbolizing upper Egypt) set in the red crown (symbolizing lower Egypt) called the pschent (⚱).
double knit	Knitted fabric made with a double set of needles to produce a double thickness of fabric which is consequently denser and has greater stability than a single knit. Popular in the 1970s.
double weave	Fabric woven with two sets of warp and filling yarns, with an extra yarn to loosely hold the two cloths together. The connecting yarn is cut, leaving two cut-pile fabrics.
doublet	In each era a doublet has slightly different characteristics. It is generally a man's close fitting buttoned jacket, sometimes short and padded with broad shoulders and tight waist, usually with sleeves and flared at the hips. Worn from the fifteenth to the seventeenth centuries.
dye house	Facility where greige goods are dyed or printed.
dyeing	The process of applying color to fiber, yarn, or fabric with natural or synthetic coloring agents.
Egyptian cotton	Fine grade of cotton known for its long staple fibers that create a smooth cotton fabric.
elasticity	Ability of a stretched material to recover its original size and shape.
elastomer	Elastic synthetic fiber with the physical properties and strength of natural rubber such as Spandex.
embades	High boots represented on Greek hunters, for example Artemis, the huntress, or other active figures, usually with shortened chiton, folded about the waist to get it out of the way.
embroidery	Basic cloth embellished with ornamental needlework.
Empire dress	Essentially a tube dress with one drawstring at a round neck and another at a high waistline. The neckline was low, the sleeves short, and the waistline high, located just under the bust. Skirts were very narrow, and because of this comparatively form-fitting silhouette, a reduction of underpinnings was necessary.
ephebe	A member of an adolescent age group or a social status, the age of young men of training age. At a certain point an official institution (*ephebia*) saw to building them into citizens, especially training them as soldiers, as part of the militia of citizens.

fabric	General term for any woven, knitted, knotted, felted, or otherwise constructed material made from fibers or yarns. Cloth, carpet, and matting are all defined as fabric.
fabric width	Crosswise measurement of cloth.
face	The side on which a fabric is finished.
fading	Color loss due to light, pollutants, cleaning, etc.
faldia, faldiglia, verducato	Farthingale or early hoop dress worn (origins in Spain) in Italian Renaissance.
falling band	A large, square, turned-down collar that rested on the shoulders.
farsetto, giubbetto, zuparello	Characteristically short upper body garment. Used in fifteenth and early sixteenth century Italian Renaissance clothing.
farthingale	A round bell-shaped hoop skirt of Spanish origin; a roll of padding, sometimes called a hoop, worn around the hips or waist extending the width of a skirt.
felt	Nonwoven fabric made of fibers joined through the application of heat, agitation, and moisture, or by mechanical treatment; woven fabric that has been treated with heat, moisture, and pressure to achieve greater strength and fullness.
fiber	The basic element of yarn and cloth. Any tough, hair-like substance, natural or manufactured, that can be spun or thrown to form yarn, or felted or otherwise joined into a fabric.
fibula	A brooch like a large safety pin used to fasten a variety of Roman garments. Like many devices meant to fasten or bind—the bride's belt, for example—it could have a symbolic meaning. So the mantle of the *flamen*, a priest, had to be *infibulatus*, fastened with a fibula in back. The bride's wedding dress was tied with a square knot, the Hercules knot. (*See* Herakles knot.)
filament fiber	Of indefinite length, either natural (silk) or manufactured. Silk filament is the actual thread of a silkworm's cocoon; manufactured filaments are produced by forcing a solution through a spinneret.
Filling yarn (or weft or woof)	In weaving, the crosswise yarn or yarns that interlace at right angles with the lengthwise warp.
filling faced	A term used to describe fabrics in which the filling picks predominate over the warp ends. The filling may conceal the warp completely.
finish	Any treatment given to a fiber, yarn, or fabric to alter its original or greige goods state.
flamen (plural flamines)	The highest rank of Roman priesthoods, at one point including four priests dedicated to the cult of particular divinities. Their costume is best represented on the Ara Pacis, where they wear the *laena, galerus* hat with *apex,* and *calcei.*
flannel	Medium weight, slightly napped plain or twill-woven cloth, most often of wool or cotton.

flapper	A flighty young girl of questionable morals in the 1920s who danced the Charleston and wore straight, uneven hemmed dresses that swung around while she danced—originated from a British word for a kind of fish that thrashed about when thrown into a hot pan.
flax plant	Plant from which linen is produced.
fleece	The woolly coat of a sheep, usually clipped in one large piece; fabric with a deep soft woolly pile.
float	Portion of warp or filling yarns covering two or more adjacent yarns to form a design or satin surface.
fontange	A tall headdress created by counting elaborate bits of lace and ribbons onto tall wires and placing it at the front and center on a woman's head.
frenello	Big jewel made with a central stone surrounded by pearls or diamonds; usually worn on the top of the head in Renaissance clothing.
frieze	A coarse, woolly woven cloth used for outerwear.
fringe	A kind of braid or tassel attached at each shoulder of a female figure's chiton in the fourth century BC was a sign of status, often marking her as a priestess or divinity.
frogging	Ornamental closures made of braid or cording.
fulling	A finishing operation dependent on the felting properties of wool that shrinks the fabric to make it heavier and thicker.
furisode kosode	Style for young Japanese women featuring long, swinging sleeves.
gabardine	Fabric of fine worsted yarns closely woven in a diagonal twill and finished with a high sheen.
galerus	The characteristic hat of the flamen, a helmet-like leather head covering, topped by a spike, the *apex*.
garibaldi	Renaissance style of shirt with a full-sleeve. Sometimes made in red or black lightweight wool, or flannel, but more often in white cotton, with the full front gathered or pleated at the neckline.
garters	Before the invention of elastic, garters were generally silk bands tied around the leg to hold up hose. Worn by both men and women, though rarely visible under the latter's dresses.
gat	Nobleman's hat; stacked onto a headband, *mangeon*, and high cap, *tanggeoun*, fastened to the head with a tie around the chin; the wide brim was positioned carefully to sit lower in the front.
gauze	Openly constructed sheer cloth of any fiber.
Geometric Period	The period of Greek art characterized by vases decorated with geometric patterns.
gilet corsage	A woman's garment made in imitation of a man's waistcoat, and front-buttoning jackets with short *basques* that extended below the waistline could all be softened by wearing underneath a

	chemisette usually in white muslin or cambric with frills showing at the neckline and cuffs.
gin (cotton gin)	A machine used to separate seeds and impurities from raw cotton fibers.
giornea	A sort of cloak opened at the sides, with a scooped neck in the back. Worn by both men and by women in fifteenth century Italy.
gokkal	Peaked hat, worn by women in warm weather made of paper or cloth that is folded repeatedly and fixed to the hair.
gorgiera	A ruff made either of thickly pleated linen trimmed with lace or linen worn in the Renaissance.
grain	The alignment of vertical (lengthwise) and horizontal (crosswise) elements in a fabric to form a right-angle relationship.
grass fibers	General class of fibers that includes abaca, sea grass, grain straw, bamboo, rattan, and cane.
grey goods (or greige goods)	Woven fabric as it comes from the loom: unbleached, not dyed or printed, unfinished.
griccia	Vertical arrangement of vegetable motifs on fabric, many of which were inspired by Persian, Chinese, and Indian patterns and used in Renaissance clothing.
grosgrain	Heavy, corded ribbon or cloth; large-scale frieze cloth with a heavy, regular warp pile.
grottesche	Composite pattern (architectural details mixed with medallions, cartouches, festoons, mermaids, sphinxes, fountains, and other heterogeneous motifs) used especially in sixteenth-century lace and inspired by the rediscovery of the frescoed decorations of Nero's Domus Aurea, in Rome.
gulle	A bonnet style embroidered hat worn by children, with a number of dangling tassels and ribbons.
hackling	Combing process as it applies to flax.
hair fibers	Animal fibers that lack the crimp and resilience of wool, such as rabbit hair and fur fibers.
hakama	Trousers worn by both men and women in Japan.
hanbok	Traditonal Korean costume bodice, made up of the ch'ma and the chogori.
hand	The tactile quality of fabric.
hand-spun yarn	Yarn spun by hand on a spinning wheel.
handwoven fabric	Cloth woven on a hand or foot-powered loom, or woven by hand without a loom.
harness	Rectangular frame on a loom that holds the heddles through which the warp yarns pass. The harnesses raise and lower the heddles in predetermined patterns so that the filling yarns can be inserted through the shed to produce the desired weave pattern.

headrail (also *conch* or *whisk*)	A wired veil worn by women that stood up from the back of the shoulders and created a heart-shaped silhouette behind the head and shoulders.
heather	Mixture of yarn composed of fibers dyed in different colors.
heddles	Needlelike wires on a loom through which the warp yarns are threaded. They are mounted in the harness, which is raised and lowered during weaving.
Hellenistic Period	Period after the death of Alexander in 323 BC and before the rule of Augustus as the first Roman emperor.
hemp	Coarse natural cellulose fiber.
Herakles knot	A strong knot created by two intertwined ribbons, used in ancient Greece and Rome as a protective amulet, for both men and women, with a variety of symbolic meanings.
hetaira	Professional female entertainer, musician, or prostitute, slave or foreign, non-citizen, hired to work at an all-male Greek drinking party, the symposium. Similar to a Japanese *geisha*.
himation	A square, large woolen mantle worn by both men and women over the chiton, draped in a variety of ways. Both men and women pulled it over the head in a mourning gesture. Typical of a bride was the gesture of holding it out as if to cover her head. In Roman times, Greek men wore the square himation with sandals, in contrast with the costume of the Roman citizen, the toga and calcei.
hinagata-bon Kosode	Design books published in Japan between 1666 and about 1820.
Homeric Greece	The early period of Greek history, when the Greek cities were ruled by the feudal monarchies described by the poet, Homer, in the *Iliad* and the *Odyssey*.
homespun	Originally, a plain-woven, fabric from hand-spun yarns; currently, a machine-woven fabric with irregular yarns to simulate the original textures.
hongnyong-po	King's robes of Choson or official costume; a long, wide sleeved, red, blue, or yellow robe decorated with large elaborate golden crests on the front chest, back, and two shoulders with the royal motif of a dragon with five claws.
hoplites	Greek foot soldiers, infantrymen, fighting in formation, in contrast to the earlier system of hand-to-hand single combat.
hopsacking	Coarse basket-weave fabric of jute, hemp, or cotton.
houndstooth	Variation of a twill weave, with a broken check pattern.
hue	Color, shade, or tint of a color.
hwanwonsam	Outer ceremonial jacket worn by the Korean queens of the Choson period; covering several layered embellished garments.
ikat	Fabric woven with tie-dyed yarns.

Incroyables	Young and fashionable French men and women born into well-to-do families who, after the end of Robespierre's bloody dictatorship, blossomed into a subculture boldly dressing in eccentric and expensive clothing proclaiming a return of individual freedom after the revolutionary terror ended. This included both ancient regime elements with revolutionary elements blending to provoke the singularity of the sans-culottes who also elevated politics above fashion.
indigo	Natural vegetable dye from the indigo plant used to color fabric deep blue or purple.
interlining	A layer of fabric between the outer, decorative fabric and the lining.
jacket bodice	Developed during the 1840s as an alternative style for day wear. It had a loose straight fit that was more masculine than the traditional fitted bodice.
jacquard	Loom attachment that uses a punched card system to raise and lower single heddles. It permits the weaving of fabrics with complex patterns such as tapestry and brocade.
jama	Generic name for a coat or outer garment worn at the Mughal Indian court.
jangot	Woman's hooded cloak, originating from the men's style of overcoat.
Japonism	Japanese-inspired styles of art and design.
jean	Sturdy cotton twill fabric (also called denim).
jeanette	Was a necklace made of a narrow braid of hair or velvet with a cross or heart charm that was worn around the neck in the later 1830s.
jegwan	Confucian horse hair hat worn by men, architecturally tiered upwards from the crown of the head in geometrical shapes and points.
jeongjagwan	Confucian hat worn by some kings.
jerkin	Short close-fitting sleeveless vest worn over the doublet by young men.
jokdur	Women's crown or headdress, small jewelled, round corner cube or architectural shape, sits forward on the head with dangling ornaments and tassels draping down the side and forehead.
juche	Knot used on Korean clothing.
justaucorps	Knee length, elegant, close-fitting men's coat usually made of rich fabrics such as velvet or brocade and decorated with cords, often with a long slightly flared skirt. Worn in the Renaissance and rococo periods.
jute	Coarse natural cellulose fiber, used primarily in burlap.
kabbadion	A Byzantine caftan or robe with an opening in the front. In the ninth century it is noted as the costume of the *ethnikoi*, probably

referring to the fact that this was a common garment in Islam. By the fourteenth century according to Pseudo-Kodinos, it is typical for many courtiers to wear a *kabbadion*. It seems that aristocrats who were influenced by Islamic culture may have been wearing these as early as the tenth century. This is also the word for knee-length quilted coats.

kalisaris	Worn by ancient Egyptian women and men. A richly ornamented narrow shell with straps. Also worn as a shift in transparent finely pleated fabric.
kamellaukia	Felt caps worn by the infantry in the tenth century.
kanoko shibori	"Fawn spot" shibori dyeing technique in which a pattern of tiny round or square dots of undyed fabric forms a design on fabric.
kapok	Natural cellulose fiber.
katabira	Summer *kosode* worn by members of the samurai class in Edo Japan.
kerchief	A large square cloth, which when folded diagonally, was worn as a head or neck covering.
khat headdress	The Egyptian king wore head-cloths arranged in two different ways; the *nemes*-headdress and the *khat*-headdress or *bag wig*. Both were made by securing a rectangular piece of cloth with a band stretching over the brow and above the ears in the manner of a kercheif. The *khat*-headdress was generally plain, with the pieces of cloth tucked up under the band instead of hanging lose around the face as on the nemes.
kil	Main body of the Korean garment.
kit	Collar of Korean dress.
knickerbockers	Pants gathered or tied at the knee known as knickers for short in the 1860s and 1870s.
knit fabric	Textile produced by continuous interlooping of one or more yarns.
kore	A type of monumental life-size stone statue representing a standing youthful woman, beautifully dressed, presented as a gift to the gods. The best known are the sixth-century Archaic korai from the Akropolis at Athens.
korum	Long sash on the chogori top in Korean women's dress.
koshimaki	Formal summer robes made of crisp fabric worn in Edo period Japan.
kouros	A type of monumental, life-size or bigger, stone statue representing a standing youthful nude male figure, which started to be made in different Greek cities in the seventh century BCE. Emphasis was placed on their nudity. They were used as votive gifts to the gods, representations of Apollo, or funerary markers.
kranea or kassidia	Iron helmets.

lace	A decorative trim created by manipulating a fine yarn or thread into a two-dimensional fabric with an open structure, often with floral or geometric patterns.
lacis (also filet)	An Italian style of cutwork where a fine piece of netting is embroidered and cut out to form a decorative trim. It is a precursor to lace.
laena	The Roman rounded garment worn by the flamines; it was draped back to front, forming a semicircle in front, and fastened with a fibula in back.
lambswool	First fleece sheared from a young sheep. The previously unclipped fiber ends are tapered, producing a very soft texture.
lappets	Flat lace caps with tapered ends that extended into long tails or *lappets* at the sides. Worn into the 1860s, this headdress was placed far back on the head.
lattughini	Small ruffles at the cuffs and neckline worn in Renaissance clothing.
lawn	Lightweight, sheer, fine cotton or linen fabric.
leading strings	Used in the walking and crawling stage, toddlers often wore sturdy ribbons, called *leading strings*, attached to the shoulders of their clothing. These kept adventurous children from wandering too far away, and helped a bodice-bound mother pick them up when the nursemaid wasn't around.
lenza	Thin silk cordonnet that crossed the forehead and from which dangled jewels or other decorations; used in the Italian Renaissance.
line	Long linen fibers that have great luster and strength.
linen	Natural cellulose yarn made from flax fibers, noted for strength, cool hand, and luster; low resilience fabric woven from linen yarn.
lining	Material attached under the principal material of a cloth or piece of clothing to protect the outer fabric and sometimes to help give stability and shape to a garment.
livery	Comes from the Old French term *livrer,* which indicates the feeding and clothing of servants provided by the employer.
llama	South American animal of the camel family whose fleece is produced in a variety of colors.
long back braid	The typical hairstyle for women in the seventh and eighth centuries BCE.
loom	Machine that produces woven textiles by interlacing warp and filling yarns at right angles to each other.
loroi	A lighter scarf used in insignia, especially for the eparch.
loros	A heavy stole worn by both the emperor and empress as much as five meters long, often studded with precious stones. Originally this formed an X over the body, coming over the

shoulders from behind, which evolved out of the *trabea trium-phalis*, the toga of the Roman consuls. During the tenth and eleventh centuries the *loros* gained a slit so that it could be pulled over the head. The empress's *loros* wrapped around the body differently and was once thought to be a different garment called a *thorakion*.

luster The gloss or sheen on the surface of a fiber, yarn or fabric.

Lycra® Trade name of a spandex fiber.

maitress en titre A royal mistress.

mandyas In Roman times, this was a light cloak, resembling the *chlamys*. The *mandyas* came to be known as the long, dark, undecorated cloak worn by both monastic men and women. The *mandyas* was knee length and slit up the front with drawstrings at the neck and waist for closure. The Bishop wore this garment over his *omophorion* when celebrating the liturgy. The emperor wore a gold *mandyas* during coronation by the fourteenth century.

mangeon Headband that the gat was stacked on top of in Korean men's adornment.

maniakion A torque, or collar, worn by barbarians and sometimes associated with soldiers. In *listes de preseances* this is the word they use for collars of insignia for certain soldiers.

manikelia Padded wool arm guards sometimes covered with mail or wood and worn by both infantrymen and cavalry.

mantle A loose cloak or wrap, usually sleeveless.

mantua A gown heavily gathered at the back and often open at the front bodice and skirts to reveal a matching or contrasting stomacher and petticoat underneath.

manufactured fiber Inclusive term for manufactured fibers of natural or synthetic origin.

maphorion A hood that covered the neck and shoulders dating back to the fourth century. Sometimes this term is used to describe the hooded part of male and female monastic garb. By the middle Byzantine era, *maphorion* were also associated with the dress of noble women. The Virgin Mary is always shown wearing a *maphorion*. The occasional man is described as wearing a *maphorion* as well. In *The Book of Ceremonies*, a member of the Senate wears a *maphorion* that covers his entire body.

maspilli Precious buttons used in Renaissance clothing.

mauveine William Perkin discovered mauveine, a bright purple dye synthesized under laboratory conditions in 1856.

mazzocchio The typical Florentine headwear worn with the long scarf called *becchetto* in Renaissance clothing.

mercerization Caustic soda treatment for cotton and linen, which makes the yarn or cloth stronger and increases luster and dye affinity.

merino	Breed of sheep yielding a high grade wool used for fine woolen and worsted cloth.
microfiber	Extremely fine fibers of one denier or less. Fibers are often spun in bicomponent form and excess material is dissolved, leaving fine, strong fibers.
mineral fiber	Natural or manufactured fiber derived from a mineral, such as asbestos or fiberglass.
Minoan	Name used by archaeologists to refer to the civilization the pre-Greek Myceneans found on Crete. The name refers to the mythological king of Crete, Minos, son of Europa and father of the Minotaur.
mitra	A gold, embroidered kerchief-like headdress or veil worn by the patriarch of Constantinople in fourteenth century Byzantium.
moccasin	Native American soft leather shoes or boots, often fur lined and decorated with intricate quill and beadwork. Worn by native Americans and settlers in the colonies of North America.
modiste	Seamstress, needlewoman, or someone who made and repaired dresses.
mohair	Processed fiber of the long, silky hair of the Angora goat.
monk's cloth	Basket-woven cotton fabric.
monmouth cap	A knitted cap, with a rounded crown and small band. Worn primarily by sailors and soldiers originally but later widely adopted.
monofilament	Single synthesized filament; fishing line is one example.
mordant	A metallic salt used to fix dyes.
motif	A pattern unit, usually repeated.
multifilament yarn	Composed of several, or hundreds, of extruded filament fibers.
muslin	Plain-woven, uncombed cotton fabric, ranging from sheer to coarse.
Mycenean	Name used by archaeologists to refer to the civilization the pre-Greek invaders brought to the Greek mainland. The name refers to the city of Mycenae in the Peloponnesus.
Nambawi	Dark fur and silk-detailed hat worn by fashionable women and offered warmth in the winter.
natural fiber	Any textile fiber obtained from an animal, vegetable, or mineral source, such as wool, cotton, or asbestos.
Nemes **headdress**	The king wore head-cloths arranged in two different ways called the *nemes*-headdress and the *khat*-headdress or *bag wig*. Both were made by securing a rectangular piece of cloth with a band stretching over the brow and above the ears in the manner of a kerchief. The *nemes*-headdress was generally made with striped fabric, and the excess fabric was left hanging at the back in a kind of tail. At the sides, two strands or lappets hung down beside the face.

new chevron	A zigzag band applied around the hem dress.
Nuishime	Japanese *shibori*-dyeing technique in which a running stitch creates lines of resist pattern.
nylon	Generic term for synthetic polyamide fiber; nylon 6,6 has 6 carbon atoms.
obi sash	Wrapped around the waist of the Japanese *kosode* and *kimono*.
off-grain	Finishing fault in which the horizontal structure is not at right angles to the vertical.
organdy	Sheer, plain-woven cotton cloth with a crisp hand.
organza	Similar to organdy but made of silk, rayon, or nylon.
ormesini	Silk fabric originally coming from Ormuz, an island in the Persian Gulf.
paenula	A short, hooded cloak worn by farmers, shepherds, and other lower-income people in late antiquity and as the cloak of a shepherd until the fifteenth century. The *chasuble*, worn by the Pope, stems from the *paenula*.
paijama	Trousers worn in South Asia. During the Mughal period the *paijama* typically was cut full through the waist, hips, and thighs and snug fitting from knee to ankle.
pajama	A loose-fitting garment consisting of trousers and a jacket, worn for sleeping or lounging; Loose-fitting trousers worn in the Far East by men and women.
paji-chogori	*Hanbok* for Korean men includes the wide-leg trouser *paji* and an earlier longer version of the chogori.
paletot	A heavy knee-length coat with three, layered capes and slit armholes; worn by young women of the 1820s.
palla	The Roman word for the square Greek *himation* worn by women over their tunics and stolas.
pallium	The Roman word for the square Greek *himation*, worn by men, usually without a tunic, when they were not dressed in the formal attire of the Roman citizen.
paludamentum	A short cloak worn by soldiers, hunters and riders. This is a Roman term and was used in late antiquity but was replaced by the term *chlamys*.
panier	Eighteenth century hoop skirts, typically very wide at the sides but flattened in the front and back.
pantalettes	Women wore long under drawers, called *pantalettes*, with lace, ruffles, or pleats at the edges that showed at the hem of dresses.
pantaloons	Very tight-fitting ankle trousers usually made from knitted jersey.
pantofle	Shoes with cork soles the name of which is derived from the Greek word *pantophellos*, meaning "cork."

parthenon   Temple of the Greek goddess Athena Parthenos, "the virgin," built on the hill of the Acropolis of Athens in the fifth century BCE (447–432), when the Athenian empire was at its height, and the goal of the Panathenaic procession. The gold and ivory statue of the goddess in the temple, and the relief frieze of a procession outside the temple, are high points of Greek art.

paternostr   Precious belts composed of large gold beads inside which are aromatic pastes and holding the hanging *pomanders*—gold or silver filigree spheres containing sponges imbued with perfumes or scented pastes—worn in Renaissance Italy.

patka   Sash from the Mughal period in India.

pattern   The arrangement of form, design, or decoration in a fabric; guide for cutting fabric.

peascod belly   The stuffing of the belly of a man's doublet. Said to derive from the shape of plate armor.

Peisistratus   Ruled as tyrant at Athens at various times (not elected), with his sons, the Peisistratids, from c. 560 to 510 BCE. He beautified the Akropolis, encouraged the Panathenaic Festival and the city's Dionysiac festival, and brought Athens to cultural prominence among the Greek city-states.

pellanda, cioppa   In Bologna called *sacco*, elsewhere *veste* or *vestito*; a corruption of the North European name of *houppelande*, indicating a garment similarly characterized by magniloquent lines, long, trailing sleeves, and decorated with precious trimmings.

pelisse   A cape-like garment with arm slits, sometimes made with a hood and worn over dresses.

peplos   Female garment, characteristic costume of Athena, and the typical dress of the Early Classical female period, though it was worn and represented in Roman times. It was made from a rectangular piece of woolen fabric draped around the body and pinned at the shoulder, usually not sewn together at the side; its simple shape contrasted with the flowing lines of the earlier fine linen Ionian chiton.

pereline   A deep cape that covered the arms to the elbows with long, broad front lappets worn over a belt.

Pericles   Political elected leader and general at Athens, active from c. 460–430 BCE, under whom Athens had its years of greatest power and influence, including the building of the Parthenon and other buildings on the Akropolis.

perizoma   Short pants worn by active males to avoid complete nudity. They are represented in Greek art, and no doubt worn in Greece before the innovation of public nudity for males, as well as elsewhere, in areas where this innovation was never accepted in real life, and only partially in art.

peruke   A wig, especially one worn by men in the seventeenth and eighteenth centuries; a periwig. French *perruque*, from Old French, head of hair, from Old Italian *perrucca*.

petticoat	An ankle- or shin-length skirt that tied around the waist or a woman's underskirt, sometimes exposed by an open-fronted robe.
pharos	A wide mantle, used as a mantle by day and a blanket by night, mentioned by Homer.
pianelle	Slippers that do not cover the heels and are characterized by a very tall wedge obtained by overlapping layers of cork covered in leather, worn in the Italian Renaissance.
picadil	A decorative trim made from a loop of fabric that was added to the hem and/or shoulder of a doublet or bodice.
pick	In weaving, a single passage of filling yarn through the warp shed.
piece dying	Dyeing of cloth after construction.
pigment	Insoluble powdered coloring agent carried in a liquid binder and printed or padded onto the surface of a cloth.
pile weave	Construction in which cut or uncut loops protrude from the ground cloth; loops may be warp or filling yarns and be produced by a double weave or with wires. The wire method uses round-tipped, removable wires to raise loops for uncut pile, and sharp-edged cut wires for cut pile such as velvet.
pinafore apron	A type of apron worn by women. It originates from "pin afore," reflecting that the bib part of an apron was earlier often secured to the chest using pins.
plaid	Pattern of unevenly spaced repeated stripes crossing at right angles.
plain weave	Simplest method of interlacing warp and weft yarns to make cloth. Each filling (weft) passes alternately under and over the warp yarns to produce a balanced construction. It is strong, inexpensive to produce, and the best ground cloth for printing; the thread count determines the fabric's strength.
plied yarn	Yarn formed by twisting together two or more single strands.
plus fours	Full knickerbockers worn by men in the 1920s and 1930s.
ply	A single strand of yarn that is twisted with one or more strands of yarn together.
points	Ribbons with metal tips that could be threaded through sleeves and attached to jackets, or could be used to lace trunkhose to doublets.
polos hat	A tall, tubular hat worn in the Orientalizing and Archaic periods in Greece by images of goddesses.
polyester	Generic term for a manufactured fiber in which the fiber-forming substance is a long-chain synthetic polymer composed on a complex ester, popular in the 1970s.
poplin	Plain-woven, warp-faced fabric with a fine crosswise rib.

posta	Silk sash worn in the Italian Renaissance.
printing	Application of color designs to the surface of cloth.
protein fiber	Natural fiber originating from an animal such as a sheep (wool) or silkworm (silk).
pteryges or kremasmata	An apron-like covering for mid-section, sometimes known as a "fighting skirt." It was generally suspended over the shoulders with leather straps and tied around the waist.
pudding cap	A padded cap, sometimes made of crossed bands, worn by toddlers to protect their heads from injury.
quilting	Compound fabric construction of two layers of cloth with a layer of padding (batting) between, stitched through all three layers.
ramie	Fine, oriental bast fiber.
raw fiber	Textile fiber in its most natural state, for example, cotton before ginning, wool before scouring.
raw silk	Silk that is not fully degummed. It is stiff, tacky, and caramel in color.
rayon	Generic term for a manufactured fiber derived from regenerated cellulose.
red crown	The royal headdress symbolizing lower Egypt called the *deshret* (⳿), this was probably made of metal.
reed	Comb-like device on a loom through which the warp ends pass.
reed mark	Vertical streak in woven fabric caused by a bent wire in the reed.
reeled silk	Continuous filament silk as it is reeled off the softened cocoon of the cultivated silkworm.
repeat	The amount of surface a single pattern covers on a fabric that is repeated over and over.
resist printing	General term for printing processes in which the motif or the ground is treated with a dye-resistant substance before dyeing the fabric.
restello	An elaborate, carved, painted, and gilded shelf that could be completed with a glass mirror and pegs used during the Italian Renaissance.
reticule	Small bags used to keep small necessary objects close at hand.
retting	Soaking of bast fiber plants to permit bacterial or chemical breakdown of the outer bark, in order to loosen the fibers.
rib	Raised ridge running lengthwise, crosswise, or diagonally on a fabric, usually formed by the insertion of a heavy thread; also formed by embossing with heated rollers.
rib weave	Modification of plain weave in which fine warp ends are closely set and two picks (or one heavier pick) interlace as one; any woven fabric construction with a horizontal rib or cord.

roba, robone	Imposing knee-length coat made of velvet or wool, completely open at the front with wide *revers* or lapels, that showed the precious furs or silk linings, worn by both men and women during the Italian Renaissance.
robe à l'anglaise	In the imported French fashion magazines this new form kept the open-fronted skirts and pointed bodice of earlier 1700s, but the waistline was higher, and the long drape formerly falling from the shoulders was drawn back into the waistline, allowing the fullness of the back draping to emphasize the rear end; often long sleeved.
roller printing	Mechanical printing of fabric with engraved rollers.
ropa (also Spanish surcote)	A long outer gown that fastened up the center front from neck to hem and could be worn open or closed. It had a high neckline and was worn unbelted in an A-line silhouette over a gown.
rotary-screen printing	A fast and accurate printing process in which the cloth moves under a series of large, patterned cylinders.
rotella	Round shield used in the Italian Renaissance.
round gown	Gowns like the Empire style dress in France, had an unstructured bodice; the shaping was provided by a drawstring around the neck opening, or by lining flaps pinned together under an apron front. The neckline shape was most often rounded, rather than wide or square. The waistline was raised to just under the bust and was formed like the neckline, by a drawstring. To support the bosom two gussets were inserted underneath the bust line at either side.
roving	Bundle of fibers that are carded and combed and arranged in parallel alignment before spinning.
ruff	A rounded, densely ruffled collar popular in the late sixteenth and early seventeenth centuries. It required extensive pleating and starching to maintain its stiff appearance. Thin strips of starched or stiffened fabric were accordion-folded or folded in a figure-eight and tacked to a band that closed at the front or the back with a hidden fastening. Ruffs were worn by men and women at the neck and wrists. Large ruffs required a *supportase* to keep them from collapsing.
sacque gown or robe à la francaise	A voluminous gown fitted tightly at the front and box-pleated at the back of the shoulders to fall in an elegant drape at the back all the way to the floor.
Sagion	A term for several types of Byzantine cloaks. Like the *chlamys*, it had a military use in its early history (sixth century are earliest mentions). But it appears to be heavier than a *chlamys* because soldiers could use it as a blanket or tent. In the middle Byzantine period it is associated with the costumes of several courtiers, such as *protospatharioi*. Monks and hermits are noted as wearing *sagia* in the twelfth century.
saio, saione	Occasionally worn by Italian women around 1520; it could have short sleeves that let the *giubbone* sleeve show. It could be made with two or more different fabrics.

sakkos	A tunic that replaced the *divetesion* for Byzantine imperial dress in Paleologan times. The origins of this garment are in the sack-cloth, worn by ascetics. In the thirteenth century it had some ecclesiastical use.
samhoejang	Chogori worn by Korean noble women on special occasions.
samjak norigai	A triple-tasselled pendant for women.
samo or coronet	Hat worn by a male public official; woven with side wings out of bamboo or horsehair. Royal men wore tall silk black cylindrical versions.
samurai	Warriors of Japan's military class who were reduced to member-ship in a highly controlled urban feudal aristocracy during the Edo period.
sans culottes	Men who wore full-length trousers instead of knee-length breeches in revolutionary France. The term referred to the ill-clad and ill-equipped volunteers of the Revolutionary army dur-ing the early years of the war.
sarabula, intercula	Briefs worn during the Italian Renaissance.
sateen	Filling-faced satin-woven fabric with horizontal rather than verti-cal floats.
satin weave	Basic weave in which the fabric face is composed almost entirely of warp or filling floats, producing a smooth, lustrous surface.
sbernie	Mantles that leave one arm free.
scarpette	Shoes that were used throughout Italy under different names; *zibre* or *zibrette* in Milan, *cibre* in other cities in North Italy, *tapine* in the South.
scarsella	A small pouch that substituted for the missing pockets in Ren-aissance garments.
scouring	Washing of fiber, yarn, or fabric to remove grease, dirt, sizing, or color.
screen printing	Hand- or machine- printing process in which a pattern-making stencil or screen held in a frame is positioned on the cloth and coloring agent applied.
segmenta	Gold patches or embroidery used to decorate a *sakkos* or other tunic.
selvage	Reinforced edge on either side of a woven or flat-knitted cloth, finished to prevent raveling.
serge	Smooth-finished fabric in a balanced twill weave, identical on face and back.
sericin	Gummy substance that holds silk fibers together as they are spun (in pairs) from the silkworm; removed from silk before spinning.
sericulture	Raising of silkworms and production of silk.
sex crines hairstyle	This special hairstyle, worn by brides and priestesses, the Vestal Virgins, was based on the Archaic Etruscan *tutulus* hairstyle,

which consisted of a high bun formed by separate strands or braids of hair. The ritual dressing of the Roman bride's hair included parting the strands with a spear, which were twisted on top of her head to form a kind of bun made up of six braids or coils.

shantung silk	Dense, plain-woven silk cloth with a slightly irregular surface due to uneven, slubbed filling yarns.
shaube	A sleeveless robe with a large shawl collar became a popular garment with mayors, sheriffs, and other men of rank.
shed	The space formed as the harnesses of a loom raise some warp yarns and lower others, through which the shuttle passes to lay in the filling.
sheer	Very thin, transparent, or semi-opaque fabric.
shenti	Hip skirt or loin cloth with pleats and decorations worn by Egyptian men.
shibori	General name for the Japanese resist dye technique often translated as "tie-dye." Shibori includes various resist techniques including clamping, stitching, and tying.
shift	The universal undergarment for women, rich or poor, was a smock-like low-necked shirt. Called a "shift" or later a "chemise," this long garment functioned as both blouse and slip.
shogun	Literally "the general who quells barbarians;" the head of the military bureaucracy that controlled Japan during the Edo period.
shuttle	Device on a loom to carry the filling yarn through the shed to interlace it with the warp.
silk	Natural protein fiber unwound from the cocoon of the silkworm.
siren suits	Suits that could be zipped into quickly for lightning-fast escapes to underground shelters in wartime London, 1940s.
sisal	Strong natural cellulose fiber used in making cord and matting.
sizing	Starch applied to warp threads to strengthen them for the weaving process, usually removed by scouring during finishing; starch applied to cotton or linen cloth that is removed when the fabric is washed.
skaranikon	A word mentioned in a twelfth century poem and Pseudo-Kodinos, according to the Oxford Dictionary of Byzantium. It is unclear whether this is a cloak or a hat similar to the *skiadion*.
skeleton suit	A young boy's outfit consisting of long trousers attached by buttons at the waist to a long-sleeved, short-waisted jacket, worn by eighteenth-century boys.
skiadion	A squarish hat worn by courtiers and sometimes the emperor in Paleologan times.
sliver	Continuous ropelike strand of loosely assembled fibers before twisting into yarns.

slub	Lump or knot in a yarn; may be a defect or purposely spun to produce a textured surface in cloth.
smock	Loose-fitting knee-length over-blouses worn by the working class for centuries. They were also a very practical fashion for children.
Socrates	Athenian philosopher (449–399 BCE) during the Golden Age of Athens, teacher of Plato, developed the Socratic method of question and answer, focusing on ethical problems, in contrast to the relativism of the sophistic philosophers.
sohme	Long curved sleeves on the Korean chogori.
soprarizzo, cesellato	Rich fabrics with textured appearance that was obtained with the alternation of cut and looped velvet. It was often brocaded with gold threads, and the details of the pattern could be highlighted with the *allucciolature*, very thin gold or silver plate loops threaded through the fabric, and variously twisted in order to achieve the desired decorative effect. Used in Renaissance clothing.
spandex	Generic term for synthetic elastic fibers composed of segmented polyurethane made popular during the 1980s fitness craze.
spencer	By 1804–5, a long sleeved, short-waisted, fitted jacket called the *Spencer* became very fashionable for women.
spinneret	Metal disc with numerous fine holes through which a chemical solution is extruded to produce synthetic fibers.
spinning	Drawing out and twisting fiber into yarn or thread; extruding manufactured filaments through a spinneret.
spoon bonnet	A hat with a narrow brim close to the ears, rising vertically above the forehead in a spoon shaped curve and sloping down behind to a very small crown.
spun yarn	Yarn spun from staple-length fiber, either natural or cut synthetic filaments.
staple	Natural or manufactured fiber that has a relatively short length.
stays	An early term for corset. A stiff undergarment tied or fastened around the torso to give a desired shape to a gown's silhouette.
stemma	A Greek crown that replaced the late antique *diadem*, or headband, for imperial head-gear. A crown is made of precious metals and gemstones, and sometimes has enameling or other luxury arts techniques used in its construction. *Perpendulia*, or simply, *pendulia*, are strings of pearls that hang from the stemma at the temples.
stola	The stola was a long garment worn by respectable upper-class Roman married women (*matronae*) over the tunic and under the palla; it can be recognized on portraits by the thin straps coming down from the shoulders.
stomacher	Stiff, triangular garment that attached to the front of a dress bodice. Sometimes embroidered or adorned with ribbons and bows.

Stratagliati, accoltellati	Fabrics, mostly simple silk satins, but also damasks and velvets, slashed and cut following specific decorative patterns such as little flowers, zigzag motifs, and crosses. Fashionable in the second half of the sixteenth century in Italy.
stretch fabrics	Constructed of stretch yarns to have much greater than normal stretch and recovery characteristics. "Comfort stretch" is a designation for fabrics with up to 30 percent stretch and recovery; "power or action stretch" describes fabrics with 30–50 percent stretch and recovery. These became popular in the 1980s.
stretch yarn	Yarn with a durable, springy elongation and exceptional recovery.
stripe	Narrow section of a fabric differing in color or texture from the adjoining area.
sugacapi	Hair towels used during the Italian Renaissance.
sugar loaf hat	A conical hat, rounded at the top with a broad brim. Similar in shape to the form in which bulk sugar was purchased in the seventeenth and eighteenth centuries. Later became identified with classic Puritan costume.
sulphur dye	Dye that produces heavy shades of black or brown in cellulosic fabrics.
sumptuary laws	Laws that governed how people of all classes were allowed to dress. Versions of these laws appear in most periods in history and most regions up until modern times. Purple, for example, has often be restricted by sumptuary law to be worn only by royalty.
sun rot	Deterioration caused by sun or light.
superhumeral	A collar with a mock turtleneck that extended out to the shoulders and down to the chest, usually decorated with gem stones and metallic threads, worn over a tunic. Worn by Byzantine aristocratic men, including the emperor in the eleventh century and beyond.
supportase (also underpropper)	A wired structure worn by both men and women that served to hold up the elaborate ruffs; wide ruffled bands worn at the neck.
synthetic fiber	Textile fiber made from a petrochemical rather than a natural base. All synthetic fibers are manufactured, but not all manufactured fibers are synthetic, e. g., rayon.
tabì, tabin, tabinetto, tabinazzo	Sometimes defined as a fabric similar to damask or as thick taffetas; characterized by a "wave" effect. Seen in the Italian Renaissance.
taffeta	Crisp, plain-woven fabric in which the filling is heavier than the warp, producing a fine, lustrous rib.
tainia	A purple headband worn by Byzantine children in the palace in the Palaeologan period. It was also acceptable for children to go without any hat.
Tanaquil	Etruscan queen, wife of the first Tarquin, legendary figure in Roman tradition. Her story is told by the first-century Roman historian, Livy.

tanggeoun	High cap onto which the gat was placed in Korean men's clothing.
tapestry	Jacquard-woven fabric with supplementary multicolored yarns that form an intricate design or scene. The finished products were often used to cover walls in cold castles in Europe.
tarquins	Etruscan dynasty who ruled at Rome in the sixth century BCE, whose fall brought about the Roman Republic. The last Tarquin especially, Tarquinius Superbus, brought to Rome many elements of Etruscan culture, including the Temple of Jupiter Capitoline, most aspects of the Roman triumph, music, and theater. Such important Roman symbols as the curved priestly *lituus*, the *fasces* and the axe of the lictor hark back to Etruscan models, and in dress, the toga, decorative purple borders, the *laena*, *calcei*, *sex crines*, and *galerus* with *apex*.
tea-gown	An unboned, loose-fitting afternoon gown, often with *watteau* style backs, that fell in folds from the neck to the hem.
tebenna	The rounded mantle worn by the Veii Apollo and other male figures from mid-sixth century Rome, the ancestor of the Roman toga.
terrycloth	Uncut warp-pile fabric, plain or jacquard; woven of cotton, linen, or rayon.
textile	Orginally, a general term for any woven cloth; now, a general term for any fabric made from fibers or yarns, natural or manufactured made into any fabric structure such as woven, knits, nonwoven etc.
thorax	From the sixth through tenth centuries cavalrymen wore this body armor made of chain mail, a shirt, with or without sleeves, made of metal links which sometimes was mounted on leather, or lamellar, small plates of iron or leather laced together or attached to a leather backing. These varied in length from ankles to waist.
thread	A strand of plied and twisted yarn with a smooth finish that is used in sewing and stitching.
thread count	The number of warp and filling yarns per square measure (inch or centimeter).
throwing	Slight twisting of filament yarns.
tippets	A short shoulder cape with a longer hanging front worn over dresses by women.
toga	The rounded mantle clearly distinguished a Roman from a Greek, who wore the rectangular himation mantle. The Romans' were by definition the *gens togata*, (Vergil, *Aeneid*). Different colors and decorations distinguished the various kinds of togas, all of them deeply symbolic of age, rank, status or office. The purple borders of the *toga praetexta*, for example, characterized the costume of the higher levels of office, the curule magistracies; it was also the dress of boys, who wore it until they discarded it for the

toga virilis, the normal plain woolen toga of adult men. A bright white *toga candida* marked the wearer as a candidate for office, a dark *toga pulla*, a mourner. Most prestigious was the *toga triumphalis*, worn by the victorious general when he celebrated a triumph.

toile   Plain, coarse twill-woven fabric, often in linen. Most noteworthy were the toiles de Jouy; eighteenth-century French fabrics printed with scenes of one color on pale cotton, linen, or silk.

tondo   The circular area in the center of a Greek vase.

tongjong   A thin, replaceable outer layer on the neckline of the Korean chogori; white woven hemp, cotton, or ramie protected the garment from wearing at the neck.

tow   Short or broken fibers of flax, hemp, or synthetic materials used for yarn, twine, or stuffing; thick bundle of continuous filaments assembled without twisting into a loose ropy strand for cutting into staple length.

trade name   Name given by manufacturer to distinguish a product produced and sold by that manufacturer, for example, Lycra.

trademark   Word, letter, or symbol used in connection with a specific product originating and owned by a particular manufacturer.

treadle   Lever or pedal on a loom that activates the lowering or raising of a harness.

Trojan War   Mythological story, the subject of Homer's *Iliad*, of the siege of the city of Troy, by the united force of the Greeks, in 1200 BC.

trunk hose   Short, puffy breeches, bound above the knee by a ribbon or garter to hold up the stockings. Worn from the sixteenth to the seventeenth centuries.

tsujigahana   Complex Japanese technique using *shibori*, painting, metallic leaf, and embroidery techniques to pattern fabric for *kosode*.

tti   Additional tie belt, fastened around the outside of jacket layers in Korean dress.

tunic   Tunics are the main piece of the Byzantine wardrobe. The T-shaped garment could be long or short, with various length sleeves. They were worn as an undergarment (this is the closest item to Byzantine underwear) and as a regular garment; typically more than one tunic was worn at one time. Or, tunic is the Roman word for the shirt or chiton worn under the mantle. The vertical purple stripes that decorated it were either broad or narrow, indicating the wearer's status.

turban   Called *phakeolis* or *phakiolion*. Worn by both Byzantine men and women by the tenth century according to evidence found on Cappadocian frescoes.

turumagi   Additional layered long overcoat in Korean dress.

tussah   Brownish silk fabric from uncultivated silkworms.

tweed	Medium-weight, rough woolen fabric, usually twill woven. Named tweeds such as Donegal, Connemara, Harris, and Galashiels are produced in Ireland and Scotland.
twill	Basic weave that produces a surface of diagonal lines by passing filling threads over two or more ends in a regular progression. Denim is a common modern example of a twill weave.
twist	The tightness and direction of the twist spun into a yarn. *S* twist is a clockwise twist and is the most common; *Z* twist is a counterclockwise twist.
twistless yarn	Yarns formed by combining fibers by means other than twisting.
uccelletti di Cipro	"Cyprus birds," solid perfumes kept in small leather cases in the shape of tiny birds, used by Italian women during the Italian Renaissance.
uchikake	Formal, outer *kosode*, worn unbelted.
ukiyo	Literally the "floating world," the pleasure quarter of Edo period Japan where prominence was determined by one's taste and ability to pay, not by position in the period's inflexible class system.
underpropper (supportase)	At the height of their fashion and their width, ruffs needed more than starch to stay rigid and were worn with this wire understructure.
ungarina	Bell-shaped Renaissance dress made from precious fabrics. The gown reached the ankles and closed in the front with frogs. Usually worn by boys aged between two and four. The name refers to the heavy braiding decorations, very common in clothing of Eastern European countries, such as Hungary.
vegetable fibers	Natural textile fibers of plant origin, such as cotton, flax, or hemp.
velour	Cut warp-pile fabric, usually of cotton or wool, with higher, less dense pile than velvet.
velvet	Close-cropped, warp-pile fabric with a smooth, rich surface, produced by double weaving or with wires. Originally woven in silk, now made with cotton or synthetic fibers as well.
velveteen	Single-woven weft pile fabric with a dense-cut surface.
vicuna	Small, wild Andean animal of the camel family, from the undercoat of which is derived a fine, lustrous fiber.
vinyl	Nonwoven fabric made from a petrochemical solution; thick or thin, it is usually soft and pliable.
virgin wool	New wool; not reused, reprocessed, or respun.
viscose rayon	The most common rayon, formed by converting cellulose into a soluble form and regenerating it into a synthetic fiber.
voile	Soft, sheer cloth, plain-woven of fine crepe (overtwisted) yarns.
waistcoat	Also called a vest. A front-buttoning, sleeveless garment worn usually by men under a jacket or coat. Occasionally had detachable sleeves.

wale	A horizontal, vertical, or diagonal rib in a fabric; the vertical rib on the face of a knitted fabric.
warp	Lengthwise yarns in a fabric, running vertically through the loom, parallel to the selvages.
weave	Structural pattern in which yarns are interlaced to produce fabric.
weaving	Process of making a fabric on a loom by interlacing horizontal yarns (weft) at right angles with vertical yarns (warp).
weft	Horizontal or crosswise element of a woven cloth.
weighted silk	Silk treated with metallic salts to increase the weight and apparent value, strictly controlled and now virtually obsolete. Historic textiles treated with this finish deteriorate quickly and damage the silk fibers.
whisk	A large unstarched falling collar, often with a deep lace trim that reaches past the shoulders.
white crown	Emblematic of Lower Egypt and probably made of metal; the white crown is also known by many names, including *hedjet* (⚱).
Windsor knot	A knot for a man's necktie named for and popularized by the Duke of Windsor in the early twentieth century.
wisk	Deep linen lace collars.
woolen	Fuzzy, loosely twisted yarn spun from carded short wool fibers. Woolen cloths are generally simple weaves and show coarser finishes than wools.
worsted	Smooth, compact yarns spun from carded and combed long wool fibers. Worsted cloths are more closely constructed and have smoother finishes than woolens.
yangban	Male aristocrats in the Korean Choson Dynasty (1392–1910).
yarn	Any form of spun, twisted or extruded fibers, natural or manufactured, that can be used in weaving, knitting, or other fabric construction.
yarn dyeing	Dyeing at the yarn stage of production, as opposed to solution, stock, or piece dyeing.
yeomnang or gangnang	Small pouches used in place of garment pockets in Korean dress.
zanana	The women's quarters at the court of Mughal India.
zebellino da mane	Fur stole worn on the shoulders during the Italian Renaissance.
zetanini avvellutati	Silk velvets originally made in the Chinese city of Zayton, worn during the Italian Renaissance.
zimarra	A Turkish-inspired overcoat, similar to a kaftan. Usually made with very expensive and showy fabrics and suitable to be worn inside the house in the Italian Renaissance.
zovi	A general word for belt, girdle or sash.

List of Museums

CLOTHING COLLECTIONS

Clothing artifacts are housed in a number of different museums around the world. In fact, most museums, from large metropolitan collections to local museums, will house at least some items of textiles and clothing in their collections even if it is not devoted to the study of clothing and costume. The staffs of dedicated employees at these museums are trained in the conservation and preservation of the textile artifacts. Specific technical skills are needed to allow costume resources to survive through time, and if only these techniques had been known long ago, there would be many more examples for study today. However, at this time in history, it is well known that climate and humidity affect textiles to a great extent and need to be controlled or the textiles will rot, fade, and disappear.

Certain types of fibers are more durable and will last longer than others. Silk is a valuable fiber that has been known to shatter rather dramatically into dust if not kept at the right temperature and moisture level. Many of the most beautiful beaded and embellished silk gowns are in desperate shape because of the fragile nature of the fabric. Often, because silk was sold by weight—and to allow the fabric to drape well—it was weighted with metals that over time have meant that the fiber has deteriorated. Hanging a heavily embellished garment can cause undue stress of the shoulder seams and rip the garment.

These garments and fabrics are sometimes hung up but more often stored in acid-free tissue paper in boxes and placed in climate-controlled rooms until they are displayed or used for research purposes to make sure there is no further degradation of the fibers. In some cases, they are never displayed for fear that they may completely fall apart. Lighting of displays is usually kept at a very low level so as not to disturb the textiles and harm them while on show for people to learn from and admire. Hats, purses, parasols, and shoes are all fitted with special supports to make sure they are not crushed further in the storage and display process.

Sometimes garments that have great historical value but are not in very good condition are received by museums. After a *condition report* is written, a plan is made to try to either restore the artifact or stabilize it so it does not decay any further. Painstaking hours are spent on single portions of garments to make sure they are saved for further study in the years to come. A single cuff may need the attention of a conservator for weeks or even months. The job of the conservator is often at odds with that of the curator, who is concerned with creating the displays and educating the public about the clothes in the collection. It is a sad day when a piece of clothing is too weak to display, especially when that item has exquisite detailing that should be seen by the museum-going public. There are thousands of historical garments stored away safely in museums around the world, many waiting to be studied.

Local museum collections will have items of interest to the history of the region, exemplifying what life was like throughout time in the community. Large urban museums will collect and house textiles and clothing from all over the world to give an idea of many different cultures and their ideas on dress and adornment.

The most famous museums with excellent costume collections include the Victoria and Albert Museum in London and the Costume Institute at the Metropolitan Museum of Art in New York. These two outstanding museums house excellent collections of all kinds of costumes from all over the world. They also have extensive study rooms with information on clothing and textile history. There are many other museums devoted to clothing artifacts, though, ranging from the purely civilian dress of the fashionable people to military uniforms.

The following is a list of collections with excellent resources that might be helpful to a student of clothing and history (websites and mailing addresses are included where available). This list by no means represents even a fraction of the many collections of costume, but it is meant to give the student of costume an idea of where to look for costume resources.

The Bata Shoe Museum
327 Bloor St. West
Toronto, ONT, Canada M5S 1W7
Phone: (416) 979-7799
www.batashoemuseum.ca

Bernberg Museum of Costume
Corner Duncombe Rd and Jan Smuts Ave
Forest Town, Johannesburg
Phone: (011) 646-0416
http://www.places.co.za/html/bernberg.html

Colonial Williamsburg
The Museums of Colonial Williamsburg
P.O. Box 1776
Williamsburg, VA 23187-1776
Phone: (757) 229-1000
http://www.history.org

Costume Museum of Canada
109 Pacific Ave
Winnipeg, MB, Canada R3B0M1
Phone: 204-999-0072
www.costumemuseum.com

Fashion and Textile Museum
83 Bermondsey Street
London SE1 3XF
http://www.ftmlondon.org/

Fashion Museum
Assembly Rooms
Bennett Street
Bath
Avon BA1 2QH
http://www.fashionmuseum.co.uk/

Fortress of Louisbourg, National Historic Site of Canada
259 Park Service Road
Louisbourg, NS, Canada B1C 2L2
Phone: (902) 733-2280
http://www.pc.gc.ca/

Gallery of Costume
Platt Hall
Rusholme
Manchester M14 5LL
http://www.manchestergalleries.org/our-other-venues/platt-hall-gallery-of-costume/

London Sewing Machine Museum
292-312 Balham High Road
Tooting Bec
London SW17 7AA
http://www.sewantique.com/

McCord Museum of Canadian History
690 Sherbrooke Street West
Montreal, QUE, Canada H3A 1E9
Phone: (514) 398-7100
http://www.mccord-museum.qc.ca/en/

The Metropolitan Museum of Art
1000 Fifth Avenue
New York, NY 10028-0198
Phone: (212) 535-7710
http://www.metmuseum.org/visitor/index.asp

Musee Carnavalet—Histoire de Paris
23 rue de Sévigné
75003 Paris
http://www.paris.fr/portail/Culture/Portal.lut?page_id=6468

Museo del Tessuto
Via Santa Chiara 24
59100 Prato (PO), Italia
Phone: +39 0574 611503
http://www.museodeltessuto.it

Museo Rubelli
Venice
Phone: +39 041-2417329
e-mail: museo@rubelli.com

Museo Stibbert
Via Stibbert 26
50134 Firenze
info@museostibbert.it

Museum of Greek Costume
7, Dimokritou Street
Kolonaki
Athens
http://www.athensinfoguide.com/wtsmuseums/greekcostume.htm

Pitti Palace Costume Collection
Florence
www.polomuseale.firenze.it

Royal Ceremonial Dress Collection
Kensington Palace
London W8 4PX
Phone: +44 (0)207 937 956
http://www.hrp.org.uk/

Royal Ontario Museum
100 Queen's Park
Toronto, ONT, Canada
M5S 2C6
Canada
www.rom.on.ca

The Shoe Museum
C&J Clark Ltd.
40 High Street
Somerset BA16 0YA

The Textile Museum
2320 S Street, NW
Washington, DC 20008-4088
Phone: (202) 667-0441
Fax: (202) 483-0994
http://www.textilemuseum.org/

Textile Museum of Canada
55 Centre Ave.
Toronto, ONT, Canada M5G 2H5
Phone: (416) 599-5321
info@textilemuseum.ca

Totnes Costume Museum
Bogan House
43 High Street
Totnes

SPECIALIZED COSTUME LIBRARIES

Centro Studi del Tessuto e del Costume di Palazzo Mocenigo, Venice: seven thousand volumes focusing on textile and costume history and textile collections from the sixteenth to twentieth centuries. http://www.museicivicivenveziani.it.

Metropolitan Museum of Art, New York, Antonio Ratti Textile Center and Reference Library: The reference library of the Textile Center contains approximately 3,400 books and journals related to the historical, technical, and cultural study of textiles. http://www.metmuseum.org/research.

Metropolitan Museum of Art, New York, Irene Lewisohn Costume Reference Library: One of the most important fashion libraries in the world, with 30,000 items related to clothing history. http://www.metmuseum.org/research.

Textile Museum, Arthur D. Jenkins Library of Textile Arts, Washington, D.C.: The materials preserved in the library's holdings, such as books, periodicals, and slides, cover every aspect related to textile and costume history, textile structures and techniques, and textile conservation. http://www.textilemuseum. org/library.htm.

COSTUME HISTORY SOCIETIES

There are a number of historical societies devoted to the study of costume history. In the United States, the Costume Society of America has a worldwide membership that represents interests in historical as well as historical theatrical costumes. This group meets every year for a national symposium that allows its members to share in the exciting developments in the areas of clothing history. Lectures and working sessions make the event highly worthwhile. The periodical *Dress* is a publication of the society. A similar organization in the United Kingdom is the British Costume Association, which also produces a journal, *Costume*, and has numerous events throughout the year for those interested in the study of clothing history.

About the Editor and Contributors

Jill Condra has taught clothing and textile history at the University of British Columbia, the University of Prince Edward Island, and the University of Manitoba. Her costume research has been largely based on using material history models to look at clothing in historical context, which has allowed her to do research at the most exciting costume collections around the world. Condra has also co-written a book on textiles called *Guide to Textiles for Interiors*, Third Edition. She is currently an independent scholar living in Minneapolis, MN, and Winnipeg, Canada.

Christel Baldia is currently assistant professor in textiles at the Florida Institute of Technology. Her research focus is forensic methods to detect and identify colorants in archaeological perishable materials, and she has applied these methods to textiles from the Hopewell culture in eastern North America.

Jennifer L. Ball is an assistant professor of art history at Brooklyn College, specializing in Western medieval, Byzantine, and Islamic art. She is the author of several articles on textiles, and her most recent book is *Byzantine Dress: Representations of Secular Dress in Eighth- to Twelfth-Century Painting* (2005).

Larissa Bonfante, professor of classics at New York University, is author of *Etruscan Dress* (1975, updated 2003). The National Endowment for the Humanities Summer Seminar she directed at the American Academy in Rome, "The Religious, Social, and Political Significance of Roman Dress," resulted in the publication of *The World of Roman Costume*, which she coedited with Judith Sebesta (1994). She is coeditor of *Etruscan News*; has written on the Roman triumph, Julian the Apostate, and nudity as a costume in classical art; and was awarded the Gold Medal for Archaeological Achievement of the Archaeological Institute of America.

Marie Botkin teaches fashion history at California State University, Sacramento. Her research interests include French fashion in medieval times and the twentieth century.

Jennifer Chi received her Ph.D. from the Institute Fine Arts, NYU, and the University of Oxford. She is currently the curator of the Collection of Shelby White and Leon Levy. In this capacity she has curated four exhibitions ranging from Greek bronze vessels and their decorative elements to the development of the Roman portrait bust. She is also the main editor and contributor to *Collecting in Context: Papers in Memory of Leon Levy* (Philip von Vabern forthcoming 2007).

Katherine Eaton received her Ph.D. from New York University in 2004. A specialist in ancient Egyptian religion and medicine, she has taught at the City College of New York, the California Institute of Technology, and the University of Pittsburgh.

Sara M. Harvey holds a master's degree in costume studies from New York University and currently teaches fashion design at the International Academy of Art and Technology in Nashville, Tennessee. She is also freelance costume designer and a novelist.

Index